Two books that influenced me are *The Letters of Vincent van Gogh* and *The Letters of Chuya Nakahara*. These are two men I deeply admire, but it wasn't just their art or poetry that impressed themselves on me, but their letters as well.

I find letters very moving because they encompass the true feelings of the speaker. A letter is a form of confession that contains a *heart* of compassion for the recipient.

For me, this manga has been a long, long letter.

—Hiroyuki Asada, 2016

Hiroyuki Asada made his debut in *Monthly Shonen Jump* in 1986. He's best known for his basketball manga *I'll*. He's a contributor to artist Range Murata's quarterly manga anthology *Robot*. *Tegami Bachi: Letter Bee* is his most recent series.

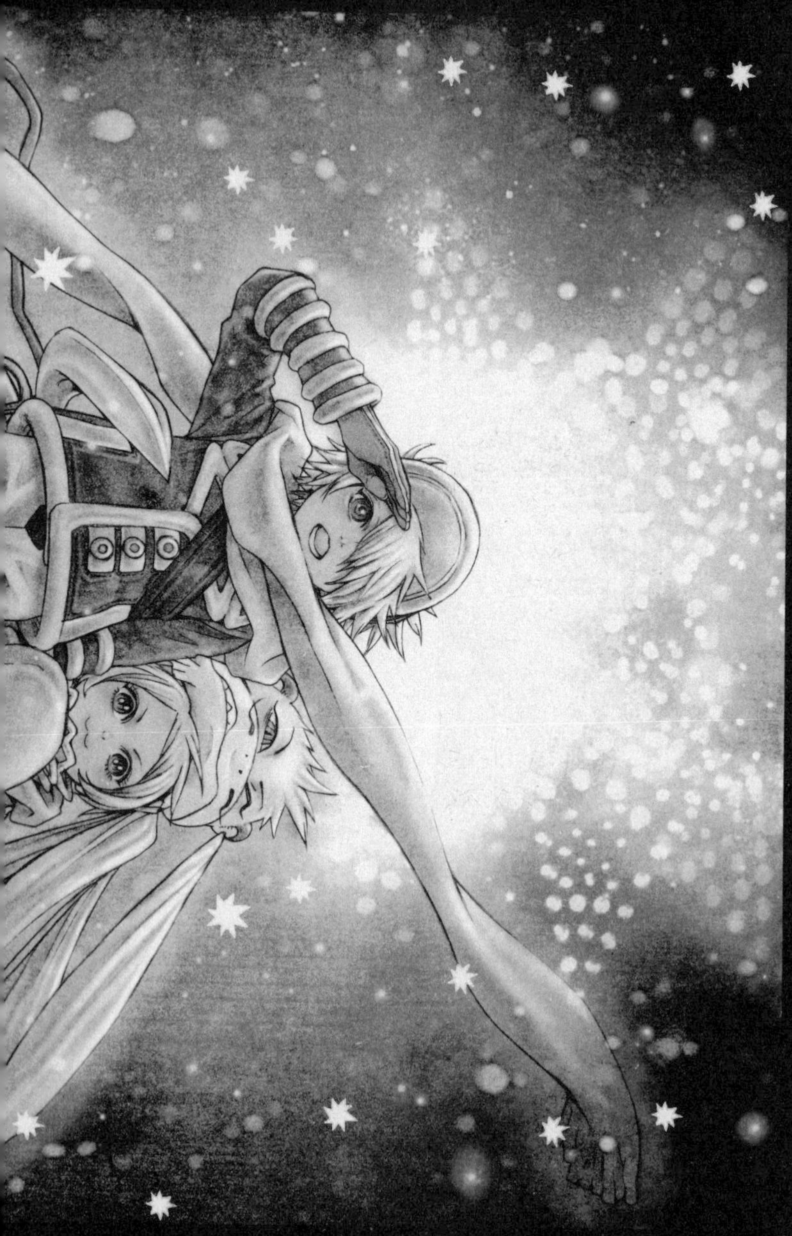

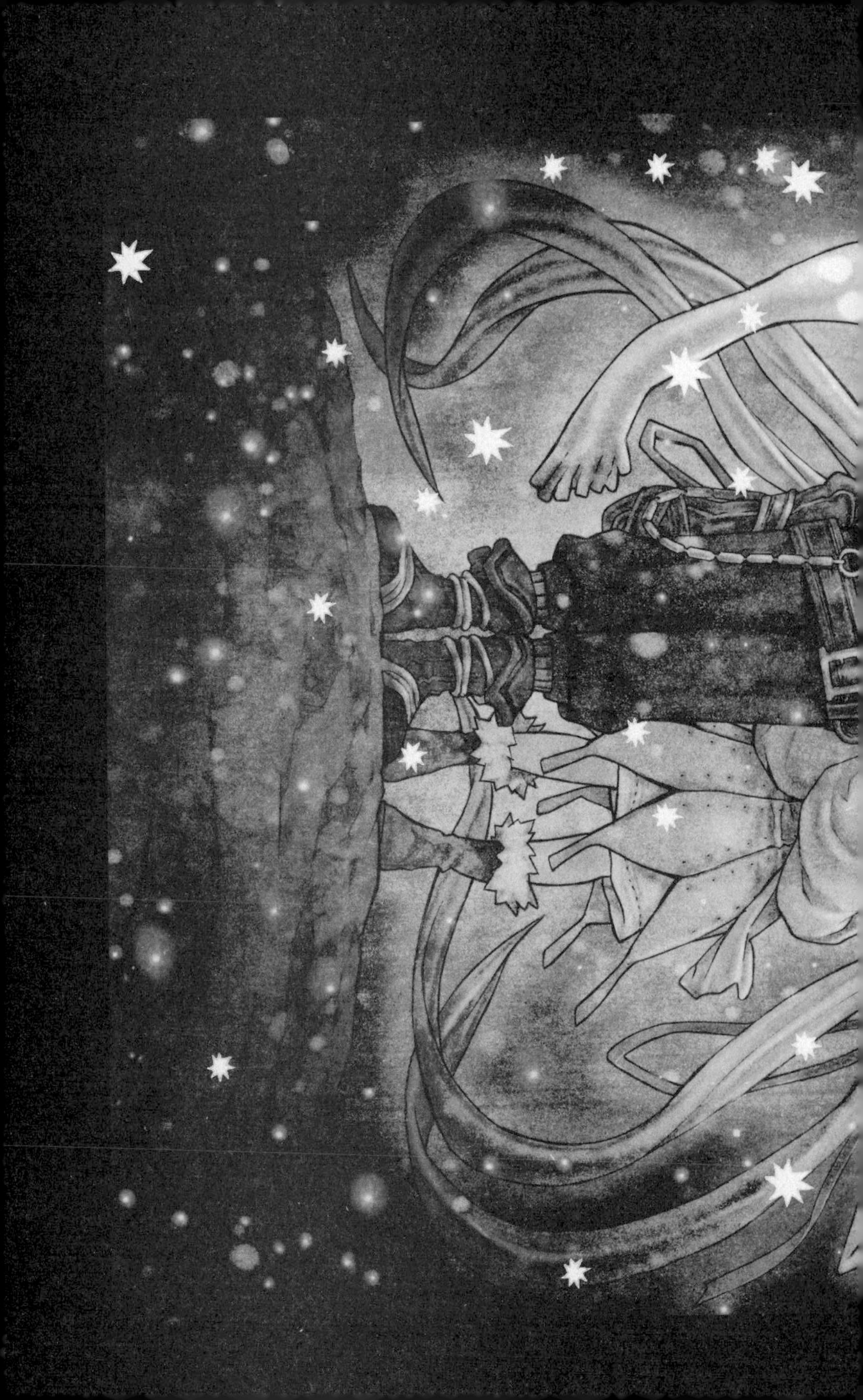

TEGAMI BACHI
LETTER · BEE

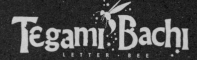

Volume 20
SHONEN JUMP Manga Edition

Story and Art by Hiroyuki Asada

English Adaptation/Rich Amtower
Translation/JN Productions
Touch-up & Lettering/Annaliese Christman
Design/Jodie Shikuma
Editor/Shaenon K. Garrity

Printed in the U.S.A.

Published by VIZ Media, LLC
P.O. Box 77010
San Francisco, CA 94107

10 9 8 7 6 5 4 3 2 1
First printing, March 2017

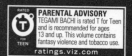

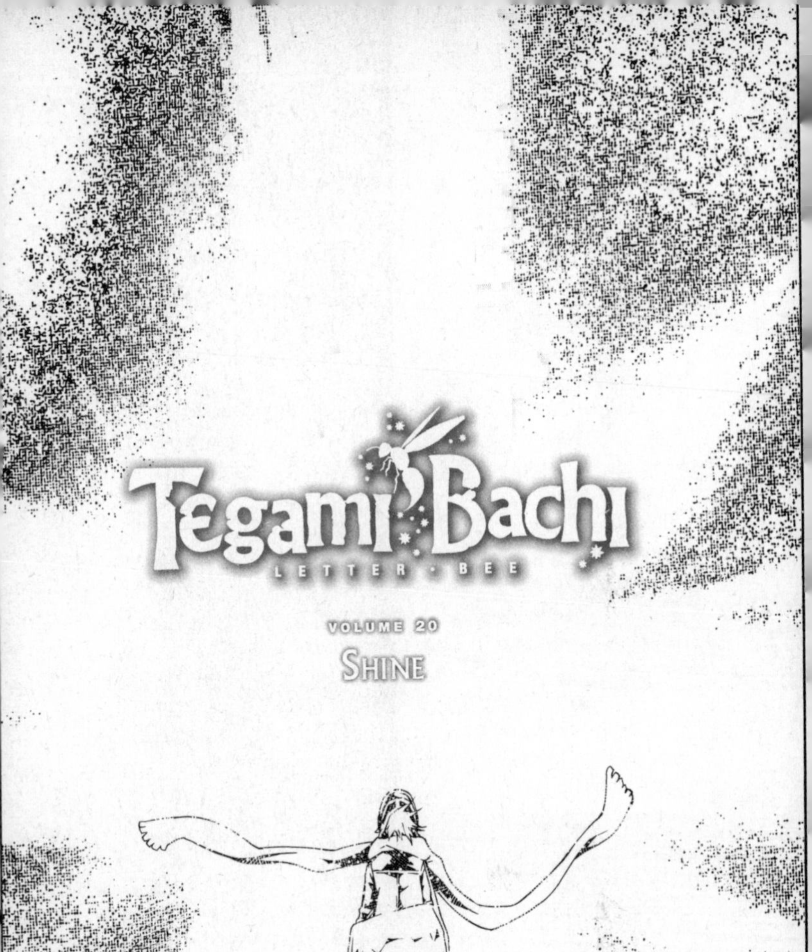
Tegami Bachi
LETTER • BEE
VOLUME 20
SHINE

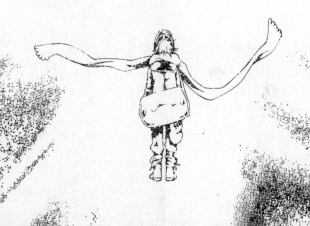

This is a country known as Amberground, where night never ends.

Its capital, Akatsuki, is illuminated by a man-made sun. The farther one strays from the capital, the weaker the light. The Yuusari region is cast in twilight; the Yodaka region survives only on pale moonlight.

Letter Bee Gauche Suede and young Lag Seeing meet in the Yodaka region— a postal worker and the "letter" he must deliver. In their short time together, they form a fast friendship, but when the journey ends, each departs down his own path. In time, Lag sets out for Yuusari to become a Letter Bee like Gauche. But Gauche is no longer there, having lost his *heart* and vanished.

Now a Bee, Lag continues delivering letters as he searches for Gauche. He discovers Gauche has taken on a new identity as Noir, a member of the rebel group Reverse. Reverse attempts to attack the capital with a massive Gaichuu, Cabernet, but the Bees foil their plan.

In the glacier town of Blue Notes Blues, Lloyd reveals to the Bees that within the sun is a massive Gaichuu called Spiritus, which the government feeds with the *hearts* of citizens. Lag goes to Sir-etok, where the last Spirit Insect lives, to prepare to save the world. Over a year later, he returns to find that Gauche's sister Sylvette has lost her *heart* to the flickering sun.

The Letter Bees are tested for their readiness to enter the capital. Lag and the Reverse spy Chico both pass. Their guide, Kuu, leads them into the darkness, where a gigantic apparatus sucks the *heart* from countless citizens...

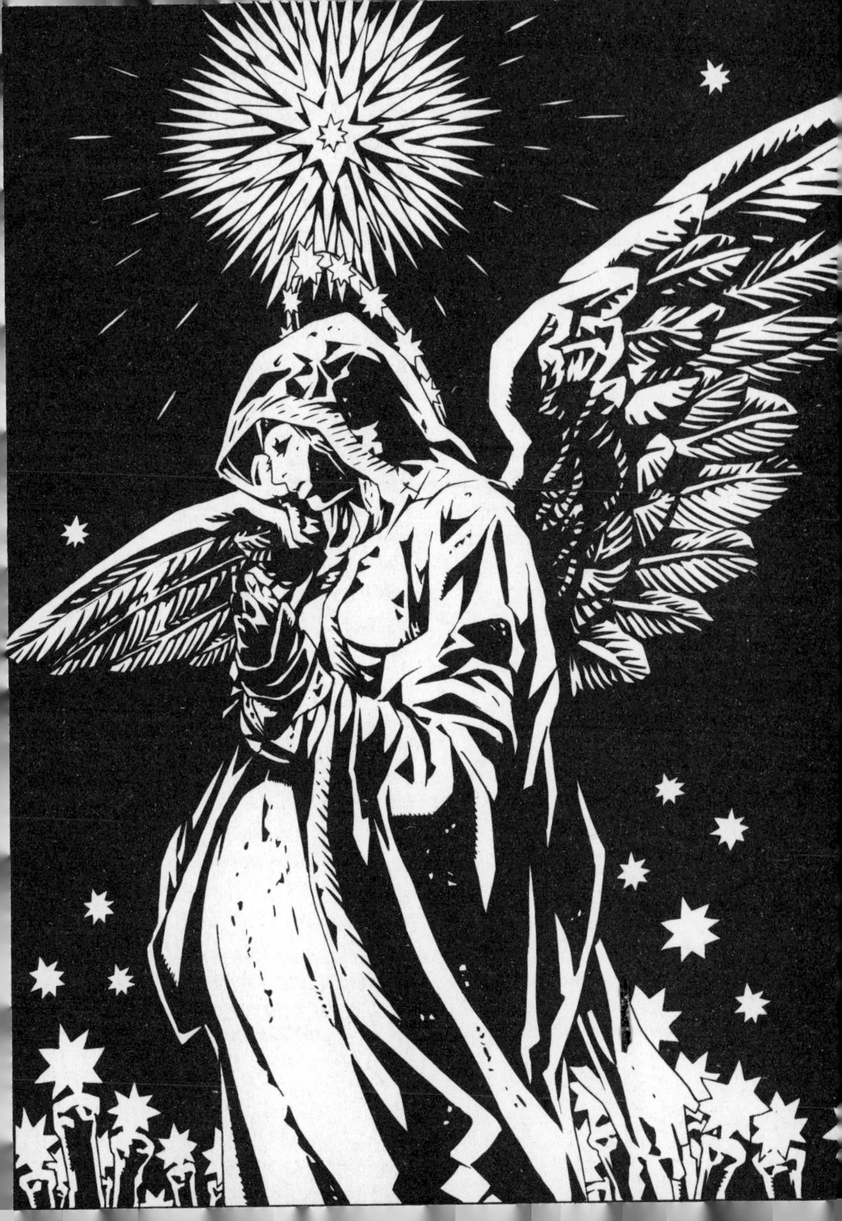

List of Characters

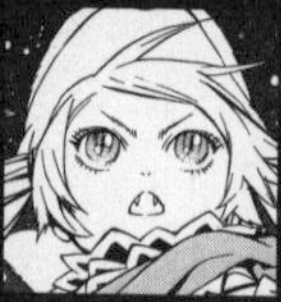

CHICO NEIGE
Letter Bee

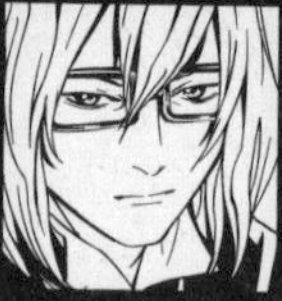

LARGO LLOYD
Ex-Beehive Director

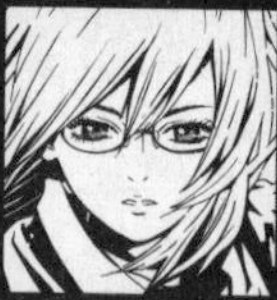

ARIA LINK
Section Chief of the Dead Letter Office

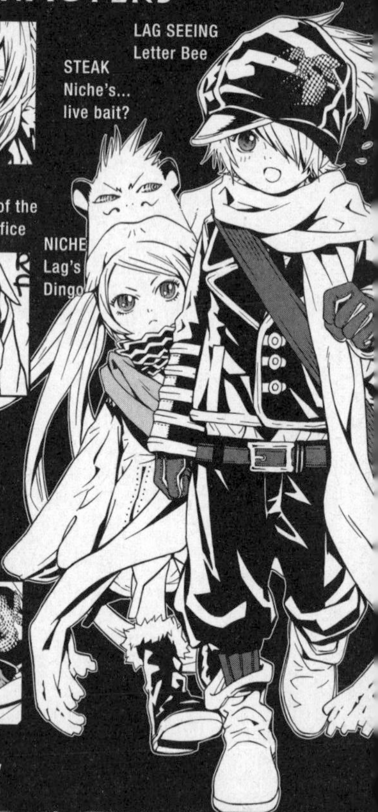

LAG SEEING
Letter Bee

STEAK
Niche's... live bait?

NICHE
Lag's Dingo

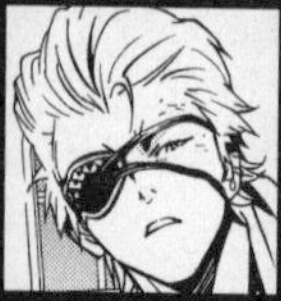

DR. THUNDERLAND, JR.
Member of the AG Biological Science Advisory Board, Third Division and head doctor at the Beehive

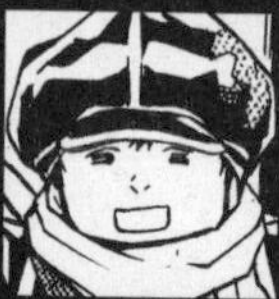

CONNOR KLUFF
Letter Bee

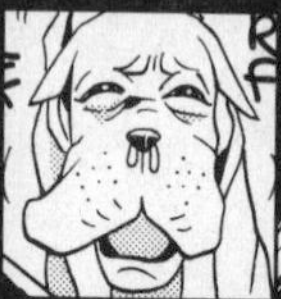

GUS
Connor's Dingo

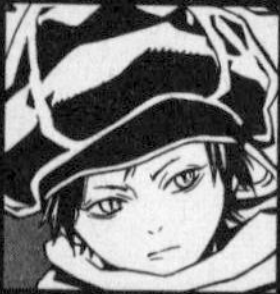

ZAZIE
Letter Bee

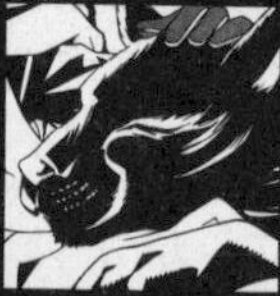

WASIOLKA
Zazie's Dingo

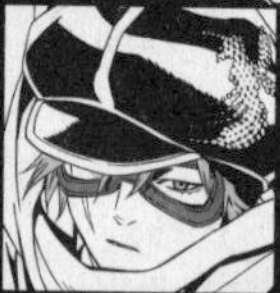

JIGGY PEPPER
Express Delivery Letter Bee

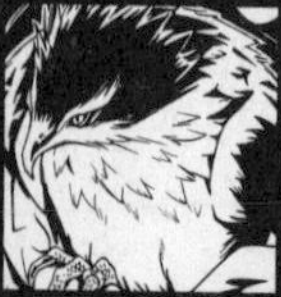

HARRY
Jiggy's Dingo

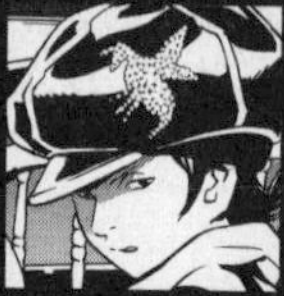

MOC SULLIVAN
Letter Bee

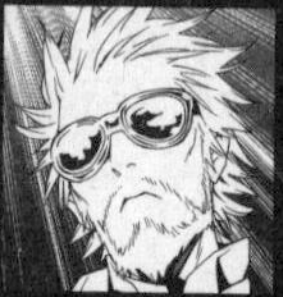

CHALYBS GARRARD
Inspector and ex-Letter Bee

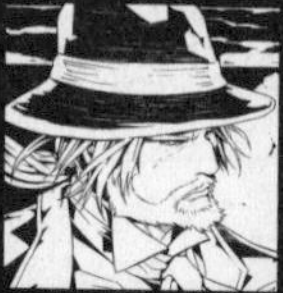

HAZEL VALENTINE
Inspector and Garrard's ex-Dingo

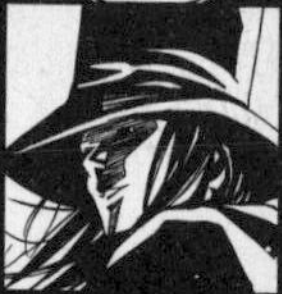

LAWRENCE
The ringleader of Reverse

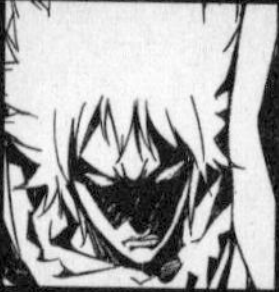

ZEAL
Marauder for Reverse

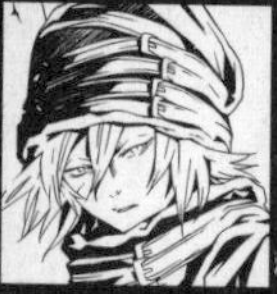

NOIR (FORMERLY GAUCHE SUEDE)
Marauder for Reverse and an ex-Letter Bee

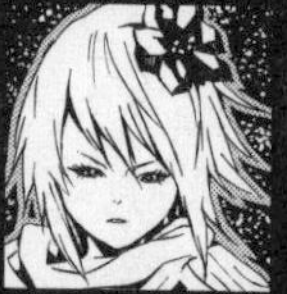

RODA
Noir's Dingo

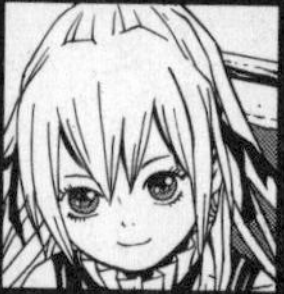

SYLVETTE SUEDE
Gauche's Sister

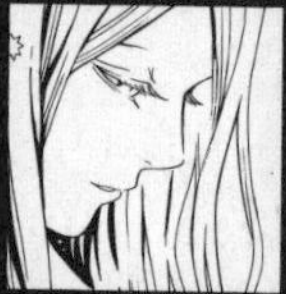

ANNE SEEING
Lag's Mother (Missing)

LETTER · BEE

VOLUME 20
SHINE

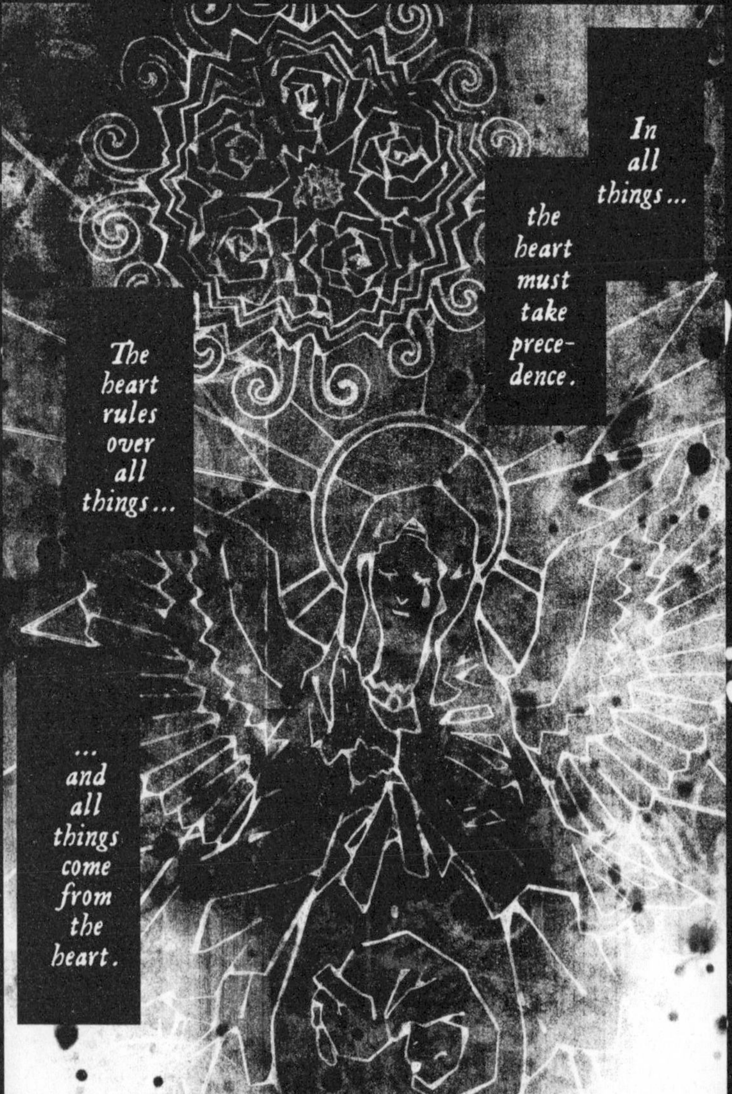
In all things... the heart must take precedence.
The heart rules over all things...
... and all things come from the heart.

–THE SCRIPTURES OF AMBERGROUND, 1st verse

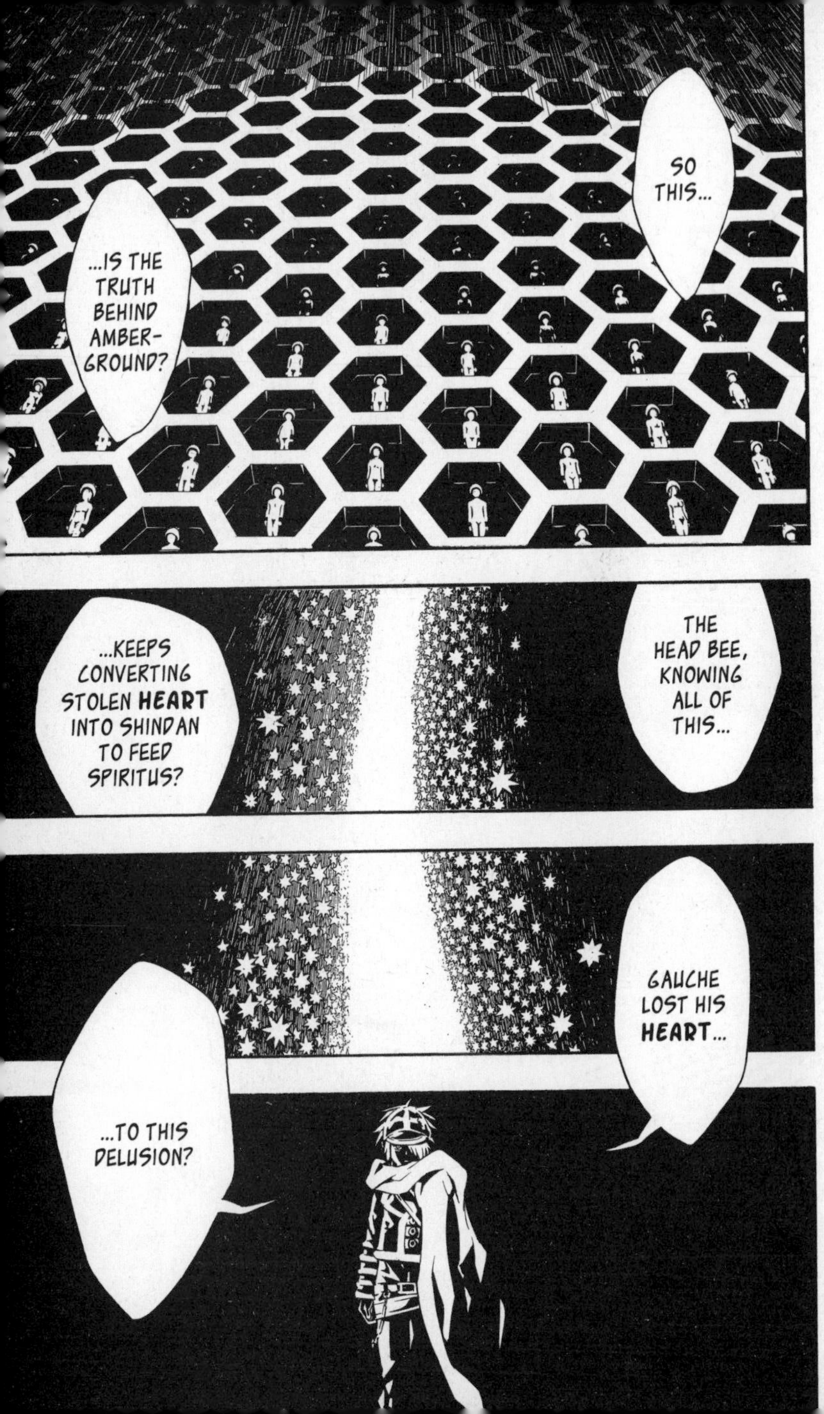
SO THIS...
...IS THE TRUTH BEHIND AMBER-GROUND?
THE HEAD BEE, KNOWING ALL OF THIS...
...KEEPS CONVERTING STOLEN HEART INTO SHINDAN TO FEED SPIRITUS?
GAUCHE LOST HIS HEART...
...TO THIS DELUSION?

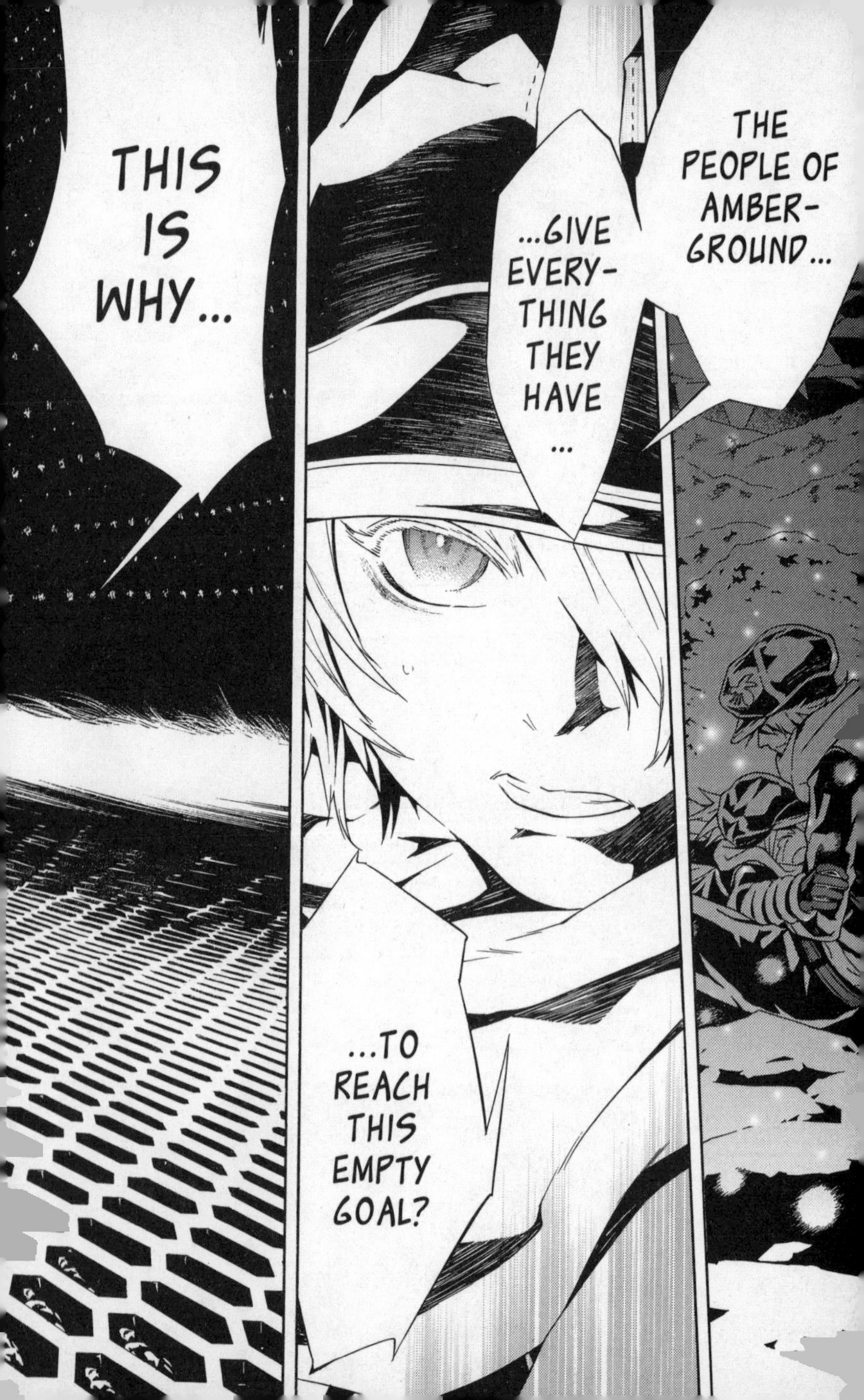
THE PEOPLE OF AMBER-GROUND...
...GIVE EVERY-THING THEY HAVE...
...TO REACH THIS EMPTY GOAL?
THIS IS WHY...

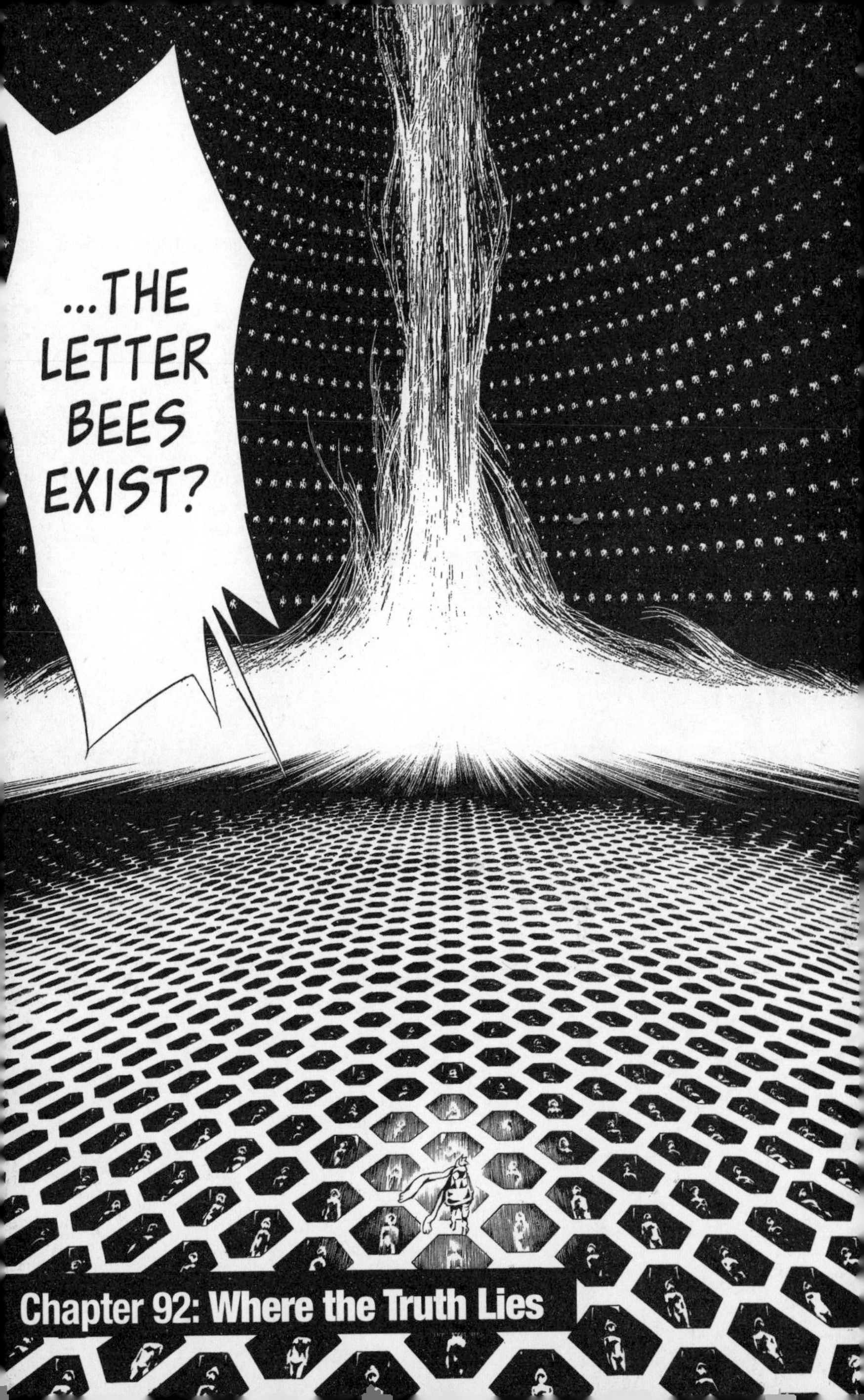
...THE LETTER BEES EXIST?

Chapter 92: Where the Truth Lies

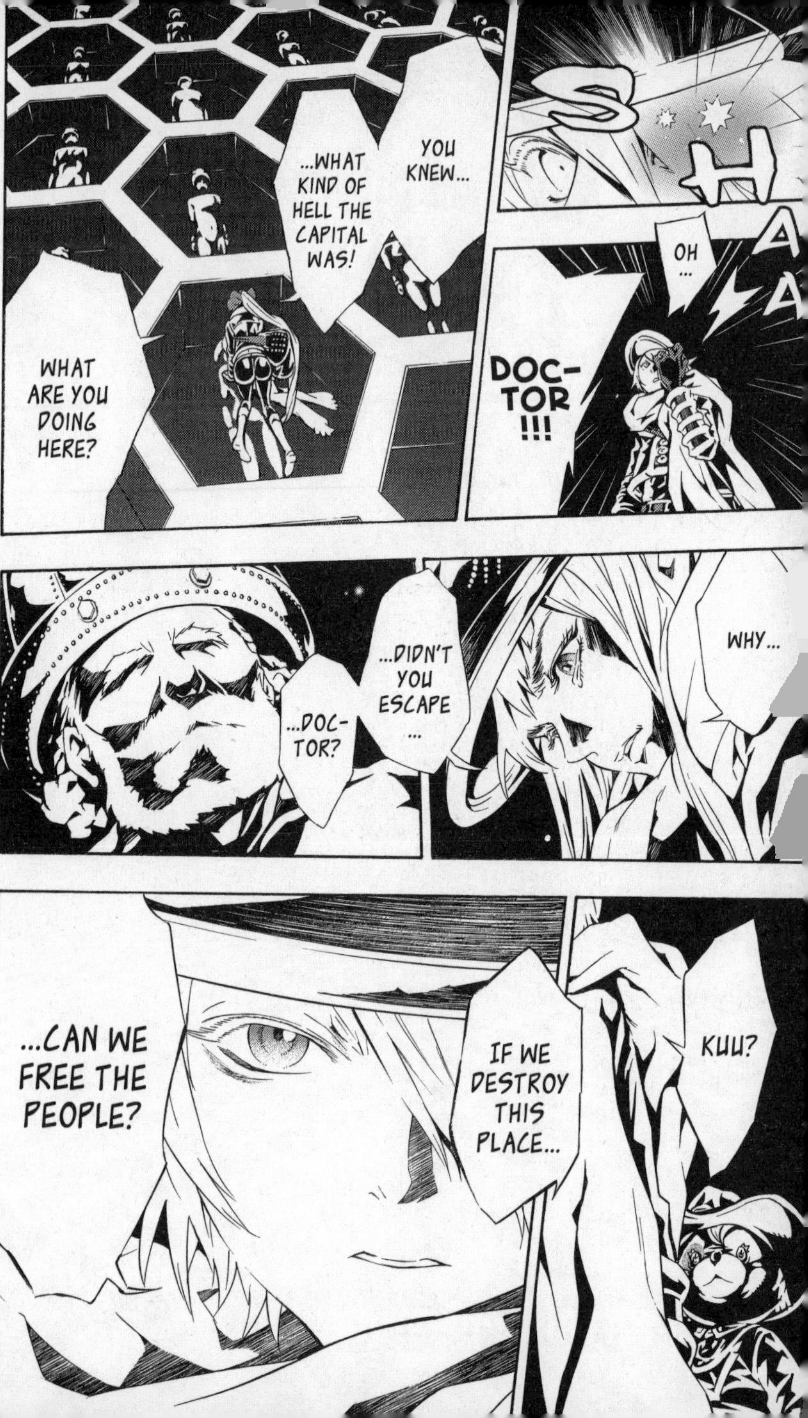
SHAA
OH...
DOCTOR!!!
YOU KNEW...
...WHAT KIND OF HELL THE CAPITAL WAS!
WHAT ARE YOU DOING HERE?
WHY...
...DIDN'T YOU ESCAPE...
...DOCTOR?
KUU?
IF WE DESTROY THIS PLACE...
...CAN WE FREE THE PEOPLE?

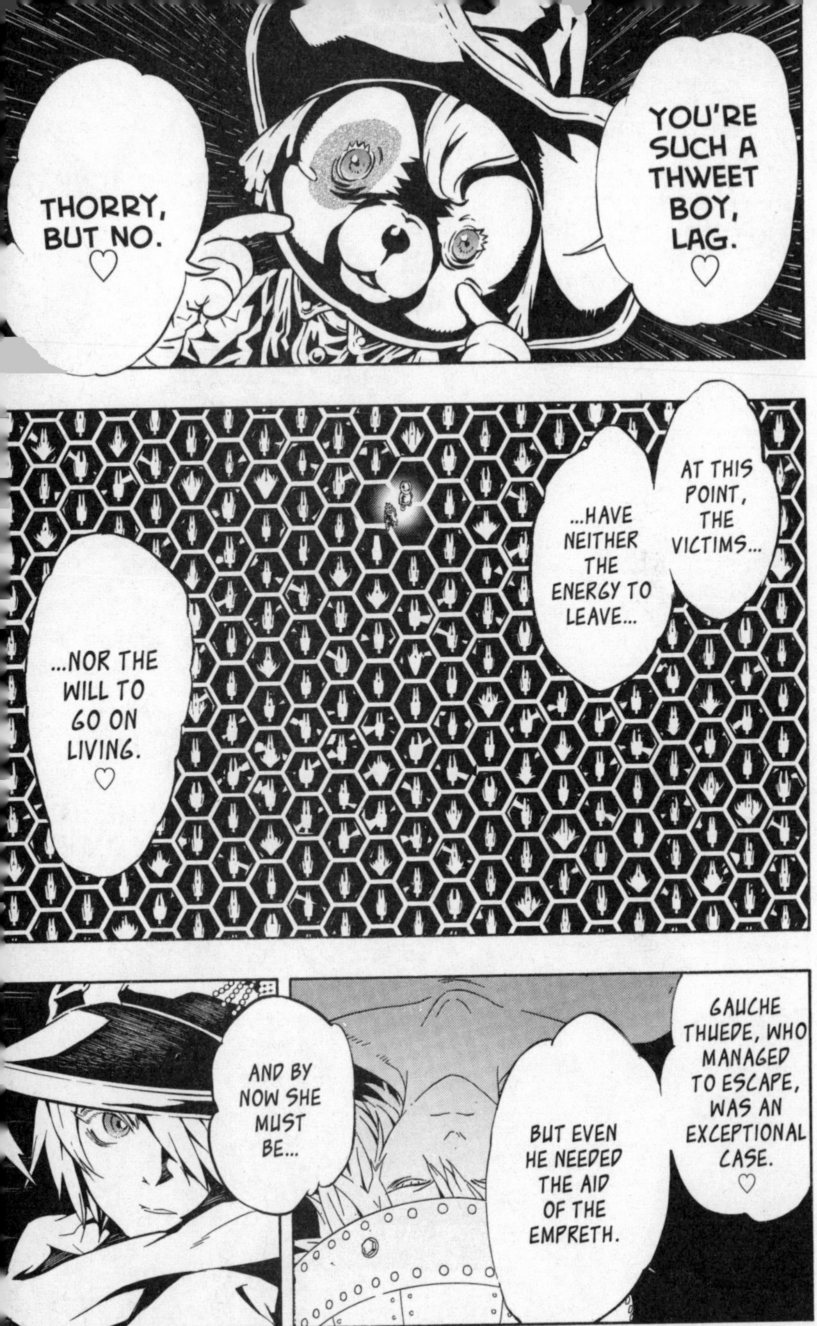
YOU'RE SUCH A THWEET BOY, LAG. ♡
THORRY, BUT NO. ♡
AT THIS POINT, THE VICTIMS...
...HAVE NEITHER THE ENERGY TO LEAVE...
...NOR THE WILL TO GO ON LIVING. ♡
GAUCHE THUEDE, WHO MANAGED TO ESCAPE, WAS AN EXCEPTIONAL CASE. ♡
BUT EVEN HE NEEDED THE AID OF THE EMPRETH.
AND BY NOW SHE MUST BE...

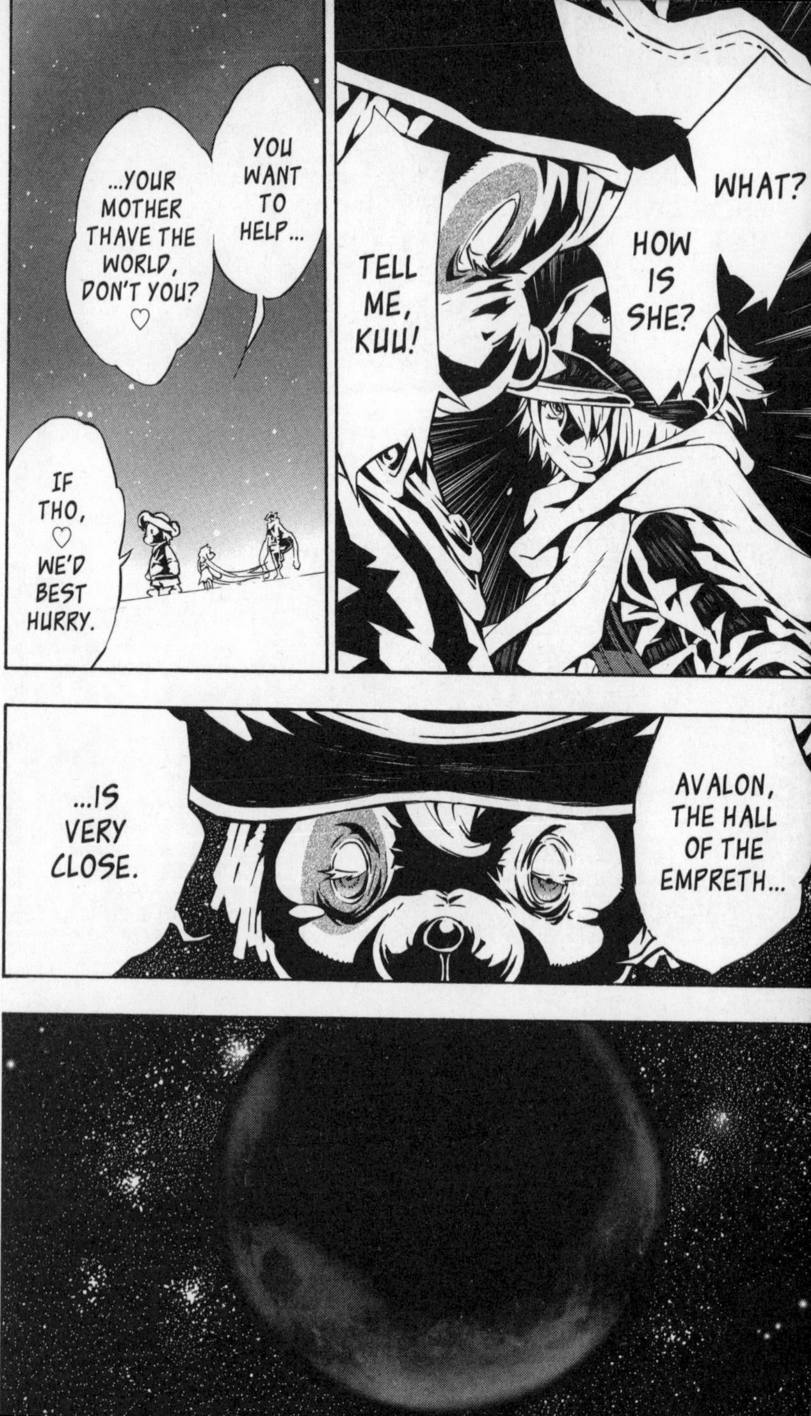
WHAT?
HOW IS SHE?
TELL ME, KUU!
YOU WANT TO HELP...
...YOUR MOTHER THAVE THE WORLD, DON'T YOU? ♡
IF THO, ♡ WE'D BEST HURRY.
AVALON, THE HALL OF THE EMPRETH...
...IS VERY CLOSE.

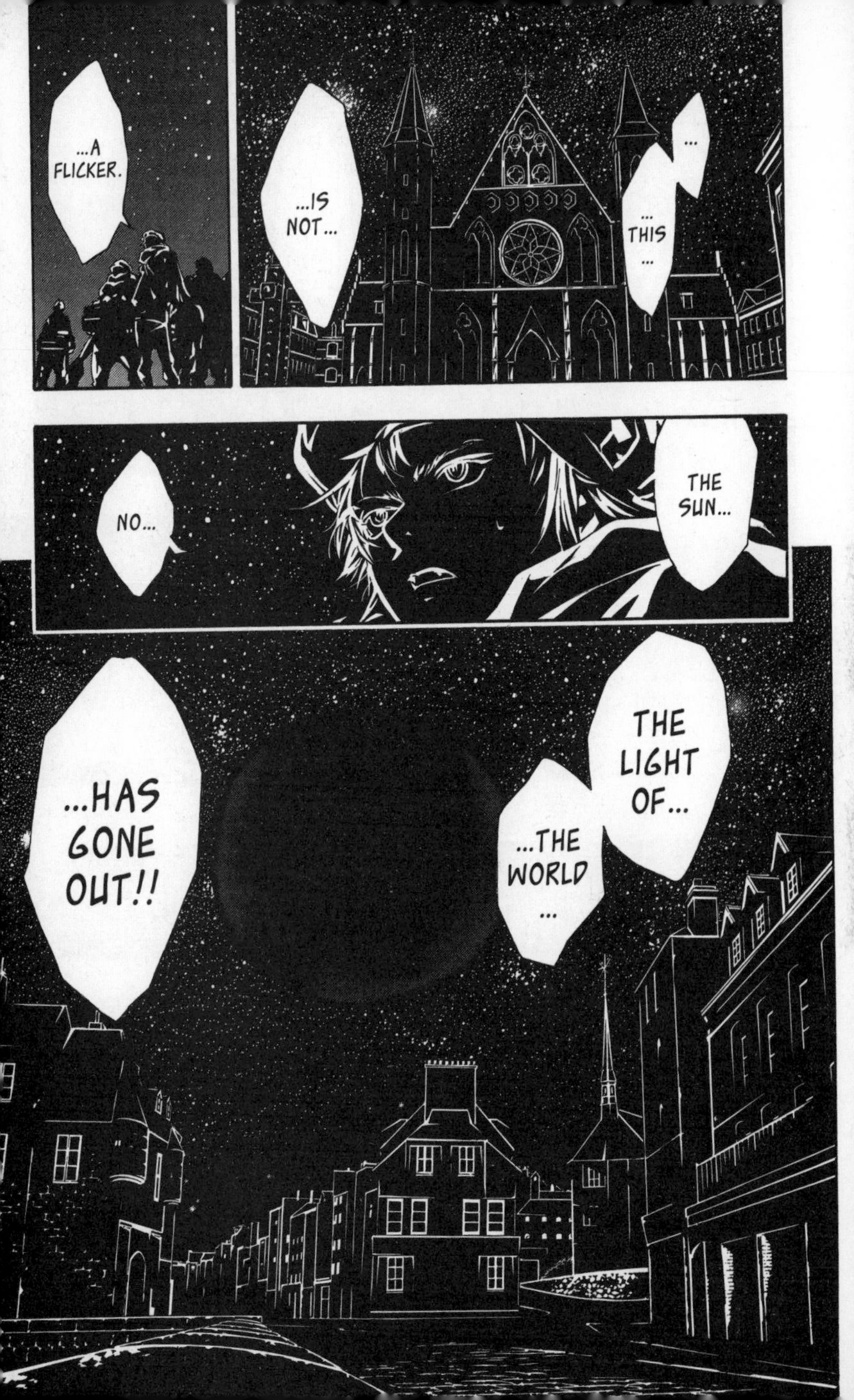
...
... THIS ...
...IS NOT...
...A FLICKER.
THE SUN...
NO...
THE LIGHT OF...
...THE WORLD ...
...HAS GONE OUT!!

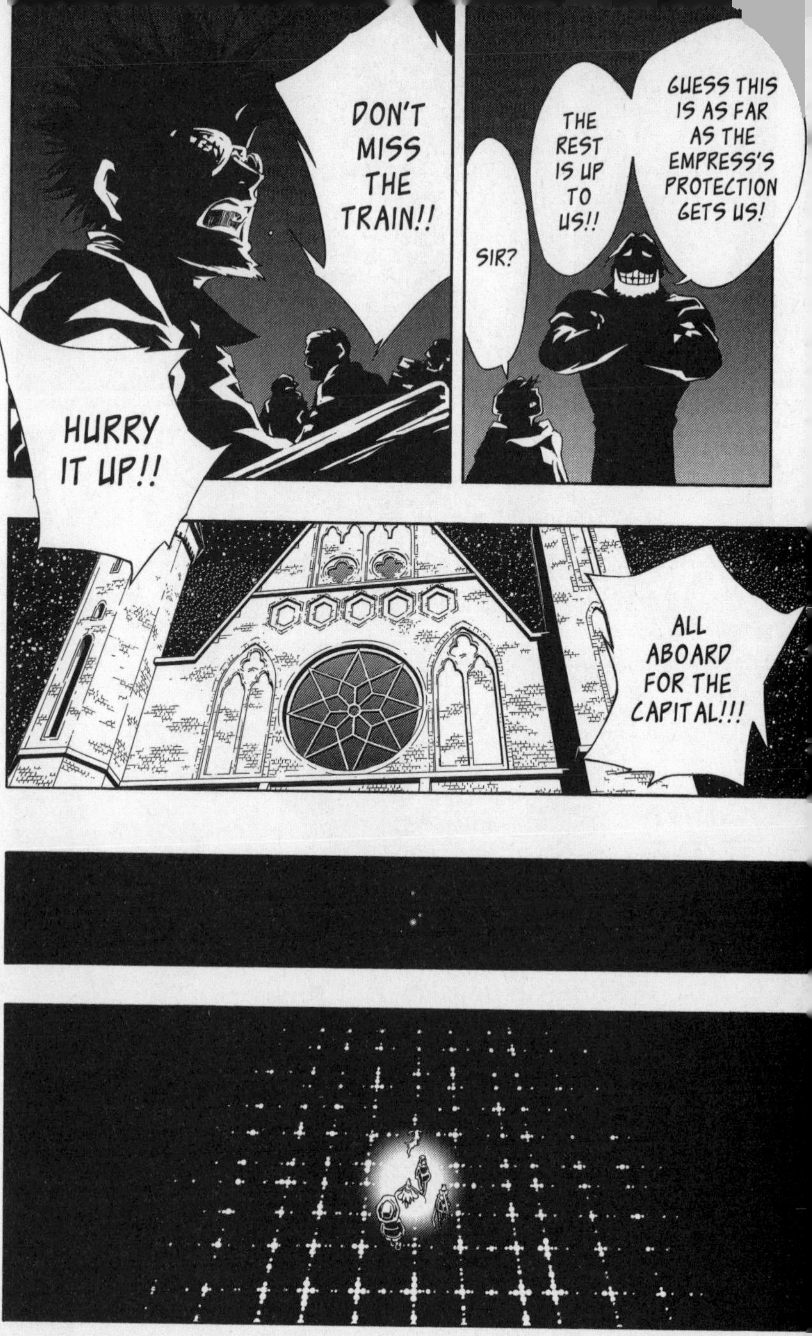
GUESS THIS IS AS FAR AS THE EMPRESS'S PROTECTION GETS US!
THE REST IS UP TO US!!
SIR?
DON'T MISS THE TRAIN!!
HURRY IT UP!!
ALL ABOARD FOR THE CAPITAL!!!

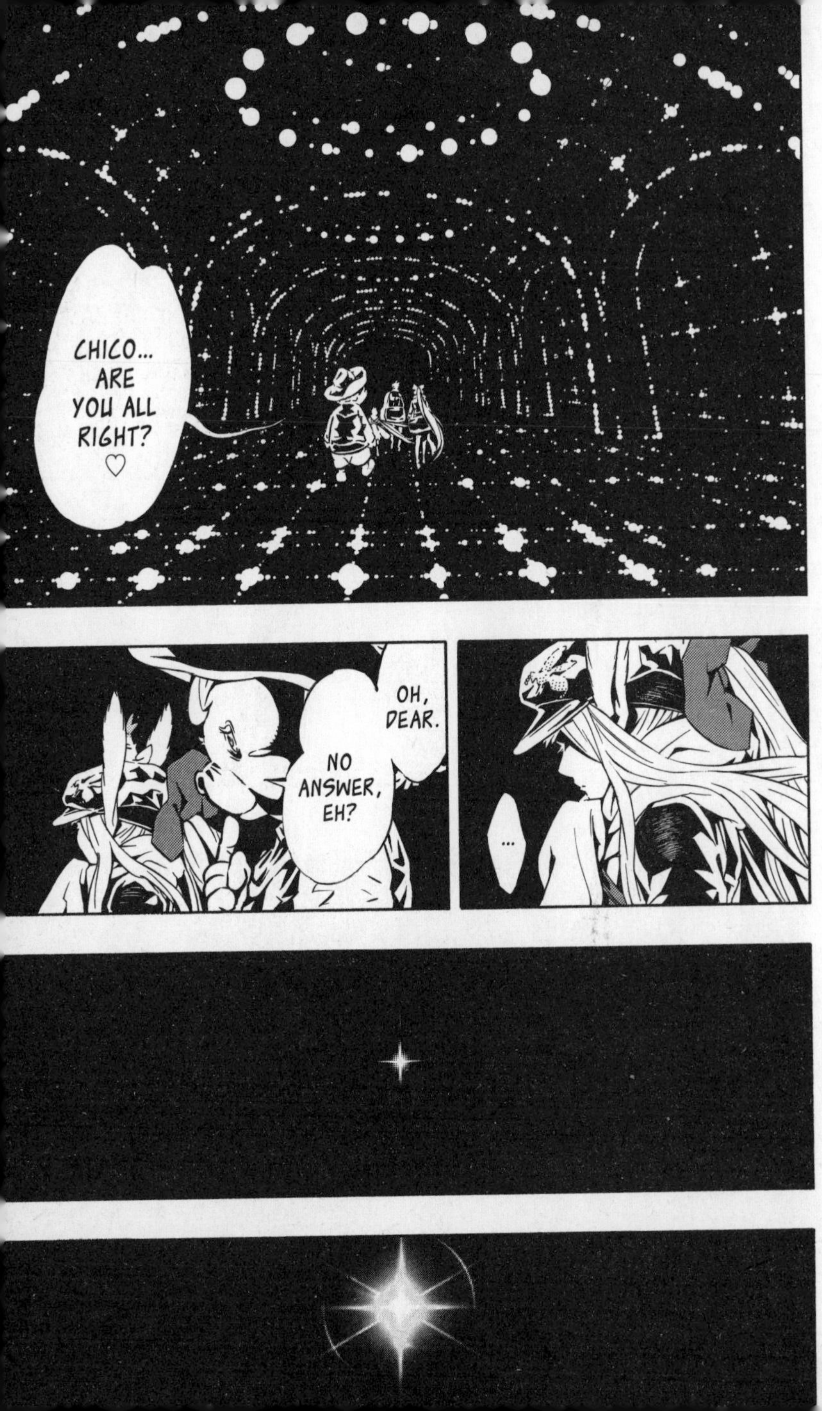
CHICO... ARE YOU ALL RIGHT? ♡
...
OH, DEAR.
NO ANSWER, EH?

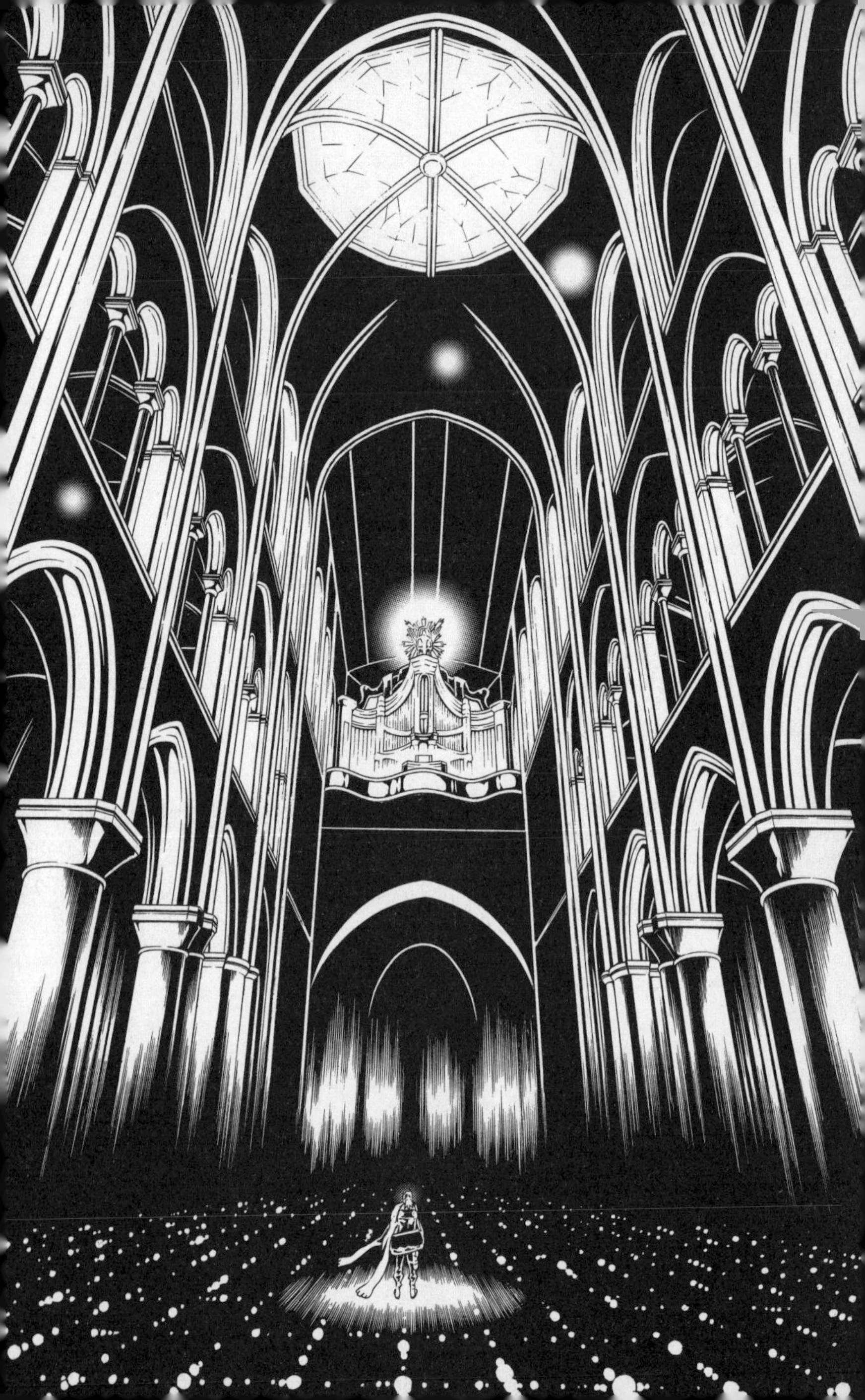

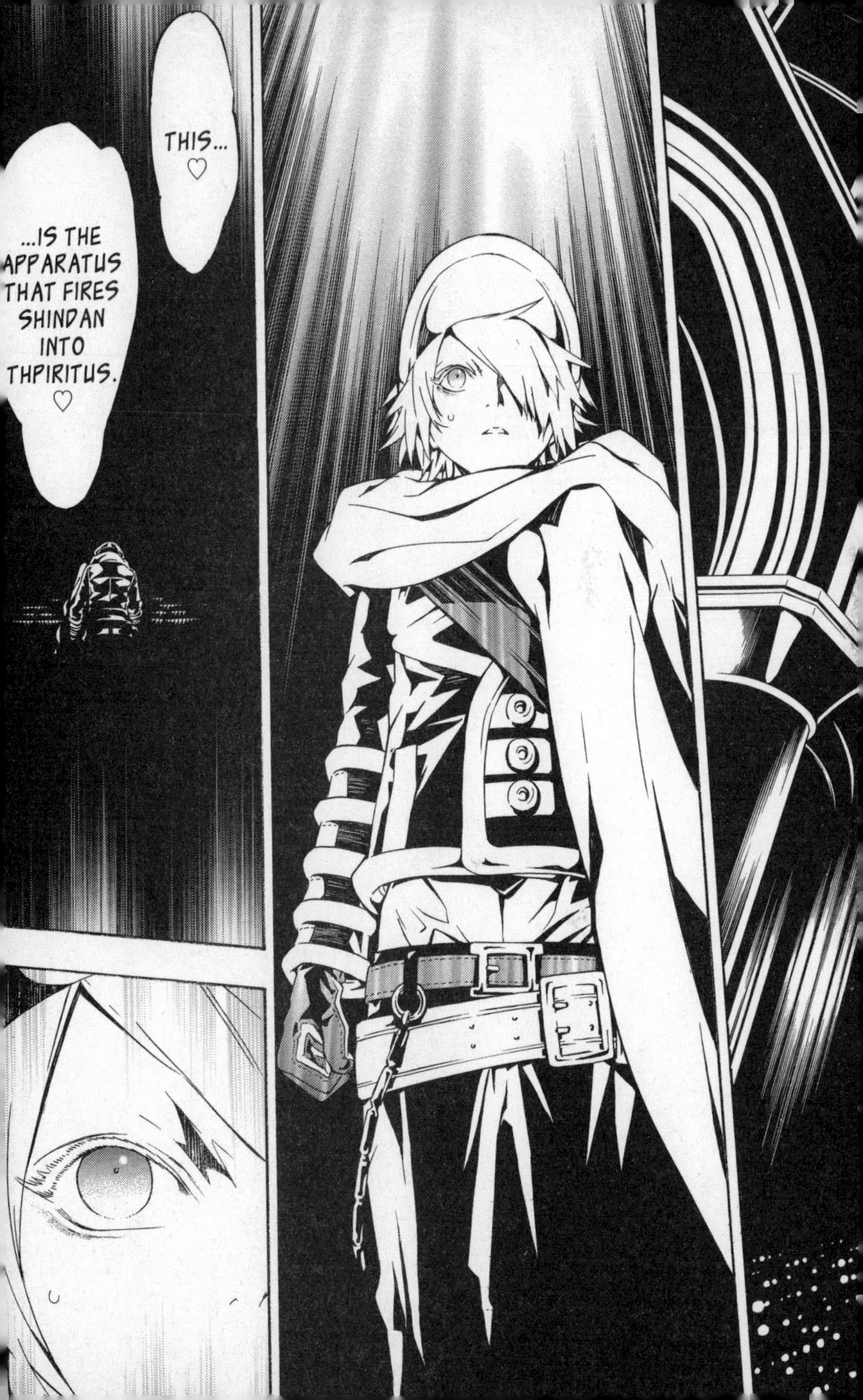
THIS... ♡
...IS THE APPARATUS THAT FIRES SHINDAN INTO THPIRITUS. ♡

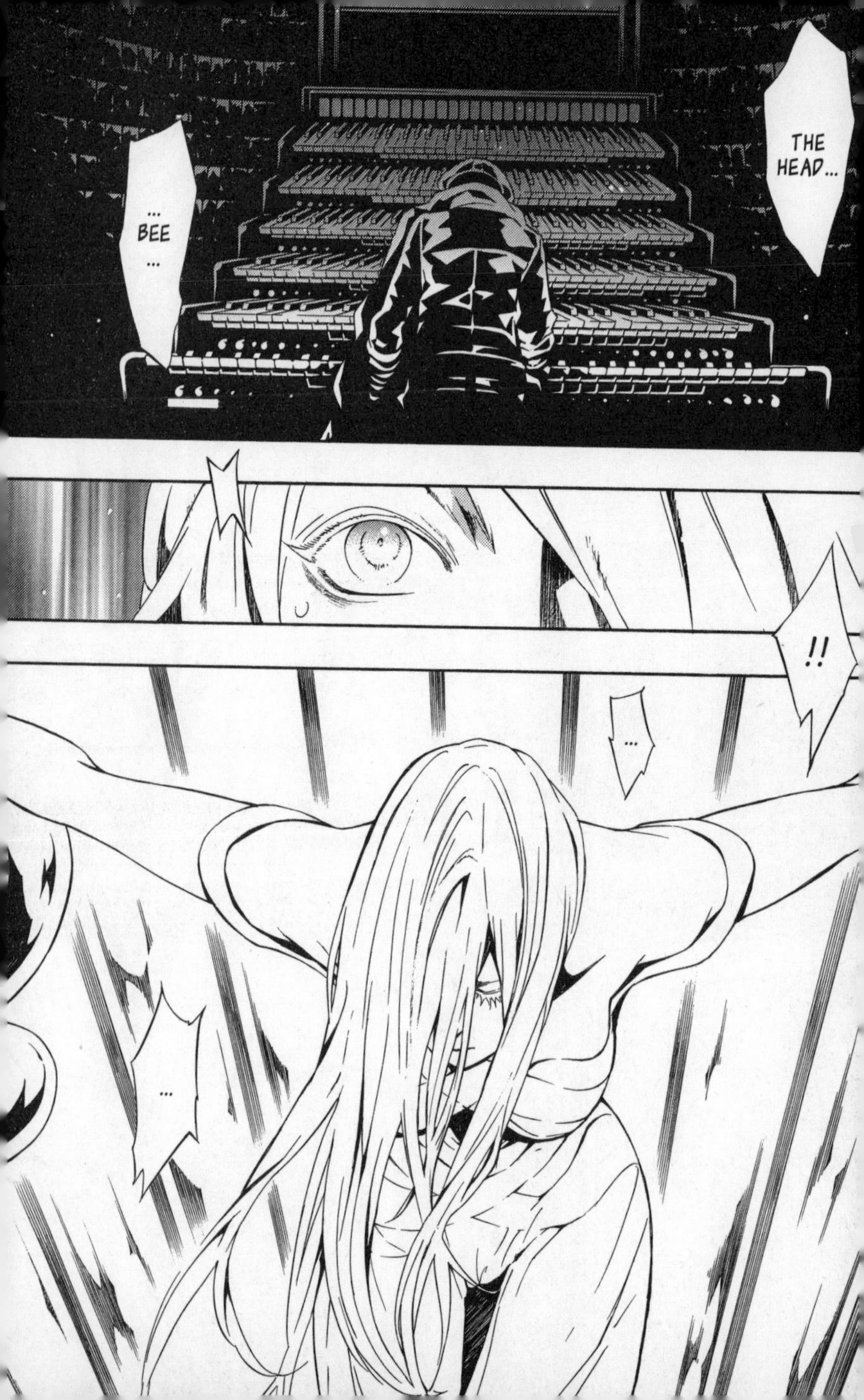
THE HEAD...
... BEE ...
!!
...
...

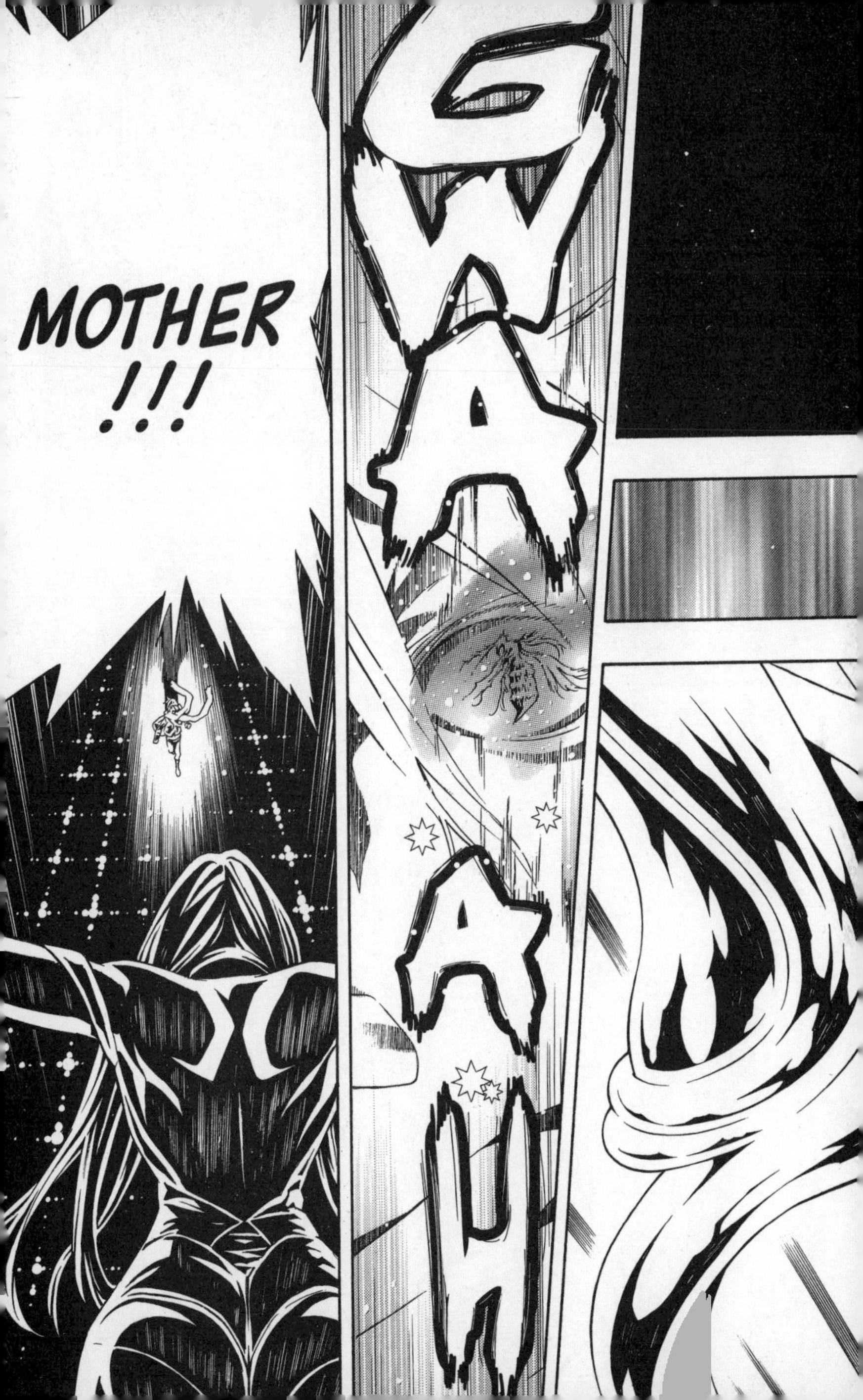
MOTHER !!!

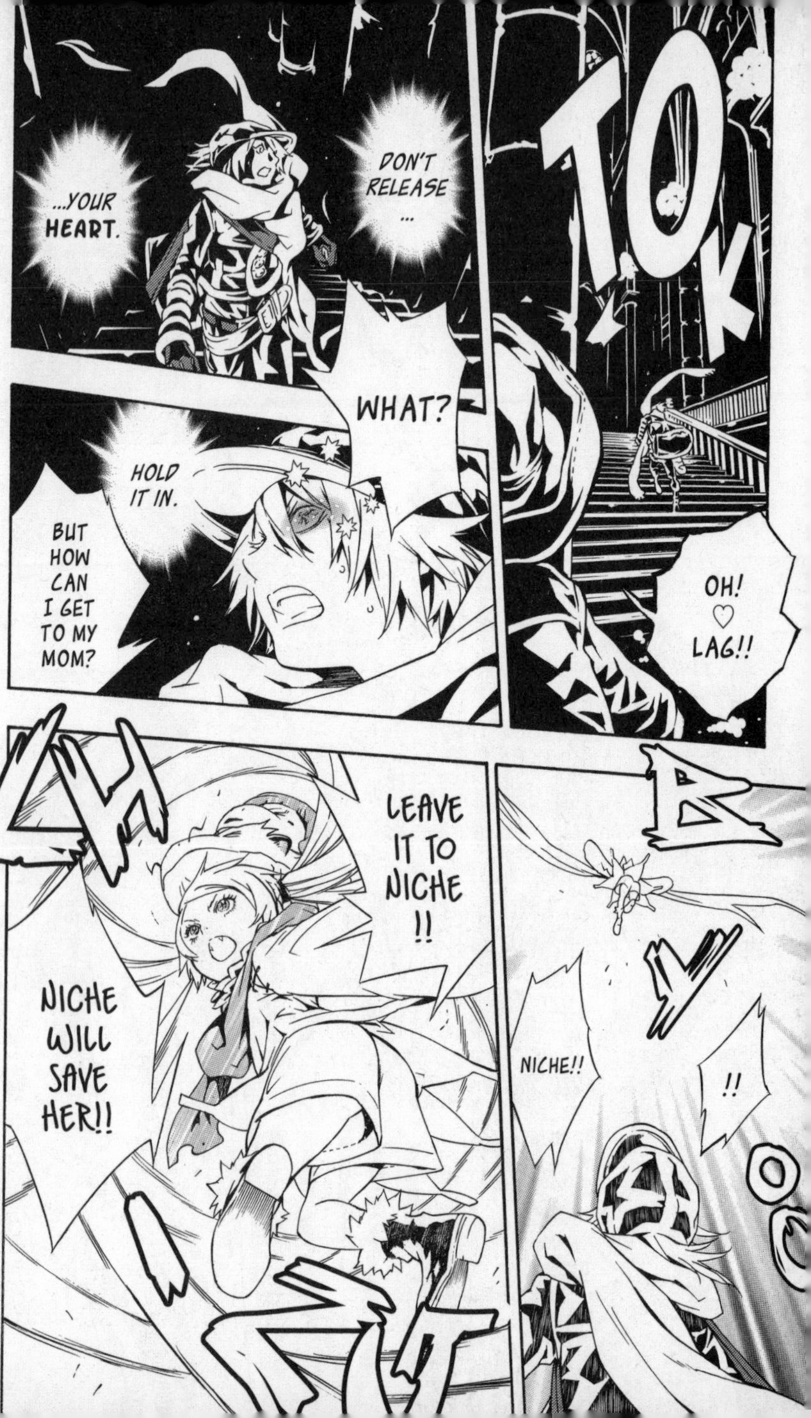
TOK
OH! ♡ LAG!!
DON'T RELEASE...
...YOUR HEART.
WHAT?
HOLD IT IN.
BUT HOW CAN I GET TO MY MOM?
BYOO
NICHE!!
!!
LEAVE IT TO NICHE!!
NICHE WILL SAVE HER!!

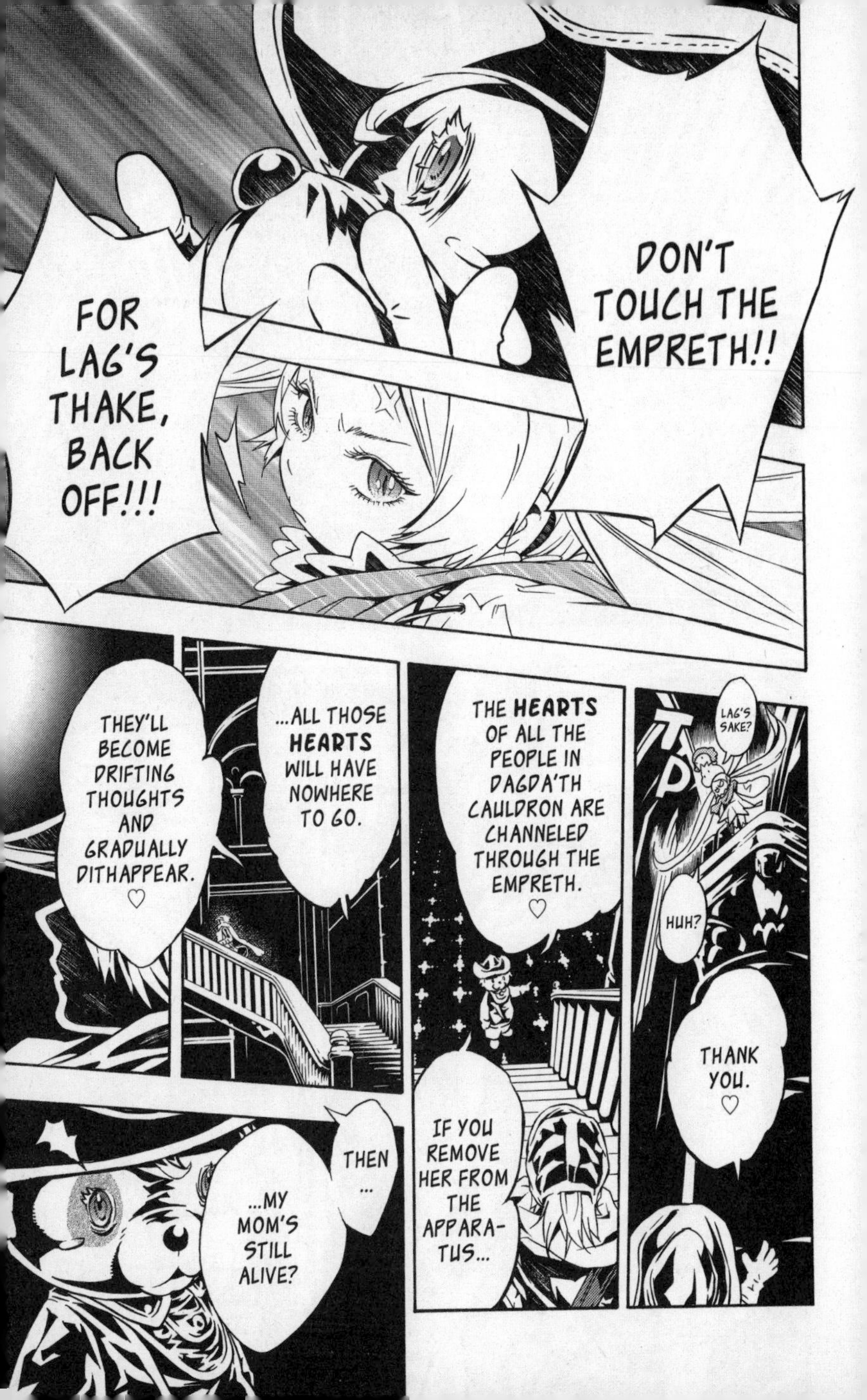
DON'T TOUCH THE EMPRETH!!
FOR LAG'S THAKE, BACK OFF!!!
LAG'S SAKE?
HUH?
THANK YOU. ♡
THE **HEARTS** OF ALL THE PEOPLE IN DAGDA'TH CAULDRON ARE CHANNELED THROUGH THE EMPRETH. ♡
IF YOU REMOVE HER FROM THE APPARA-TUS...
...ALL THOSE **HEARTS** WILL HAVE NOWHERE TO GO.
THEY'LL BECOME DRIFTING THOUGHTS AND GRADUALLY DITHAPPEAR. ♡
THEN ...
...MY MOM'S STILL ALIVE?

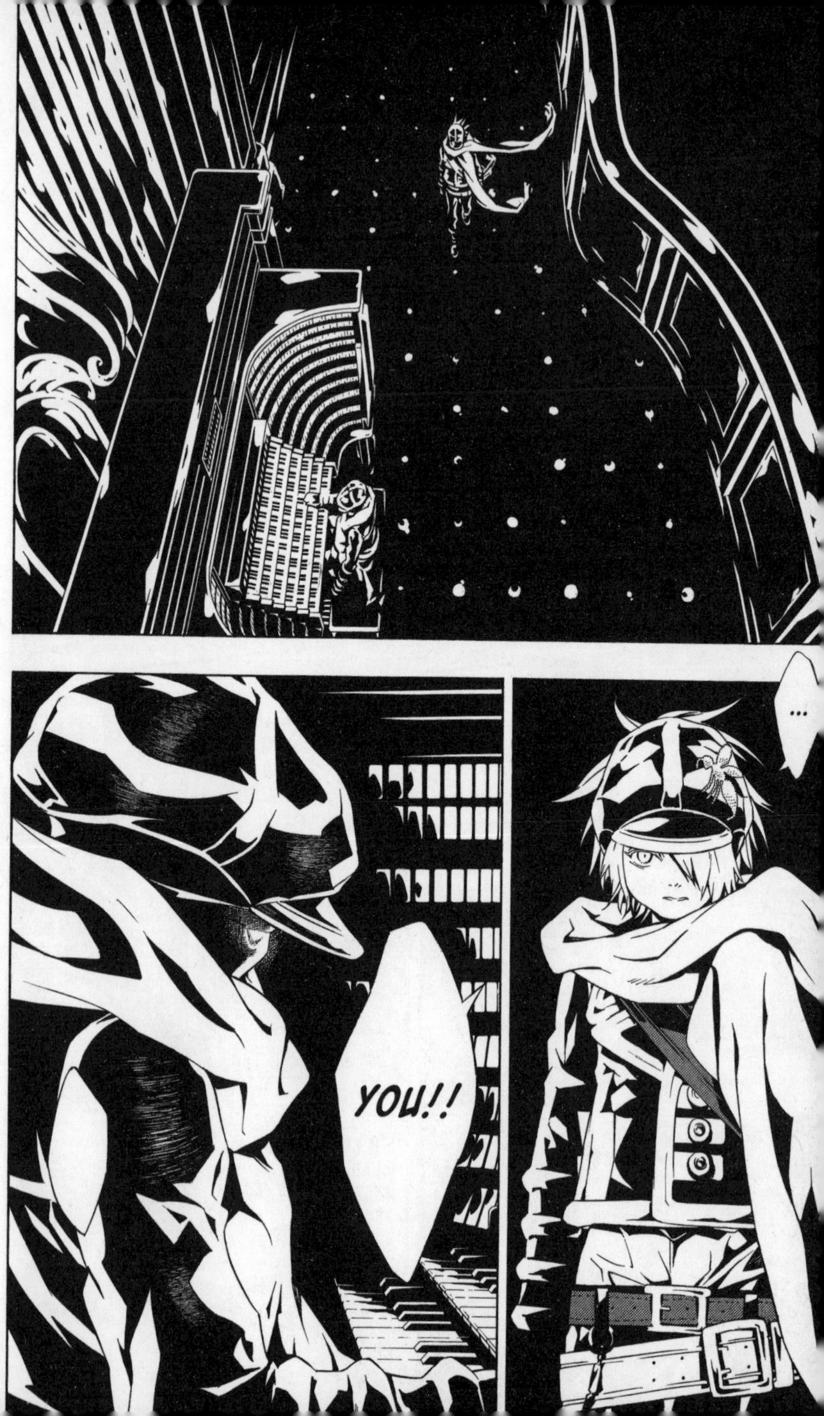
...
YOU!!

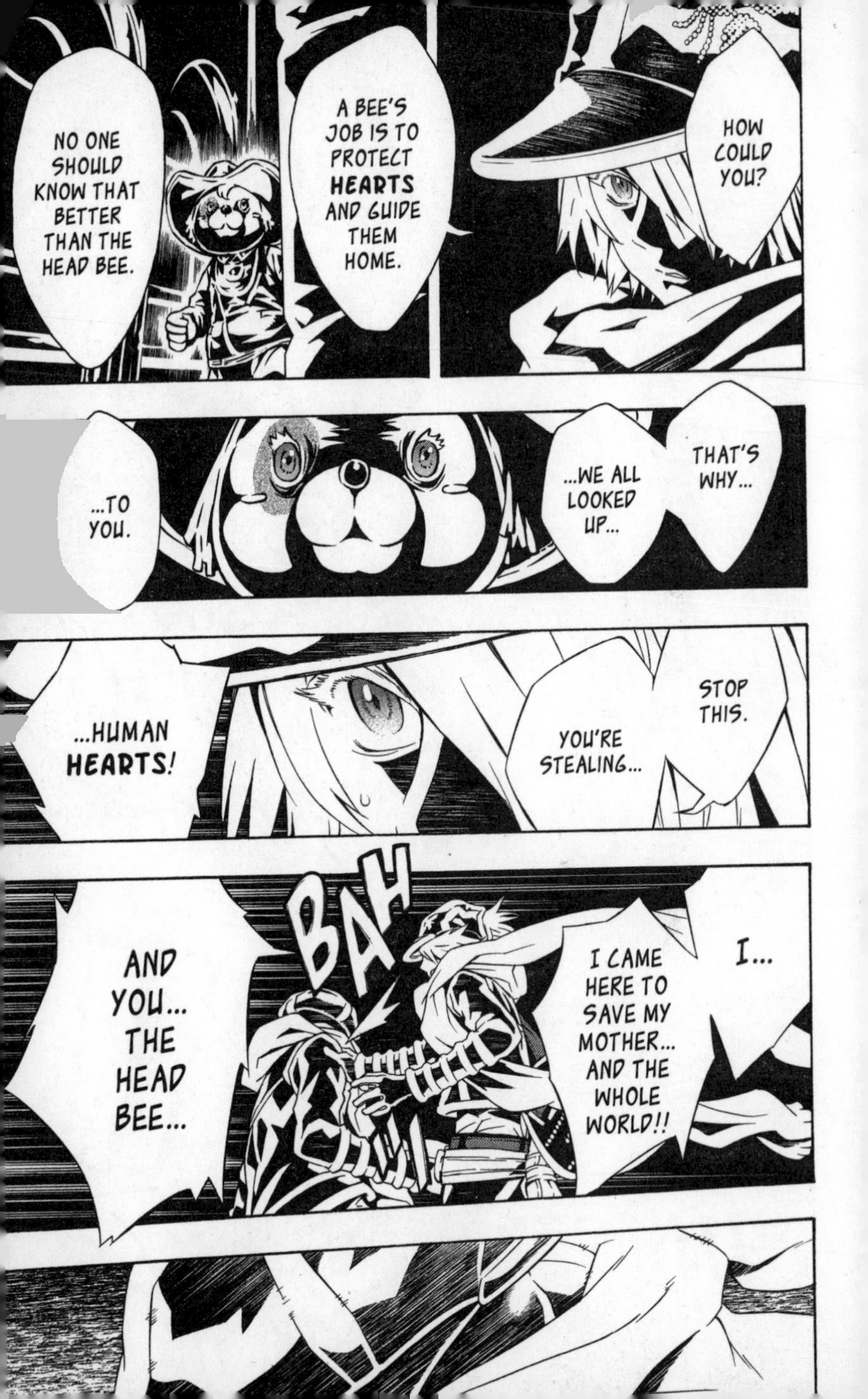
HOW COULD YOU?
A BEE'S JOB IS TO PROTECT **HEARTS** AND GUIDE THEM HOME.
NO ONE SHOULD KNOW THAT BETTER THAN THE HEAD BEE.
THAT'S WHY...
...WE ALL LOOKED UP...
...TO YOU.
STOP THIS.
YOU'RE STEALING...
...HUMAN **HEARTS**!
I...
I CAME HERE TO SAVE MY MOTHER... AND THE WHOLE WORLD!!
BAH
AND YOU... THE HEAD BEE...

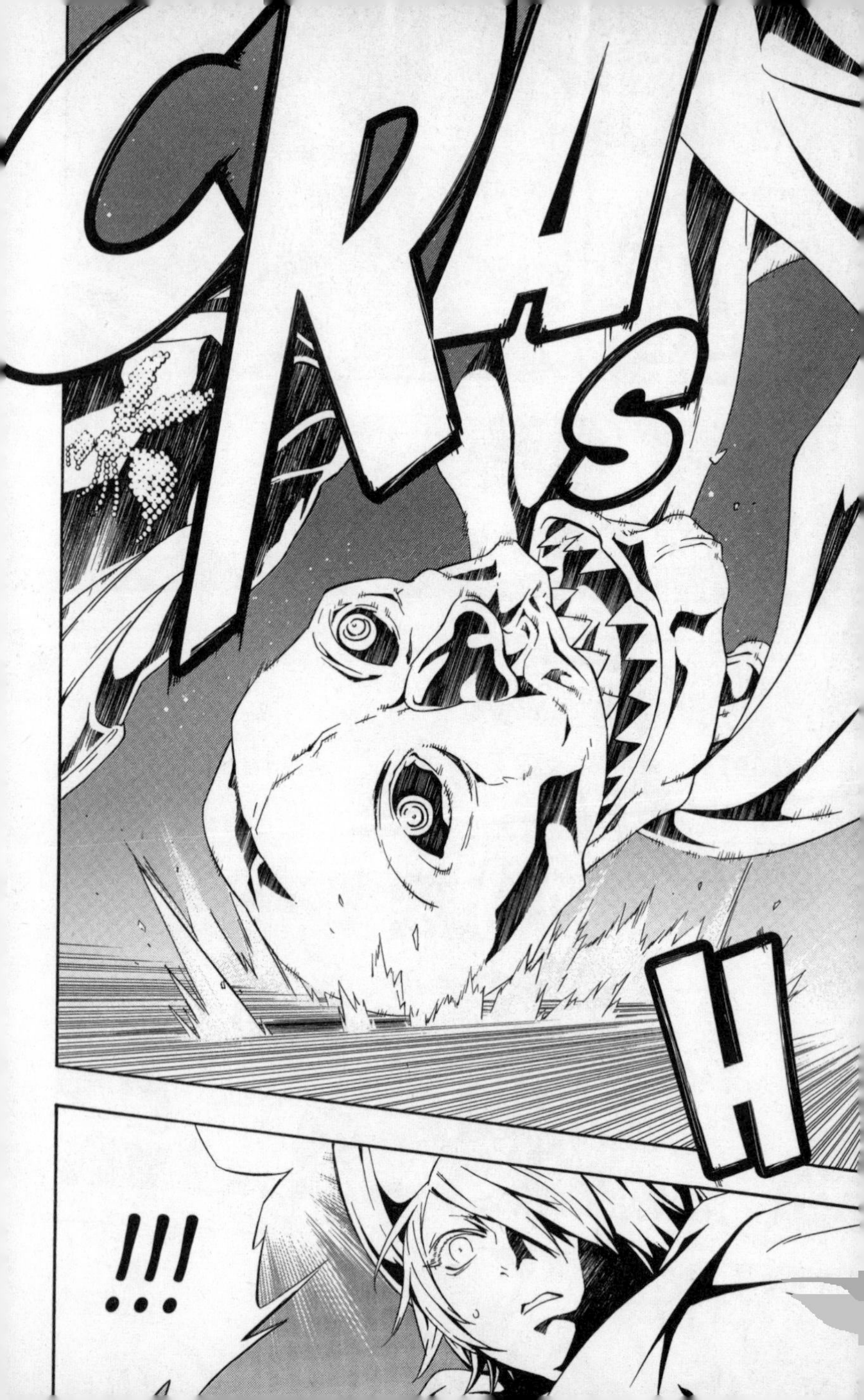
CRASH
!!!

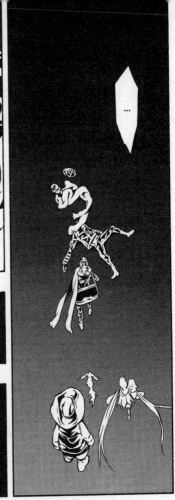

A...

...DOLL?

WHAT'S THE MEANING OF THIS?

WHERE'S ...

OR WAS THERE *NEVER* A HEAD BEE?

...THE REAL ONE?

I'LL TAKE OVER!!

OH, NEVER MIND.

IT DOESN'T MATTER.

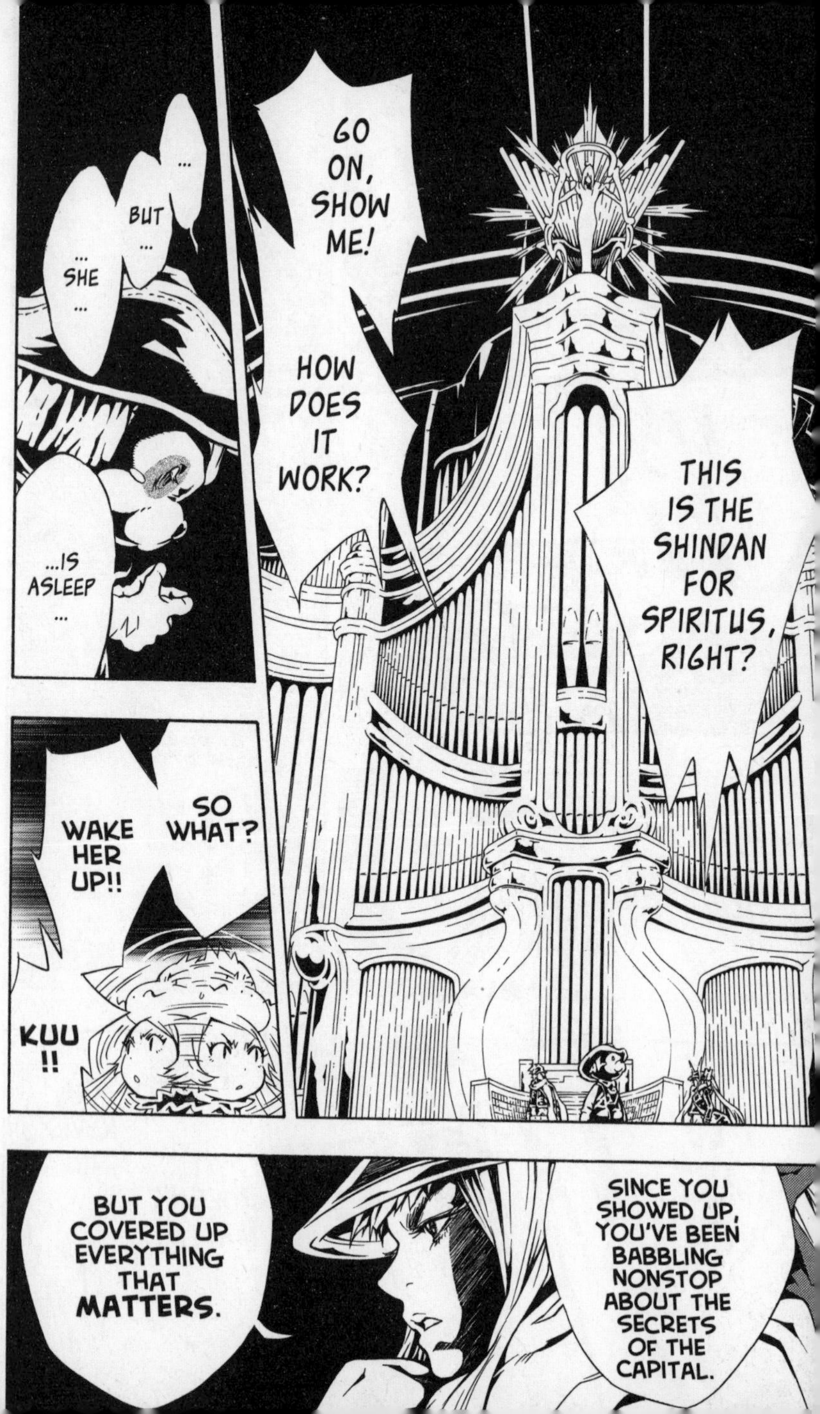
THIS IS THE SHINDAN FOR SPIRITUS, RIGHT?
GO ON, SHOW ME!
HOW DOES IT WORK?
...
BUT ...
... SHE ...
...IS ASLEEP ...
SO WHAT?
WAKE HER UP!!
KUU !!
SINCE YOU SHOWED UP, YOU'VE BEEN BABBLING NONSTOP ABOUT THE SECRETS OF THE CAPITAL.
BUT YOU COVERED UP EVERYTHING THAT MATTERS.

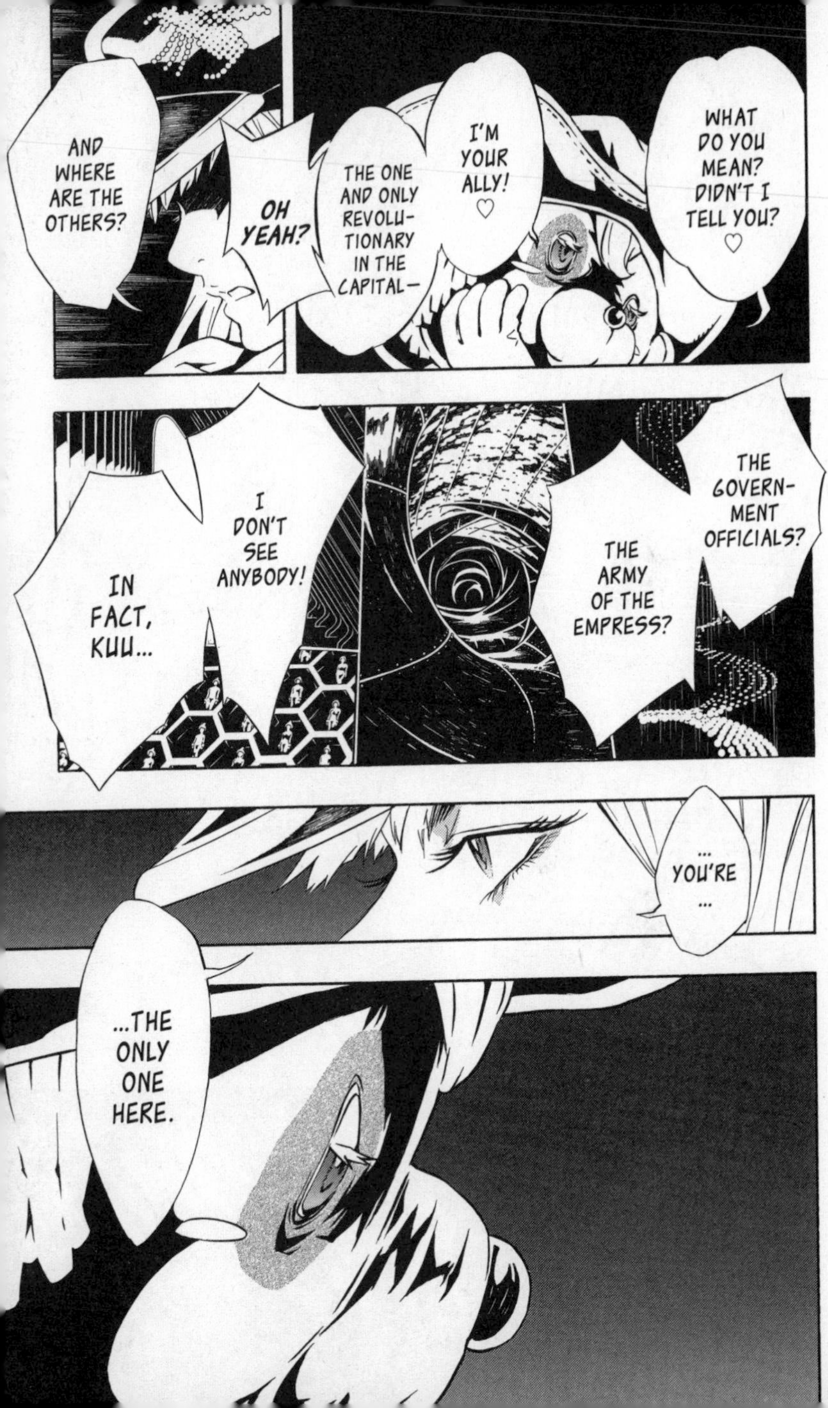
WHAT DO YOU MEAN? DIDN'T I TELL YOU? ♡
I'M YOUR ALLY! ♡
THE ONE AND ONLY REVOLUTIONARY IN THE CAPITAL—
OH YEAH?
AND WHERE ARE THE OTHERS?
THE GOVERNMENT OFFICIALS?
THE ARMY OF THE EMPRESS?
I DON'T SEE ANYBODY!
IN FACT, KUU...
... YOU'RE ...
...THE ONLY ONE HERE.

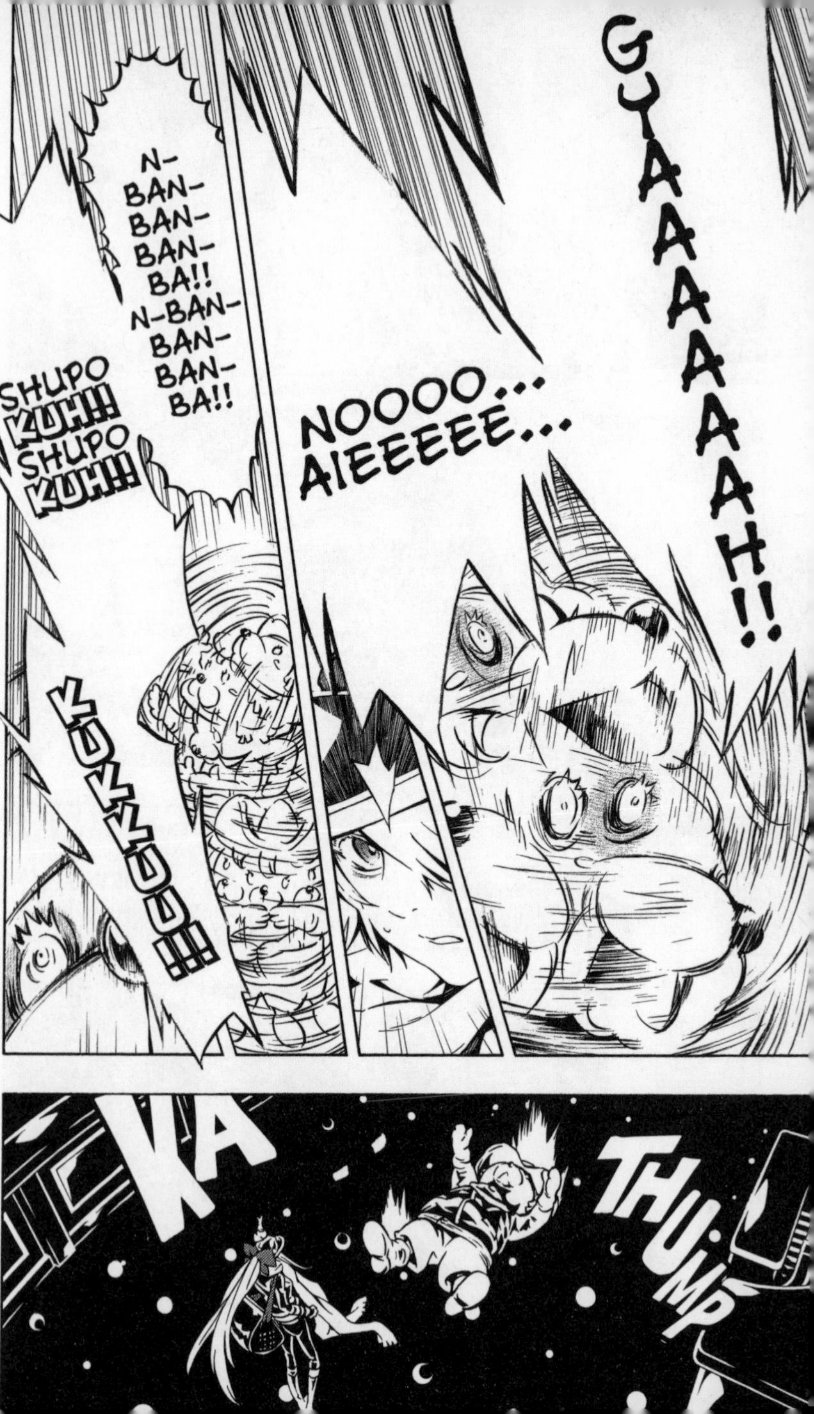
GYAAAAAAAH!!
NOOOO... AIEEEEEE...
N-BAN-BAN-BAN-BA!! N-BAN-BAN-BAN-BA!!
SHUPO KUH!! SHUPO KUH!!
KUKKUUU!!!
KA
THUMP

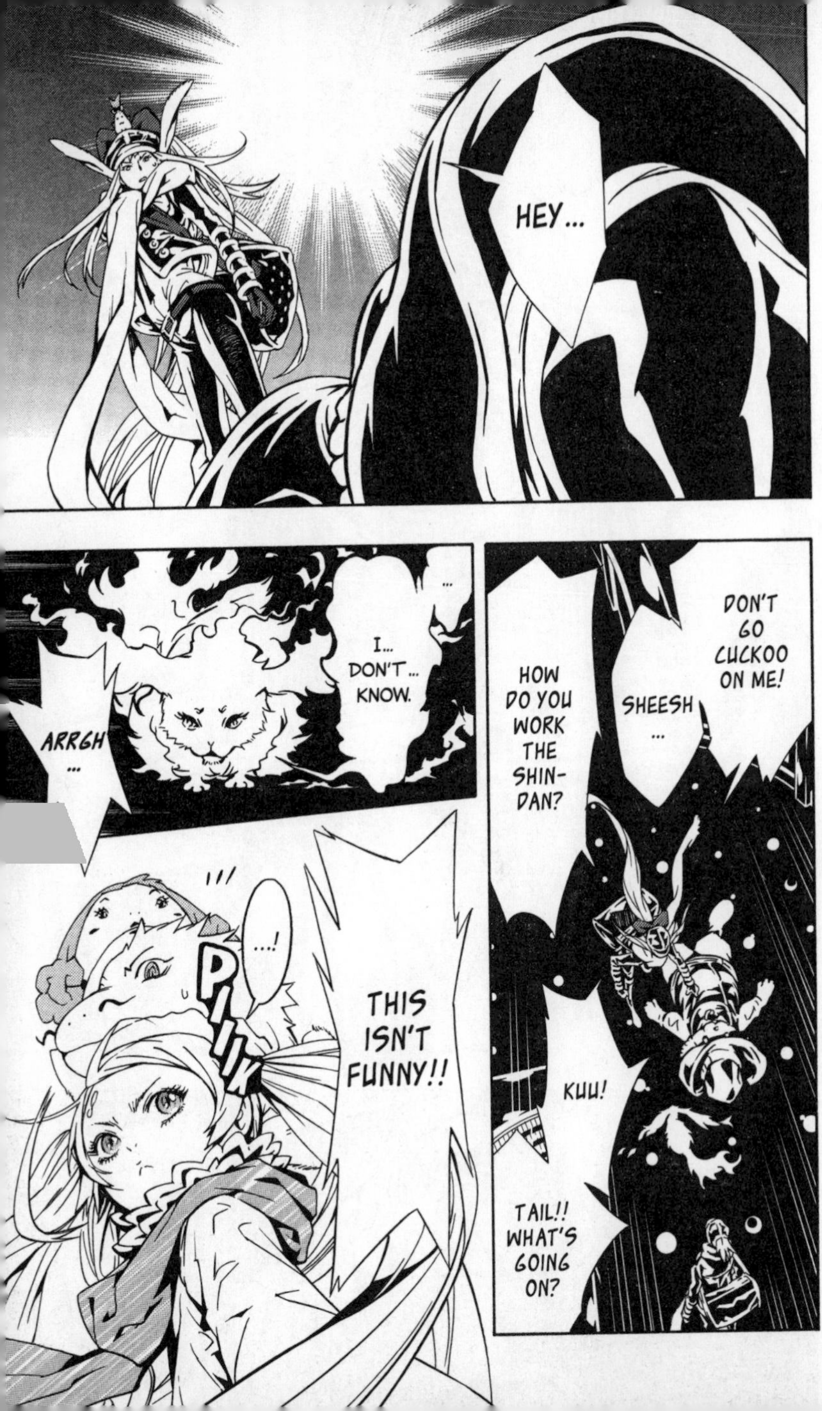
HEY...
DON'T GO CUCKOO ON ME!
SHEESH...
HOW DO YOU WORK THE SHIN-DAN?
KUU!
TAIL!! WHAT'S GOING ON?
...
I... DON'T... KNOW.
ARRGH...
THIS ISN'T FUNNY!!
PIIIK
...!

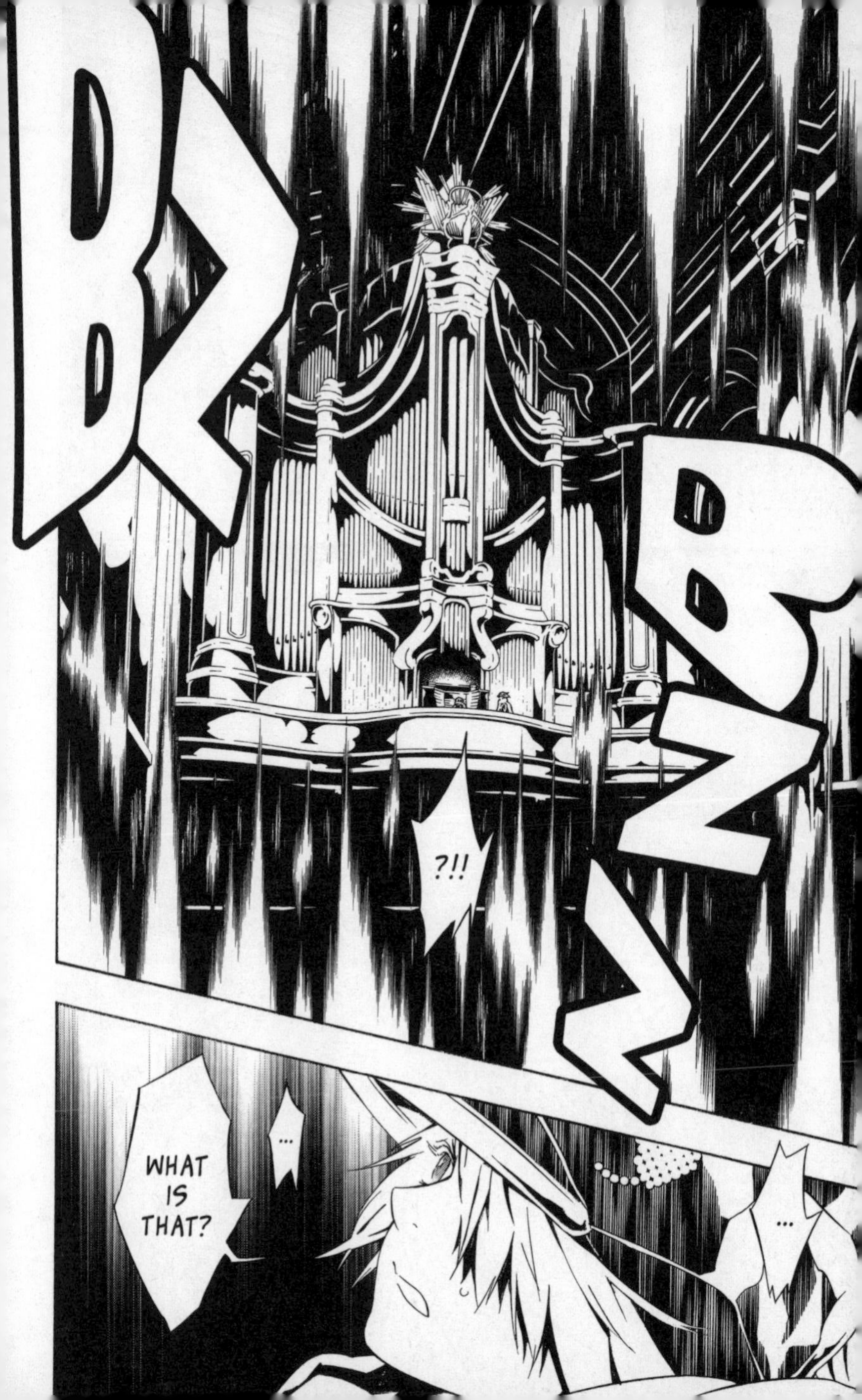
?!!
...
...
WHAT IS THAT?

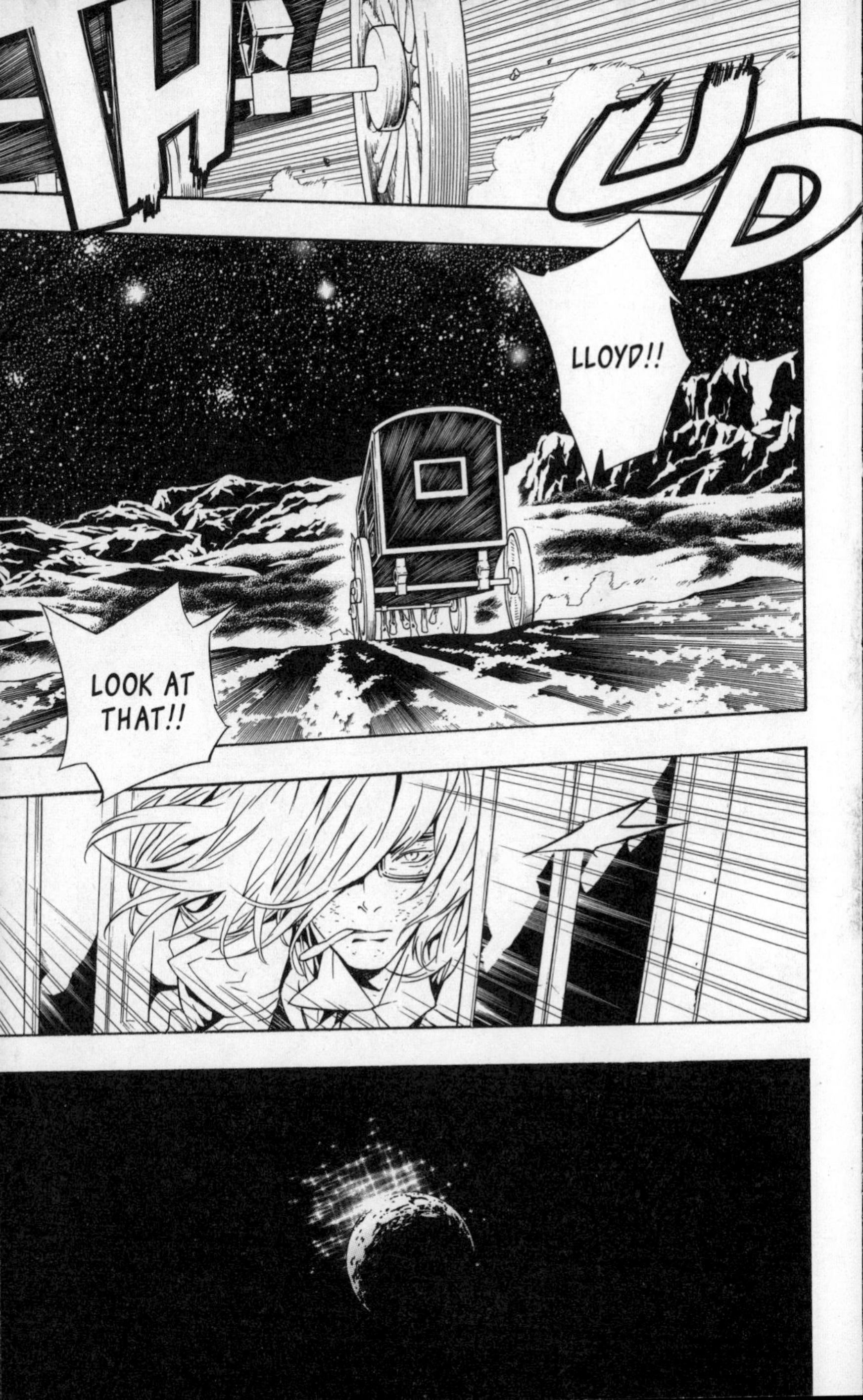
LLOYD!!
LOOK AT THAT!!

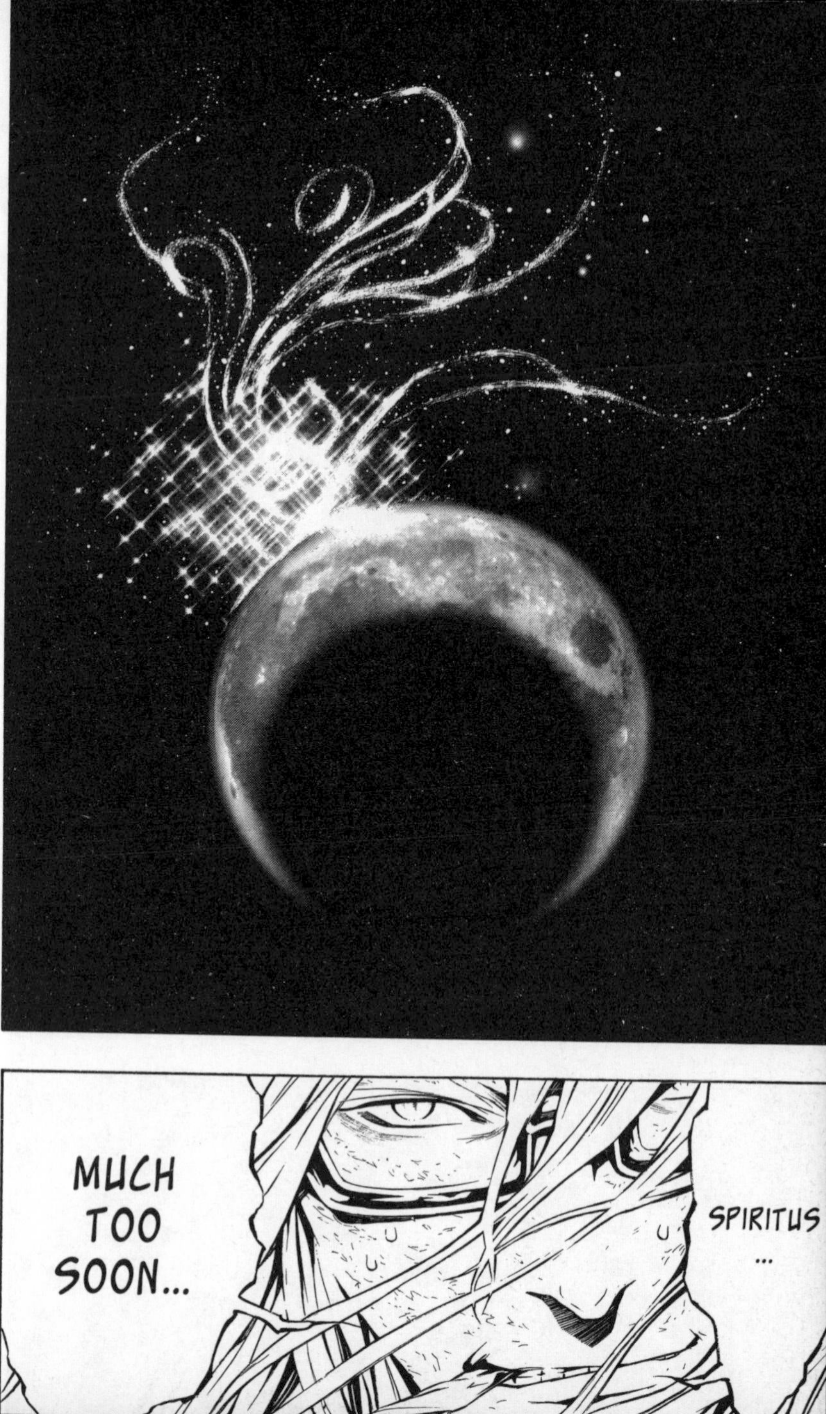
SPIRITUS ...
MUCH TOO SOON...

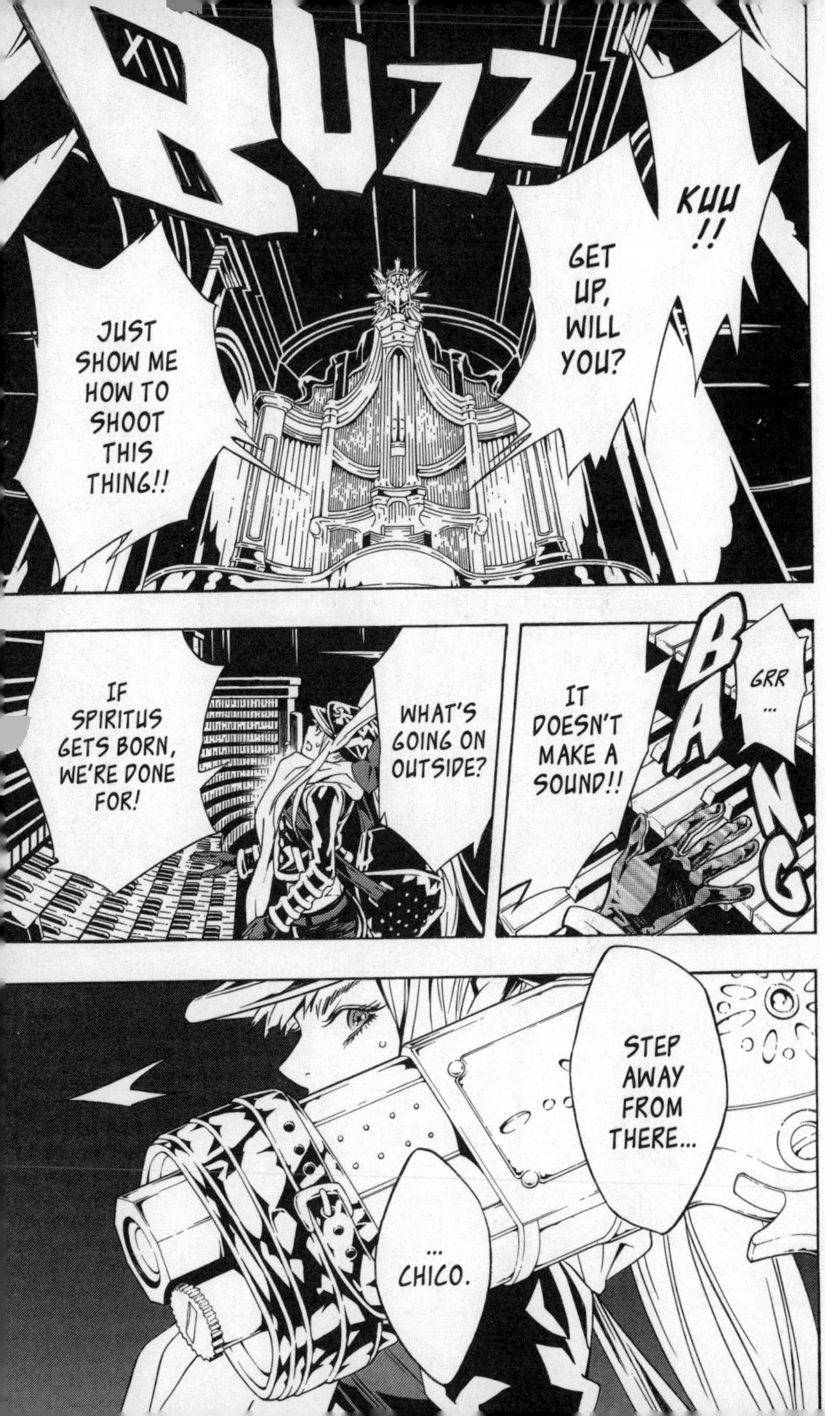
BUZZ
KUU!!
GET UP, WILL YOU?
JUST SHOW ME HOW TO SHOOT THIS THING!!
BANG
GRR...
IT DOESN'T MAKE A SOUND!!
WHAT'S GOING ON OUTSIDE?
IF SPIRITUS GETS BORN, WE'RE DONE FOR!
STEP AWAY FROM THERE...
...CHICO.

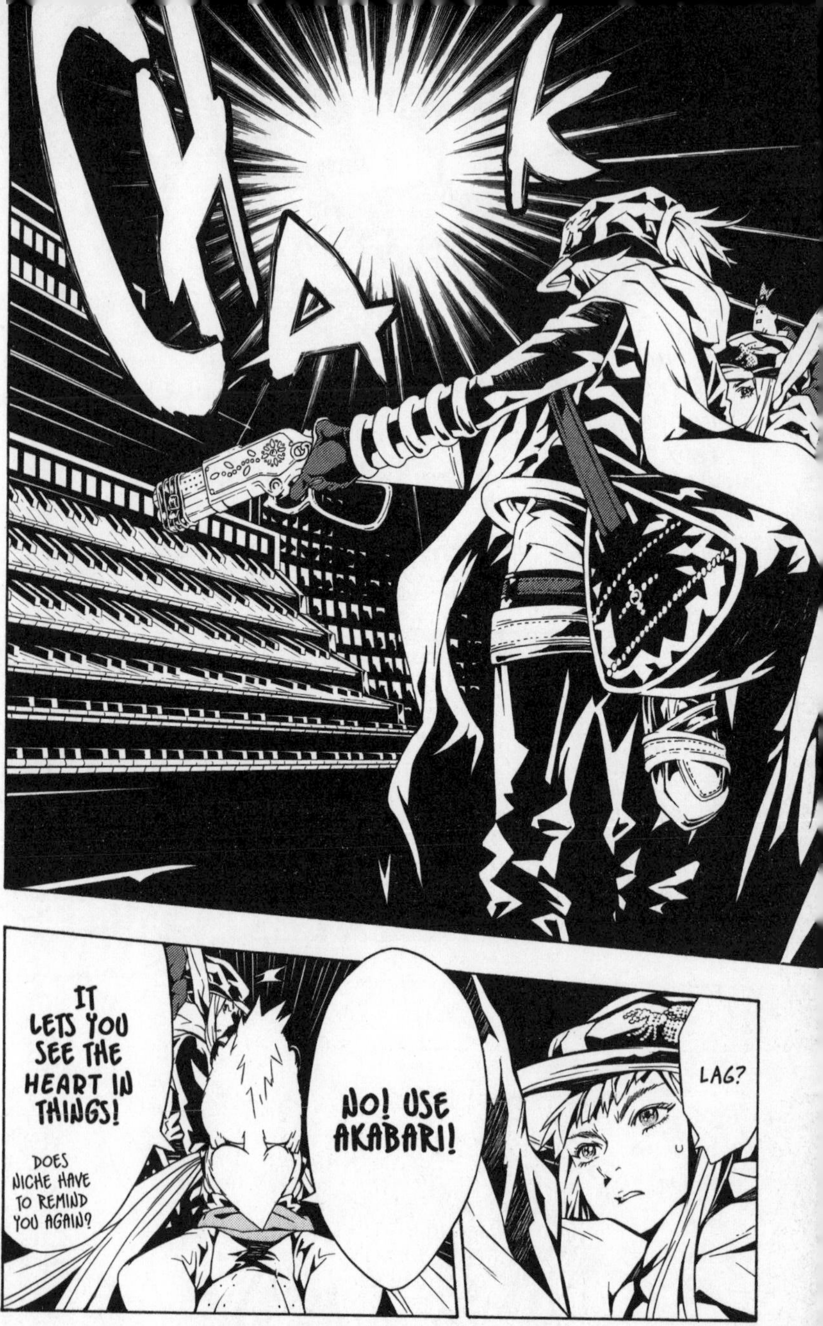
CHAK
LAG?
NO! USE AKABARI!
IT LETS YOU SEE THE HEART IN THINGS!
DOES NICHE HAVE TO REMIND YOU AGAIN?

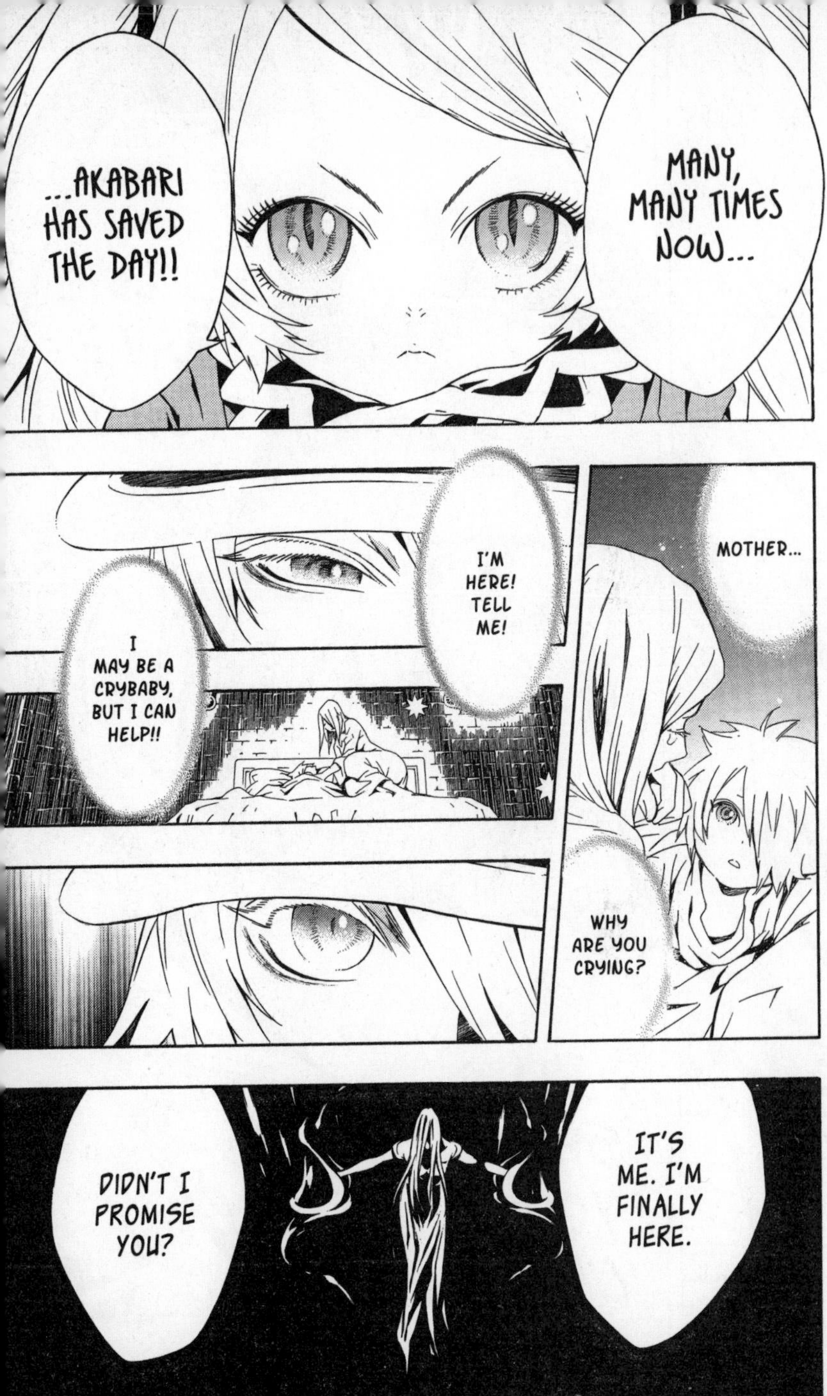
MANY, MANY TIMES NOW...
...AKABARI HAS SAVED THE DAY!!
MOTHER...
WHY ARE YOU CRYING?
I'M HERE! TELL ME!
I MAY BE A CRYBABY, BUT I CAN HELP!!
IT'S ME. I'M FINALLY HERE.
DIDN'T I PROMISE YOU?

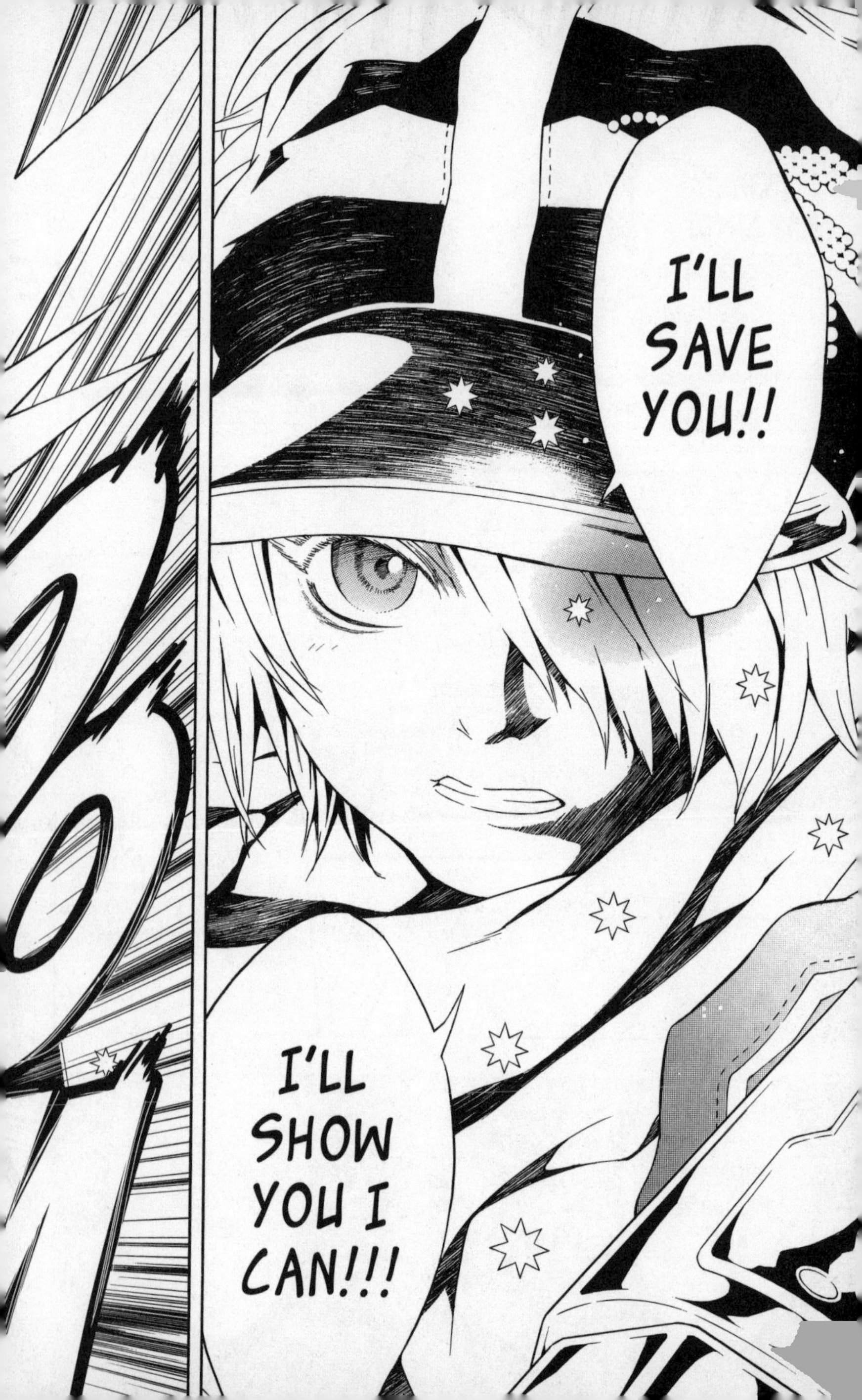
I'LL SAVE YOU!!
I'LL SHOW YOU I CAN!!!

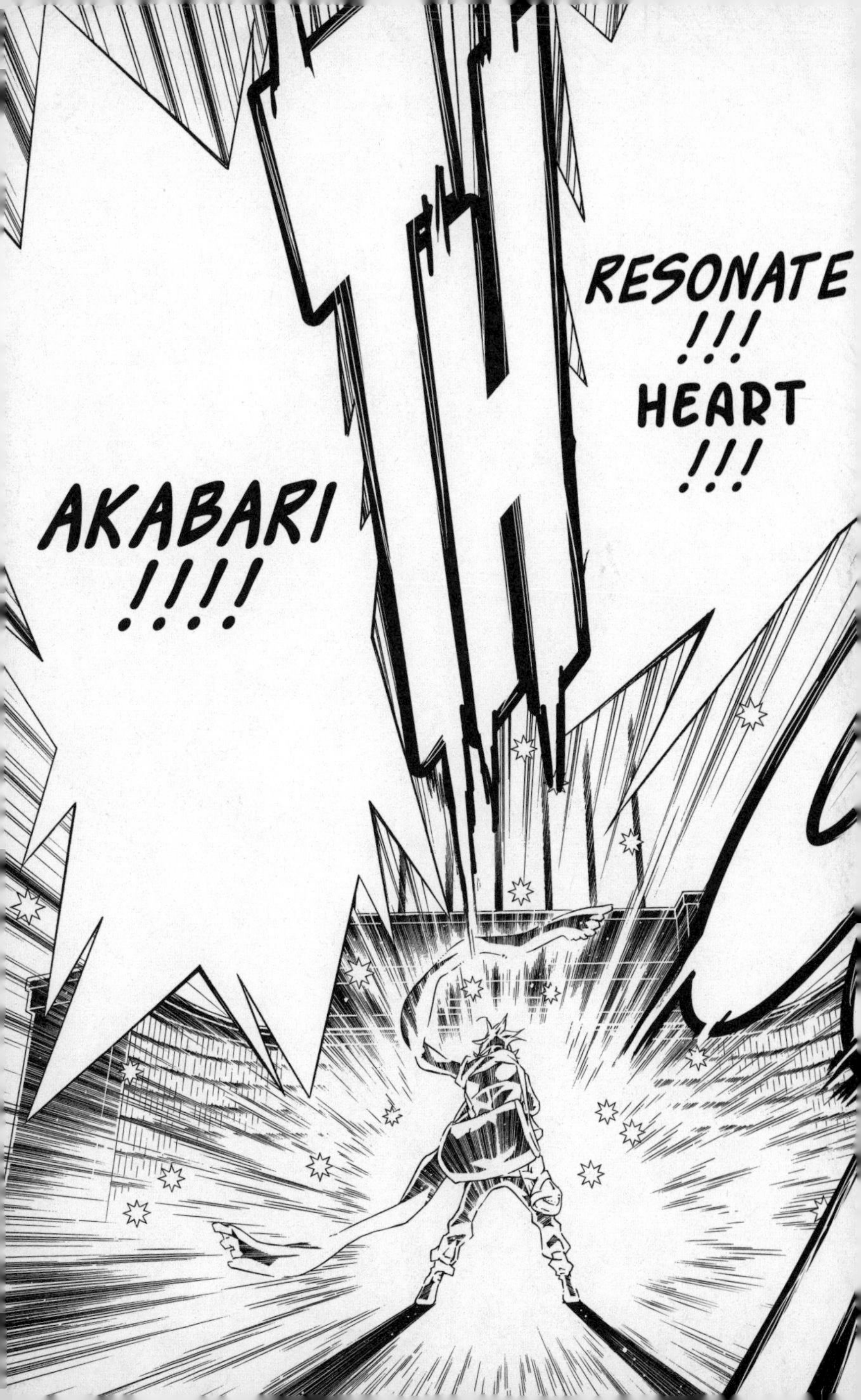
RESONATE !!!
HEART !!!
AKABARI !!!!

Chapter 93: The Head Bee

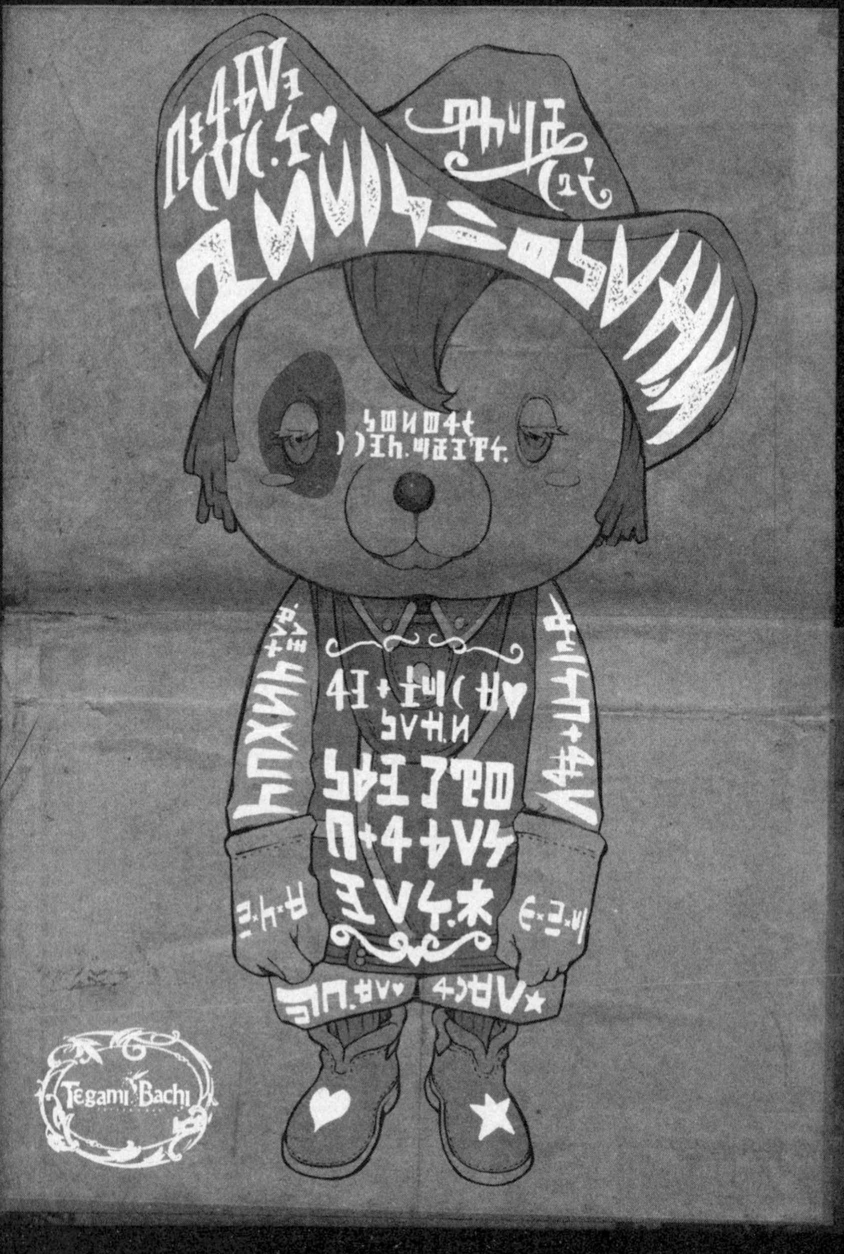
Tegami Bachi

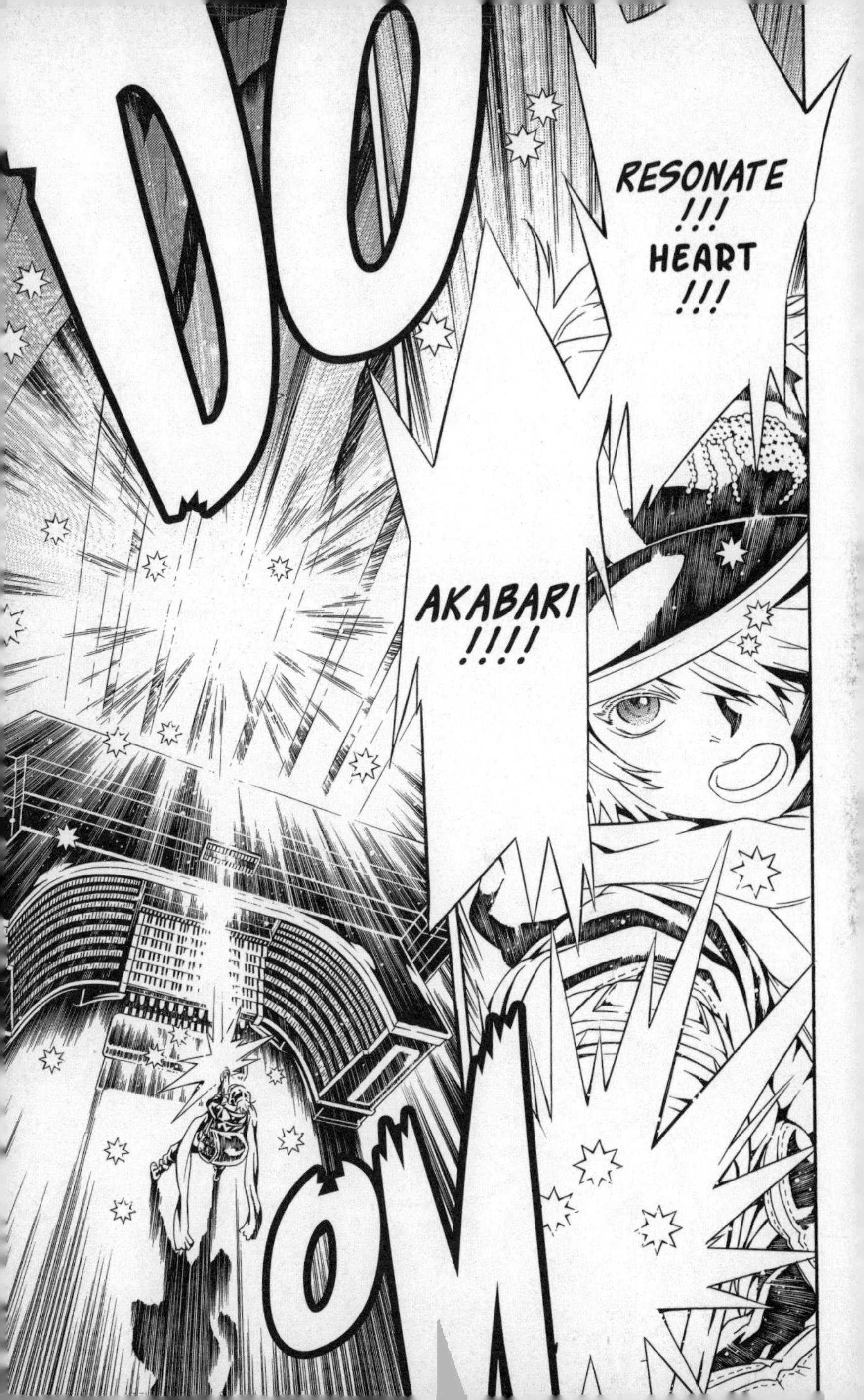
RESONATE!!! HEART!!!
AKABARI!!!!

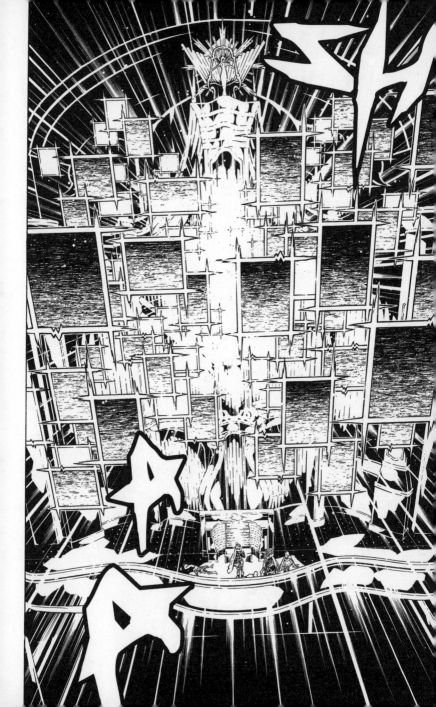

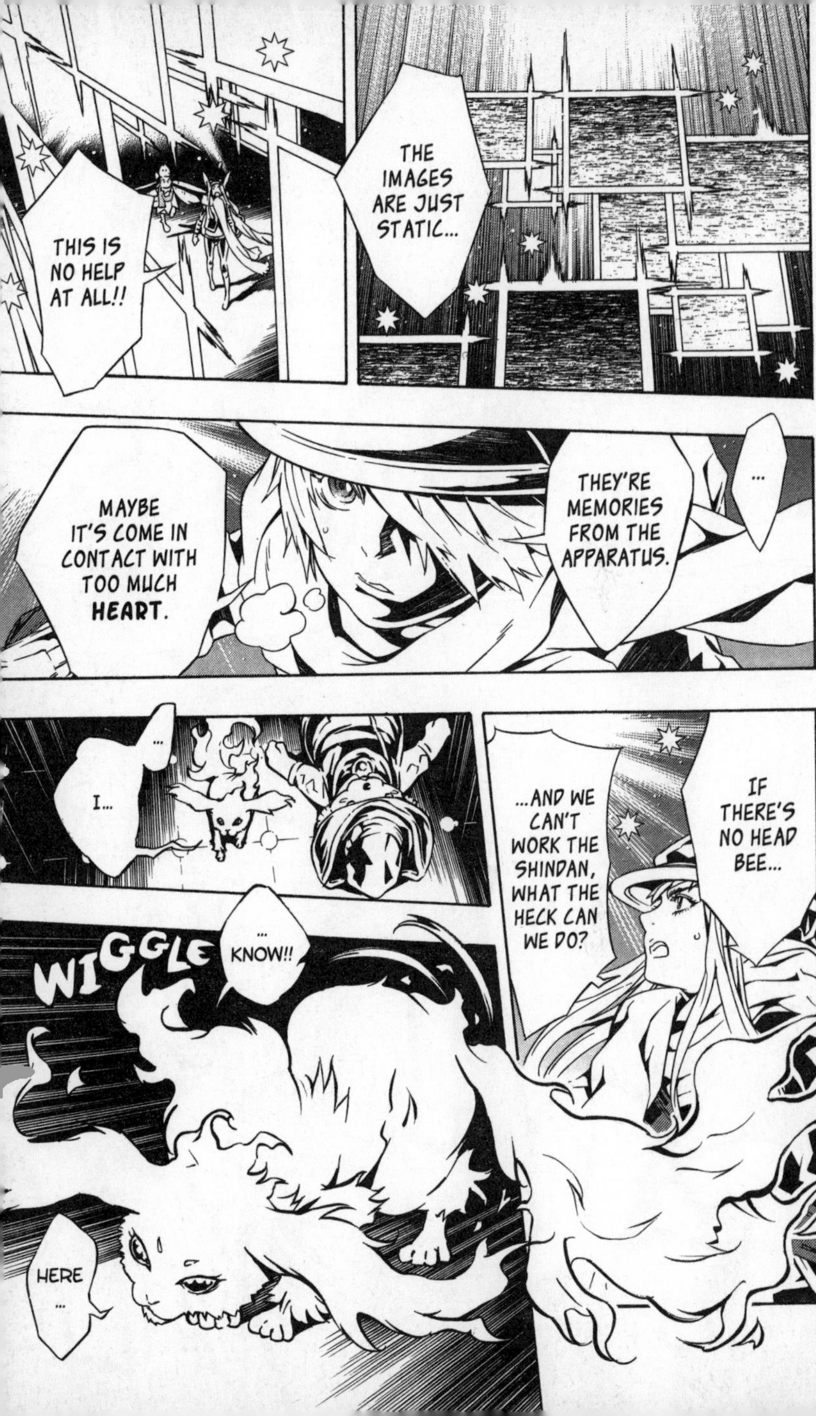
THE IMAGES ARE JUST STATIC...
THIS IS NO HELP AT ALL!!
...
THEY'RE MEMORIES FROM THE APPARATUS.
MAYBE IT'S COME IN CONTACT WITH TOO MUCH **HEART**.
IF THERE'S NO HEAD BEE...
...AND WE CAN'T WORK THE SHINDAN, WHAT THE HECK CAN WE DO?
...
I...
... KNOW!!
WIGGLE
HERE ...

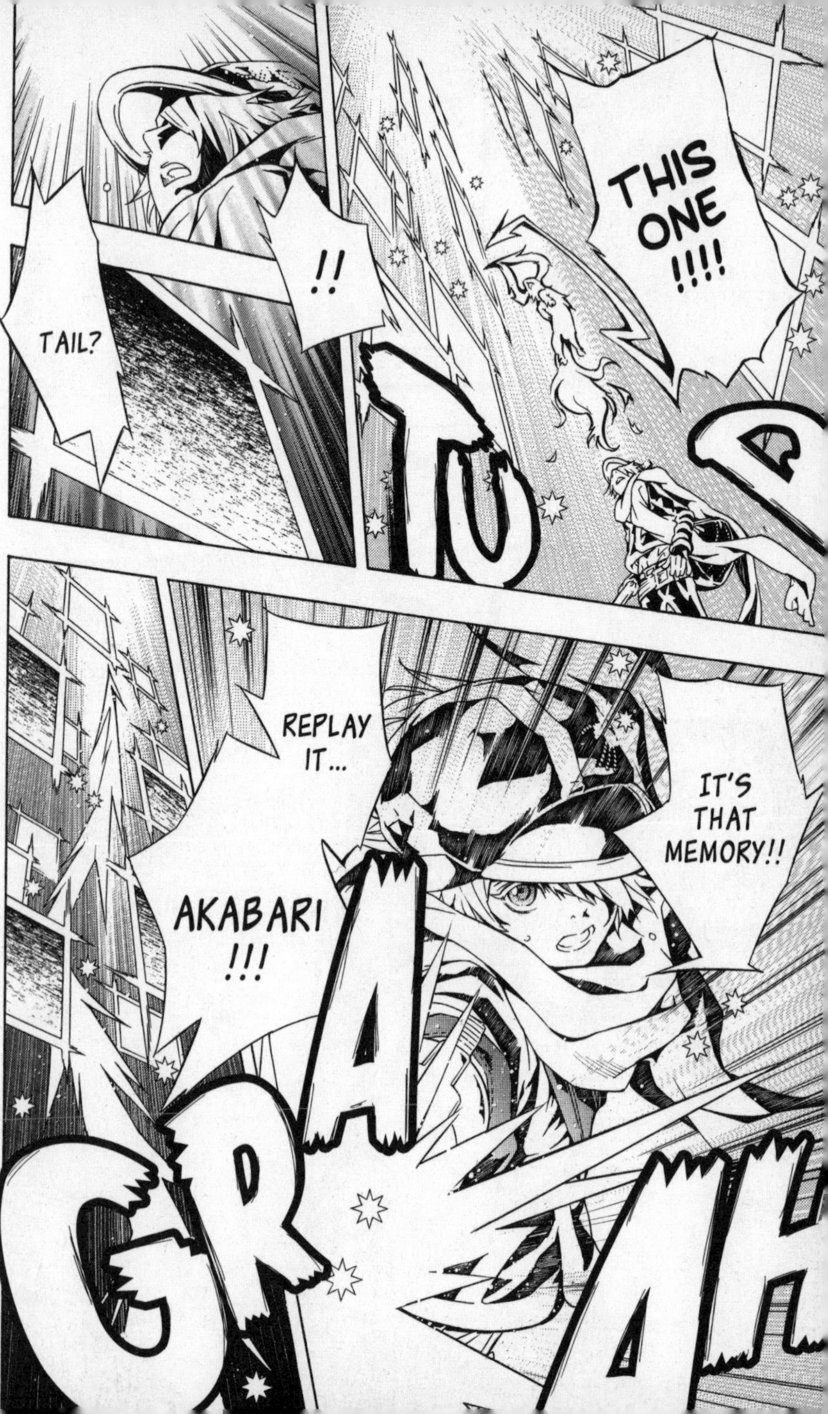
THIS ONE !!!!
TUD
!!
TAIL?
IT'S THAT MEMORY!!
REPLAY IT...
AKABARI !!!
GRAAH

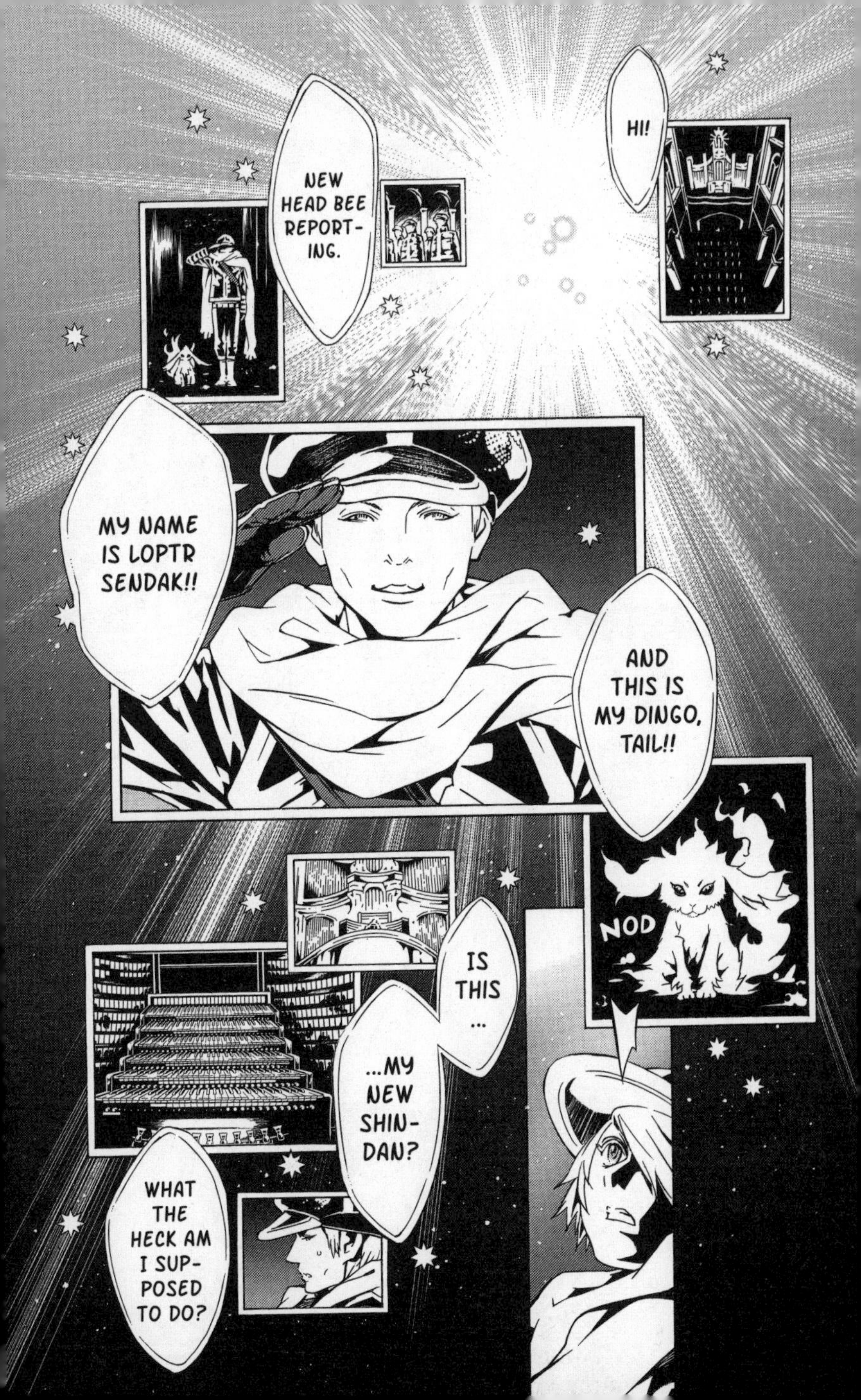
HI!
NEW HEAD BEE REPORTING.
MY NAME IS LOPTR SENDAK!!
AND THIS IS MY DINGO, TAIL!!
NOD
IS THIS...
...MY NEW SHINDAN?
WHAT THE HECK AM I SUPPOSED TO DO?

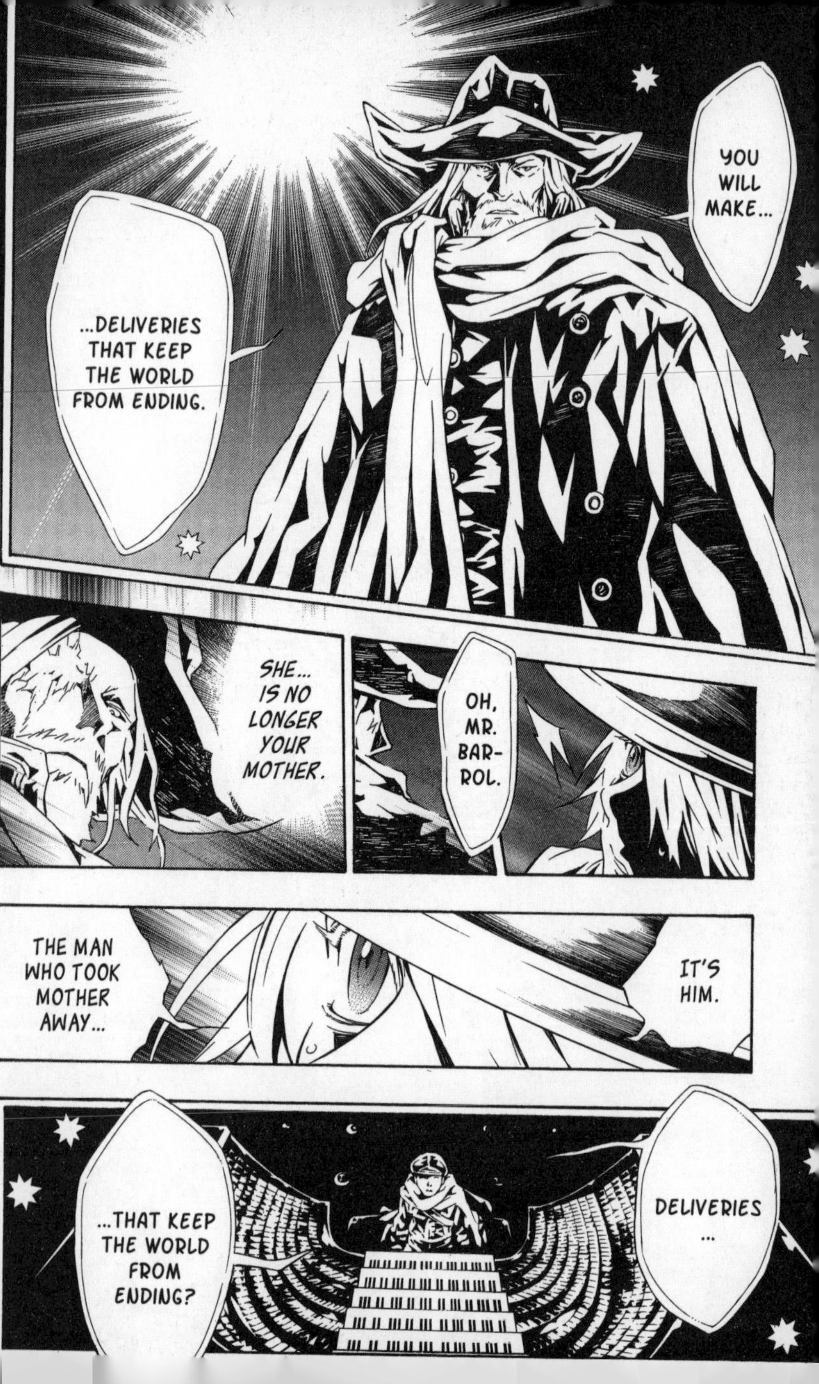
YOU WILL MAKE...
...DELIVERIES THAT KEEP THE WORLD FROM ENDING.
OH, MR. BAR-ROL.
SHE... IS NO LONGER YOUR MOTHER.
IT'S HIM.
THE MAN WHO TOOK MOTHER AWAY...
DELIVERIES...
...THAT KEEP THE WORLD FROM ENDING?

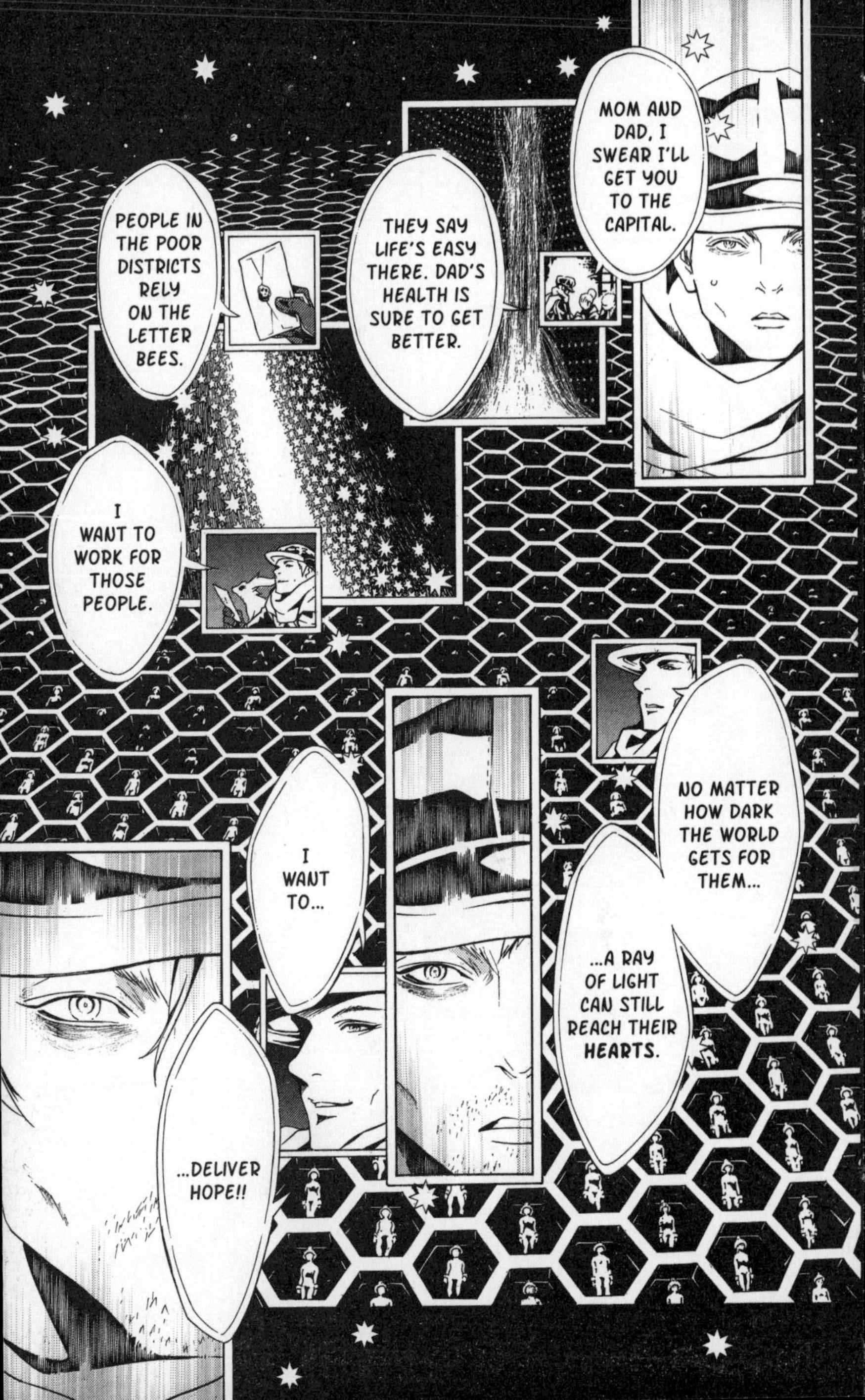
MOM AND DAD, I SWEAR I'LL GET YOU TO THE CAPITAL.
THEY SAY LIFE'S EASY THERE. DAD'S HEALTH IS SURE TO GET BETTER.
PEOPLE IN THE POOR DISTRICTS RELY ON THE LETTER BEES.
I WANT TO WORK FOR THOSE PEOPLE.
NO MATTER HOW DARK THE WORLD GETS FOR THEM...
...A RAY OF LIGHT CAN STILL REACH THEIR HEARTS.
I WANT TO...
...DELIVER HOPE!!

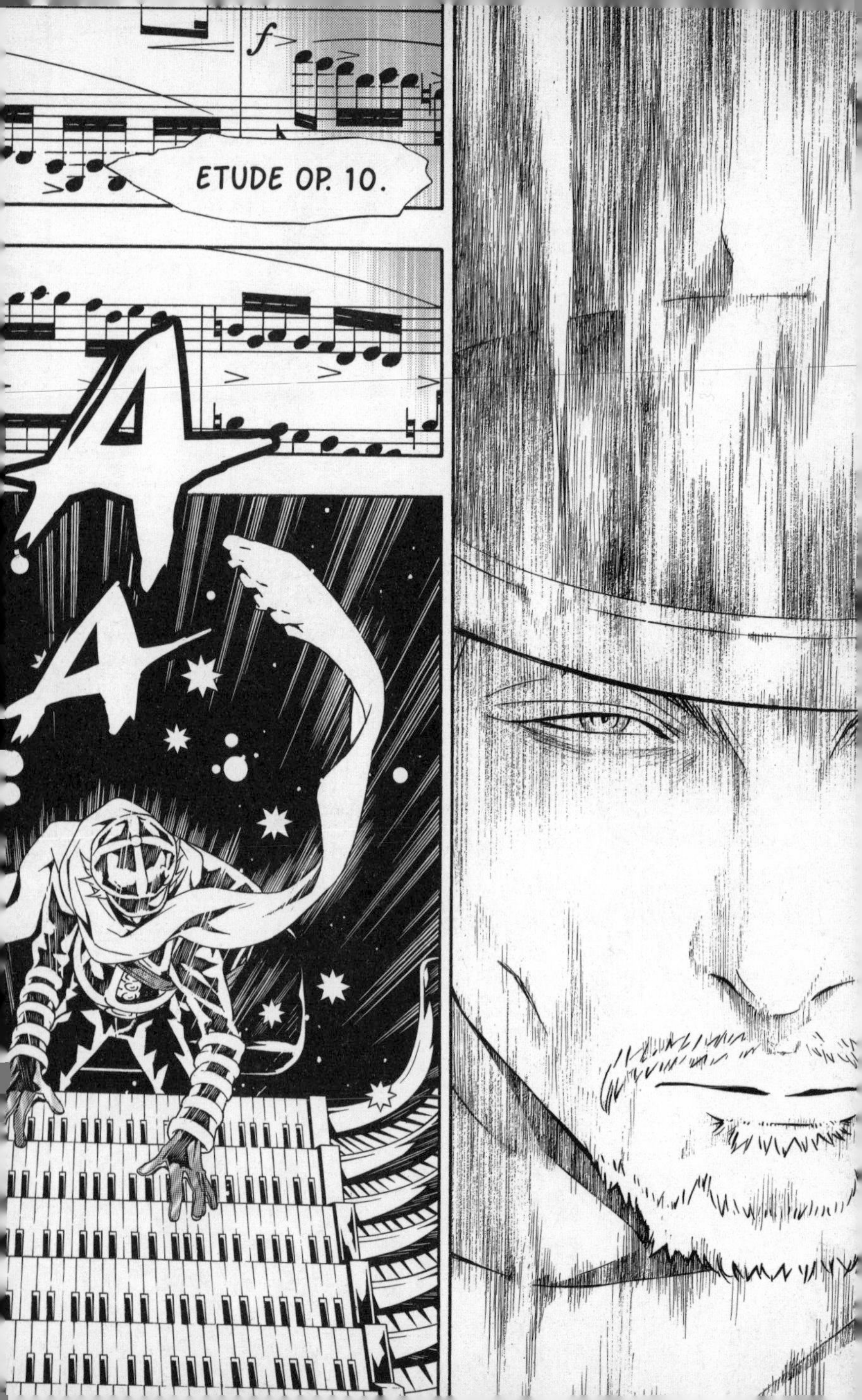
ETUDE OP. 10.

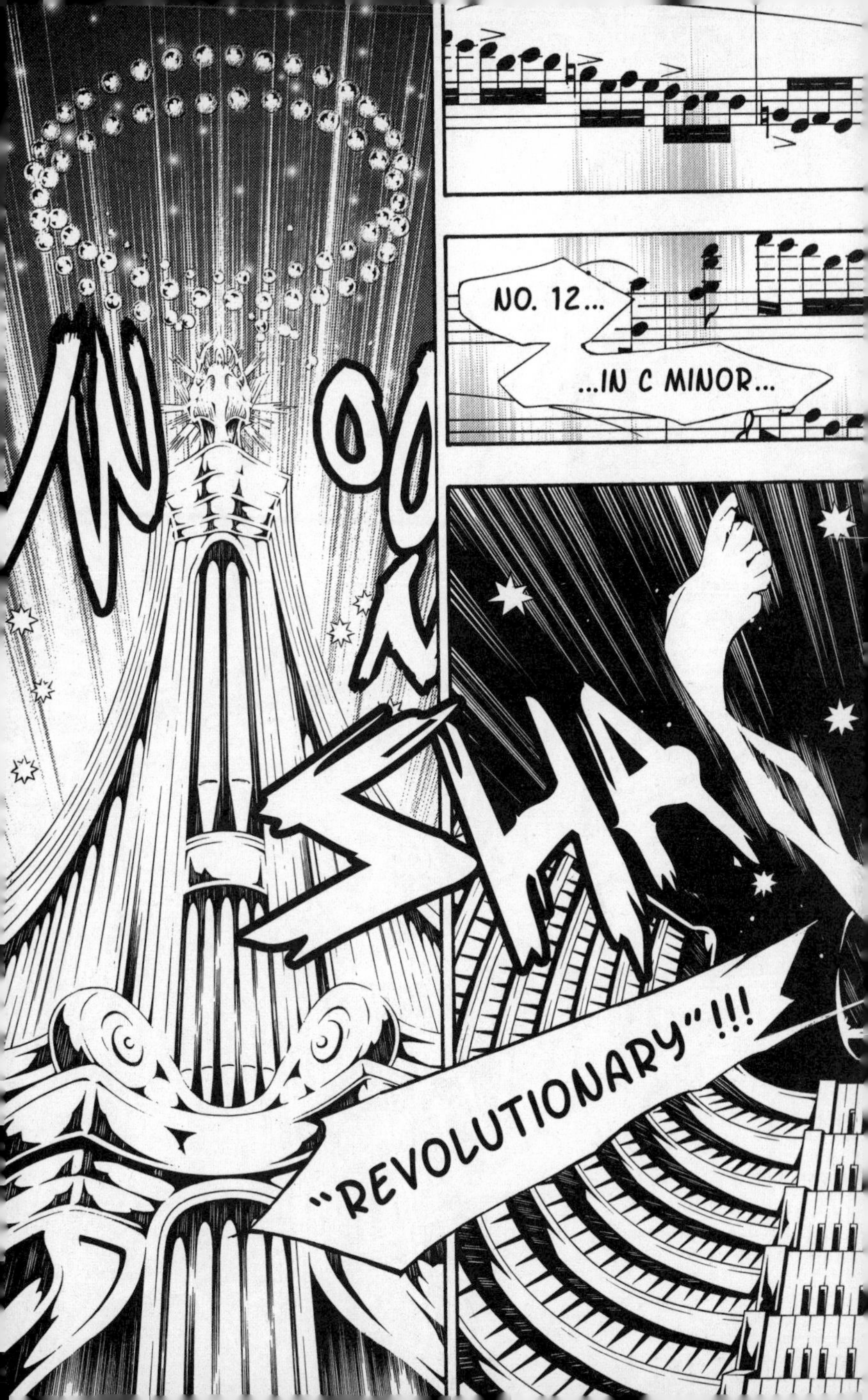
NO. 12...
...IN C MINOR...
SHA
"REVOLUTIONARY"!!!

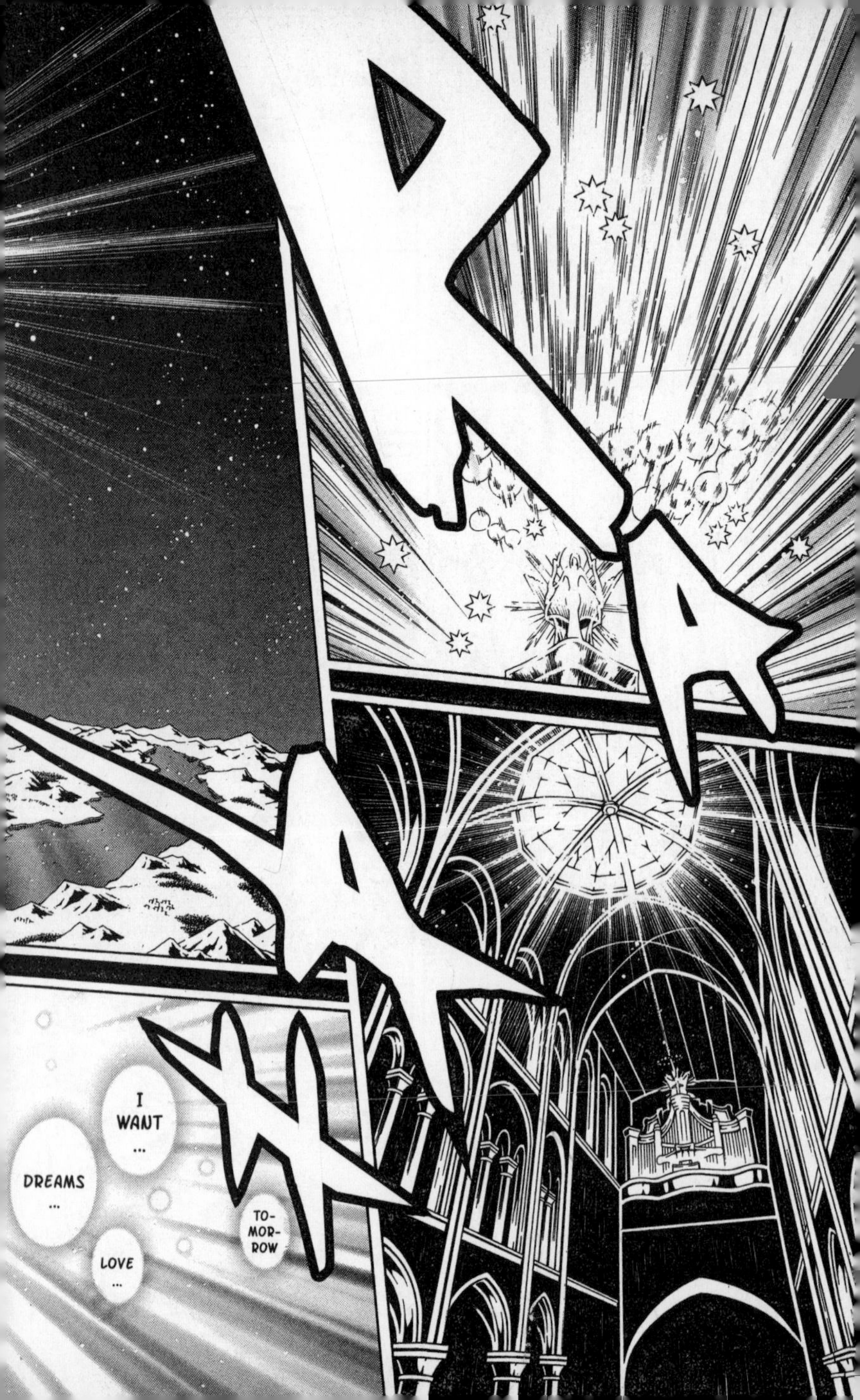
I WANT ...
DREAMS ...
TO-MOR-ROW
LOVE ...

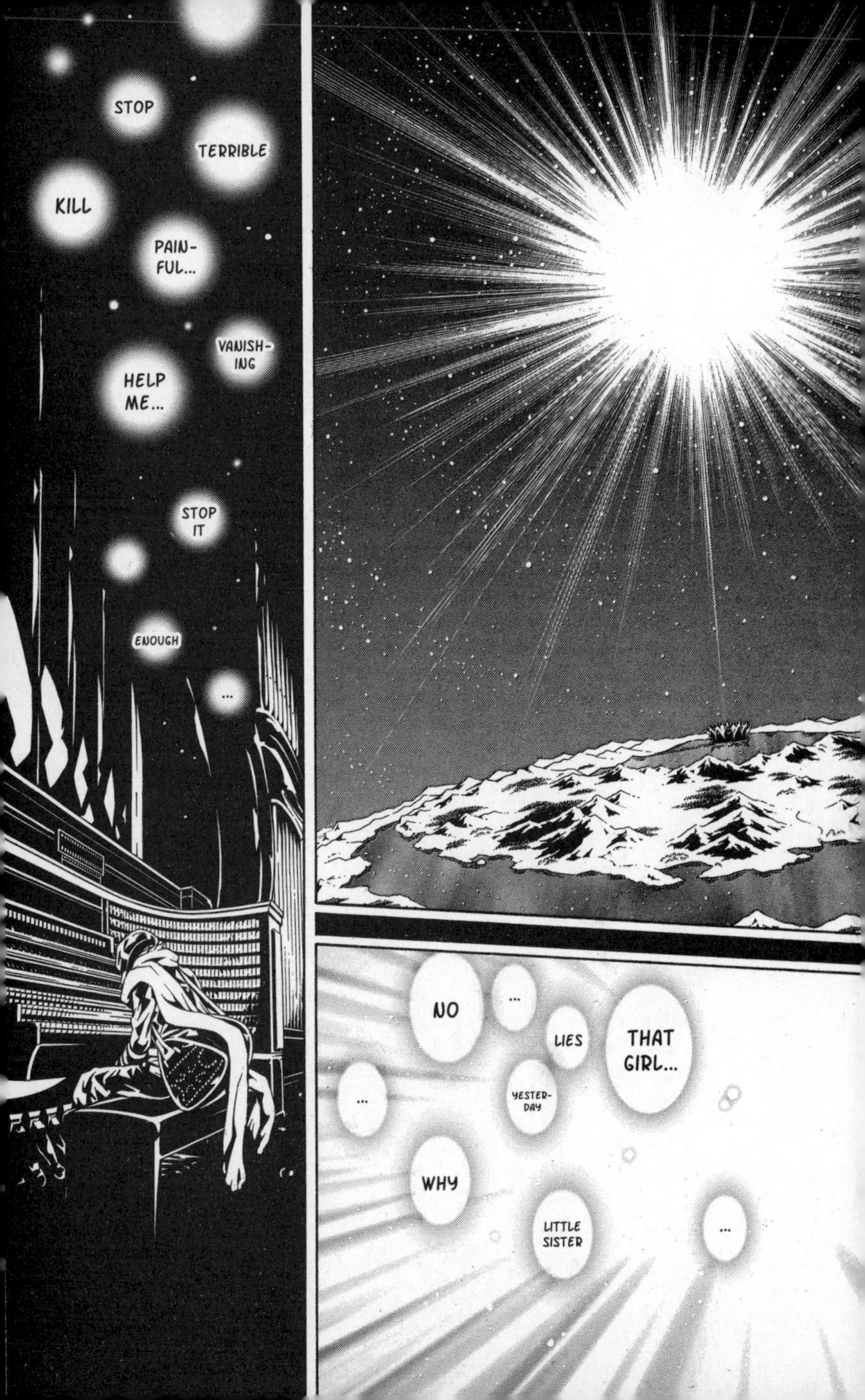
THAT GIRL...
LIES
...
NO
YESTER-DAY
...
...
LITTLE SISTER
WHY
TERRIBLE
STOP
KILL
PAIN-FUL...
VANISH-ING
HELP ME...
STOP IT
ENOUGH
...

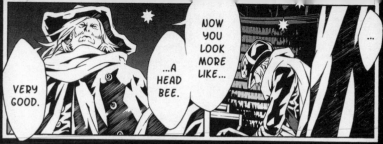

...
NOW YOU LOOK MORE LIKE...
...A HEAD BEE.
VERY GOOD.
AS WE HAVE NO USE FOR YOUR HEART, TAKE PRIDE IN YOUR PLACE...
...AS ONE OF THE COGS THAT KEEPS THE WORLD RUNNING.
ALL THE HEAD BEES WHO CAME BEFORE YOU HAVE DONE THE SAME.
A FLICKER...
THEY SAY...THE EMPRESS... HAS DIED.
THE FLOW OF HEART FROM DAGDA'S CAULDRON HAS STOPPED.
...
OHH...
HOW CALM IT IS...

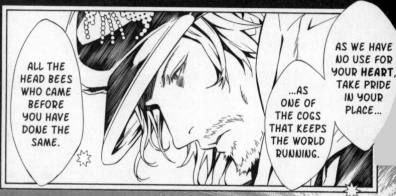

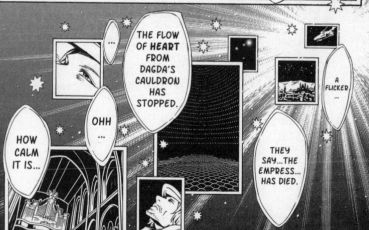

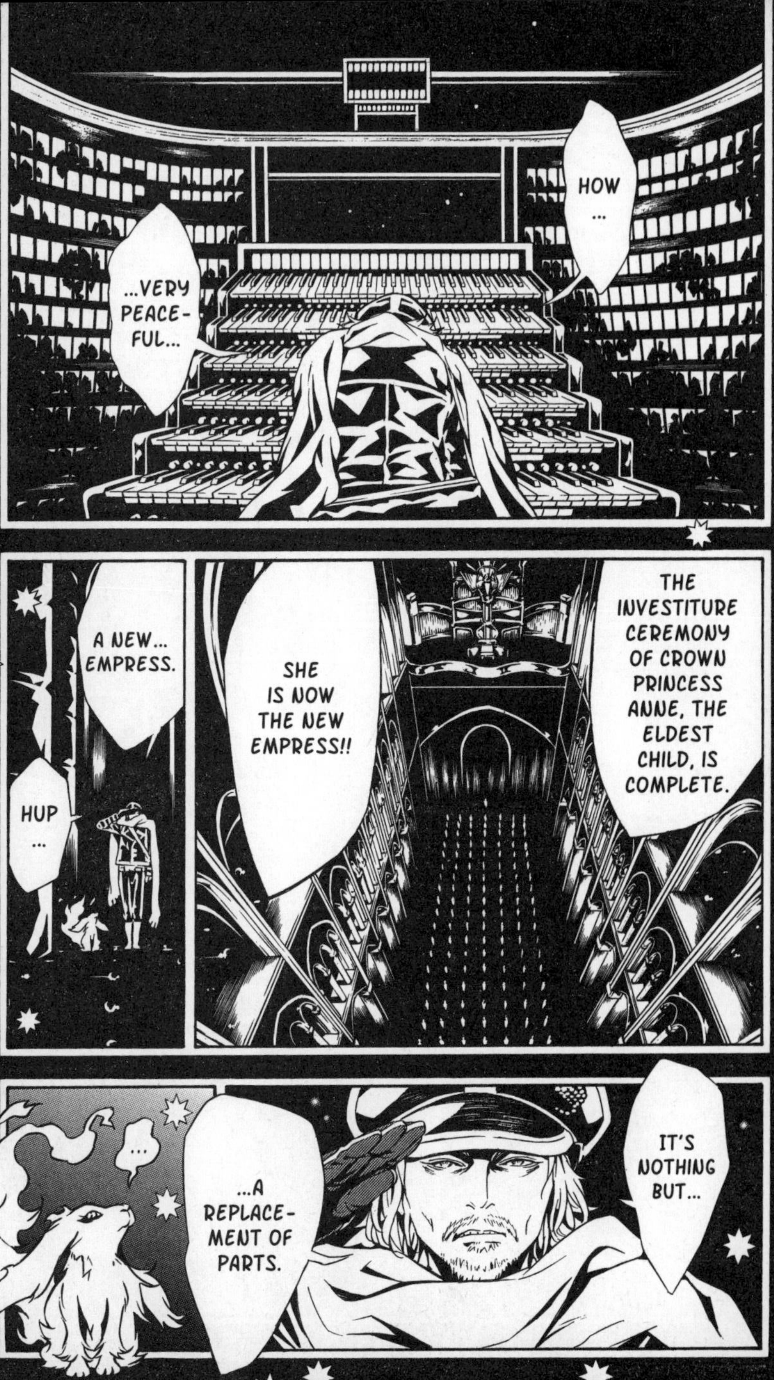
HOW...
...VERY PEACEFUL...
THE INVESTITURE CEREMONY OF CROWN PRINCESS ANNE, THE ELDEST CHILD, IS COMPLETE.
SHE IS NOW THE NEW EMPRESS!!
A NEW... EMPRESS.
HUP...
IT'S NOTHING BUT...
...A REPLACEMENT OF PARTS.
...

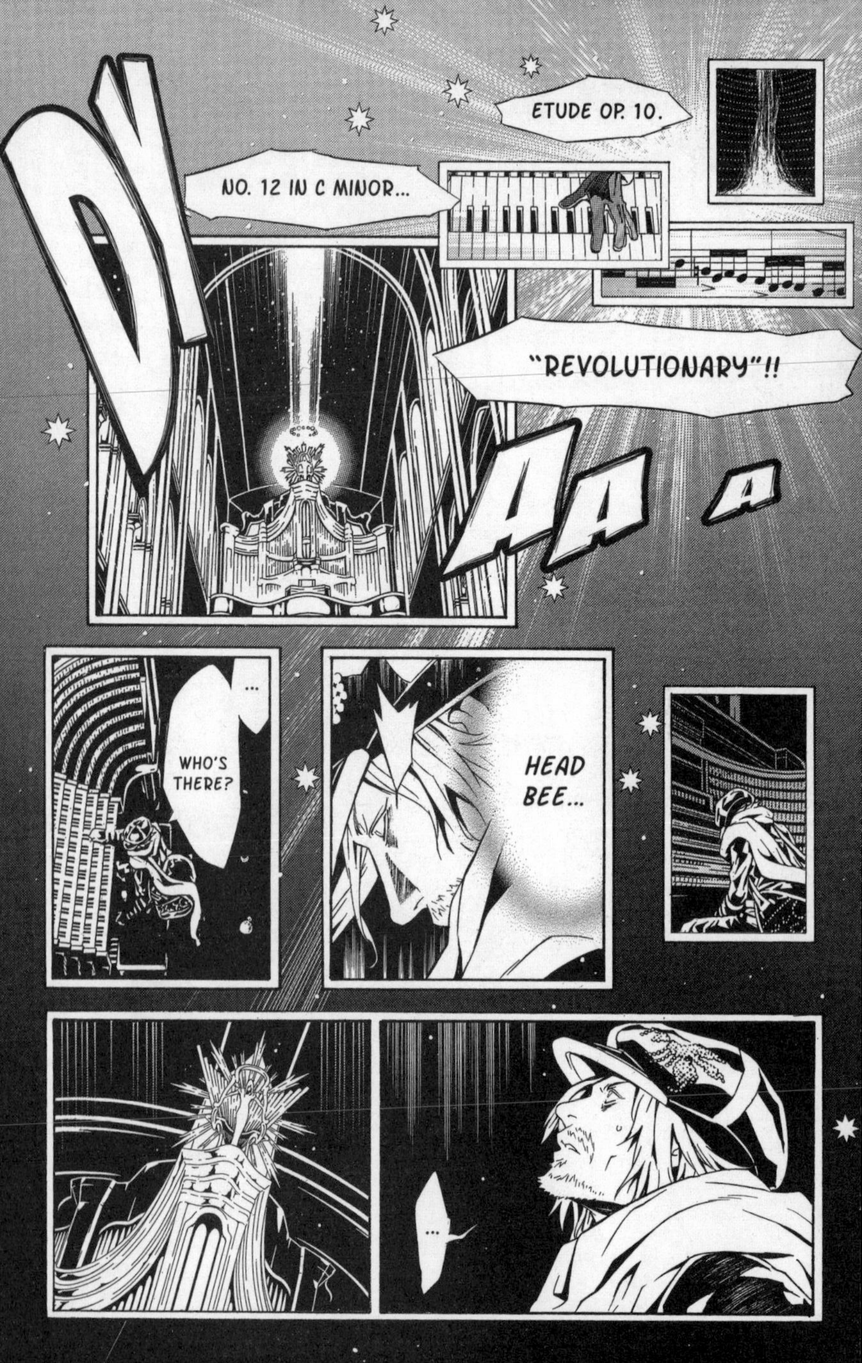
ETUDE OP. 10.
NO. 12 IN C MINOR...
"REVOLUTIONARY"!!
DVAAA
HEAD BEE...
...
WHO'S THERE?
...

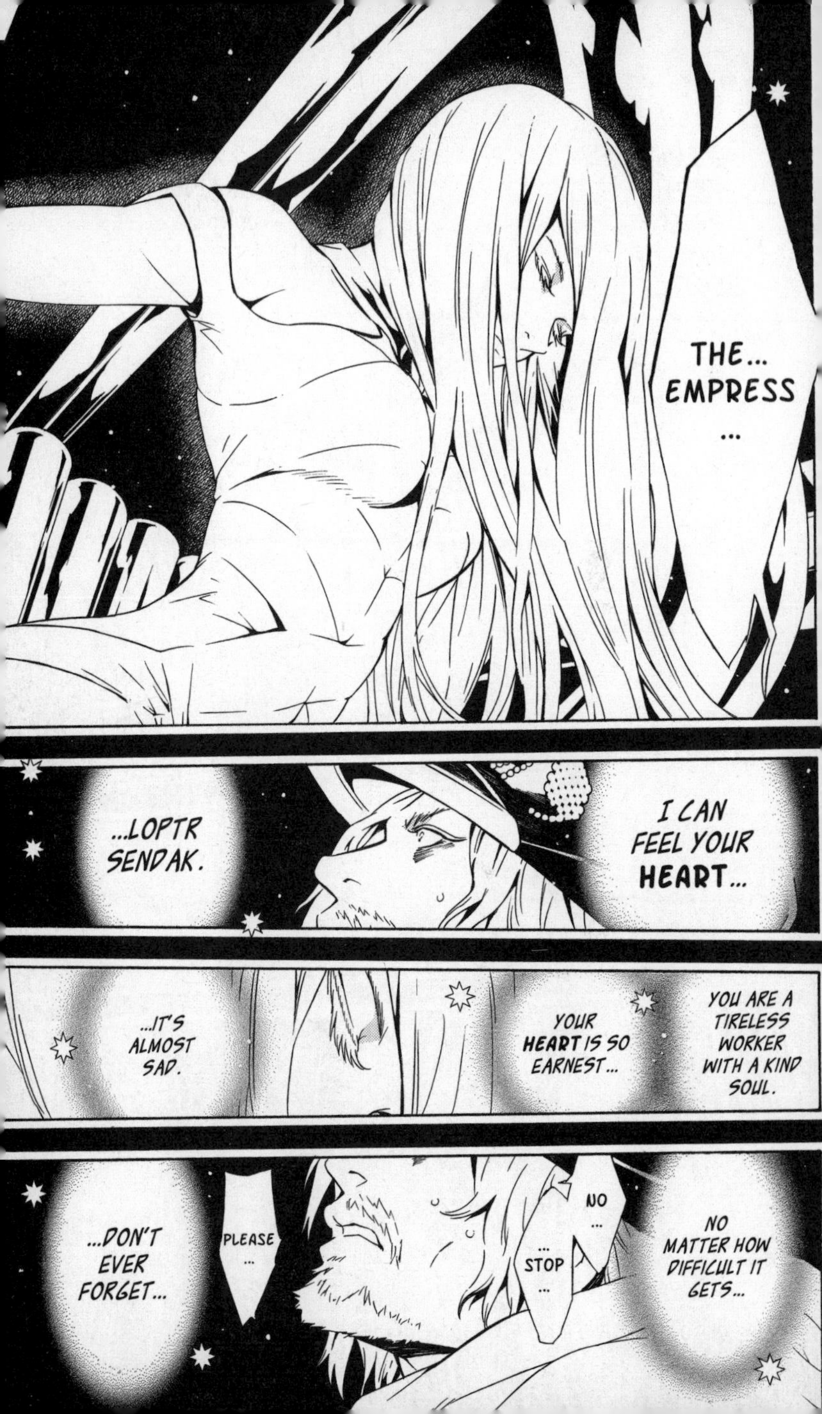
THE... EMPRESS ...
I CAN FEEL YOUR HEART...
...LOPTR SENDAK.
YOU ARE A TIRELESS WORKER WITH A KIND SOUL.
YOUR HEART IS SO EARNEST...
...IT'S ALMOST SAD.
NO MATTER HOW DIFFICULT IT GETS...
NO ...
... STOP ...
PLEASE ...
...DON'T EVER FORGET...

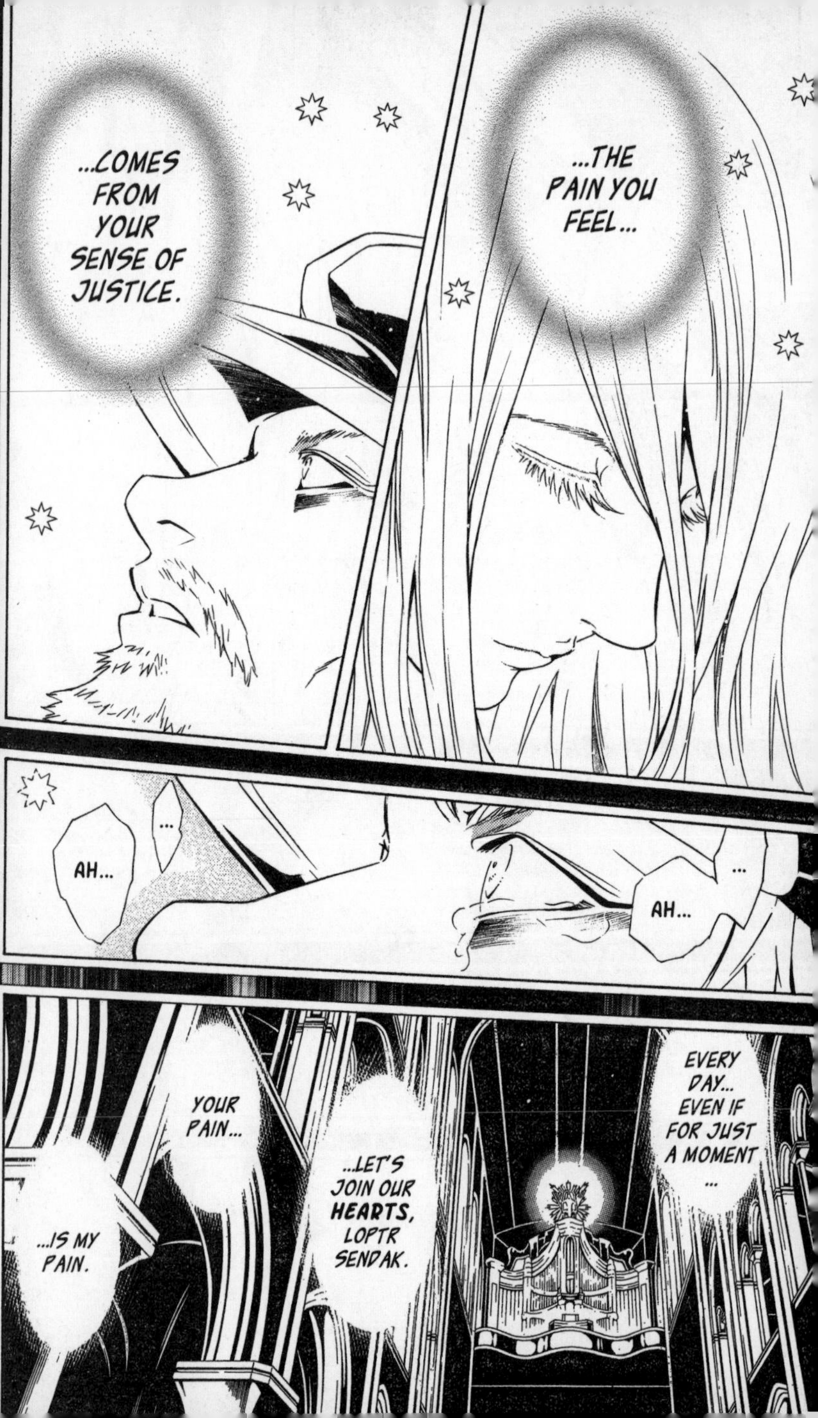
...THE PAIN YOU FEEL...
...COMES FROM YOUR SENSE OF JUSTICE.
...
AH...
...
AH...
EVERY DAY... EVEN IF FOR JUST A MOMENT...
...LET'S JOIN OUR HEARTS, LOPTR SENDAK.
YOUR PAIN...
...IS MY PAIN.

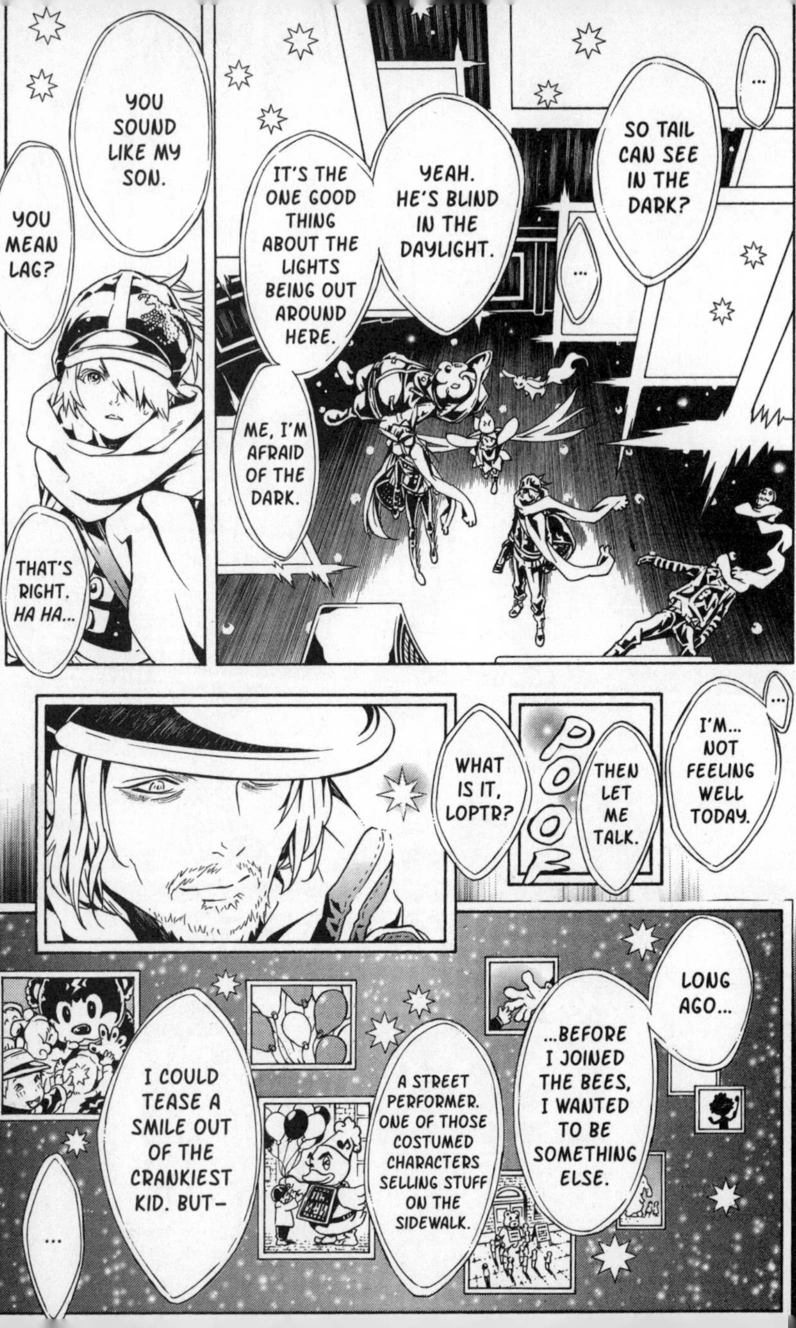

...
SO TAIL CAN SEE IN THE DARK?
...
YEAH. HE'S BLIND IN THE DAYLIGHT.
IT'S THE ONE GOOD THING ABOUT THE LIGHTS BEING OUT AROUND HERE.
ME, I'M AFRAID OF THE DARK.
YOU SOUND LIKE MY SON.
YOU MEAN LAG?
THAT'S RIGHT. HA HA...
...
I'M... NOT FEELING WELL TODAY.
THEN LET ME TALK.
POOF
WHAT IS IT, LOPTR?
LONG AGO...
...BEFORE I JOINED THE BEES, I WANTED TO BE SOMETHING ELSE.
A STREET PERFORMER. ONE OF THOSE COSTUMED CHARACTERS SELLING STUFF ON THE SIDEWALK.
I COULD TEASE A SMILE OUT OF THE CRANKIEST KID. BUT-
...

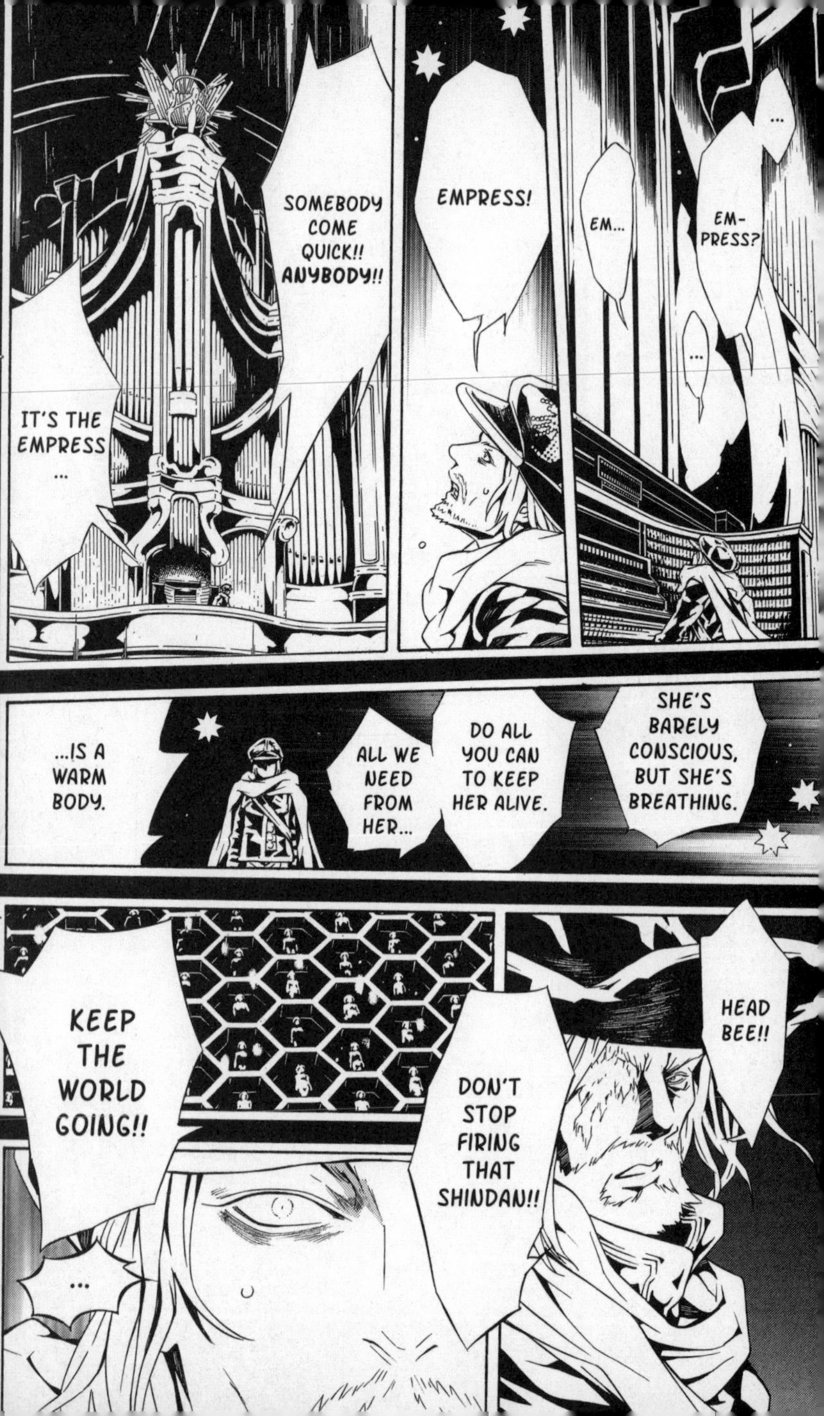
...
EM-PRESS?
EM...
...
EMPRESS!
SOMEBODY COME QUICK!! ANYBODY!!
IT'S THE EMPRESS ...
SHE'S BARELY CONSCIOUS, BUT SHE'S BREATHING.
DO ALL YOU CAN TO KEEP HER ALIVE.
ALL WE NEED FROM HER...
...IS A WARM BODY.
HEAD BEE!!
DON'T STOP FIRING THAT SHINDAN!!
KEEP THE WORLD GOING!!
...

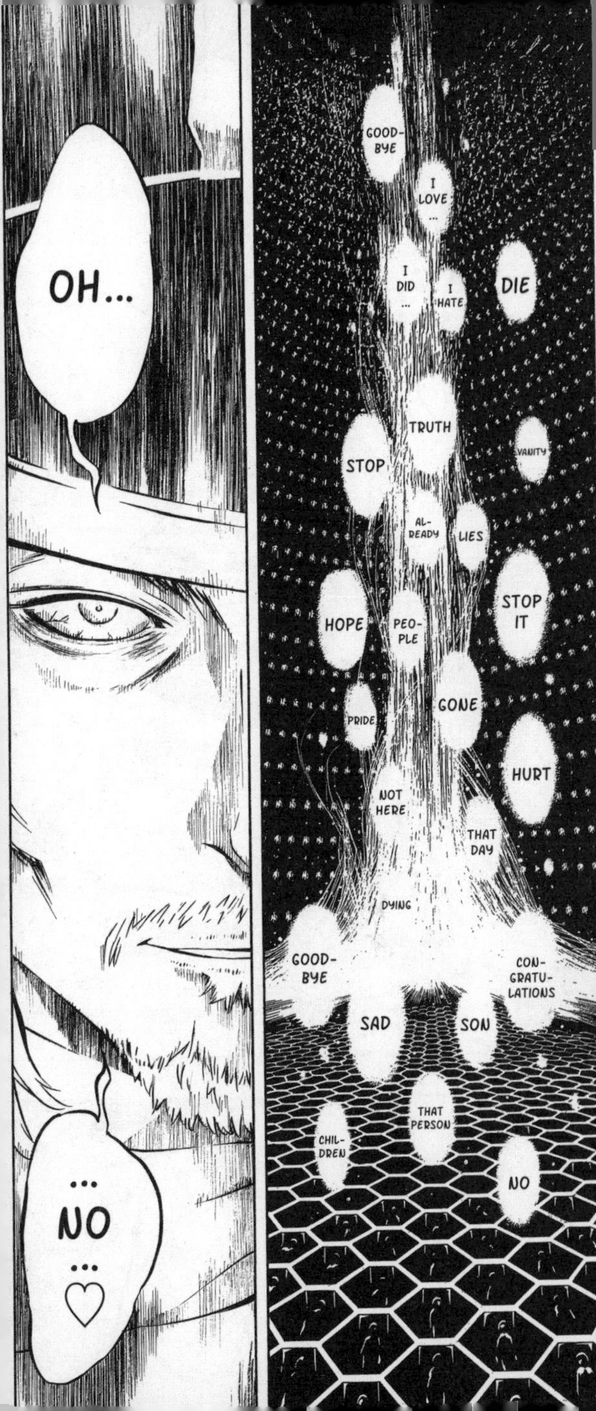
GOOD-BYE
I LOVE...
DIE
I HATE
I DID...
VANITY
TRUTH
STOP
LIES
AL-READY
STOP IT
PEO-PLE
HOPE
GONE
PRIDE
HURT
NOT HERE
THAT DAY
DYING
CON-GRATU-LATIONS
GOOD-BYE
SON
SAD
THAT PERSON
NO
CHIL-DREN
OH...
...NO...♥

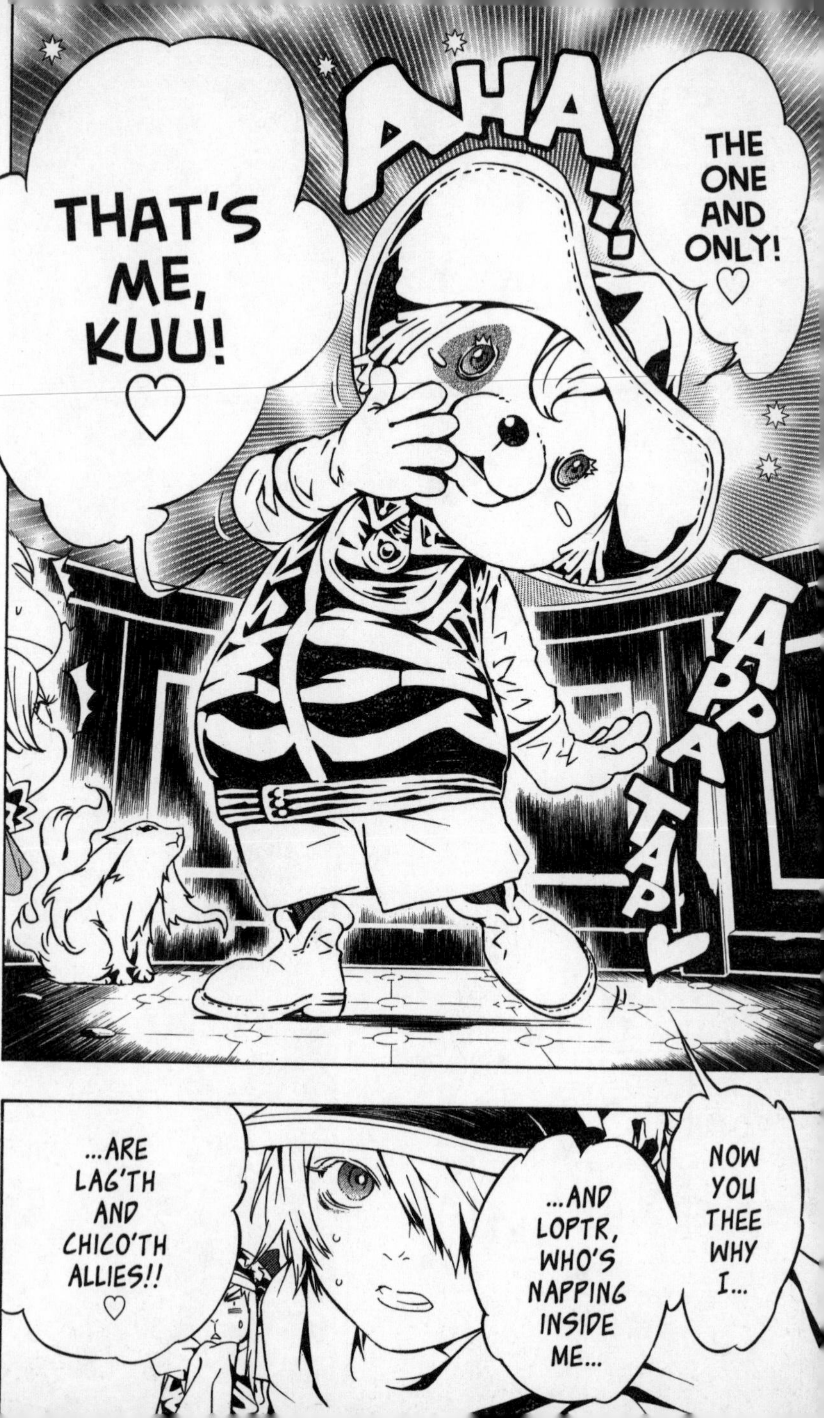
AHA...
THE ONE AND ONLY! ♡
THAT'S ME, KUU! ♡
TAPPATAP♡
NOW YOU THEE WHY I...
...AND LOPTR, WHO'S NAPPING INSIDE ME...
...ARE LAG'TH AND CHICO'TH ALLIES!! ♡

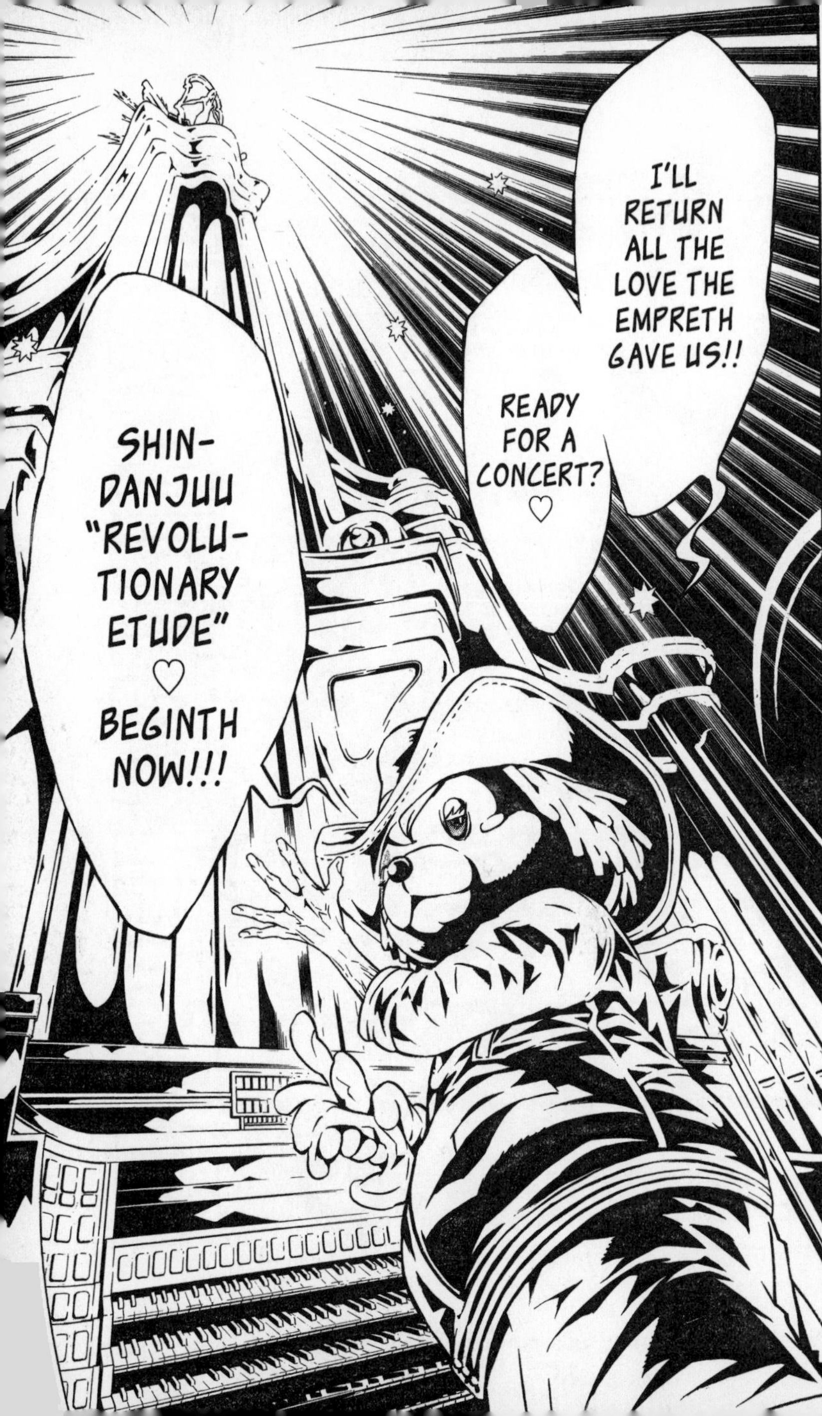
I'LL RETURN ALL THE LOVE THE EMPRETH GAVE US!!
READY FOR A CONCERT? ♡
SHIN-DANJUU "REVOLUTIONARY ETUDE" ♡ BEGINTH NOW!!!

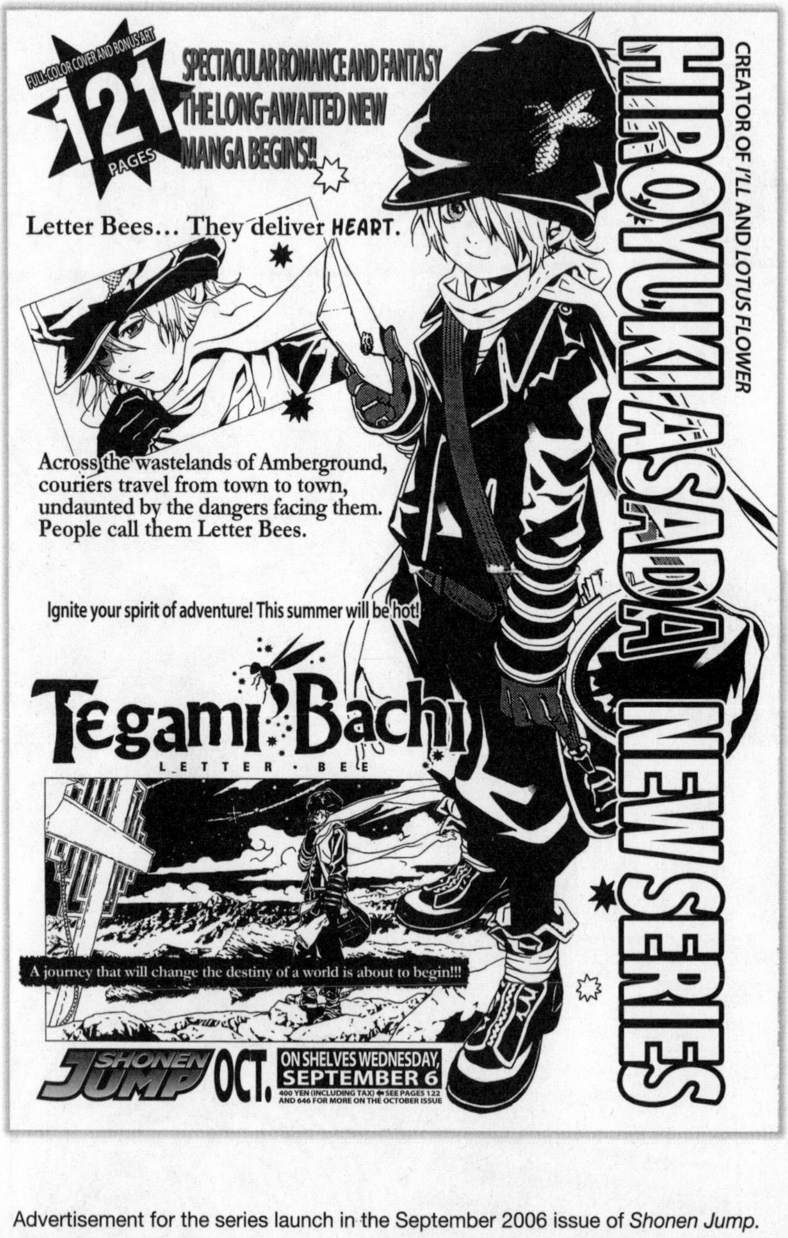
FULL-COLOR COVER AND BONUS ART
121
PAGES
SPECTACULAR ROMANCE AND FANTASY
THE LONG-AWAITED NEW
MANGA BEGINS!!
HIROYUKI ASADA NEW SERIES
CREATOR OF I'LL AND LOTUS FLOWER
Letter Bees... They deliver HEART.
Across the wastelands of Amberground,
couriers travel from town to town,
undaunted by the dangers facing them.
People call them Letter Bees.
Ignite your spirit of adventure! This summer will be hot!
Tegami Bachi
LETTER · BEE
A journey that will change the destiny of a world is about to begin!!!
SHONEN JUMP
OCT.
ON SHELVES WEDNESDAY,
SEPTEMBER 6
400 YEN (INCLUDING TAX) SEE PAGES 122
AND 646 FOR MORE ON THE OCTOBER ISSUE

Advertisement for the series launch in the September 2006 issue of *Shonen Jump*.

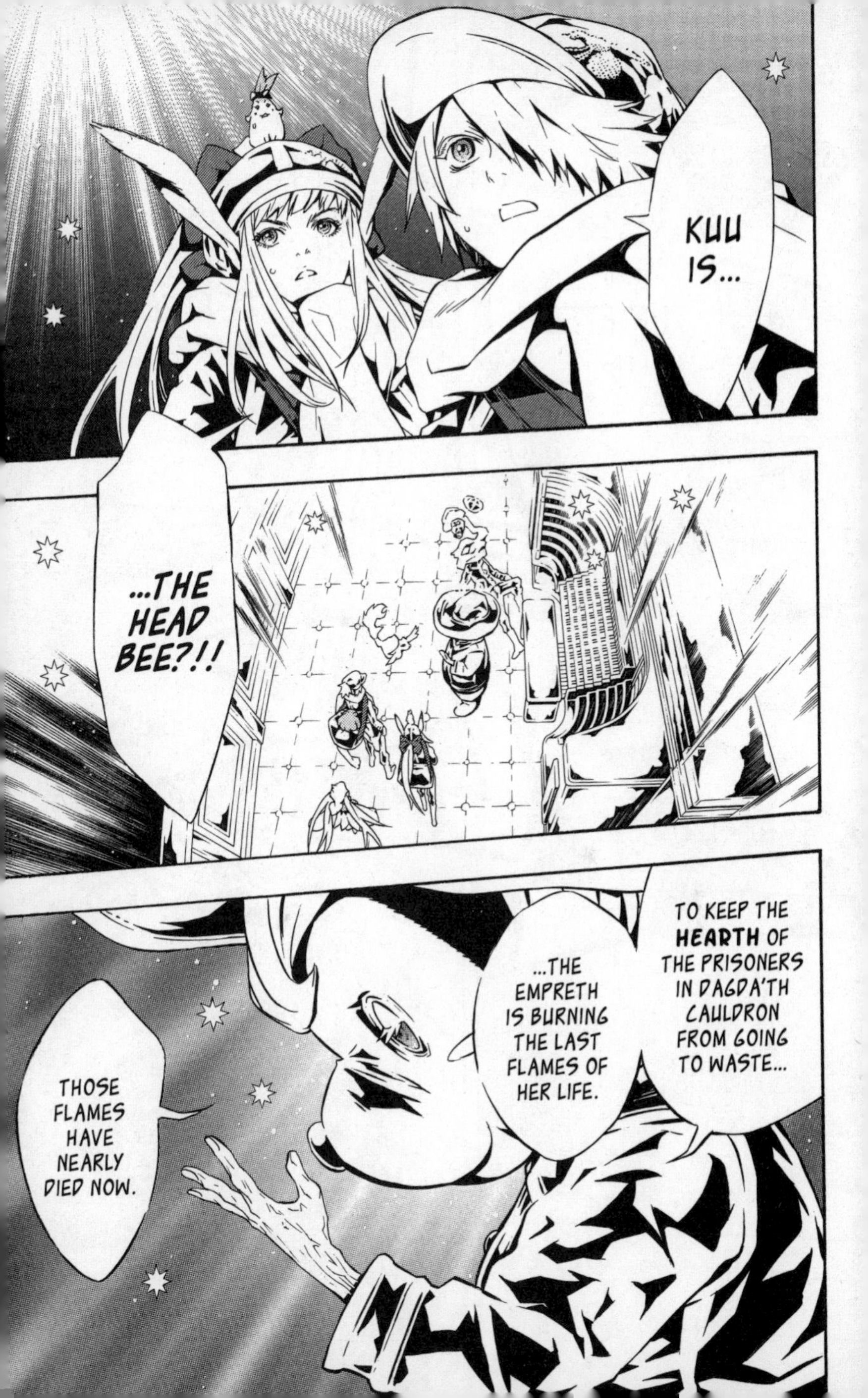
KUU IS...
...THE HEAD BEE?!!
TO KEEP THE **HEARTH** OF THE PRISONERS IN DAGDA'TH CAULDRON FROM GOING TO WASTE...
...THE EMPRETH IS BURNING THE LAST FLAMES OF HER LIFE.
THOSE FLAMES HAVE NEARLY DIED NOW.

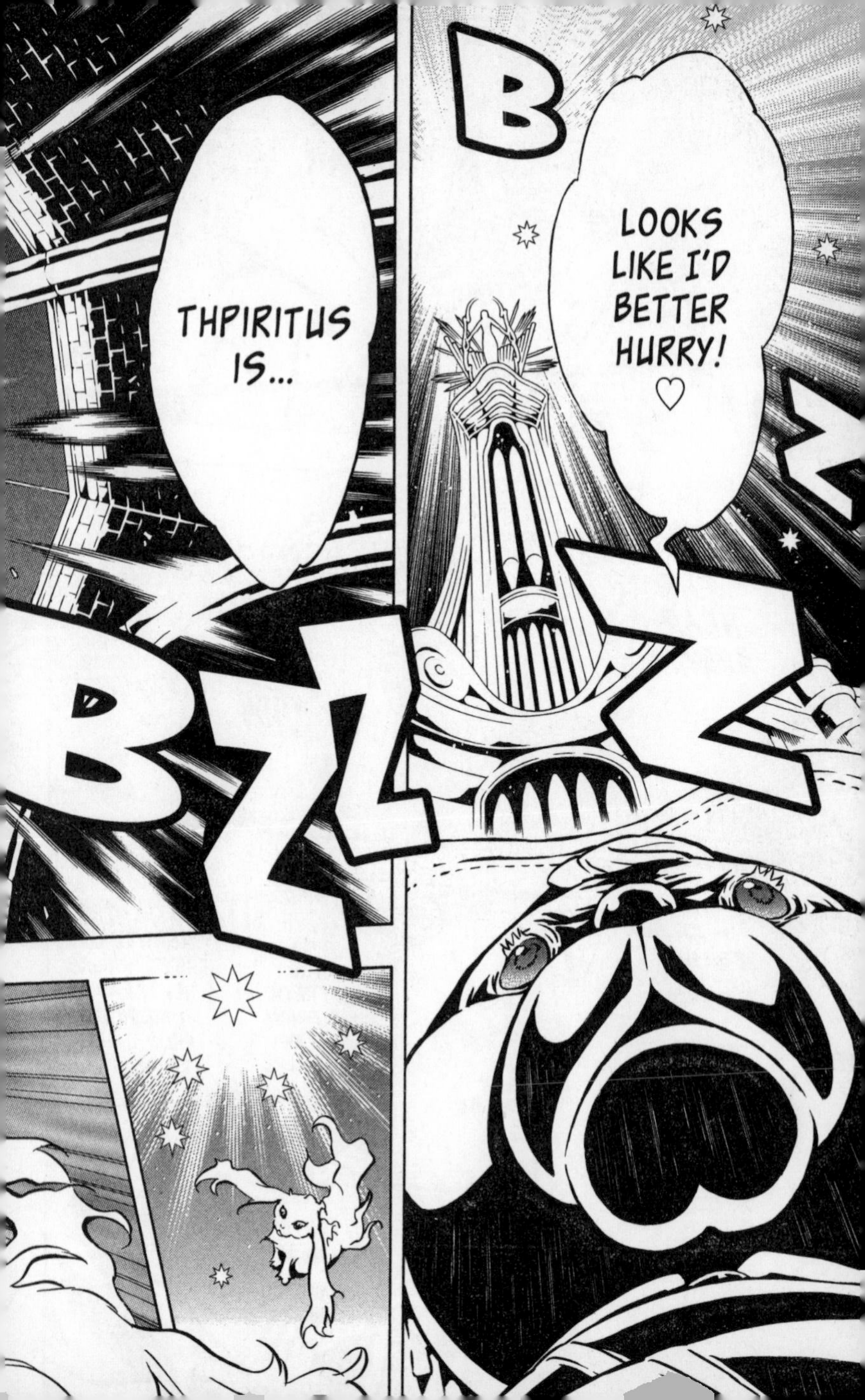
B
LOOKS LIKE I'D BETTER HURRY! ♡
THPIRITUS IS...
BZZ

Chapter 94: Lloyd's Chance Meeting

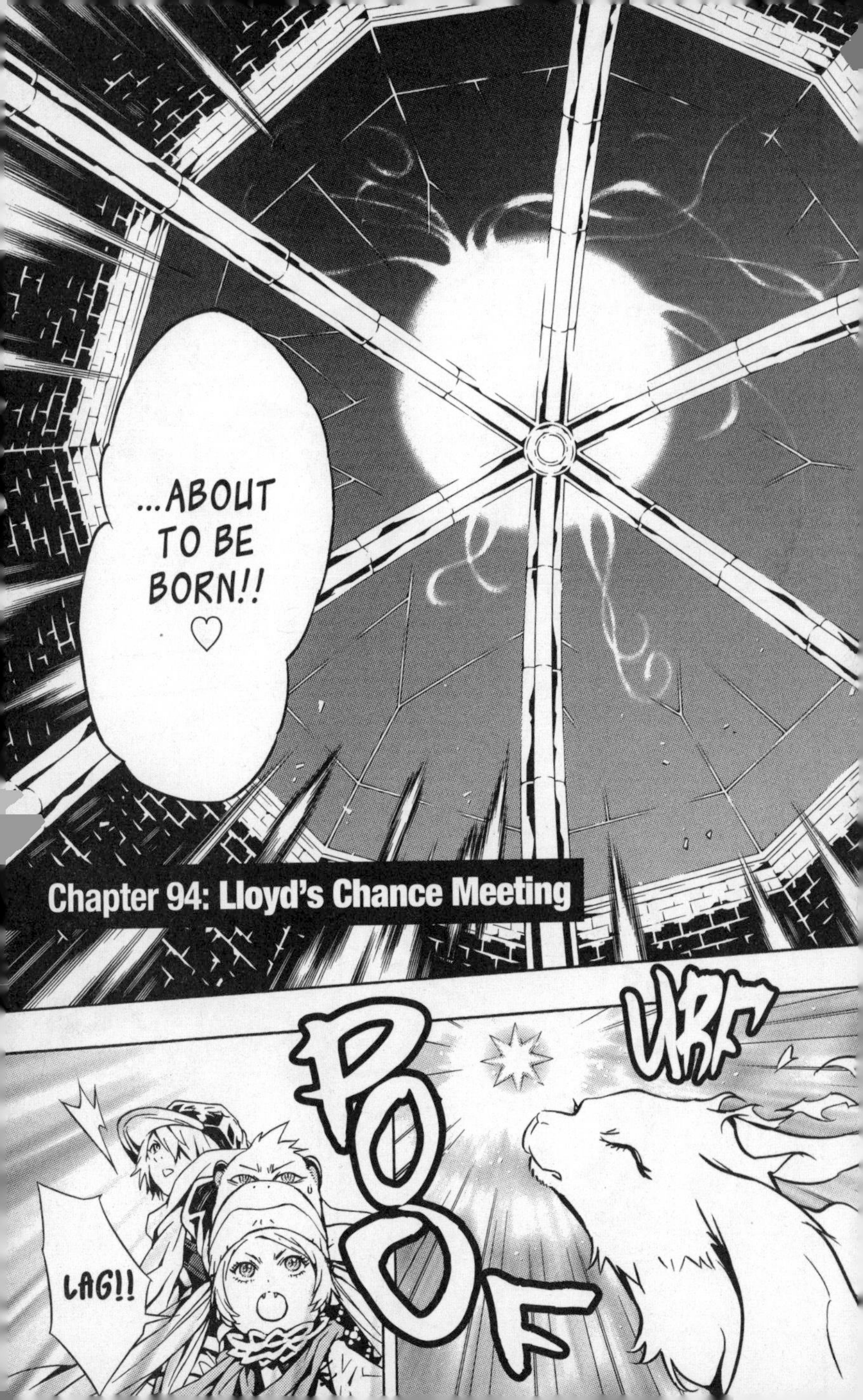
...ABOUT TO BE BORN!! ♡
URF
POOF
LAG!!

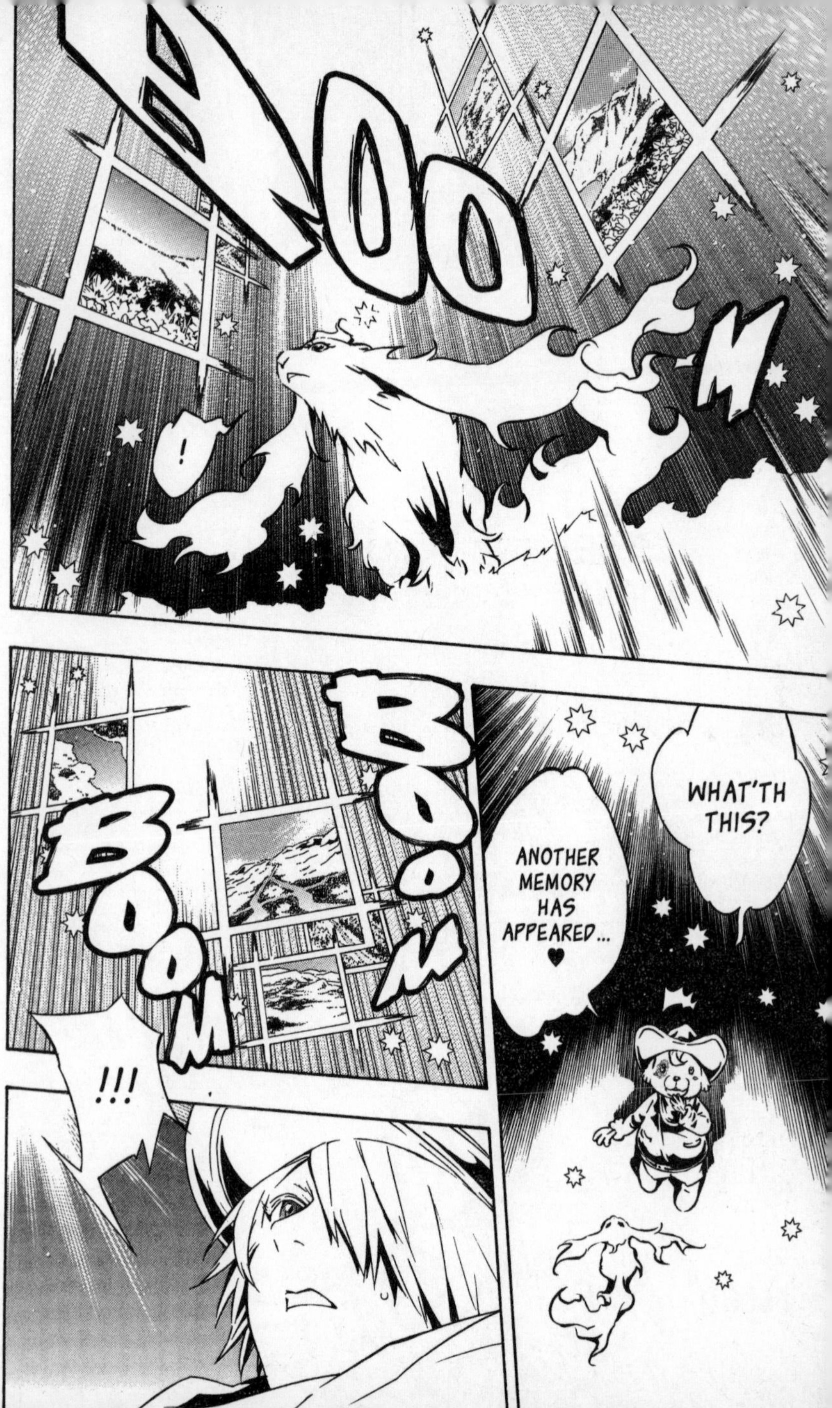
!
WHAT'TH THIS?
ANOTHER MEMORY HAS APPEARED... ♥
BOOOM
BOOOM
!!!

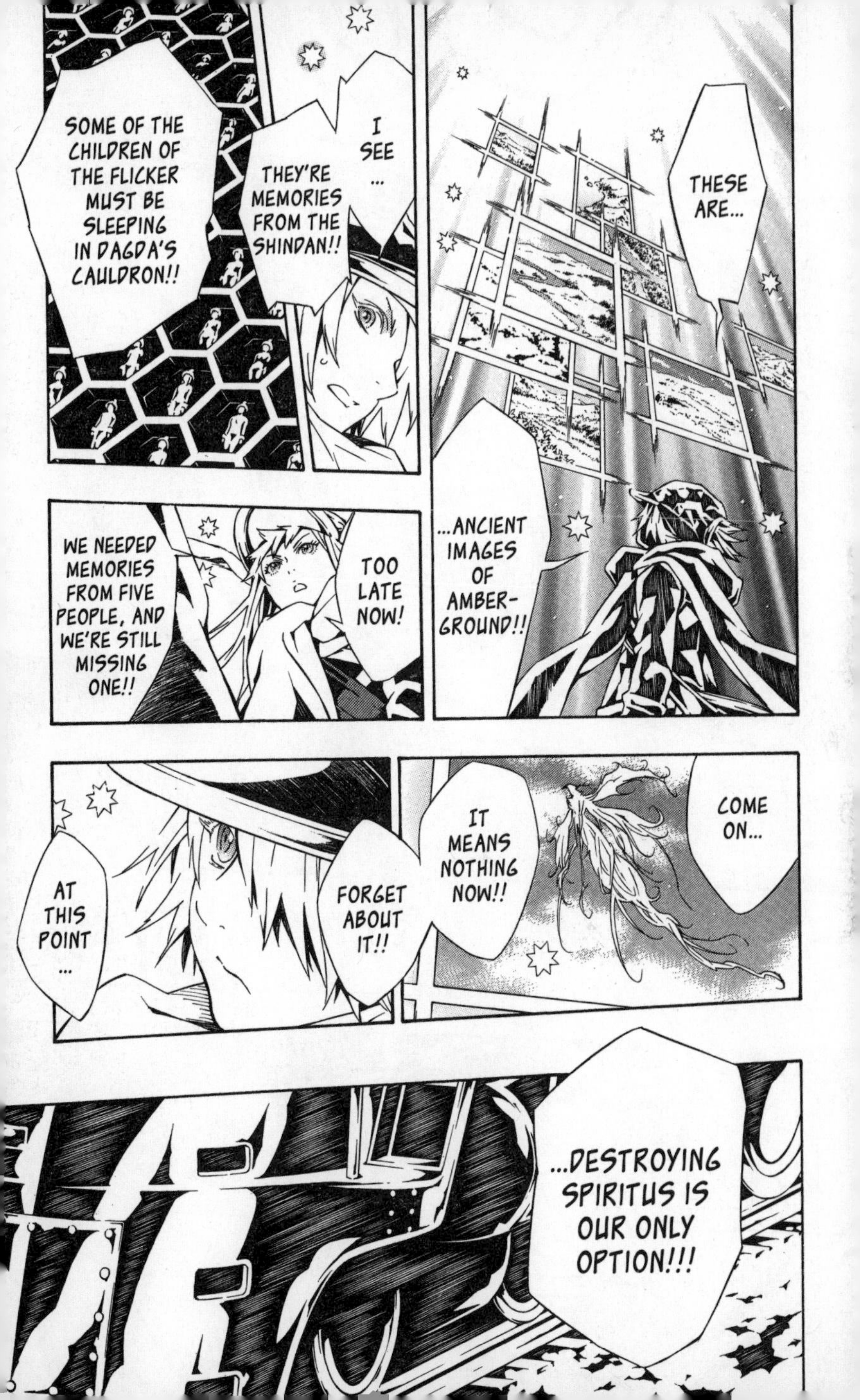
THESE ARE...
...ANCIENT IMAGES OF AMBER-GROUND!!
I SEE ...
THEY'RE MEMORIES FROM THE SHINDAN!!
SOME OF THE CHILDREN OF THE FLICKER MUST BE SLEEPING IN DAGDA'S CAULDRON!!
TOO LATE NOW!
WE NEEDED MEMORIES FROM FIVE PEOPLE, AND WE'RE STILL MISSING ONE!!
COME ON...
IT MEANS NOTHING NOW!!
FORGET ABOUT IT!!
AT THIS POINT ...
...DESTROYING SPIRITUS IS OUR ONLY OPTION!!!

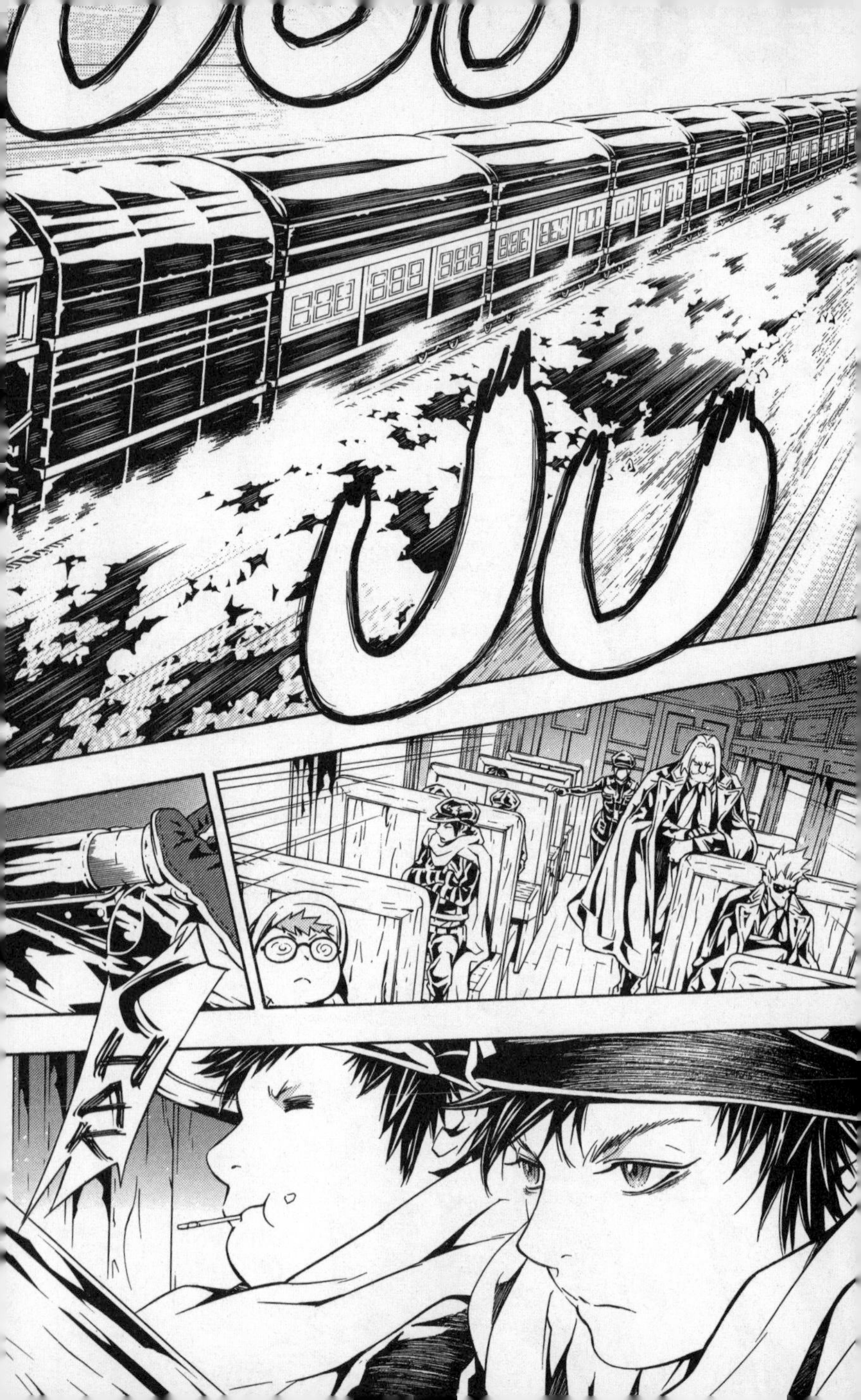
HAK

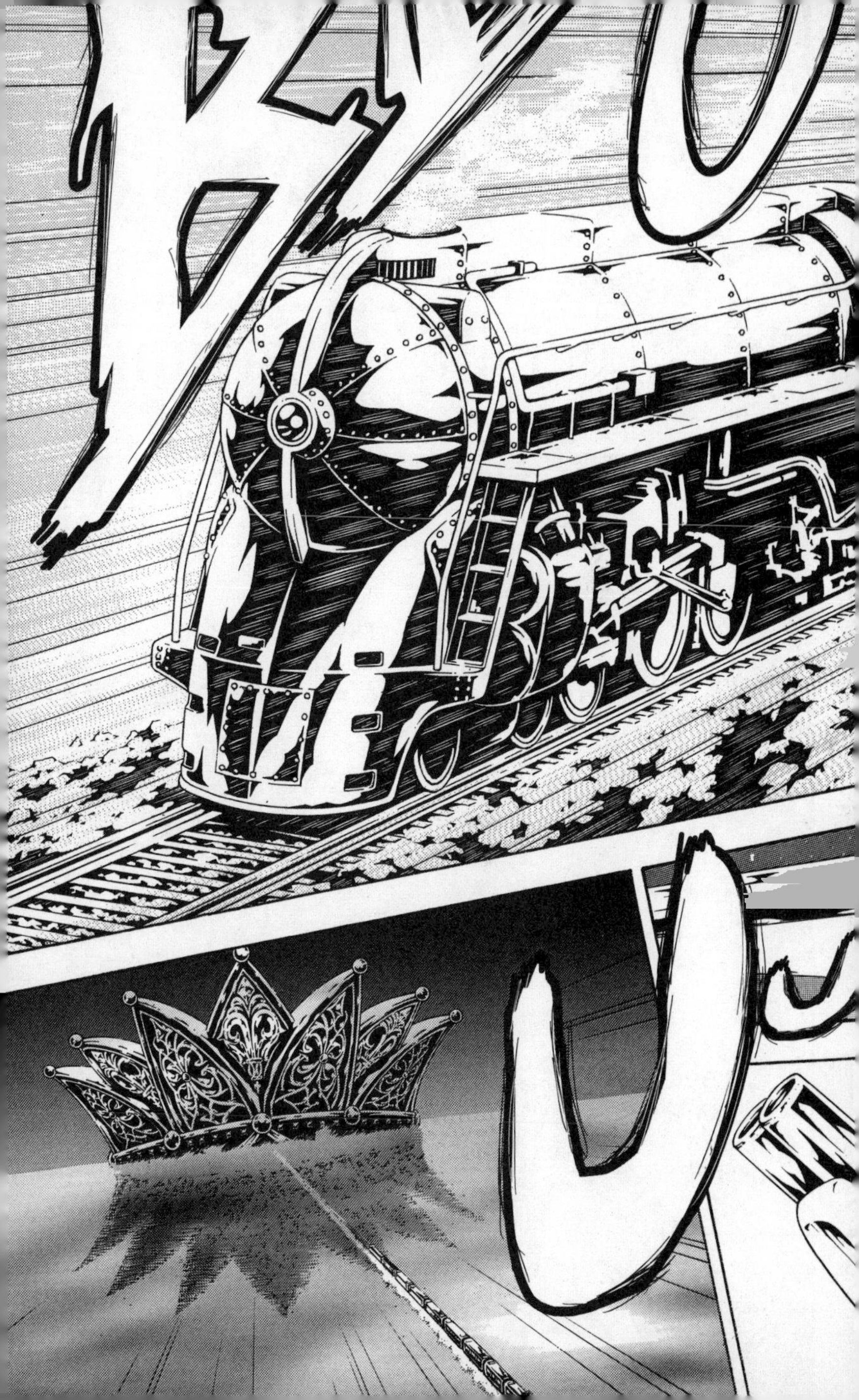

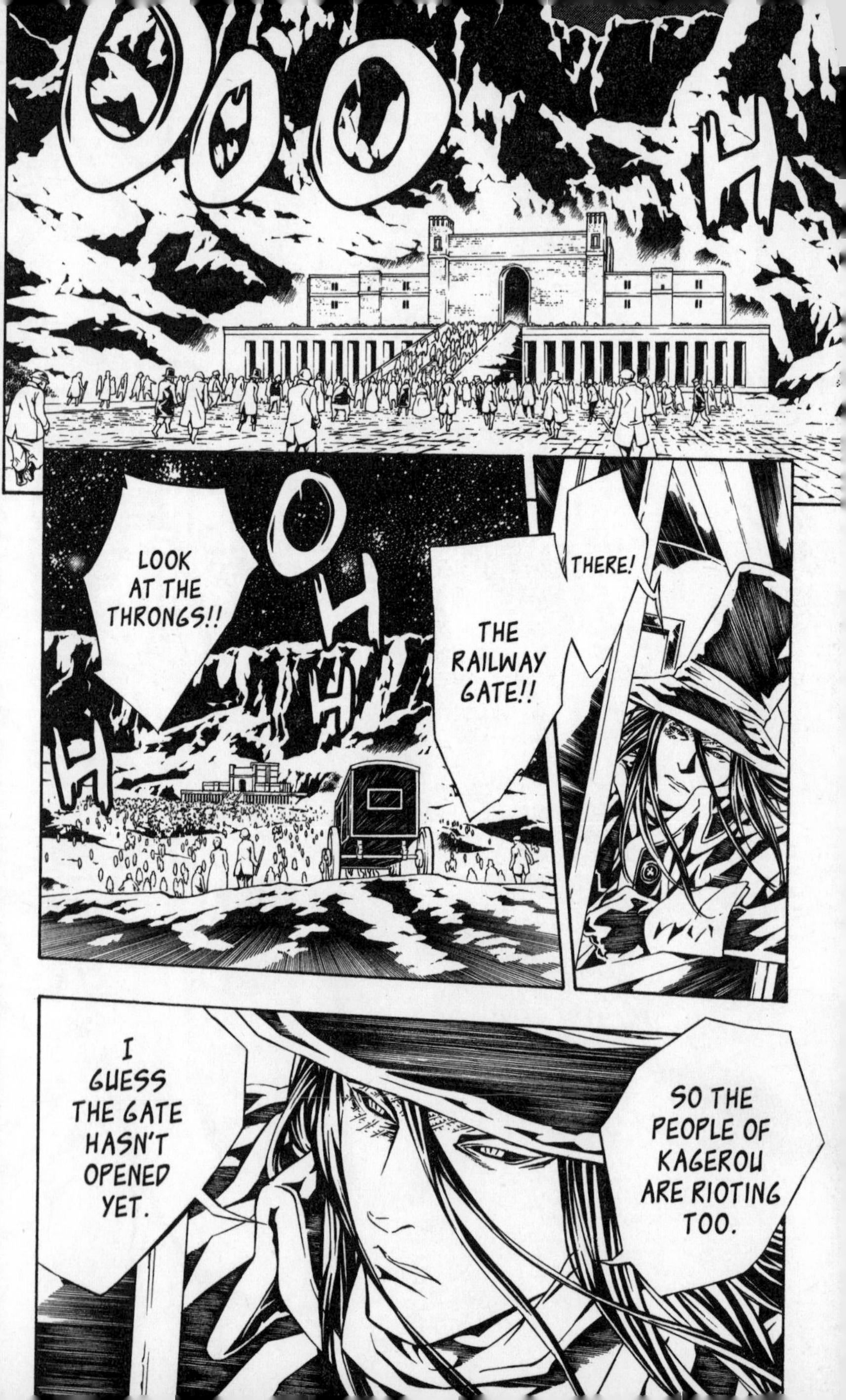
OOOH
THERE!
THE RAILWAY GATE!!
LOOK AT THE THRONGS!!
OHHH
SO THE PEOPLE OF KAGEROU ARE RIOTING TOO.
I GUESS THE GATE HASN'T OPENED YET.

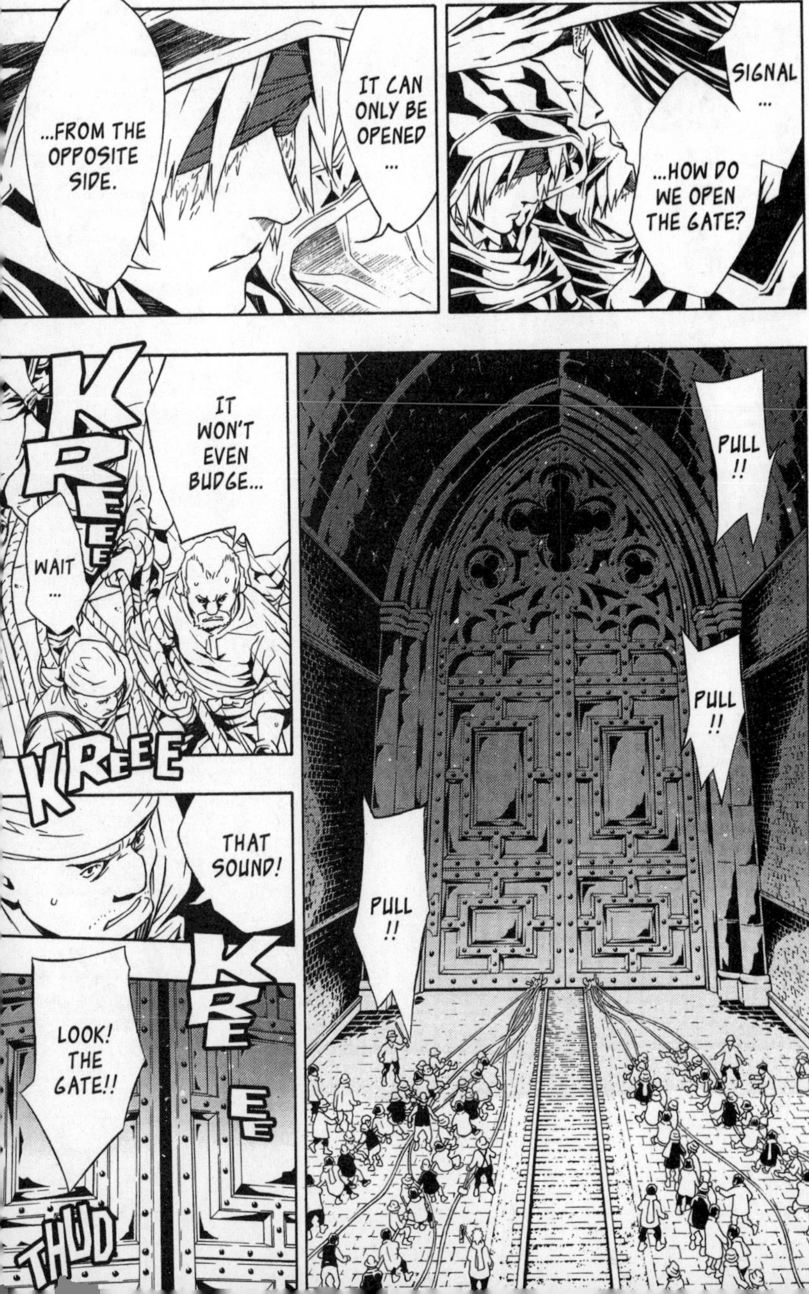
SIGNAL ...
...HOW DO WE OPEN THE GATE?
IT CAN ONLY BE OPENED ...
...FROM THE OPPOSITE SIDE.
PULL !!
PULL !!
PULL !!
KREEE
IT WON'T EVEN BUDGE...
WAIT ...
KREEE
THAT SOUND!
KREEE
LOOK! THE GATE!!
THUD

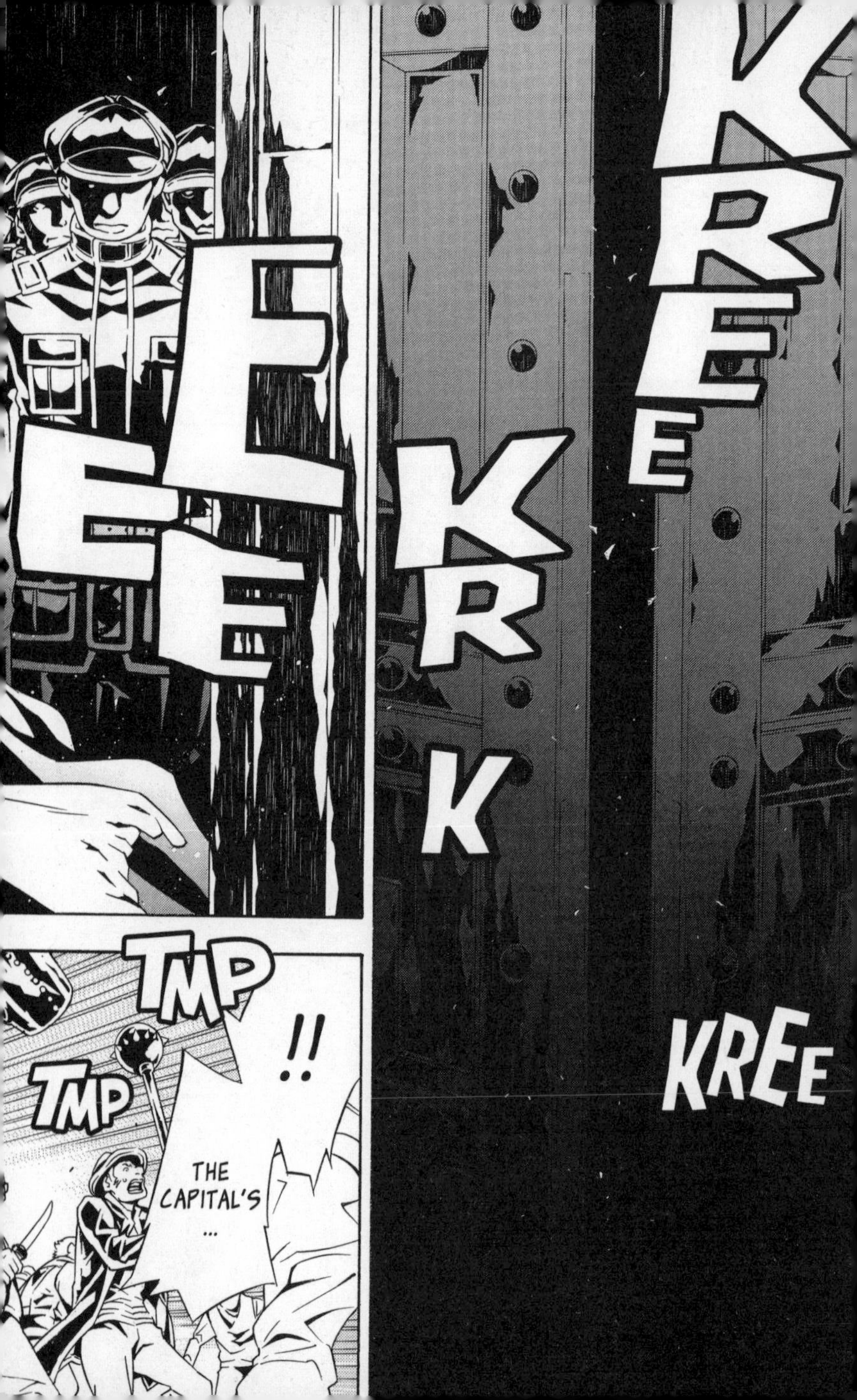
KREEE
KRK
KREe
EEE
TMP
TMP
!!
THE CAPITAL'S ...

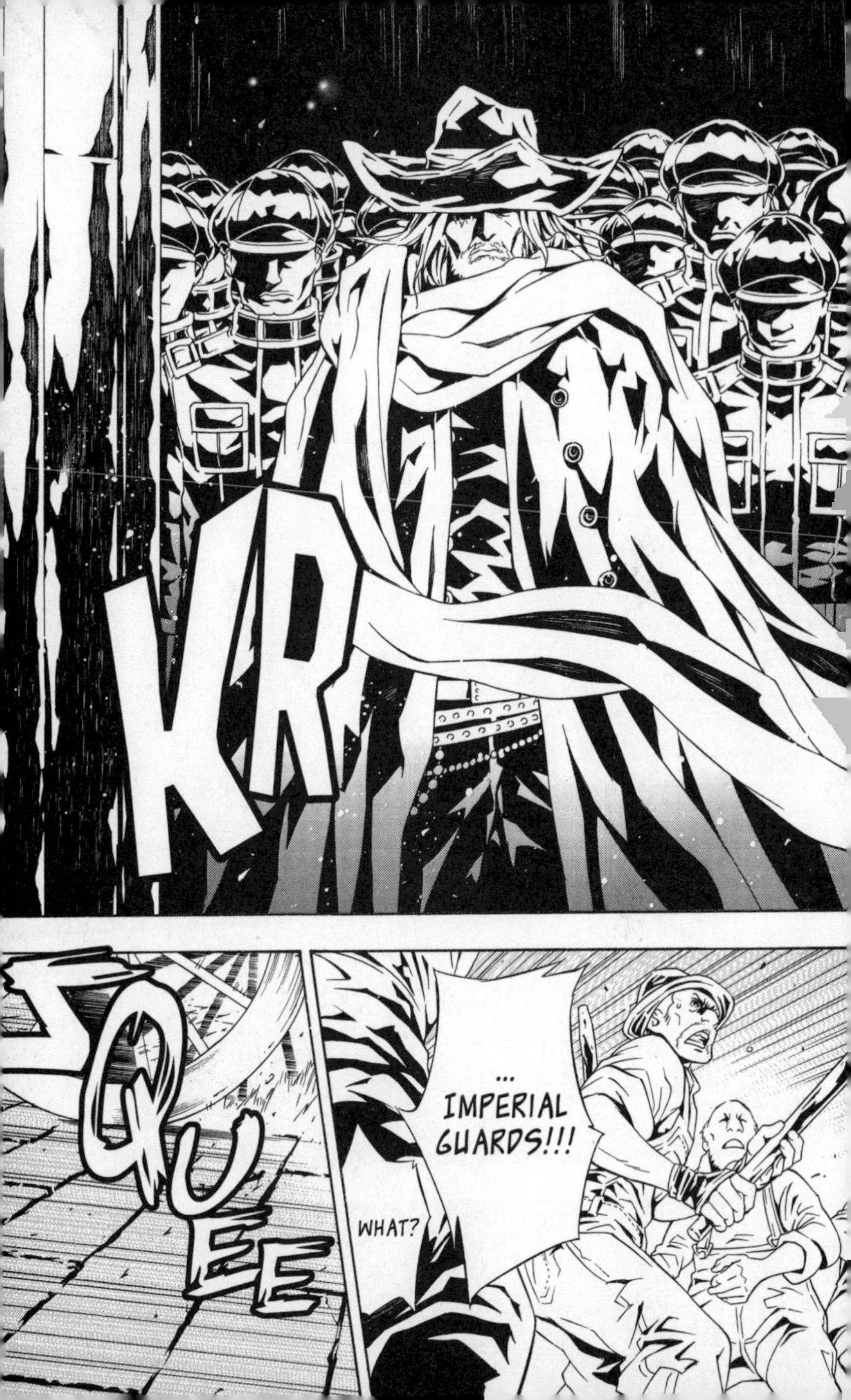
KR
... IMPERIAL GUARDS!!!
WHAT?
SQUEEE

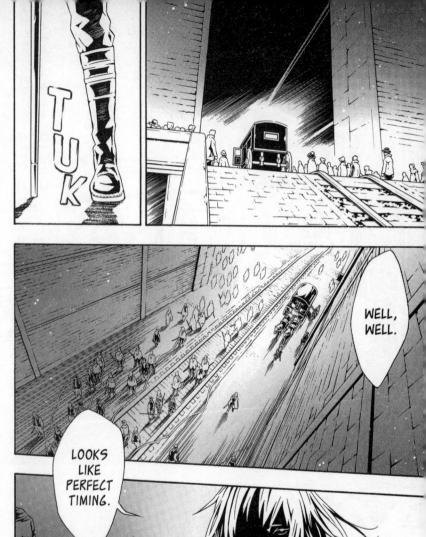

TUK

WELL, WELL.

LOOKS LIKE PERFECT TIMING.

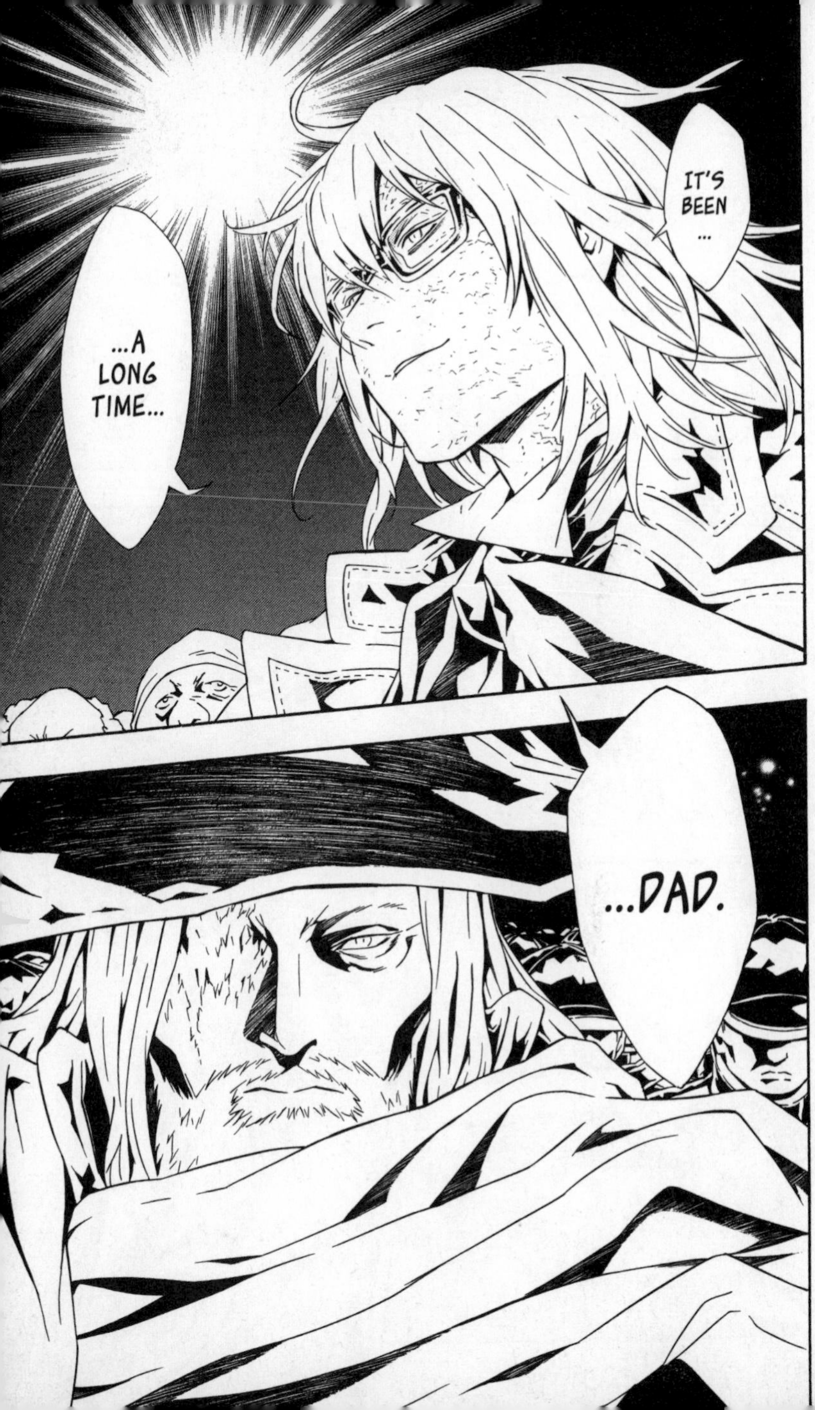
IT'S BEEN ...
...A LONG TIME...
...DAD.

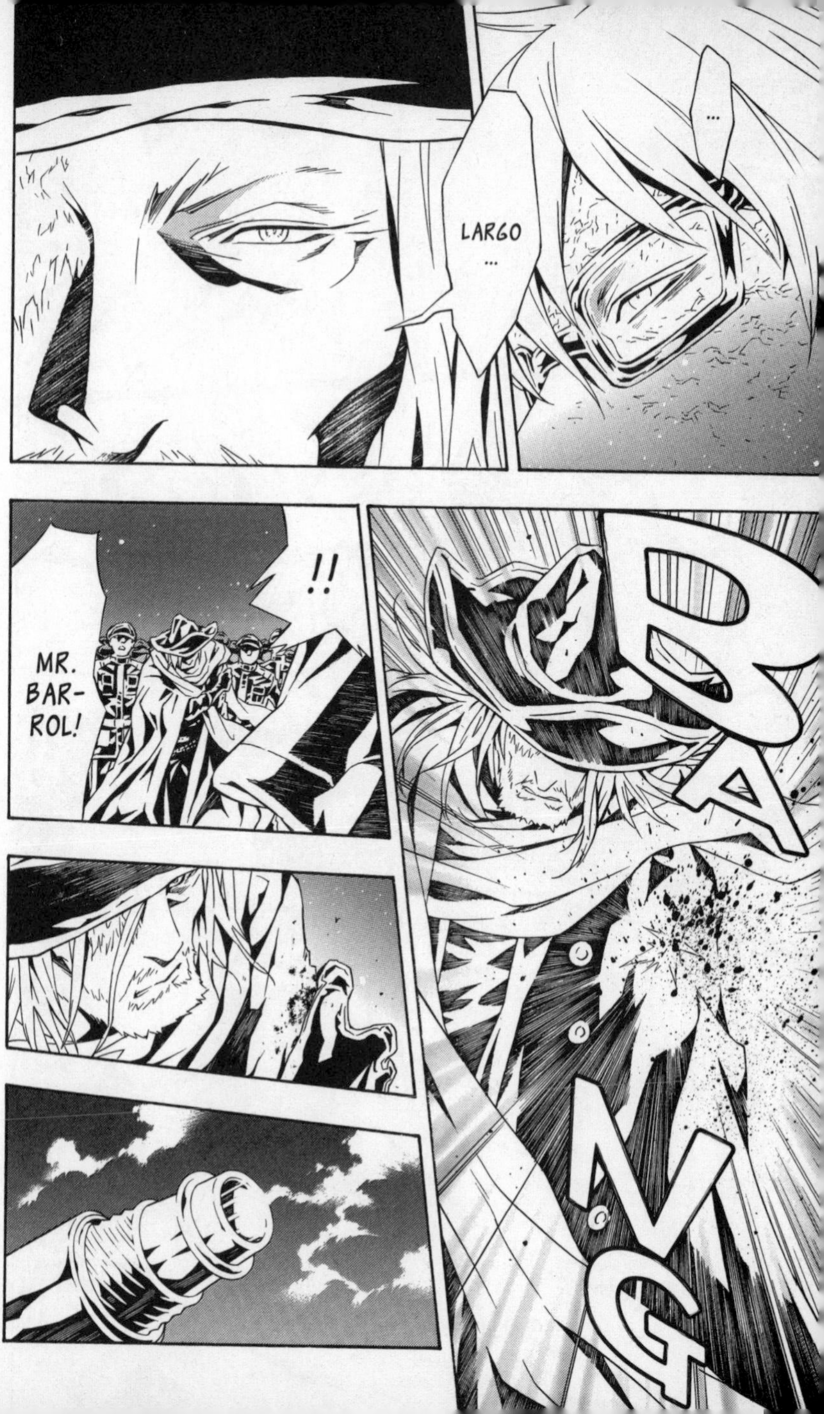
...
LARGO ...
BANG
!!
MR. BAR-ROL!

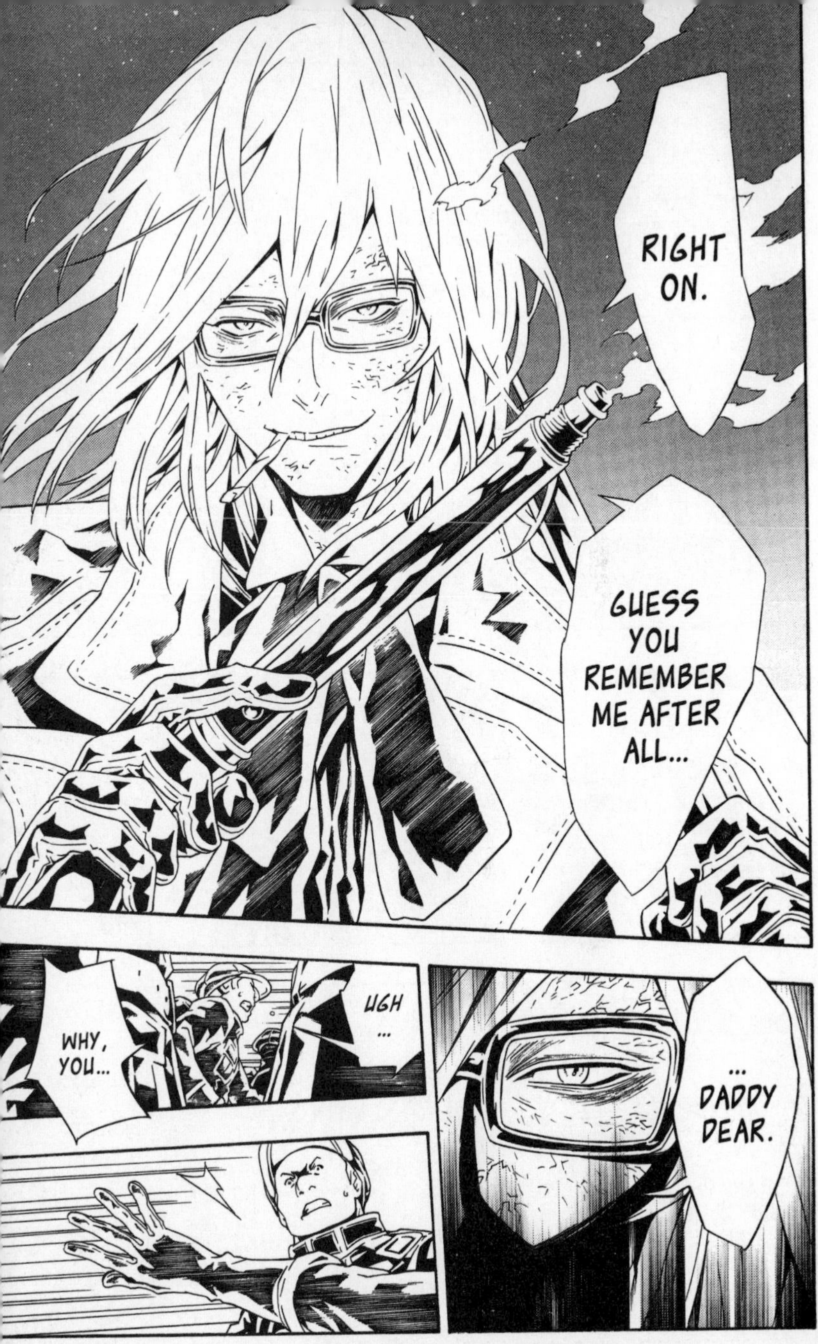
RIGHT ON.
GUESS YOU REMEMBER ME AFTER ALL...
... DADDY DEAR.
UGH ...
WHY, YOU...

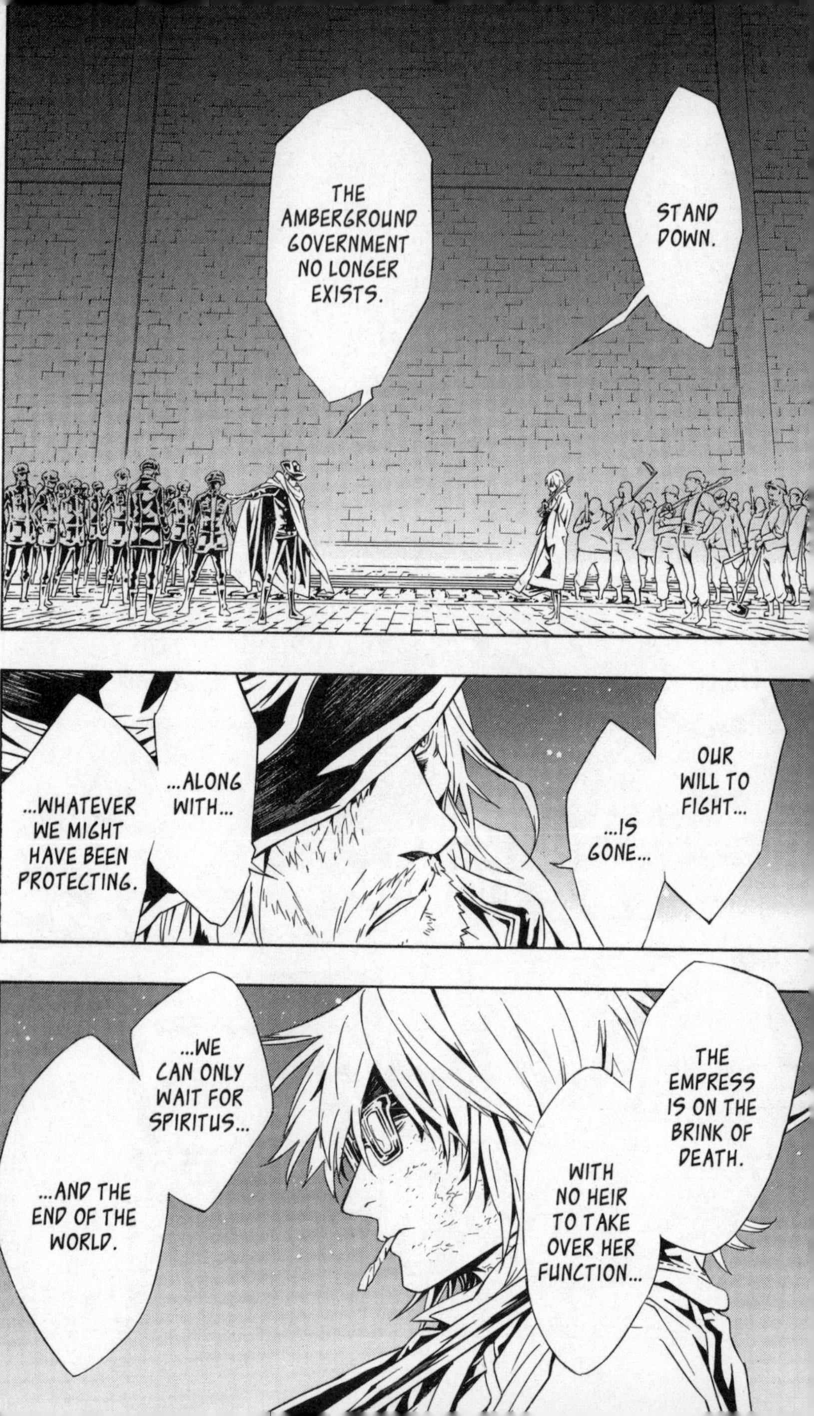
STAND DOWN.
THE AMBERGROUND GOVERNMENT NO LONGER EXISTS.
OUR WILL TO FIGHT...
...IS GONE...
...ALONG WITH...
...WHATEVER WE MIGHT HAVE BEEN PROTECTING.
THE EMPRESS IS ON THE BRINK OF DEATH.
WITH NO HEIR TO TAKE OVER HER FUNCTION...
...WE CAN ONLY WAIT FOR SPIRITUS...
...AND THE END OF THE WORLD.

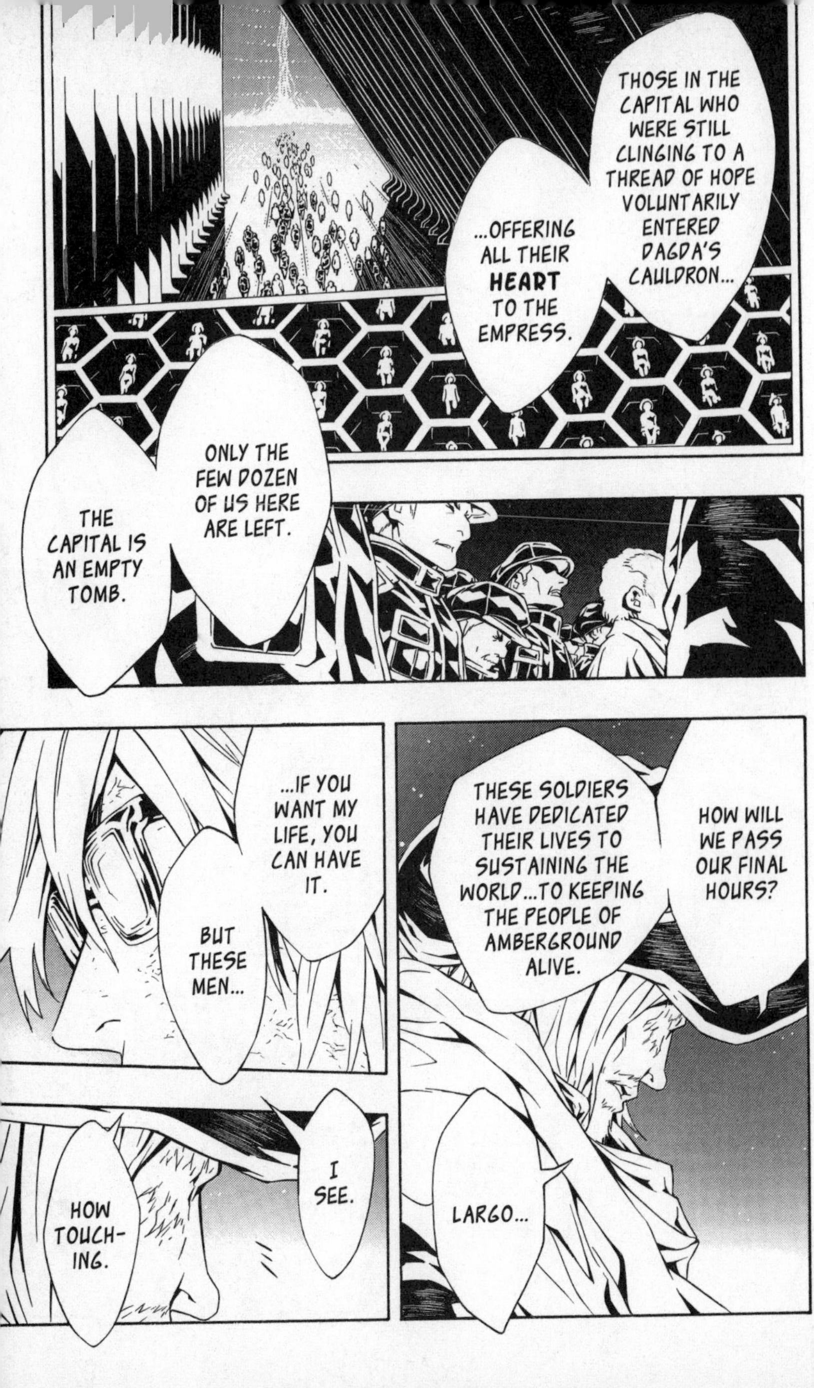
THOSE IN THE CAPITAL WHO WERE STILL CLINGING TO A THREAD OF HOPE VOLUNTARILY ENTERED DAGDA'S CAULDRON...
...OFFERING ALL THEIR **HEART** TO THE EMPRESS.
ONLY THE FEW DOZEN OF US HERE ARE LEFT.
THE CAPITAL IS AN EMPTY TOMB.
HOW WILL WE PASS OUR FINAL HOURS?
THESE SOLDIERS HAVE DEDICATED THEIR LIVES TO SUSTAINING THE WORLD...TO KEEPING THE PEOPLE OF AMBERGROUND ALIVE.
LARGO...
...IF YOU WANT MY LIFE, YOU CAN HAVE IT.
BUT THESE MEN...
I SEE.
HOW TOUCHING.

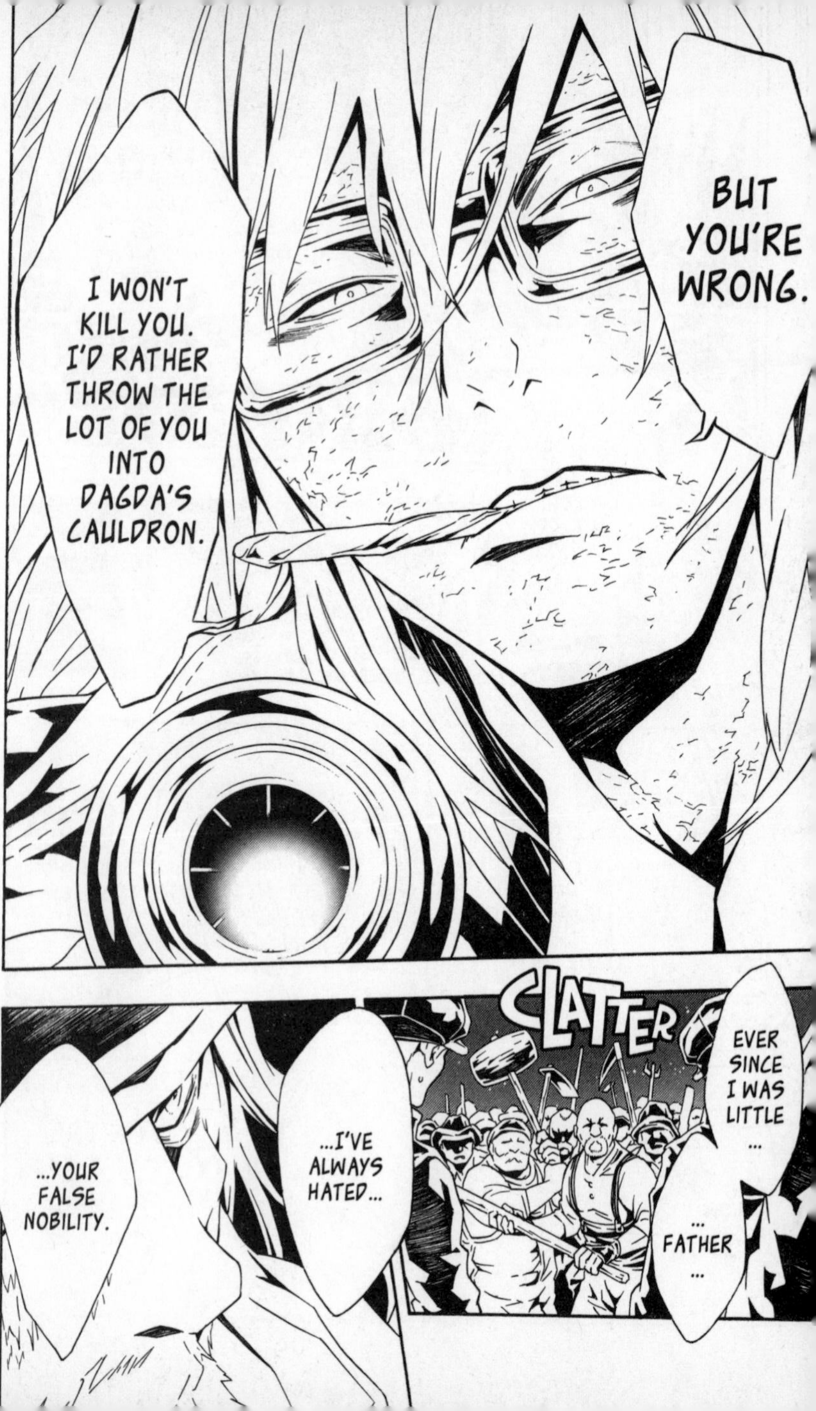
BUT YOU'RE WRONG.
I WON'T KILL YOU. I'D RATHER THROW THE LOT OF YOU INTO DAGDA'S CAULDRON.
CLATTER
EVER SINCE I WAS LITTLE...
...FATHER...
...I'VE ALWAYS HATED...
...YOUR FALSE NOBILITY.

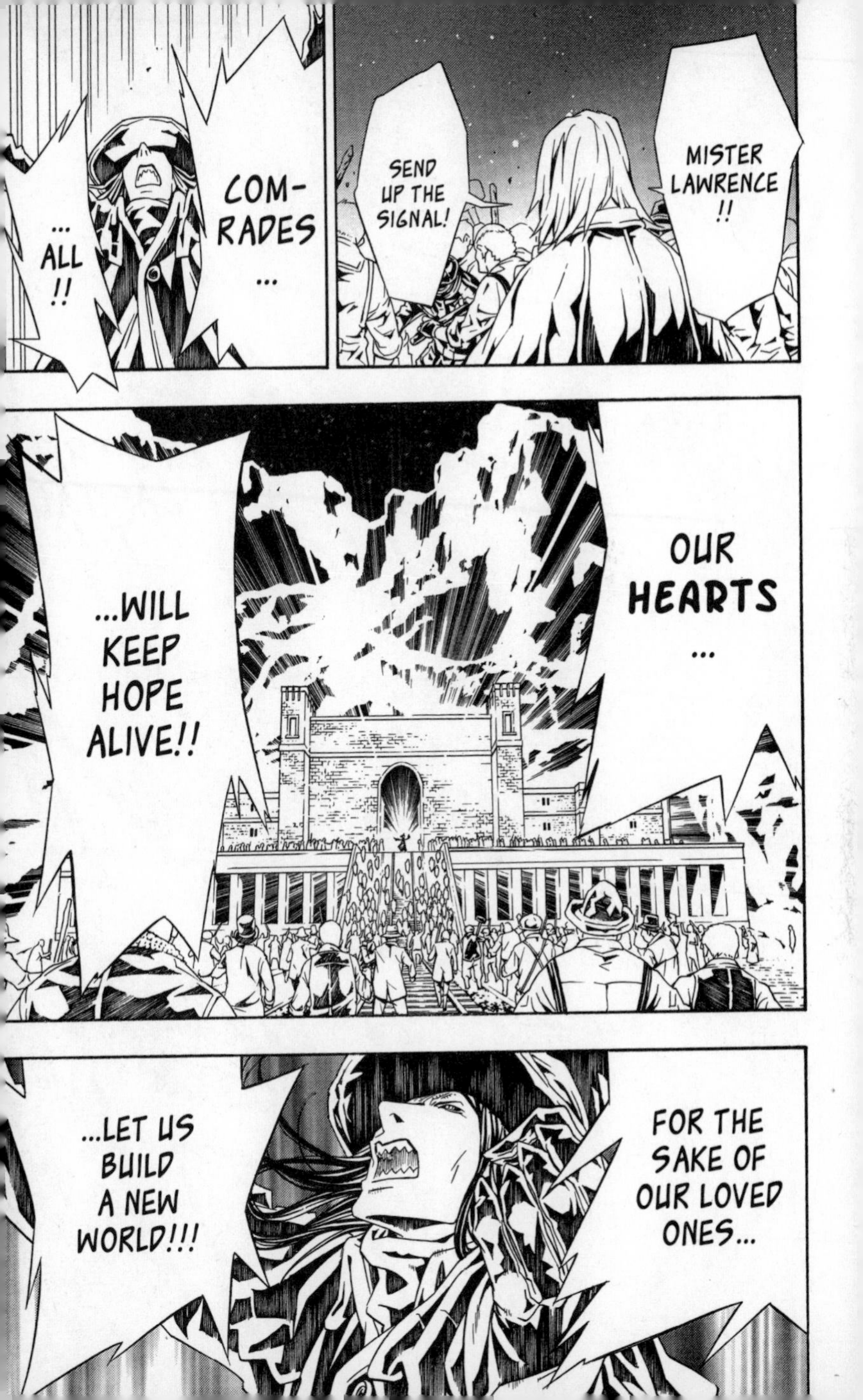
MISTER LAWRENCE !!
SEND UP THE SIGNAL!
COM-RADES ...
... ALL !!
OUR HEARTS ...
...WILL KEEP HOPE ALIVE!!
FOR THE SAKE OF OUR LOVED ONES...
...LET US BUILD A NEW WORLD!!!

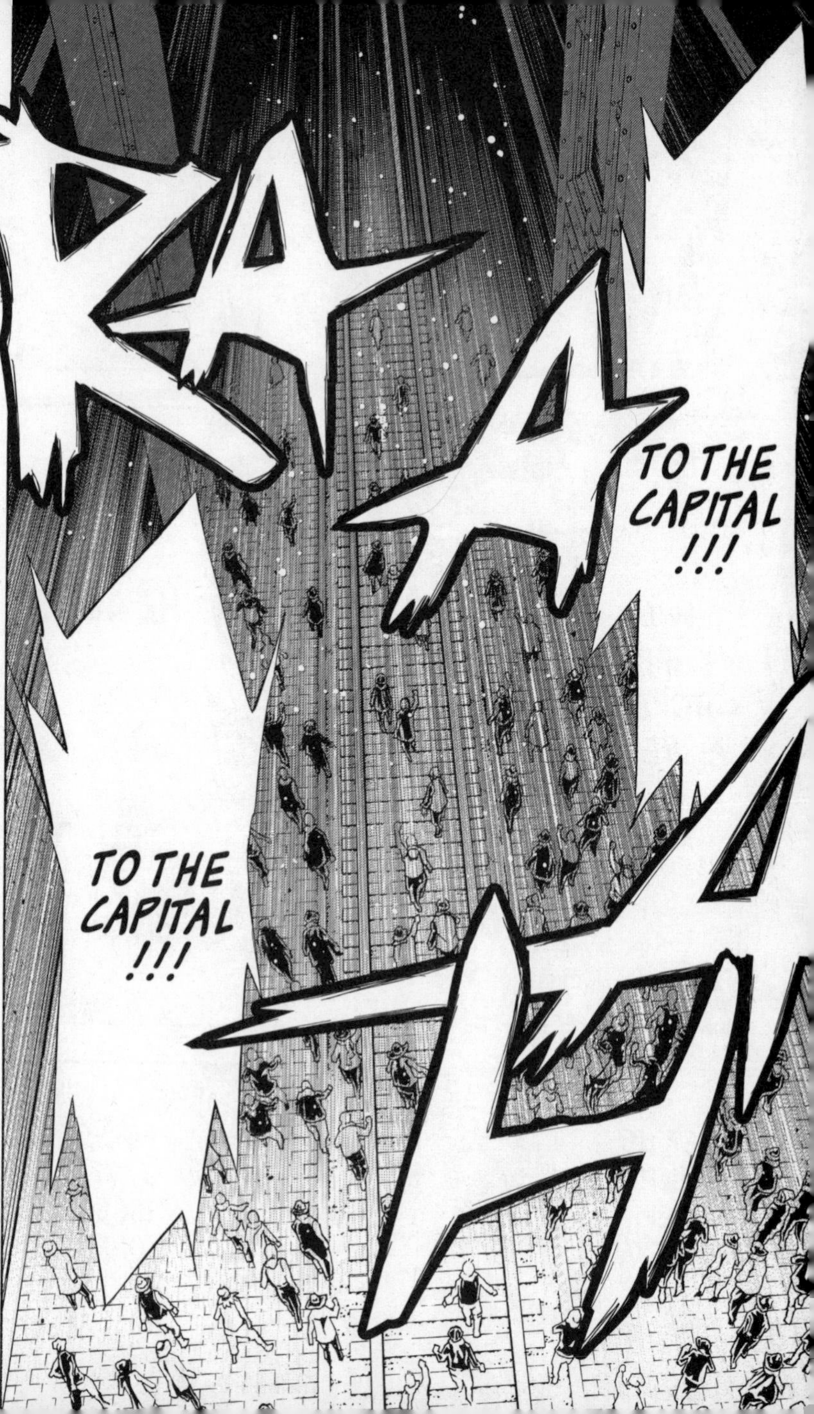
TO THE CAPITAL !!!
TO THE CAPITAL !!!

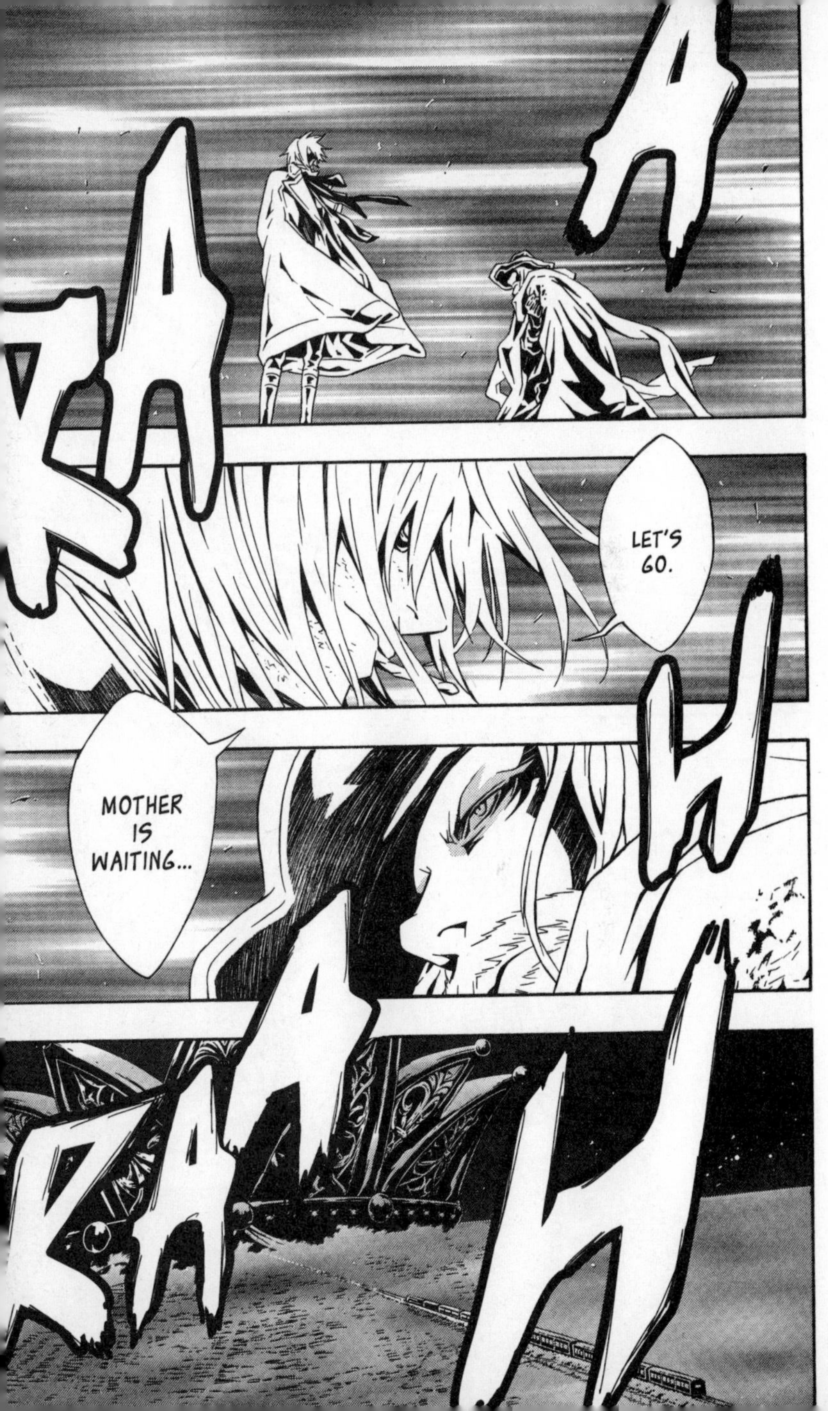
LET'S GO.
MOTHER IS WAITING...

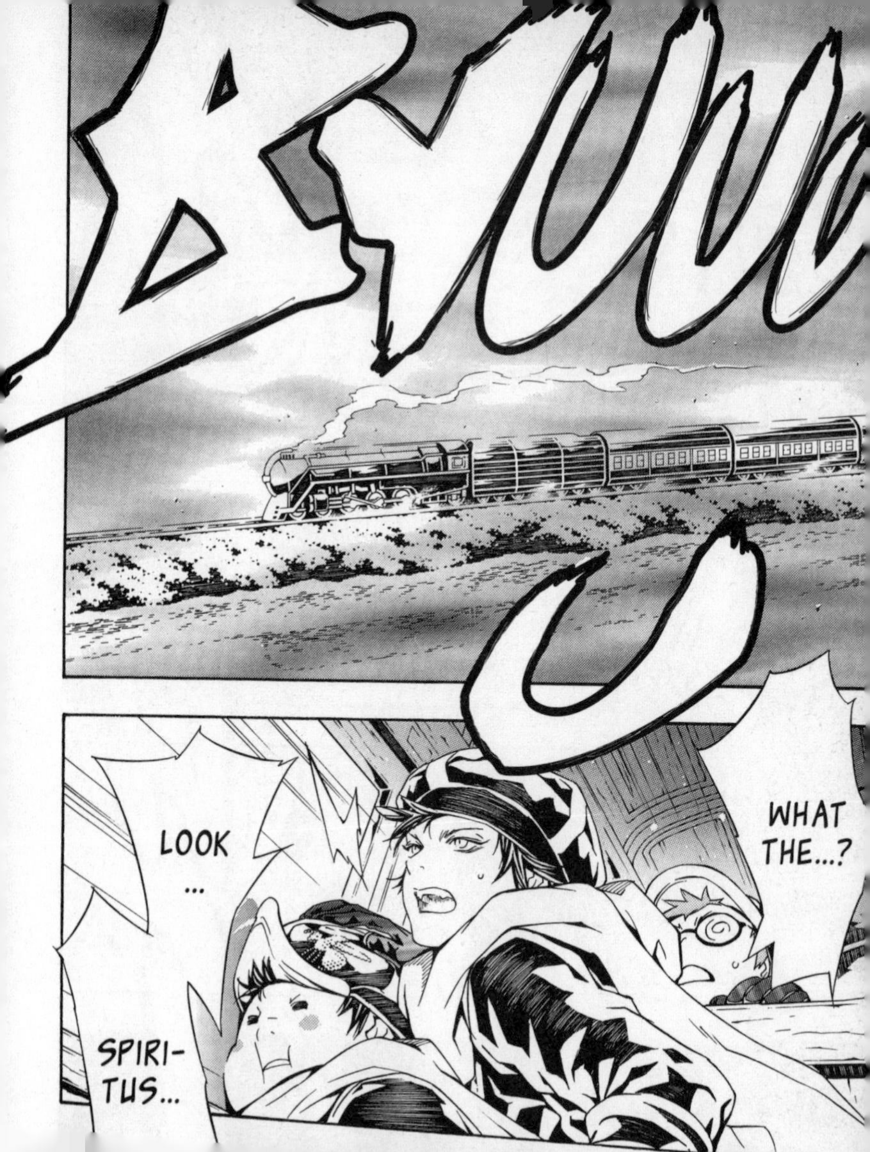
WHAT THE...?
LOOK ...
SPIRI-TUS...

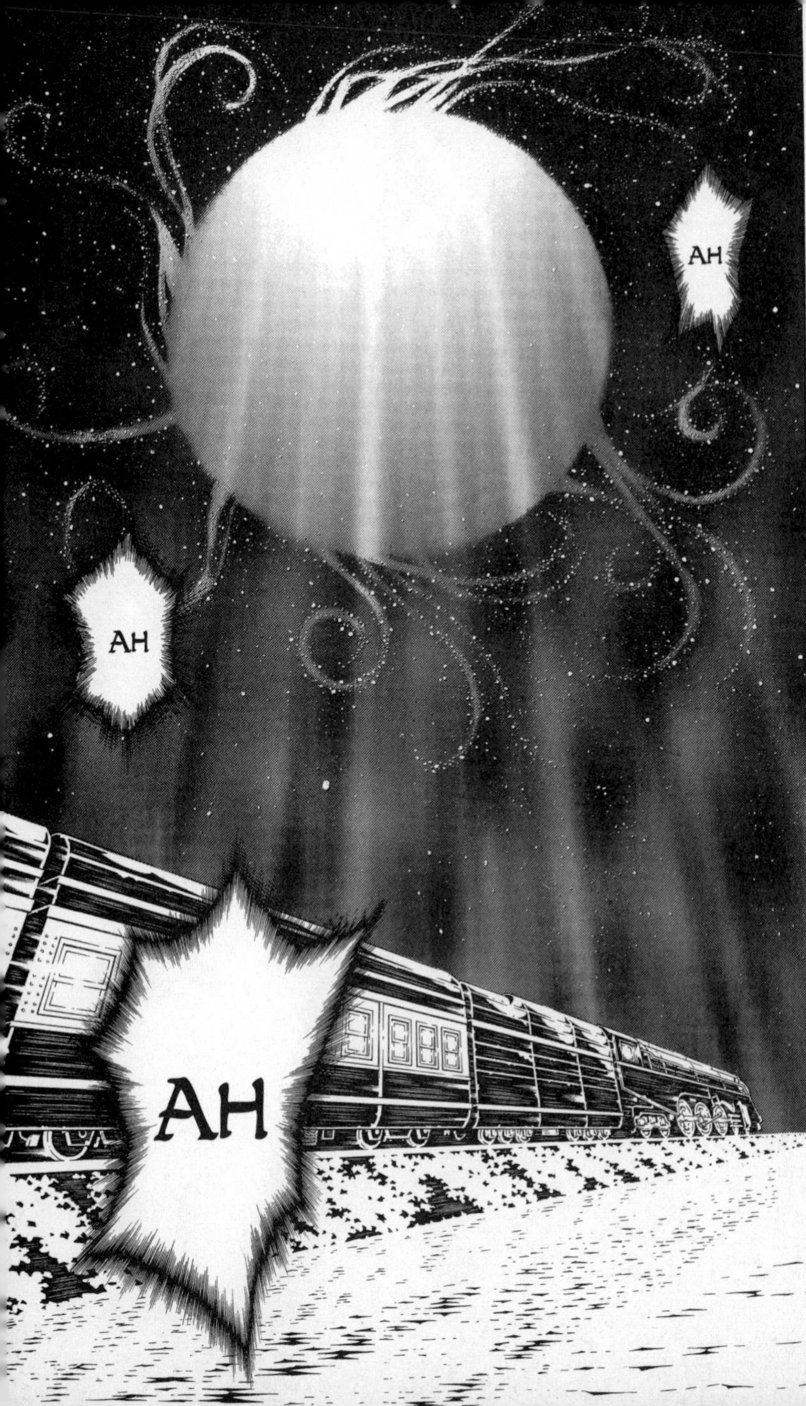
AH
AH
AH

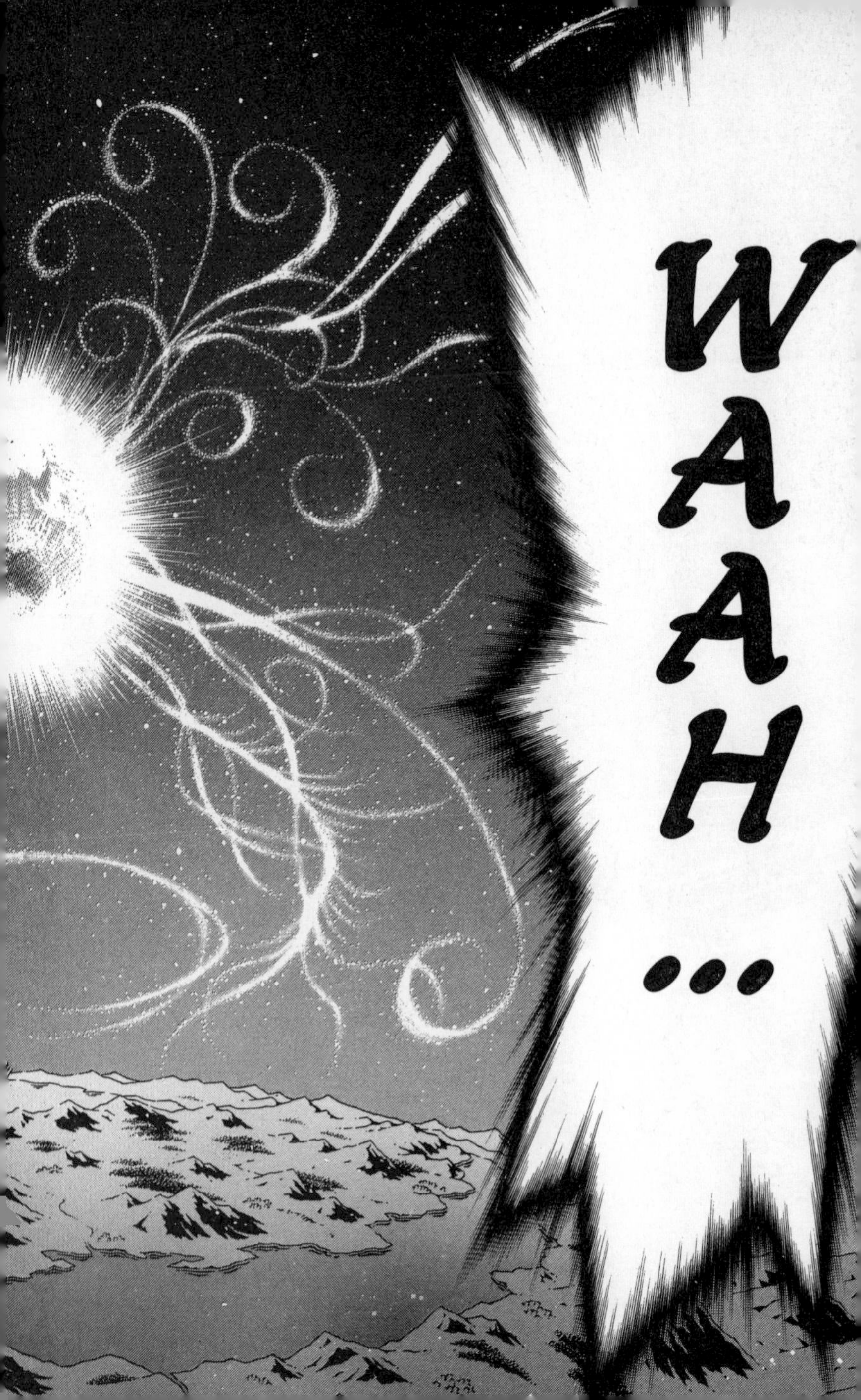
WAAH...

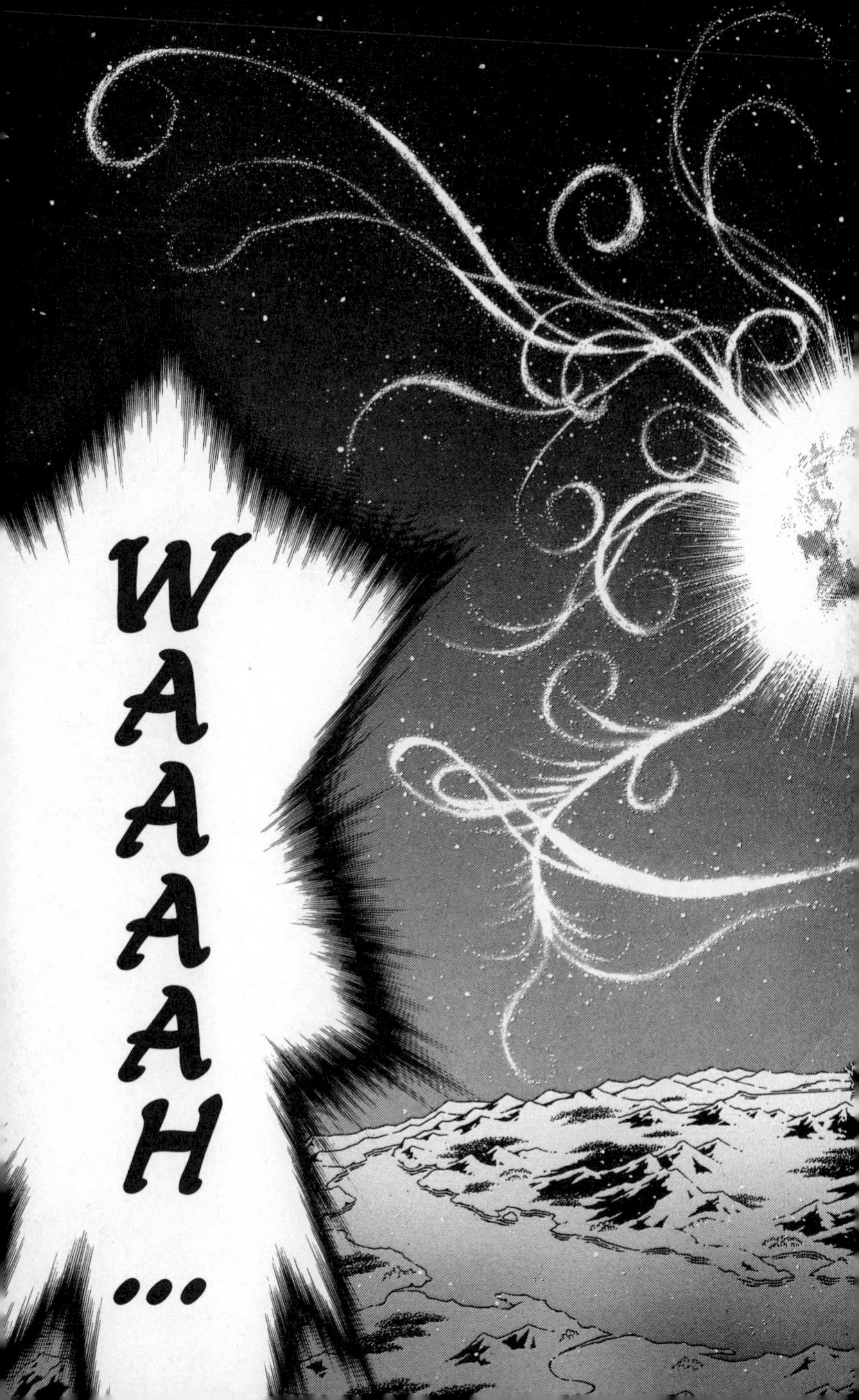
WAAAAAH...

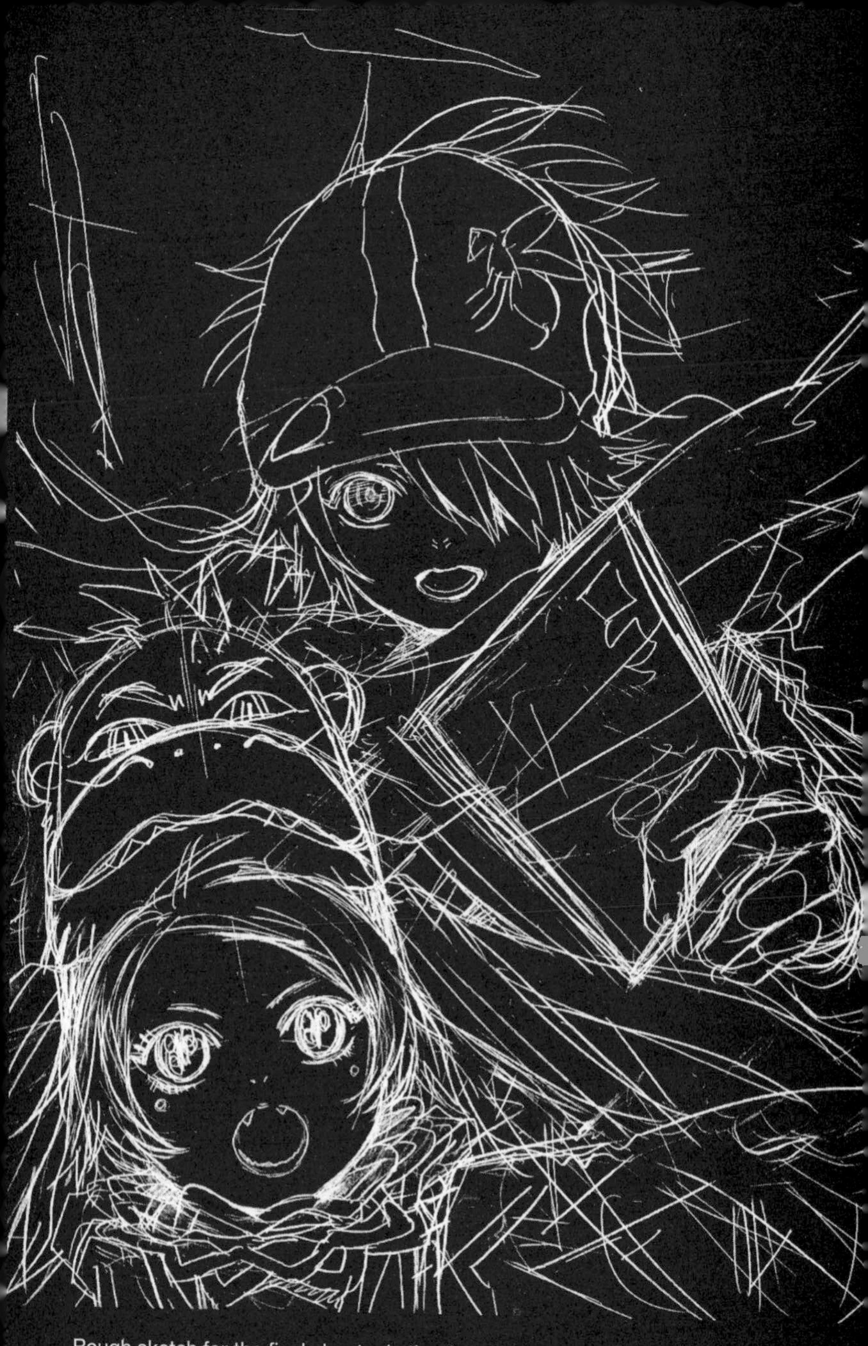

Rough sketch for the final chapter in the *Jump Square* December 2015 issue.

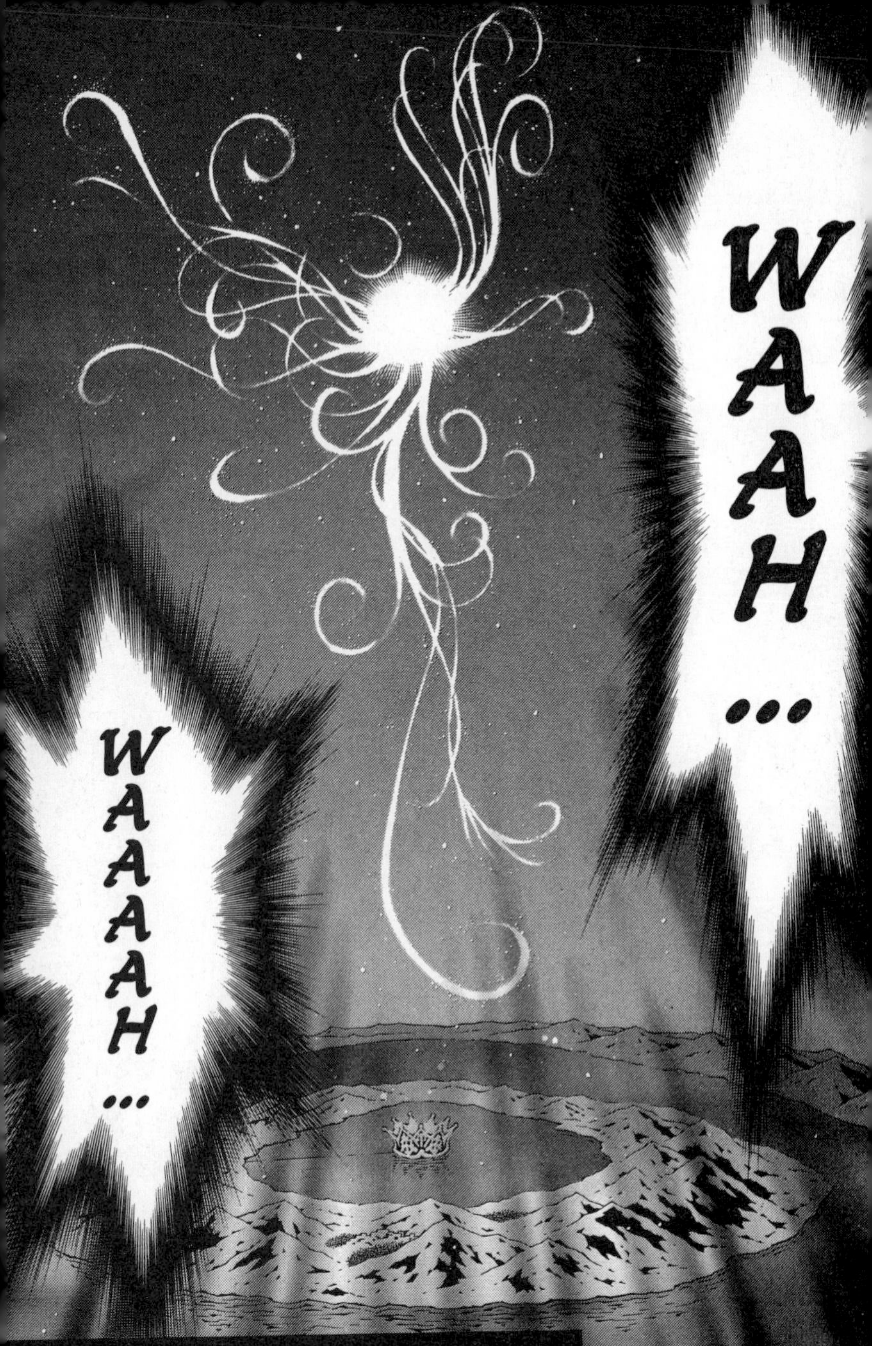
WAAH...
WAAAAAH...

Chapter 95: Goodbye

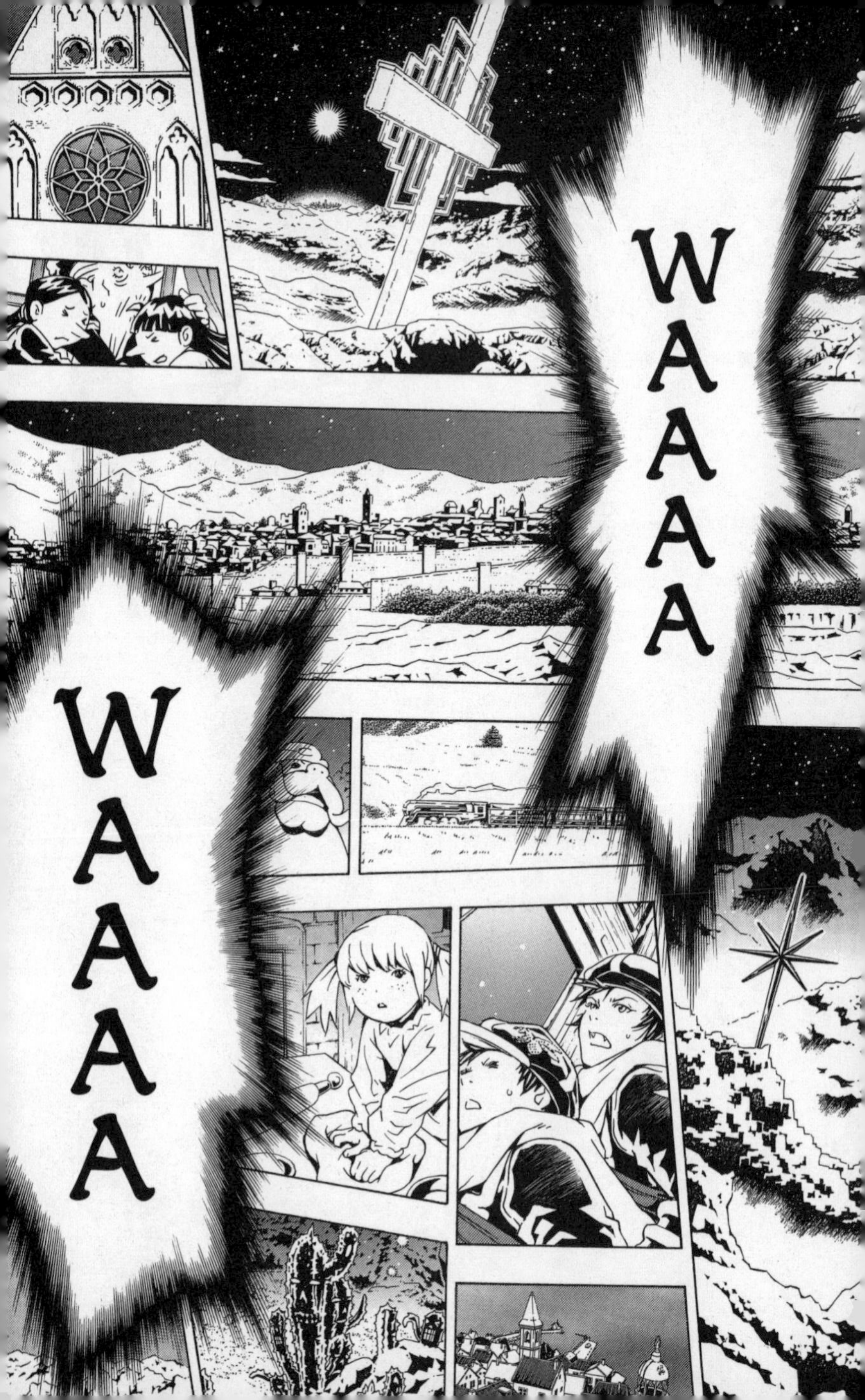
WAAAA
WAAAA

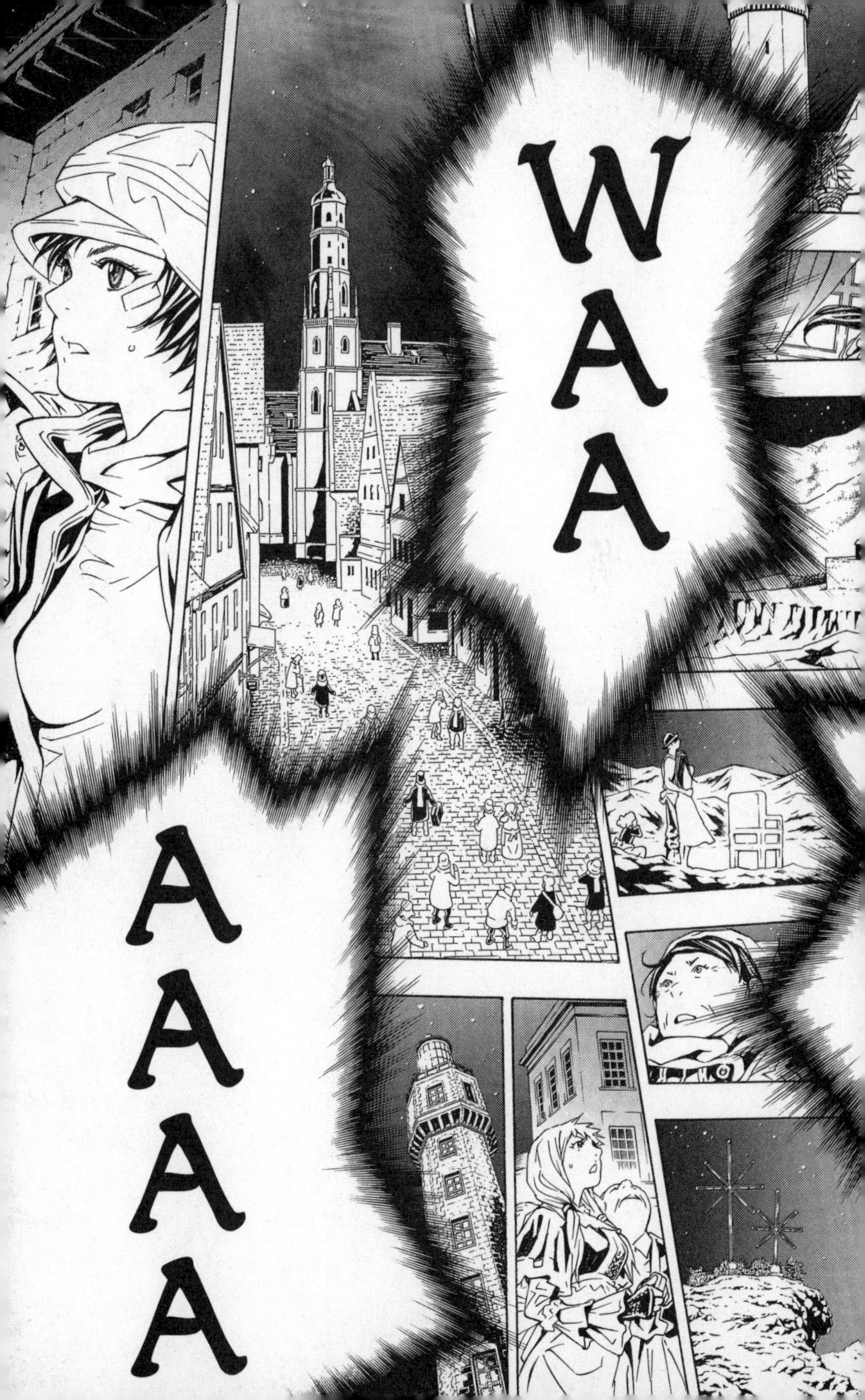
WAA
AAAA

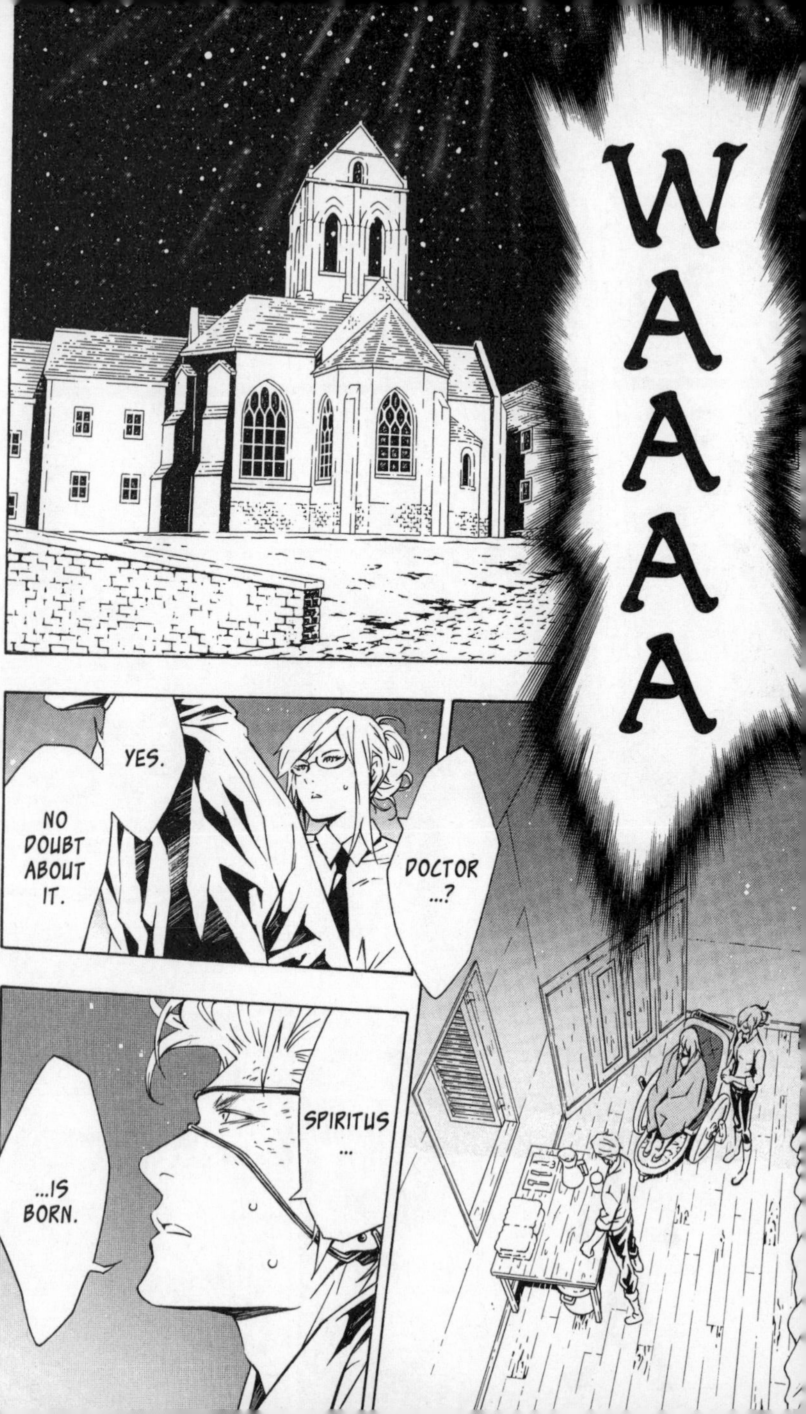
WAAAA
DOCTOR ...?
YES.
NO DOUBT ABOUT IT.
SPIRITUS ...
...IS BORN.

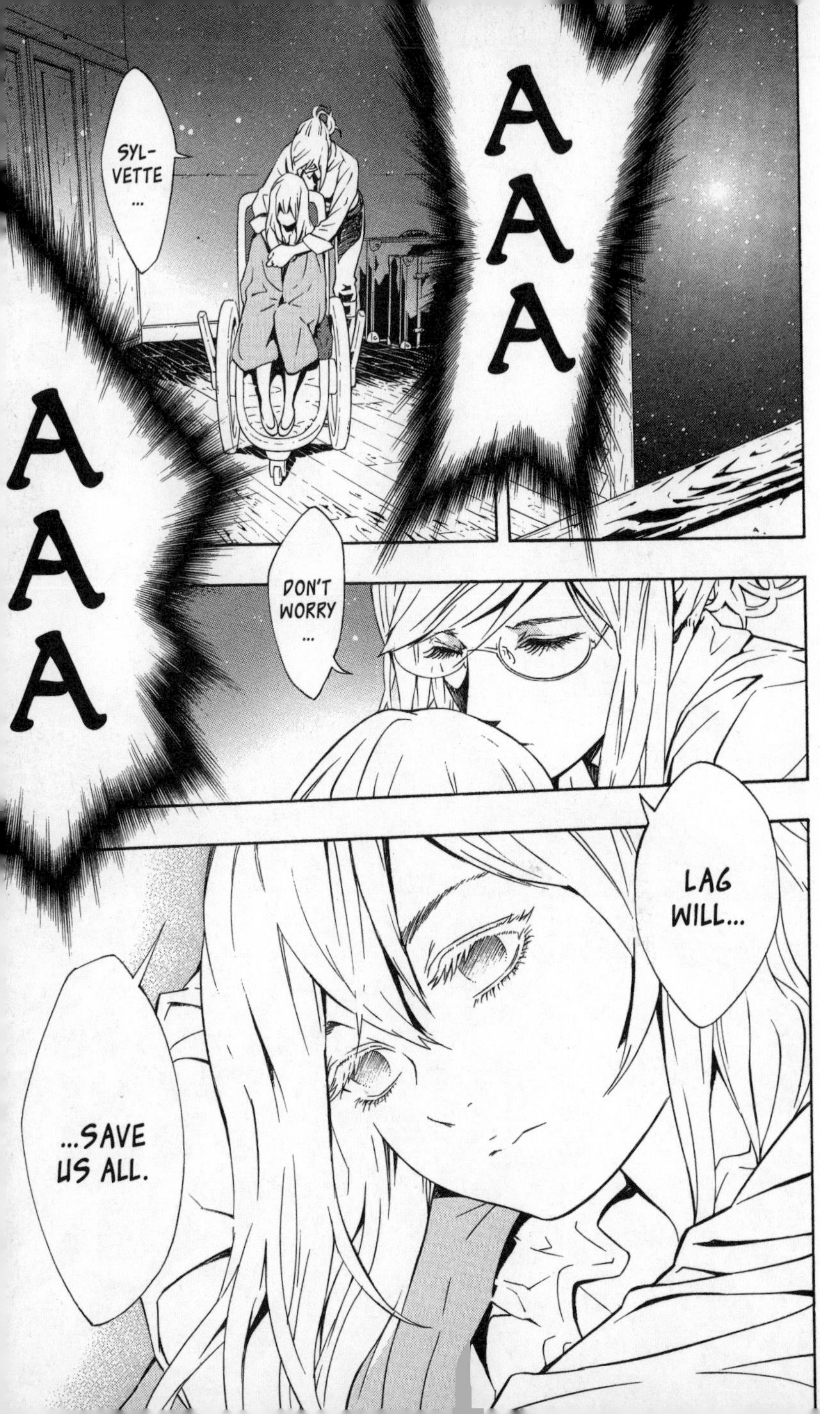
AAA
AAA
SYL-VETTE ...
DON'T WORRY ...
LAG WILL...
...SAVE US ALL.

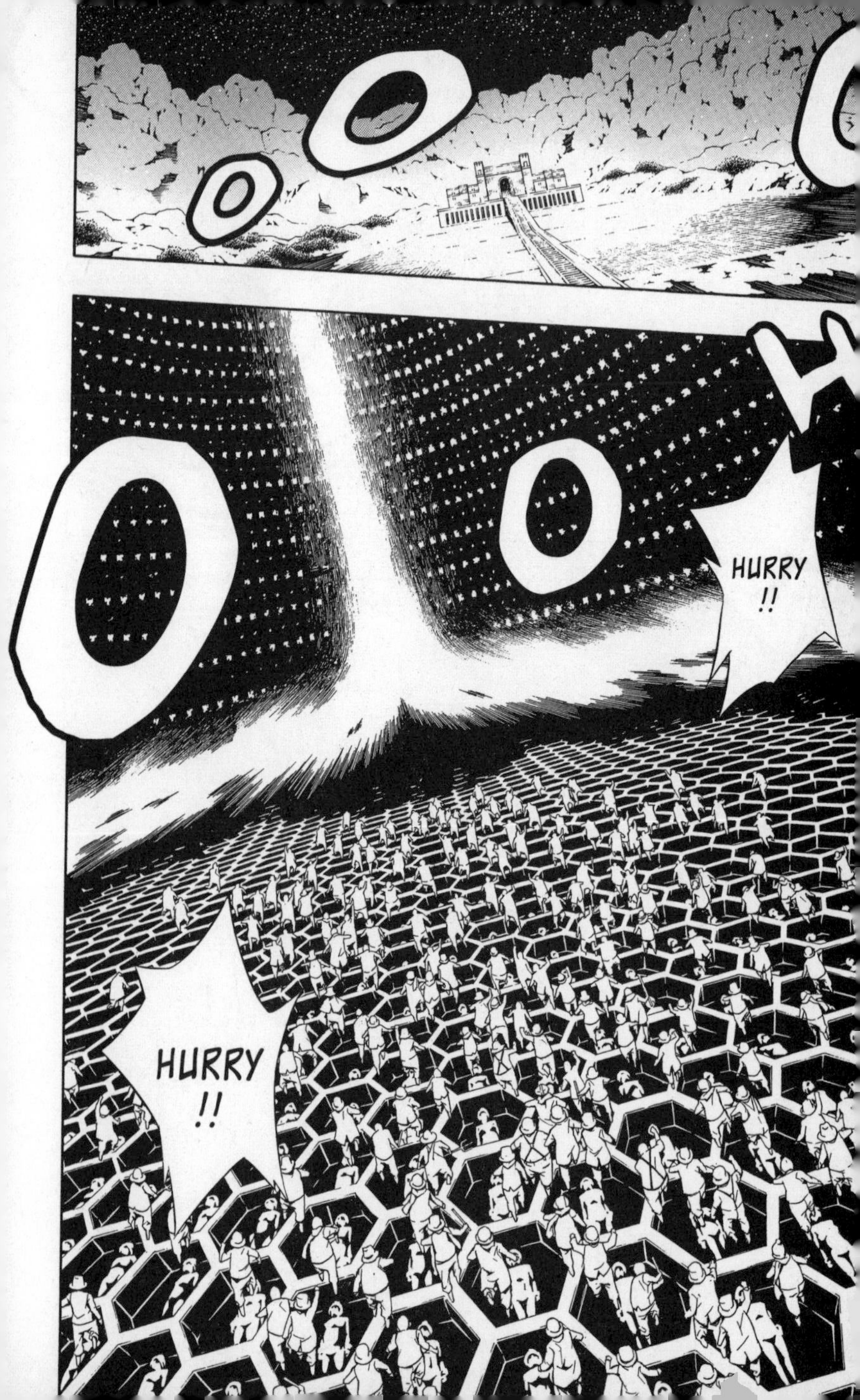
HURRY !!
HURRY !!

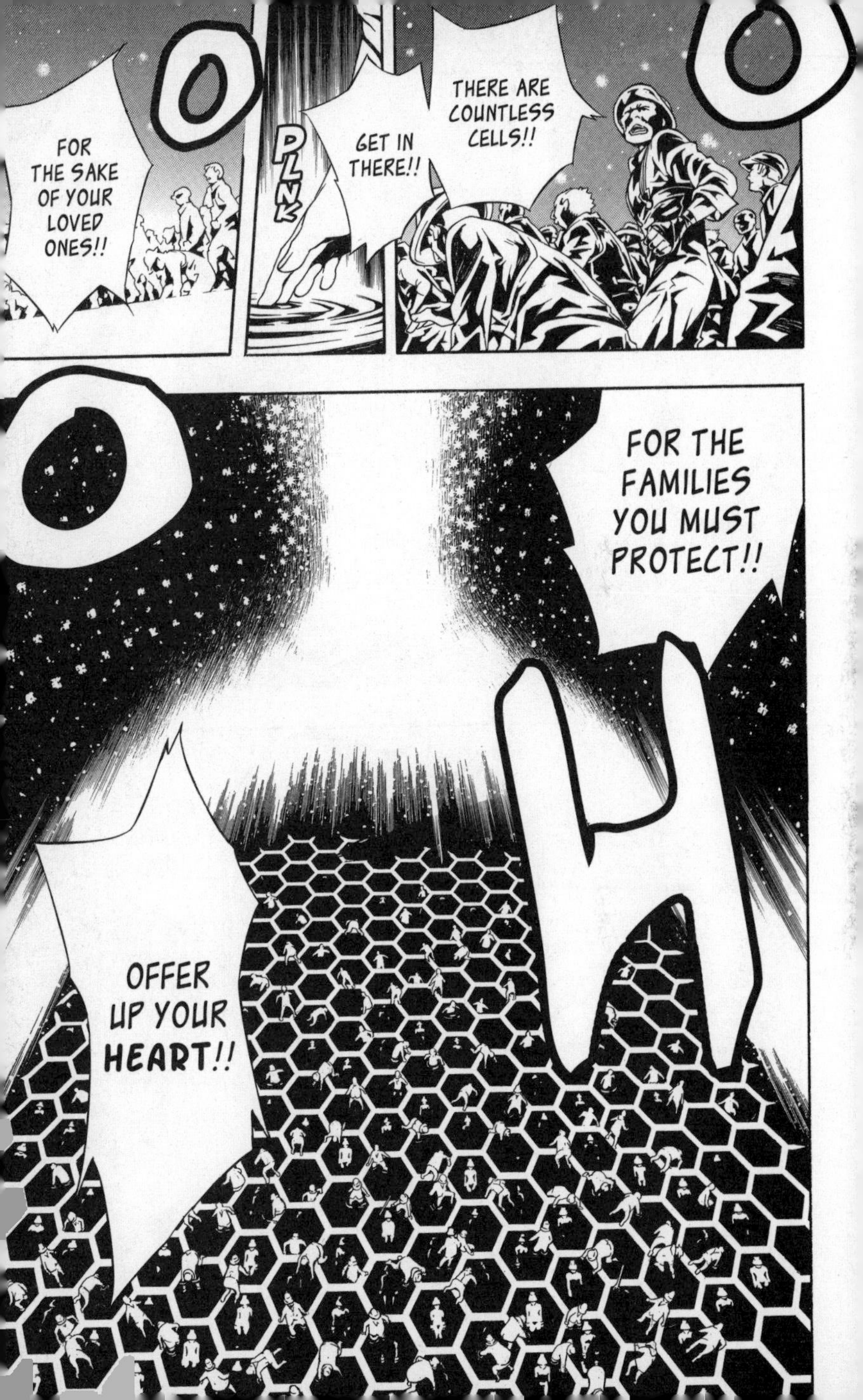
THERE ARE COUNTLESS CELLS!!
GET IN THERE!!
PLNK
FOR THE SAKE OF YOUR LOVED ONES!!
FOR THE FAMILIES YOU MUST PROTECT!!
OFFER UP YOUR **HEART**!!

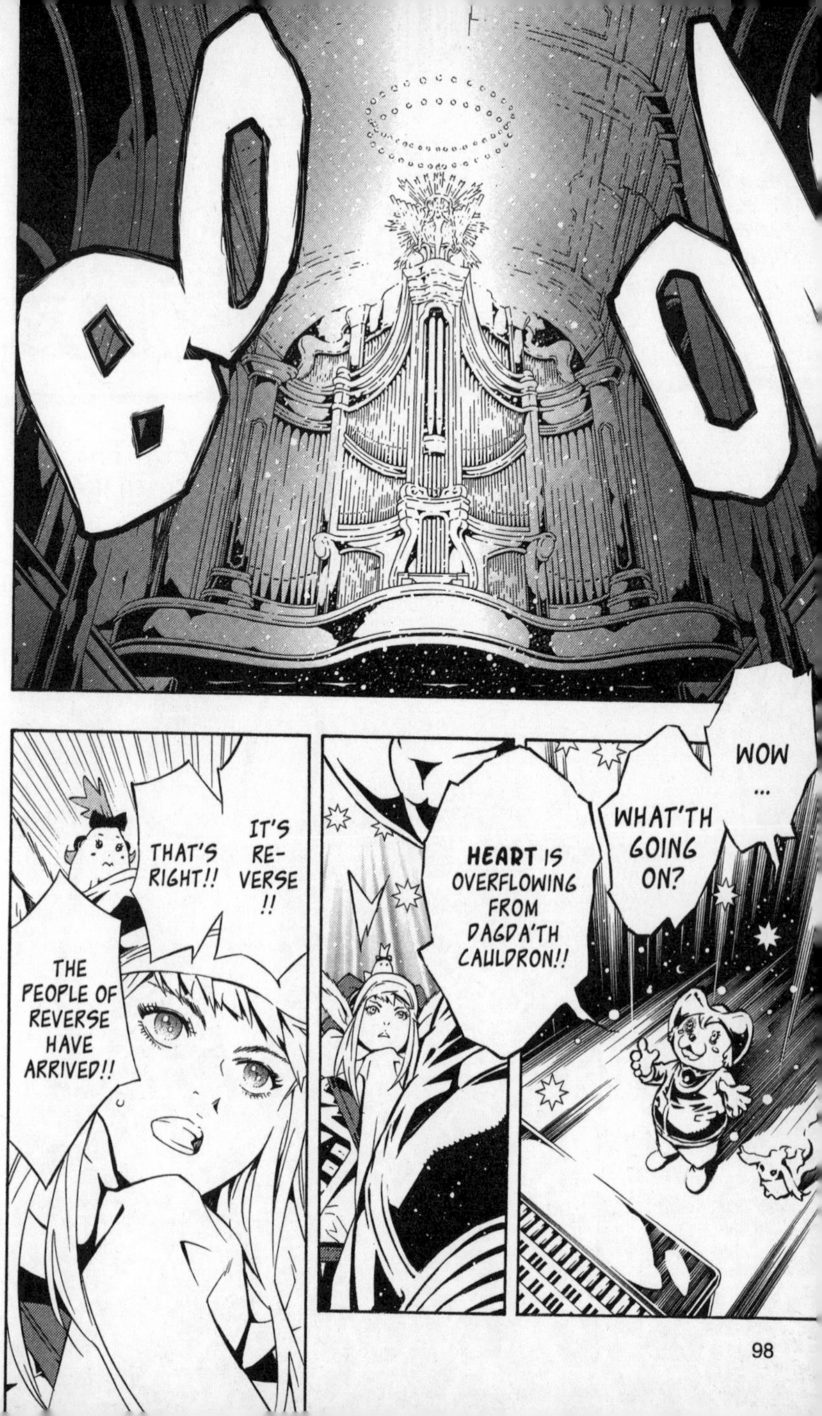
WOW ...
WHAT'TH GOING ON?
HEART IS OVERFLOWING FROM DAGDA'TH CAULDRON!!
IT'S RE-VERSE!!
THAT'S RIGHT!!
THE PEOPLE OF REVERSE HAVE ARRIVED!!

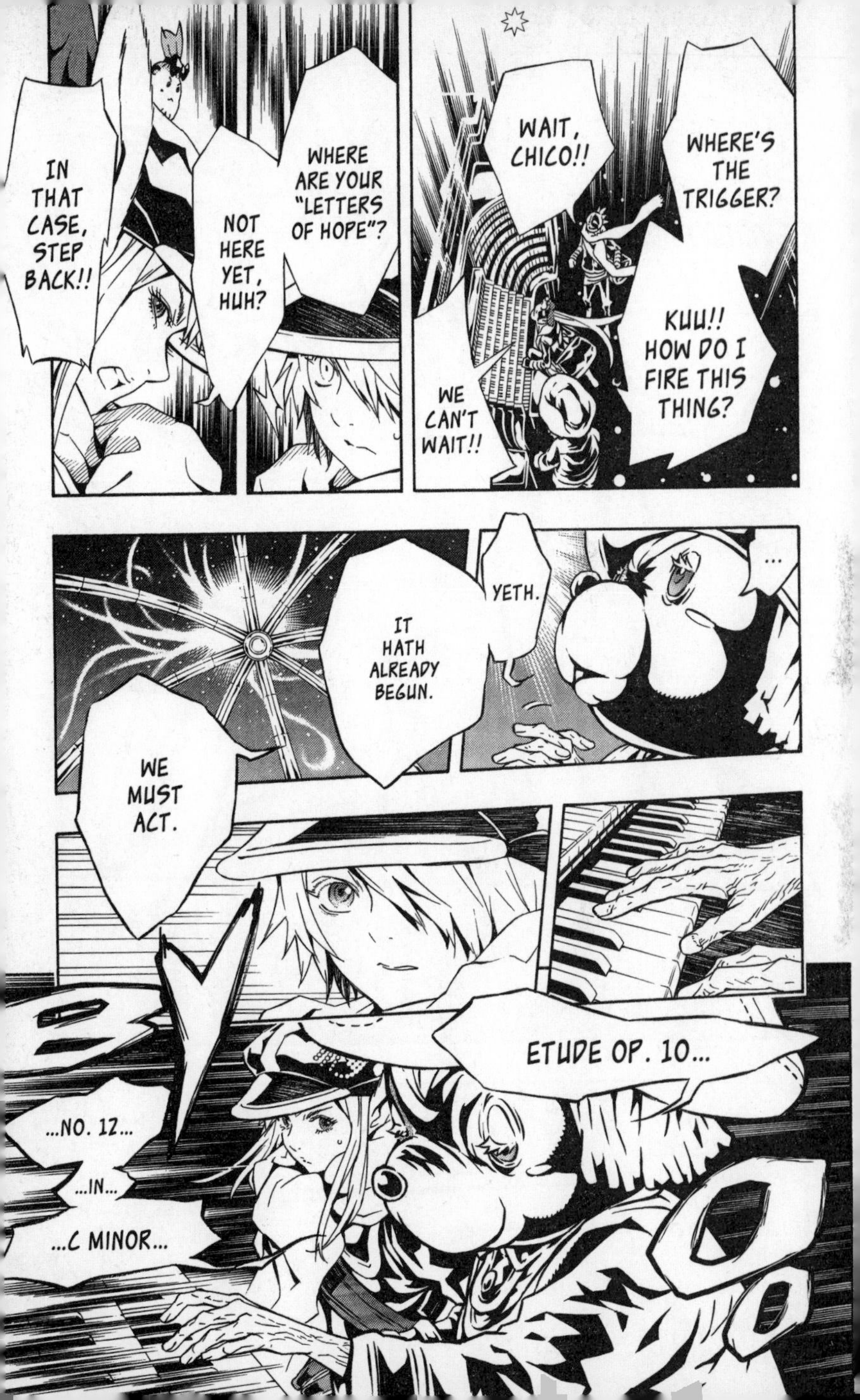
WHERE'S THE TRIGGER?
WAIT, CHICO!!
KUU!! HOW DO I FIRE THIS THING?
WE CAN'T WAIT!!
WHERE ARE YOUR "LETTERS OF HOPE"?
NOT HERE YET, HUH?
IN THAT CASE, STEP BACK!!
...
YETH.
IT HATH ALREADY BEGUN.
WE MUST ACT.
ETUDE OP. 10...
...NO. 12...
...IN...
...C MINOR...

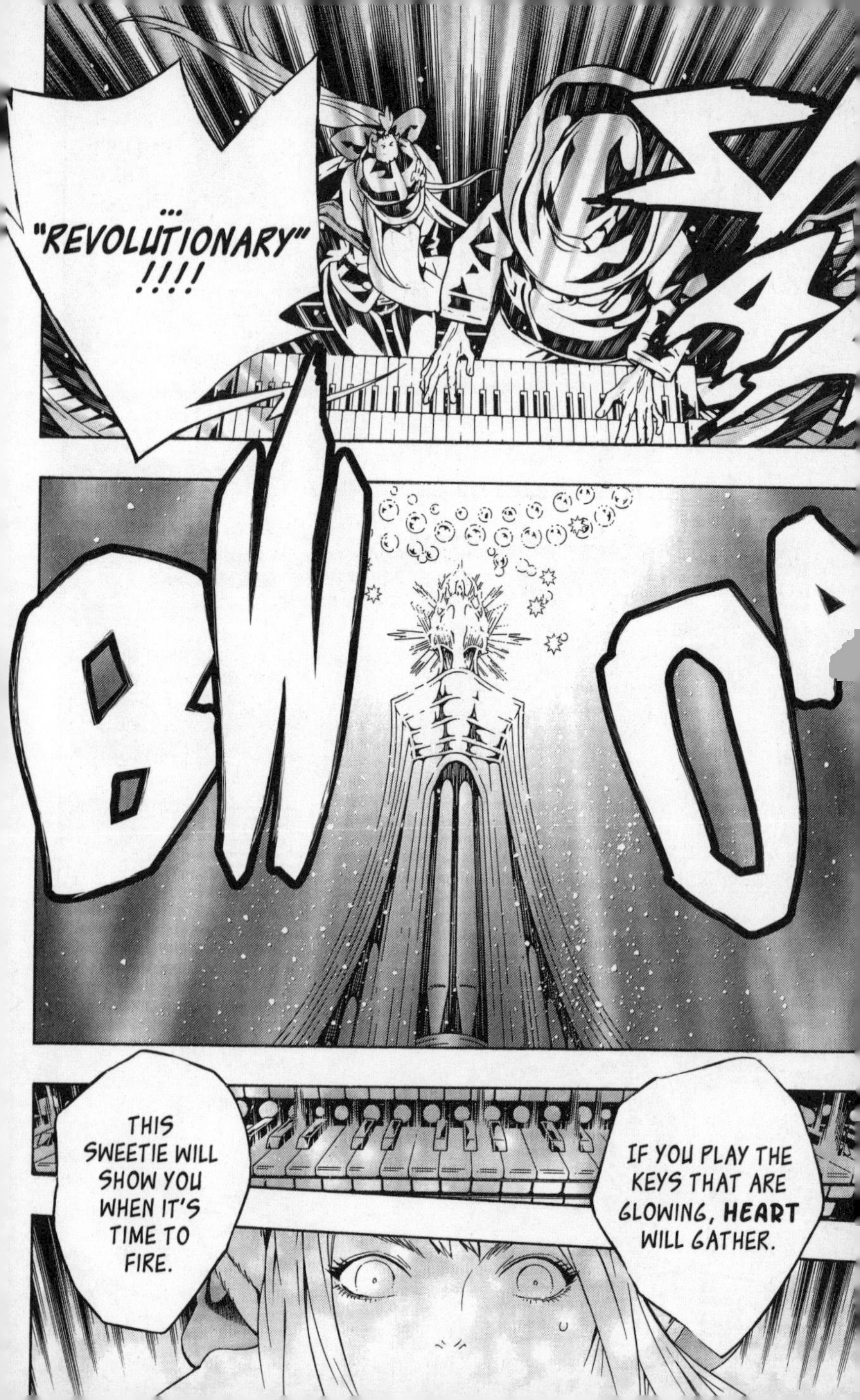
..."REVOLUTIONARY"!!!!
BWOA
IF YOU PLAY THE KEYS THAT ARE GLOWING, HEART WILL GATHER.
THIS SWEETIE WILL SHOW YOU WHEN IT'S TIME TO FIRE.

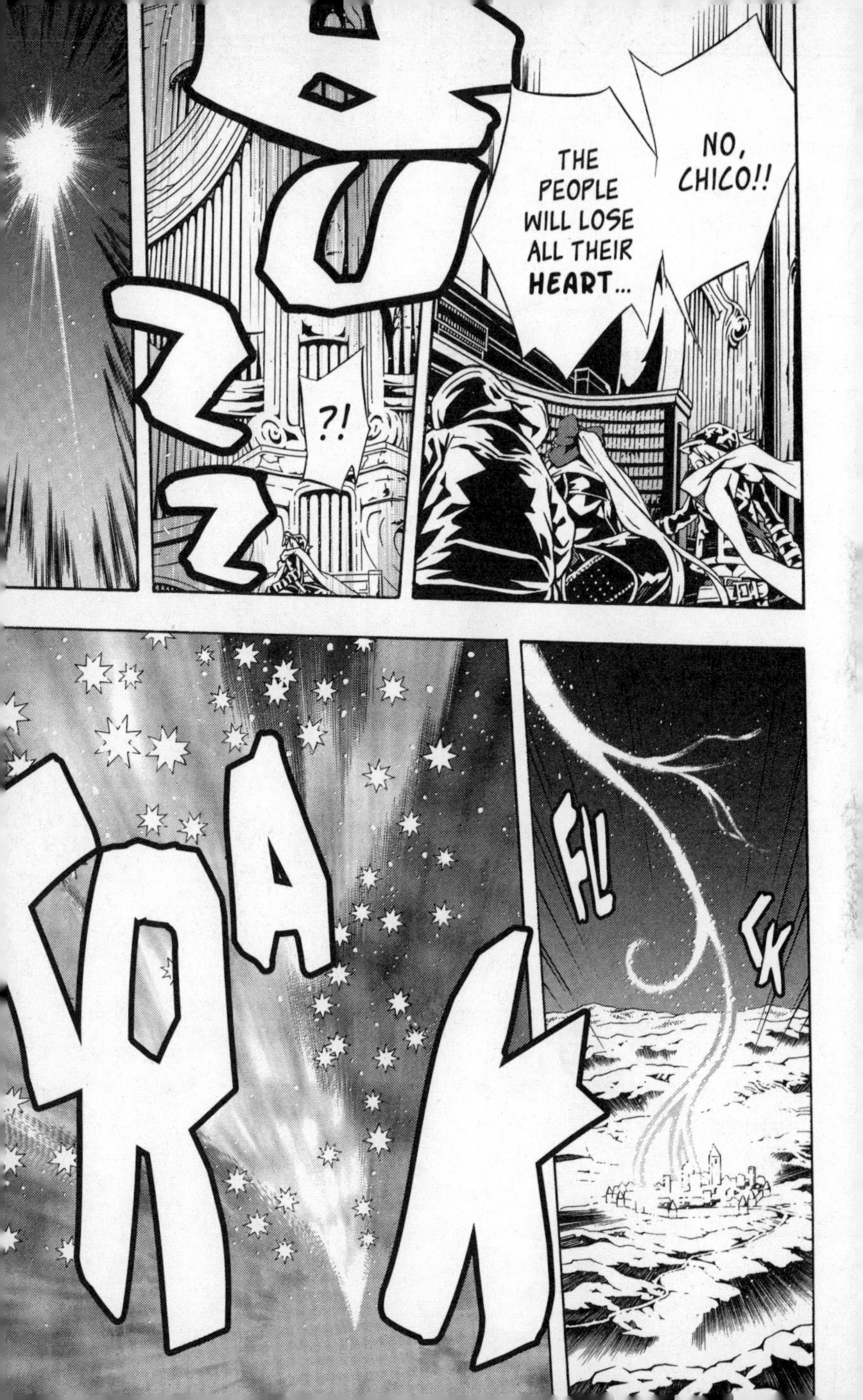
NO, CHICO!!
THE PEOPLE WILL LOSE ALL THEIR HEART...
?!
FL
CK

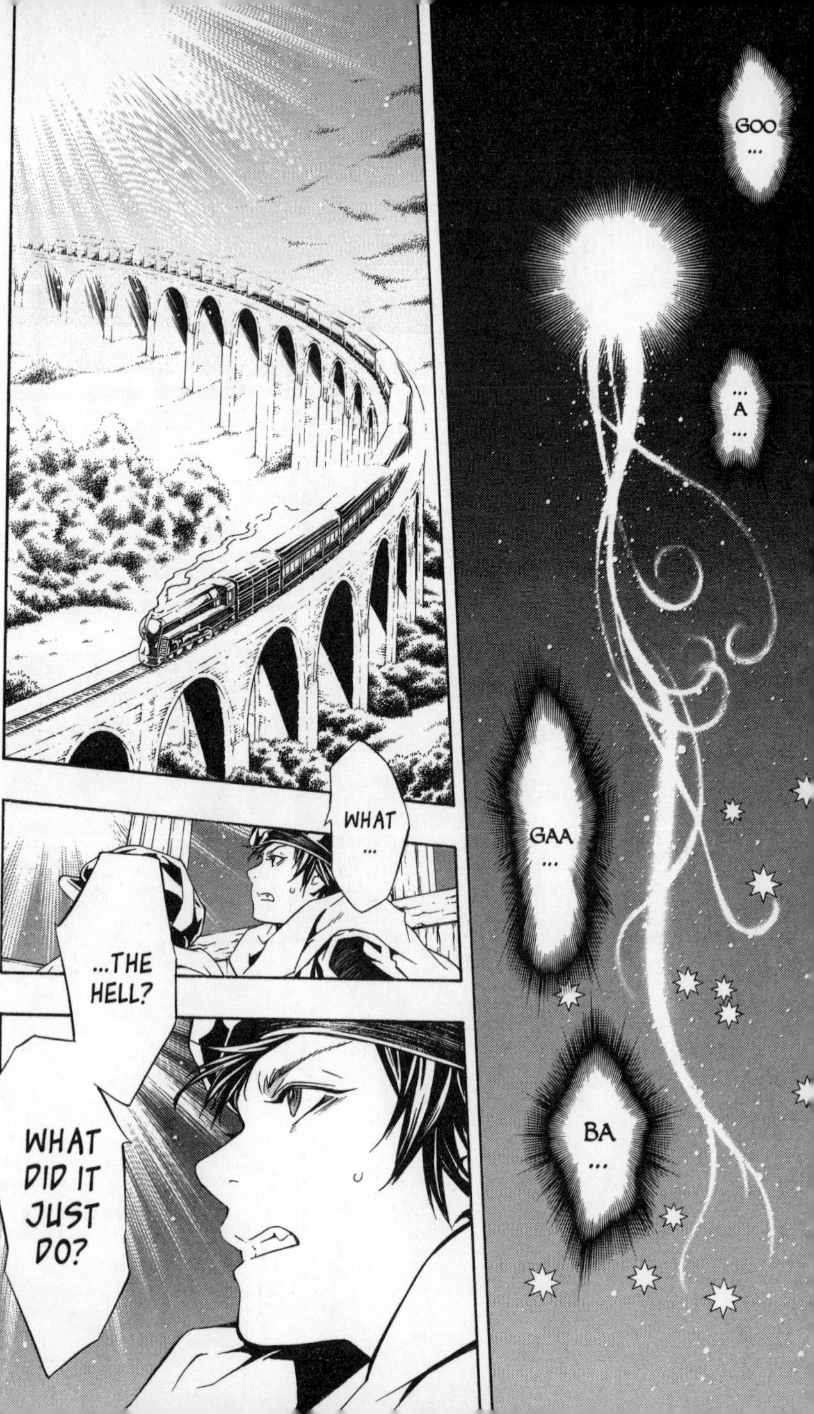
GOO ...
... A ...
GAA ...
BA ...
WHAT ...
...THE HELL?
WHAT DID IT JUST DO?

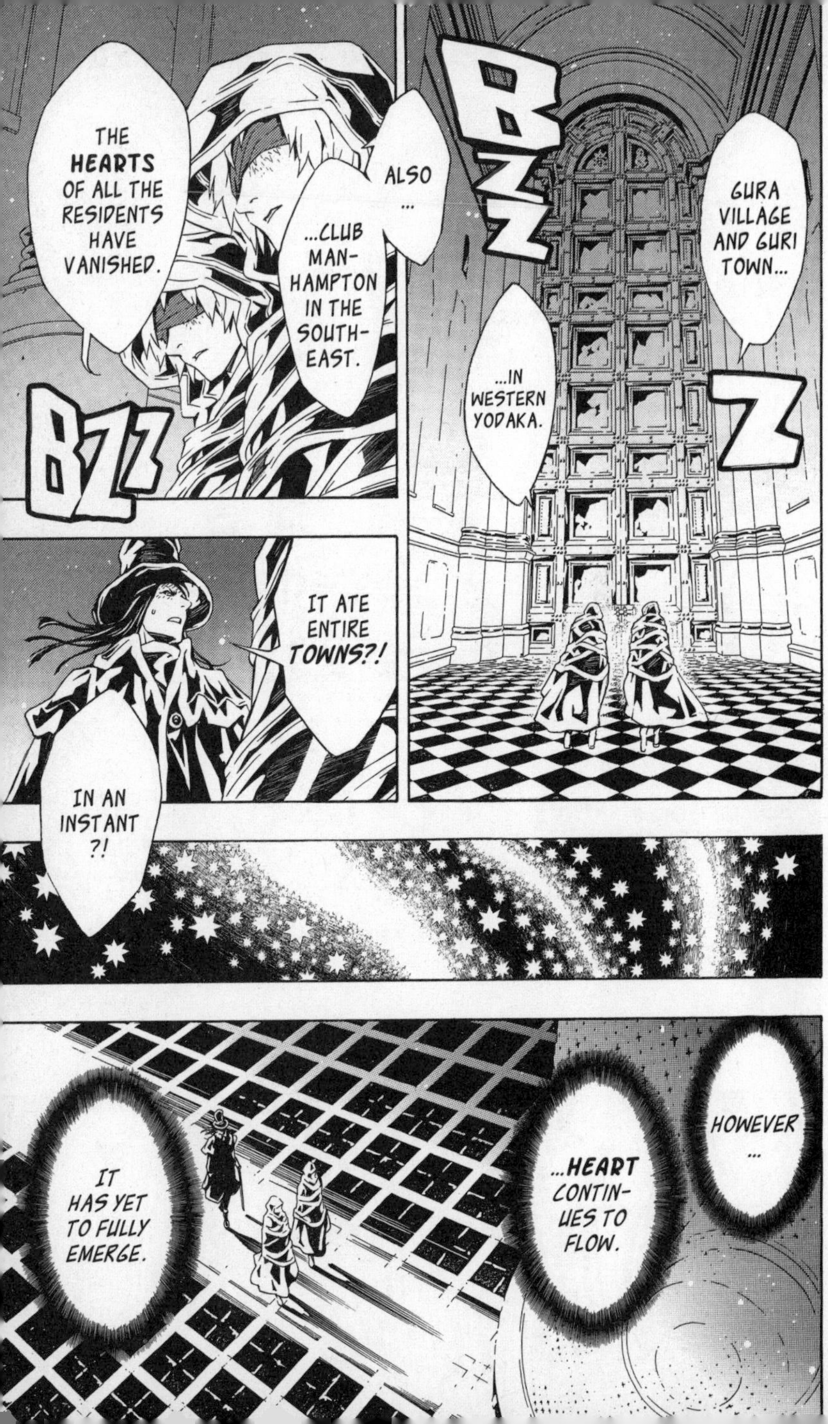
BZZ
GURA VILLAGE AND GURI TOWN...
...IN WESTERN YODAKA.
Z
ALSO ...
...CLUB MAN-HAMPTON IN THE SOUTH-EAST.
THE **HEARTS** OF ALL THE RESIDENTS HAVE VANISHED.
BZZ
IT ATE ENTIRE *TOWNS?!*
IN AN INSTANT ?!
HOWEVER ...
...**HEART** CONTIN-UES TO FLOW.
IT HAS YET TO FULLY EMERGE.

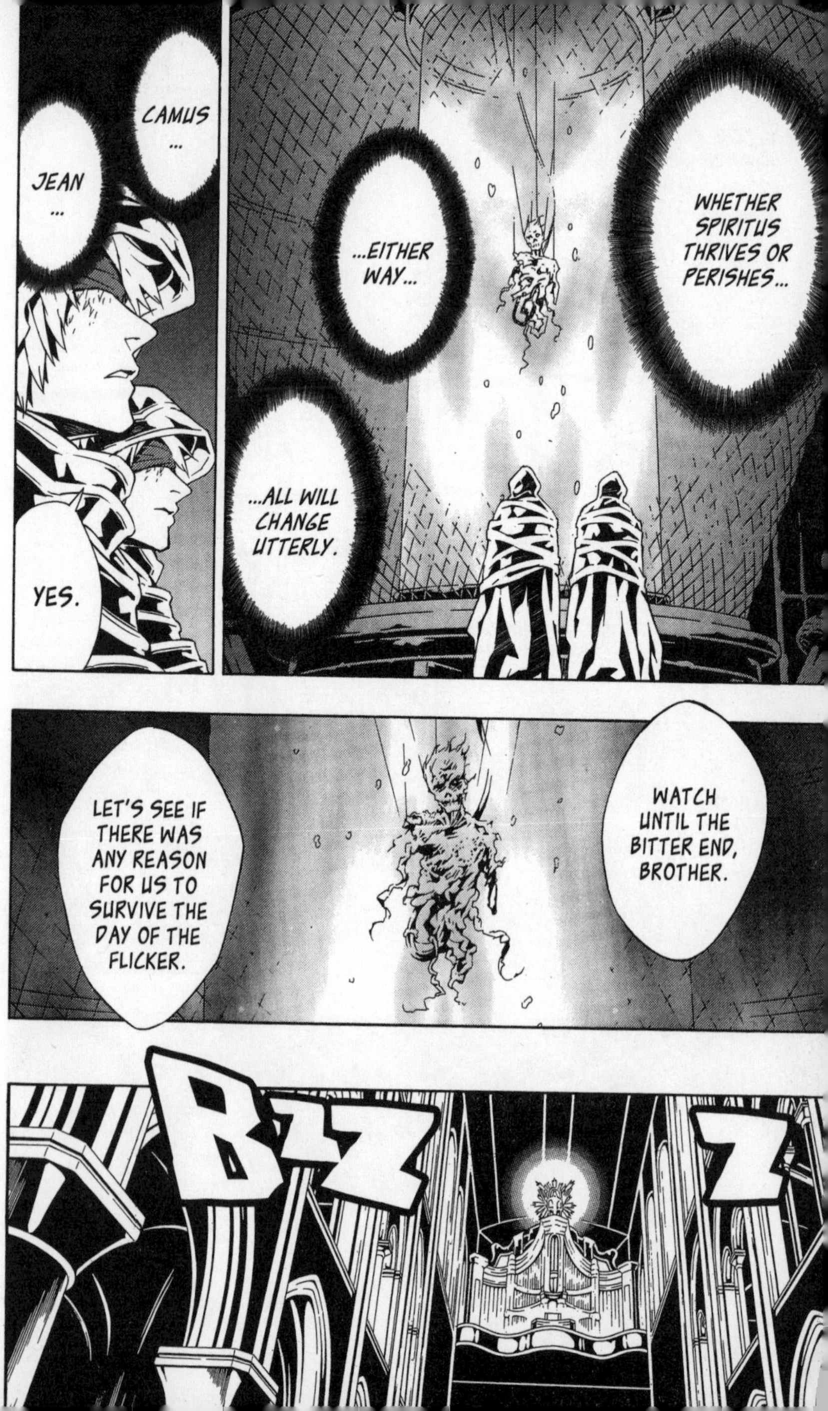
WHETHER SPIRITUS THRIVES OR PERISHES...
...EITHER WAY...
...ALL WILL CHANGE UTTERLY.
CAMUS ...
JEAN ...
YES.
WATCH UNTIL THE BITTER END, BROTHER.
LET'S SEE IF THERE WAS ANY REASON FOR US TO SURVIVE THE DAY OF THE FLICKER.
BZZ

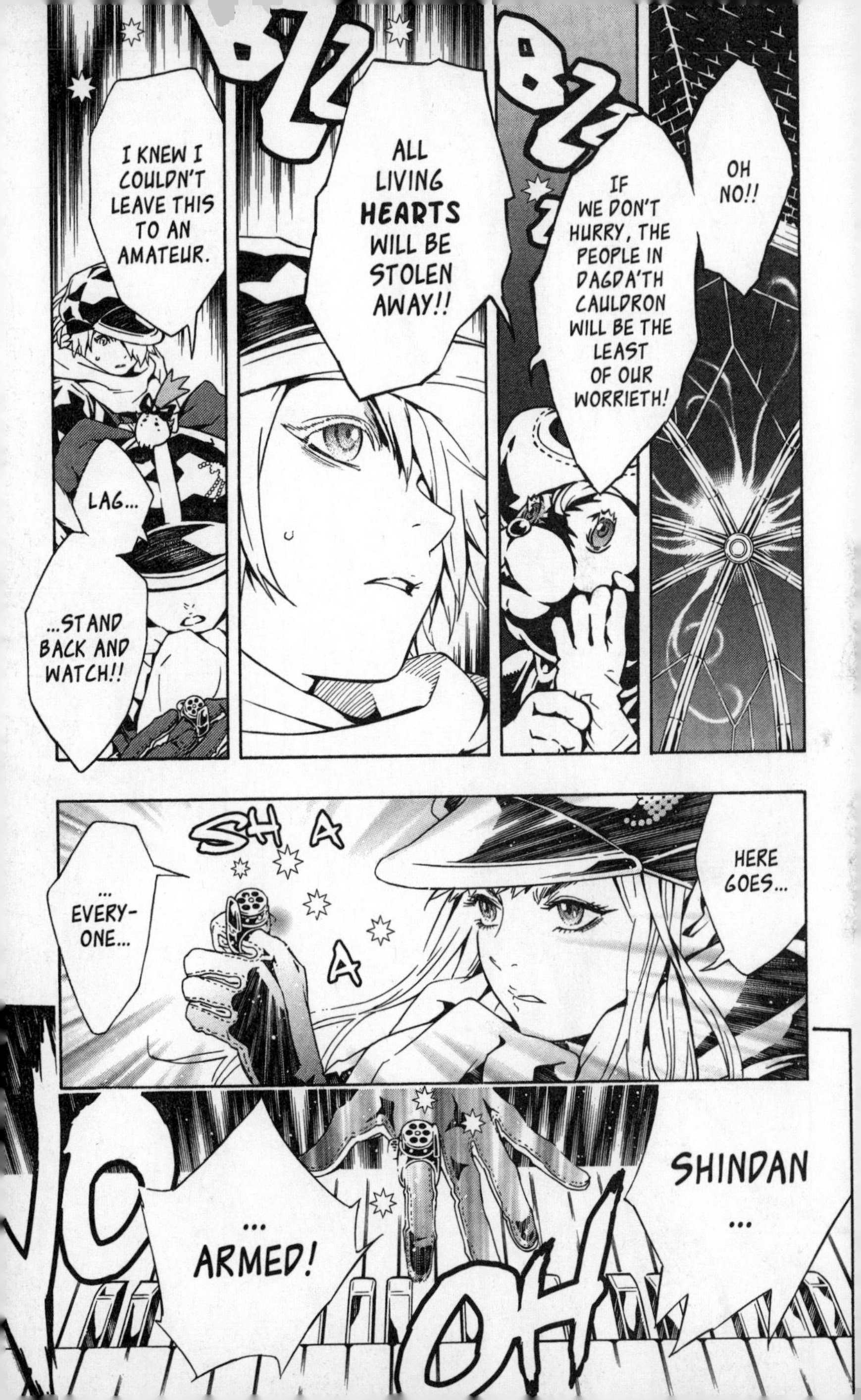

OH NO!!
BZZ BZZ
IF WE DON'T HURRY, THE PEOPLE IN DAGDA'TH CAULDRON WILL BE THE LEAST OF OUR WORRIETH!
ALL LIVING **HEARTS** WILL BE STOLEN AWAY!!
I KNEW I COULDN'T LEAVE THIS TO AN AMATEUR.
LAG...
...STAND BACK AND WATCH!!
HERE GOES...
SHAA
...EVERY-ONE...
SHINDAN...
...ARMED!

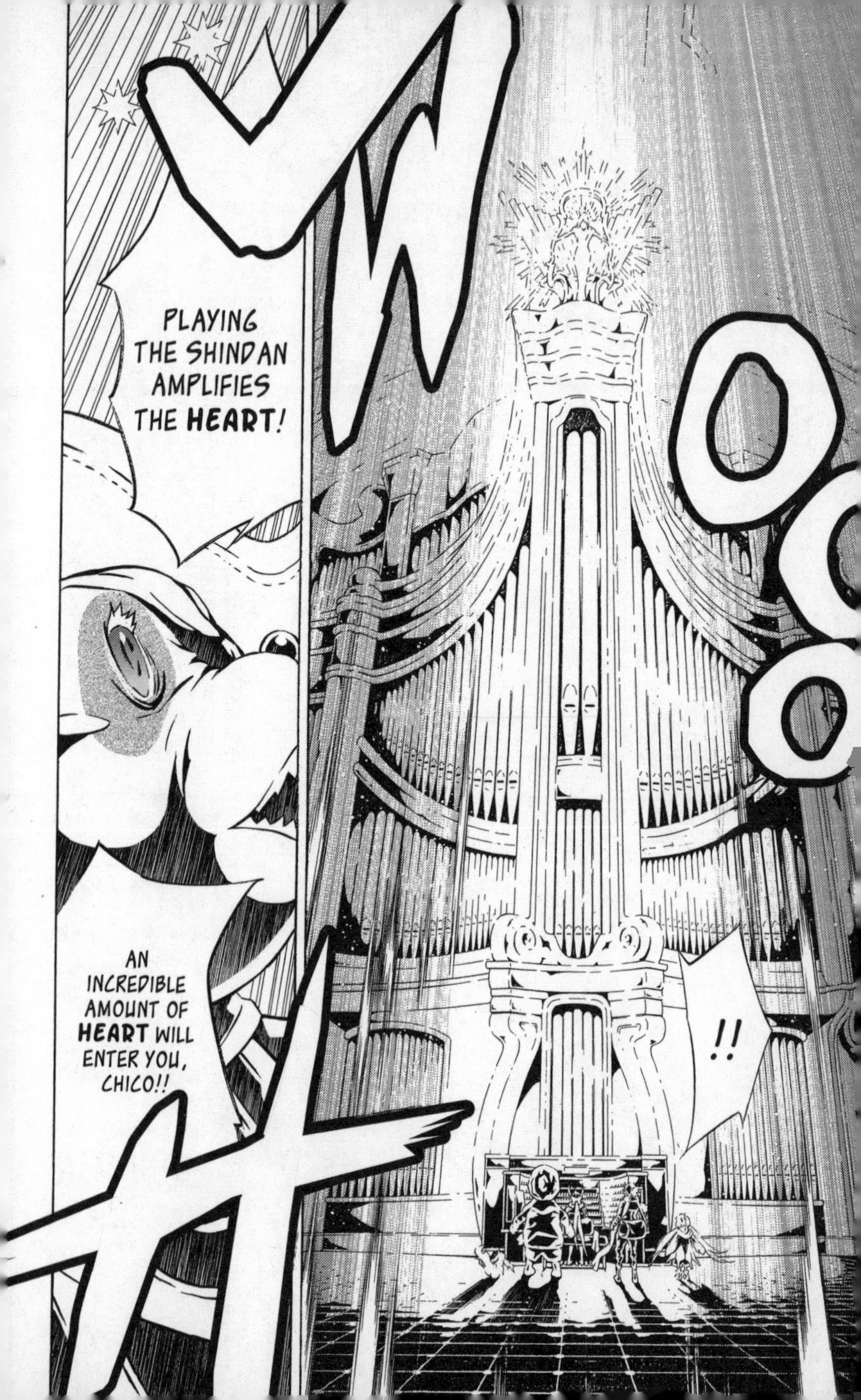
VWOOO
!!
PLAYING THE SHINDAN AMPLIFIES THE **HEART**!
AN INCREDIBLE AMOUNT OF **HEART** WILL ENTER YOU, CHICO!!

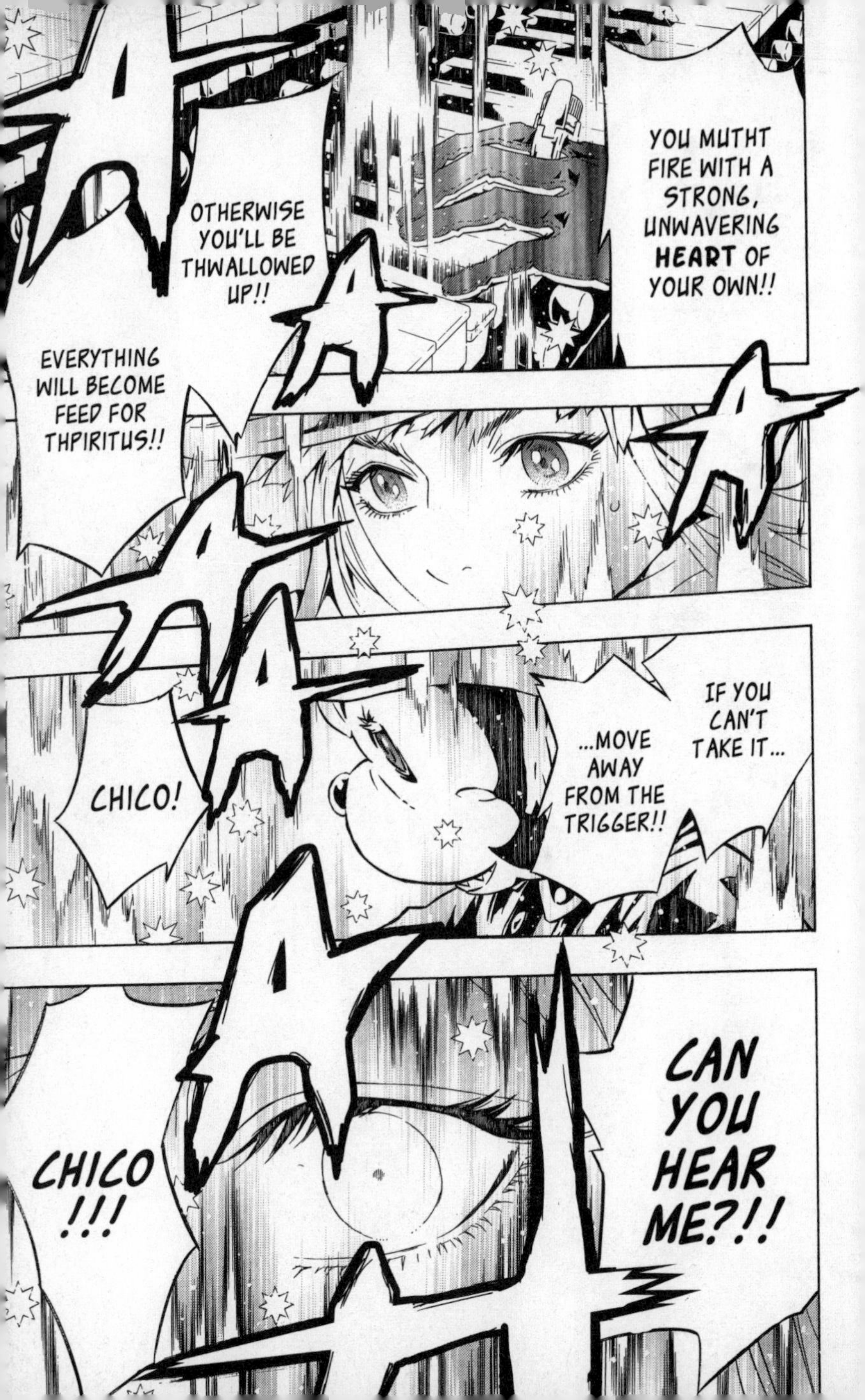
YOU MUTHT FIRE WITH A STRONG, UNWAVERING **HEART** OF YOUR OWN!!
OTHERWISE YOU'LL BE THWALLOWED UP!!
EVERYTHING WILL BECOME FEED FOR THPIRITUS!!
IF YOU CAN'T TAKE IT...
...MOVE AWAY FROM THE TRIGGER!!
CHICO!
CAN YOU HEAR ME?!!
CHICO!!!

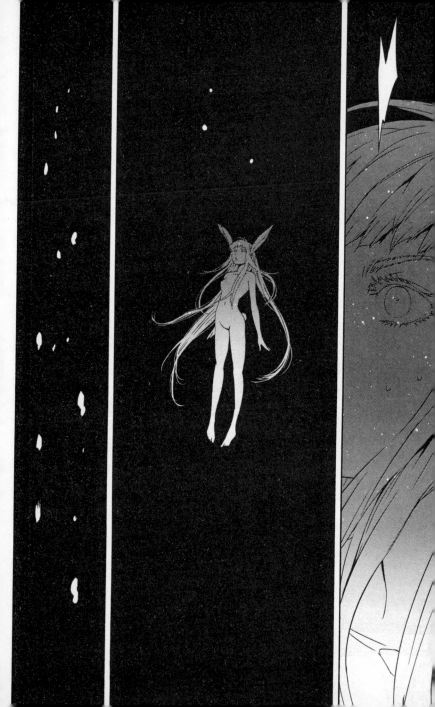

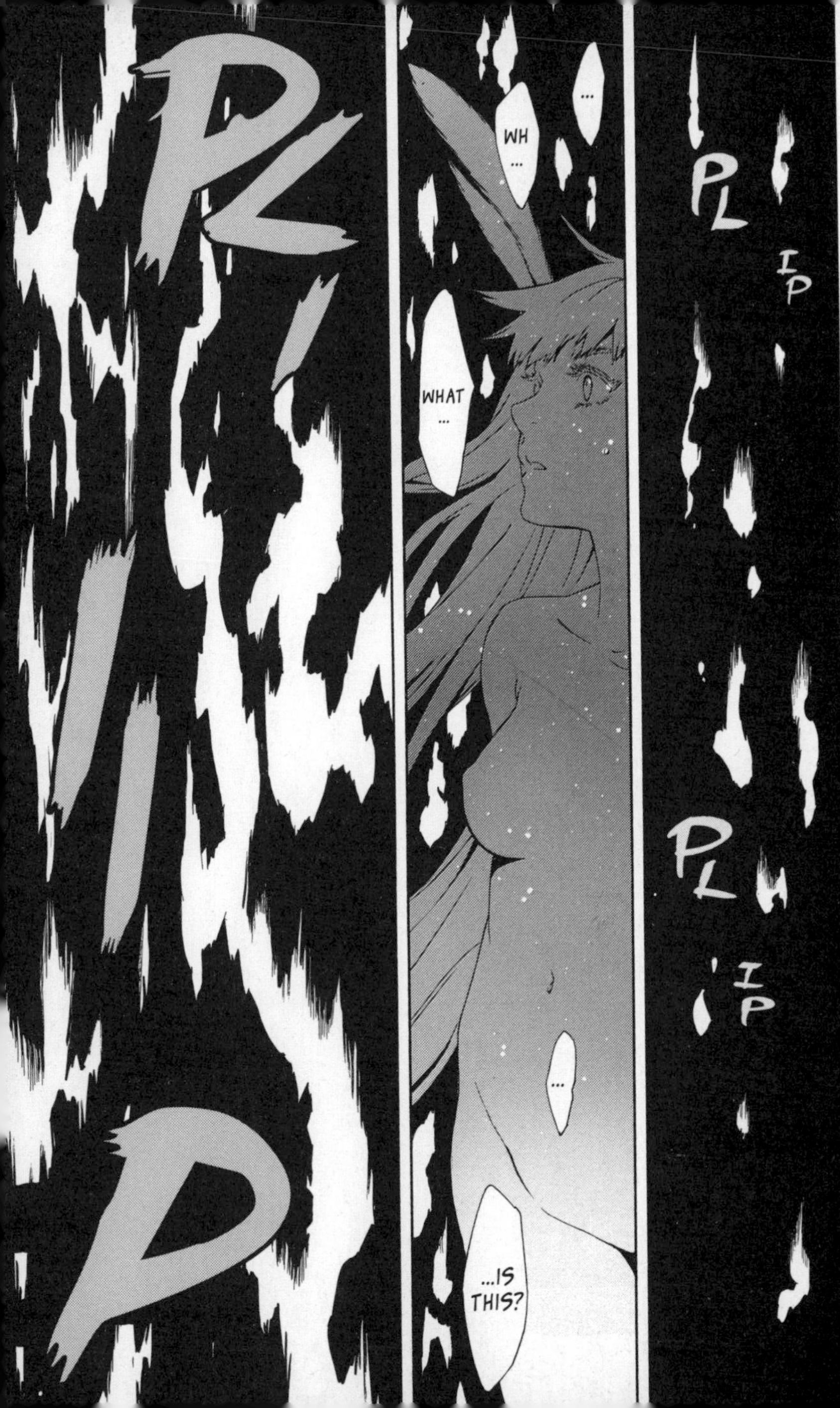
PLIP
PLIP
...
WH...
WHAT...
...
...IS THIS?
PLIP

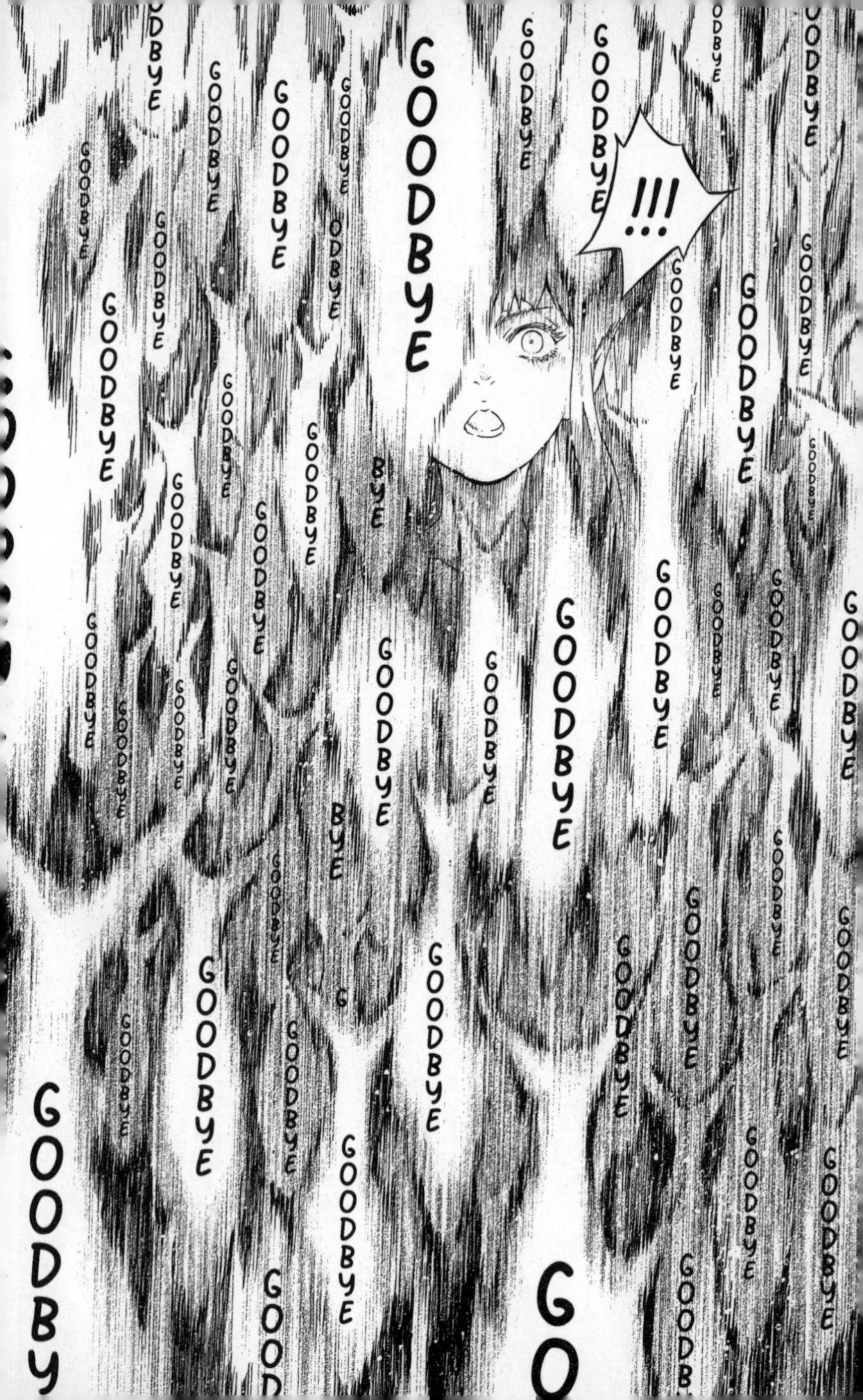
GOODBYE
GOODBYE
GOODBYE
GOODBYE
!!!...
GOODBYE
GOODBYE
GOODBYE
GOODBYE
GOODBYE
GOODBYE
GOODBYE
GOODBYE
GOODBYE
GOODBYE

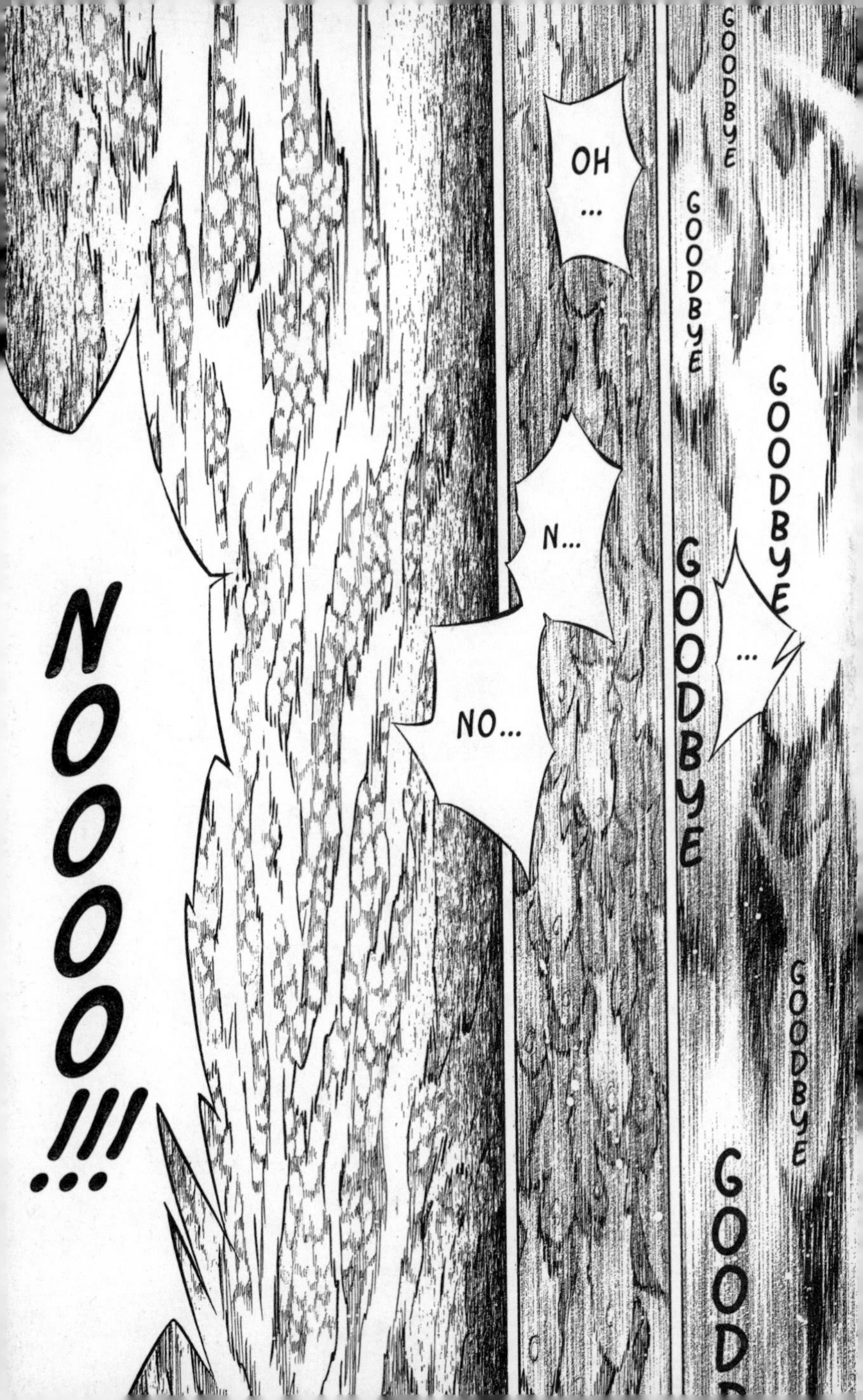
GOODBYE
GOODBYE
GOODBYE
...
GOODBYE
GOODBYE
GOOD
OH ...
N...
NO...
NOOOO!!!

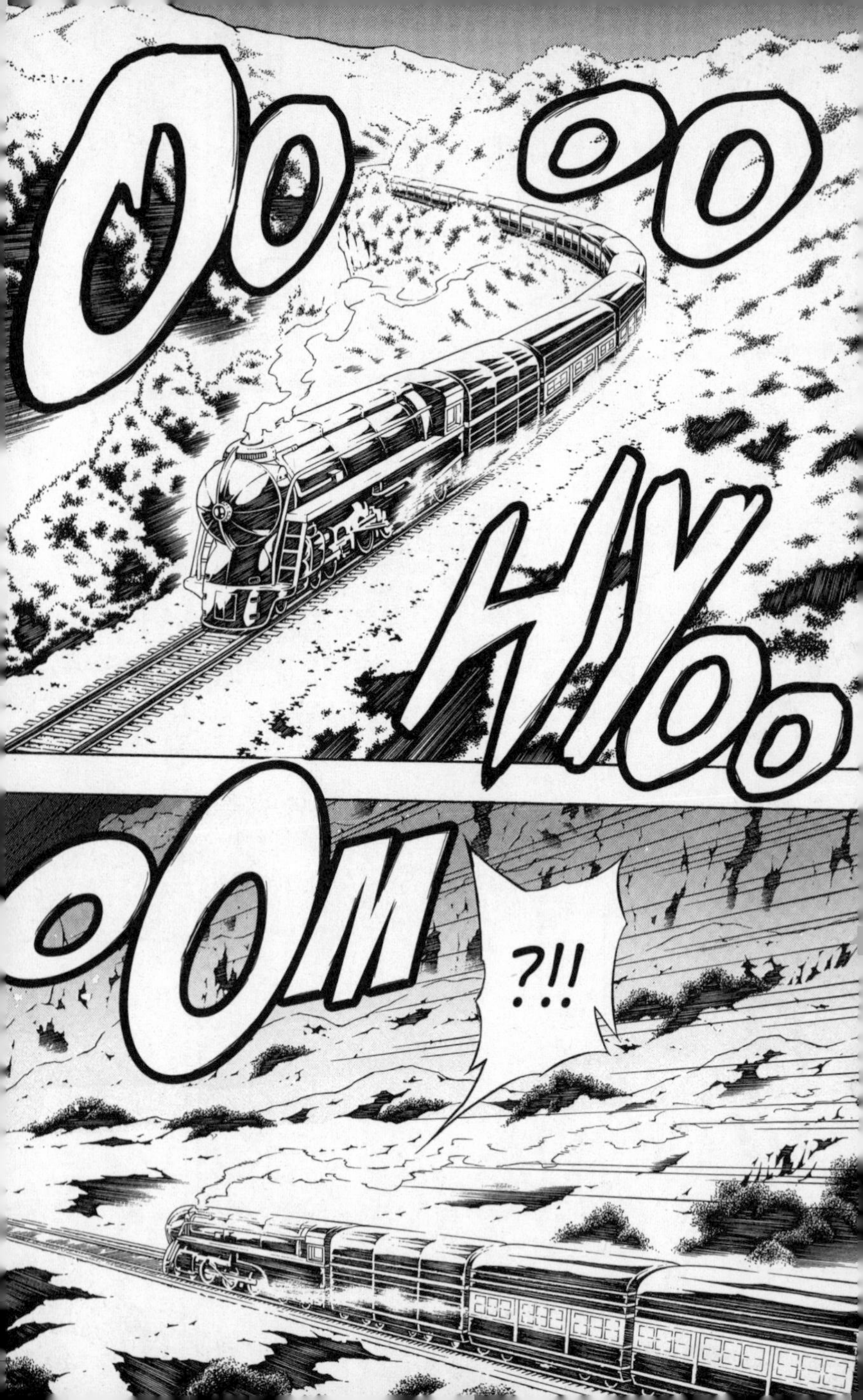
OOOO HWOO OOM
?!!

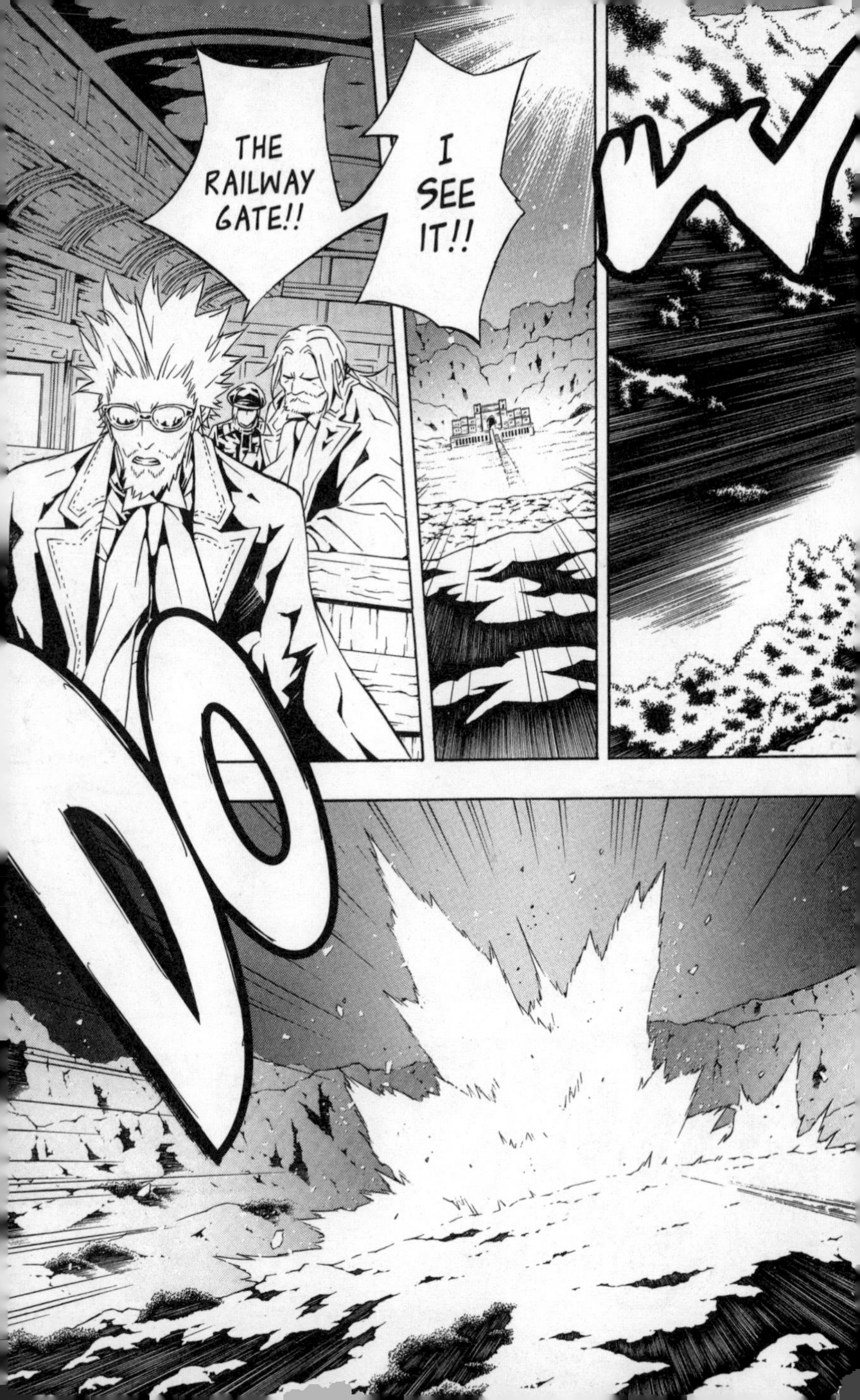
I SEE IT!!
THE RAILWAY GATE!!

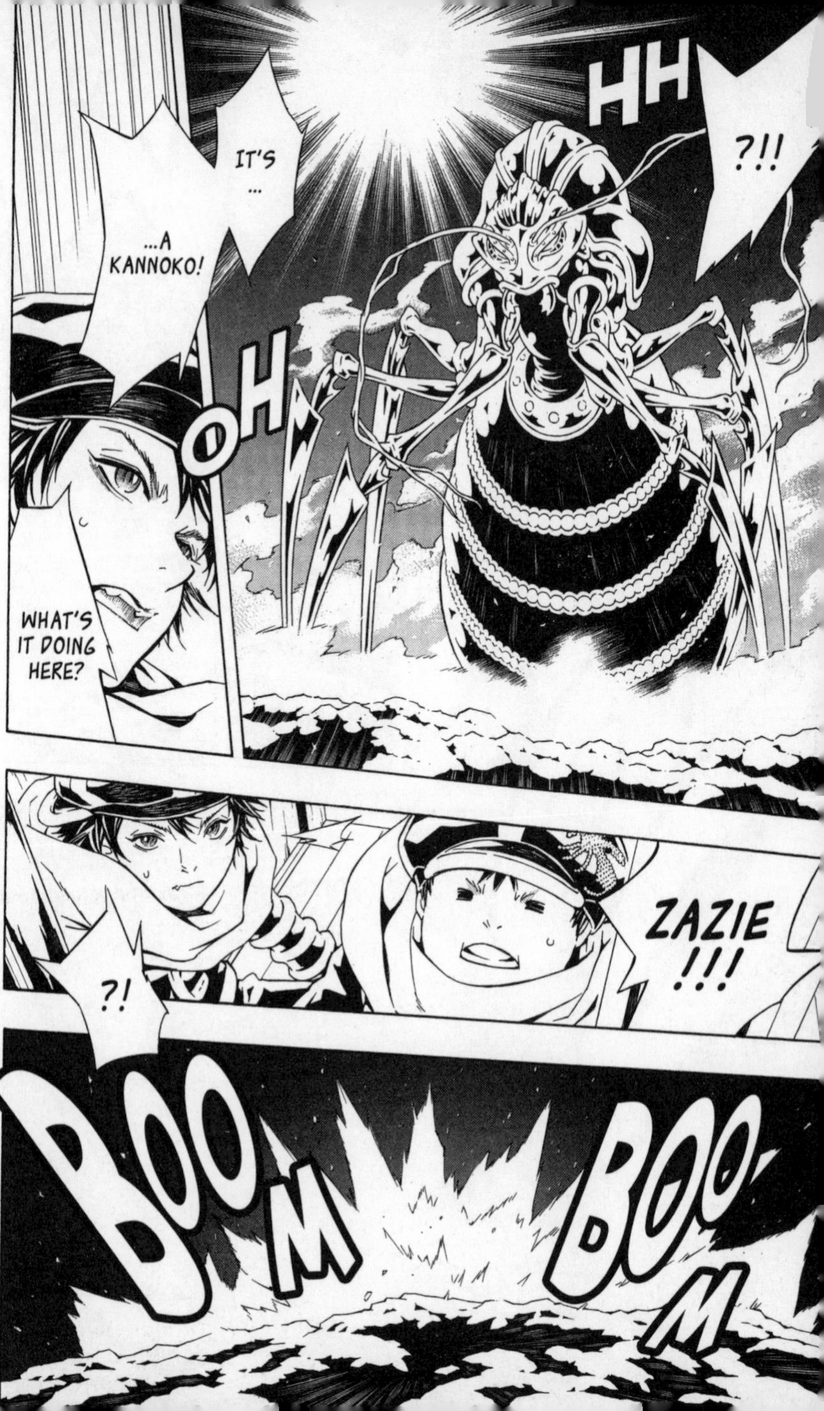

HH
?!!
IT'S ...
...A KANNOKO!
OH
WHAT'S IT DOING HERE?
ZAZIE !!!
?!
BOOM
BOOM

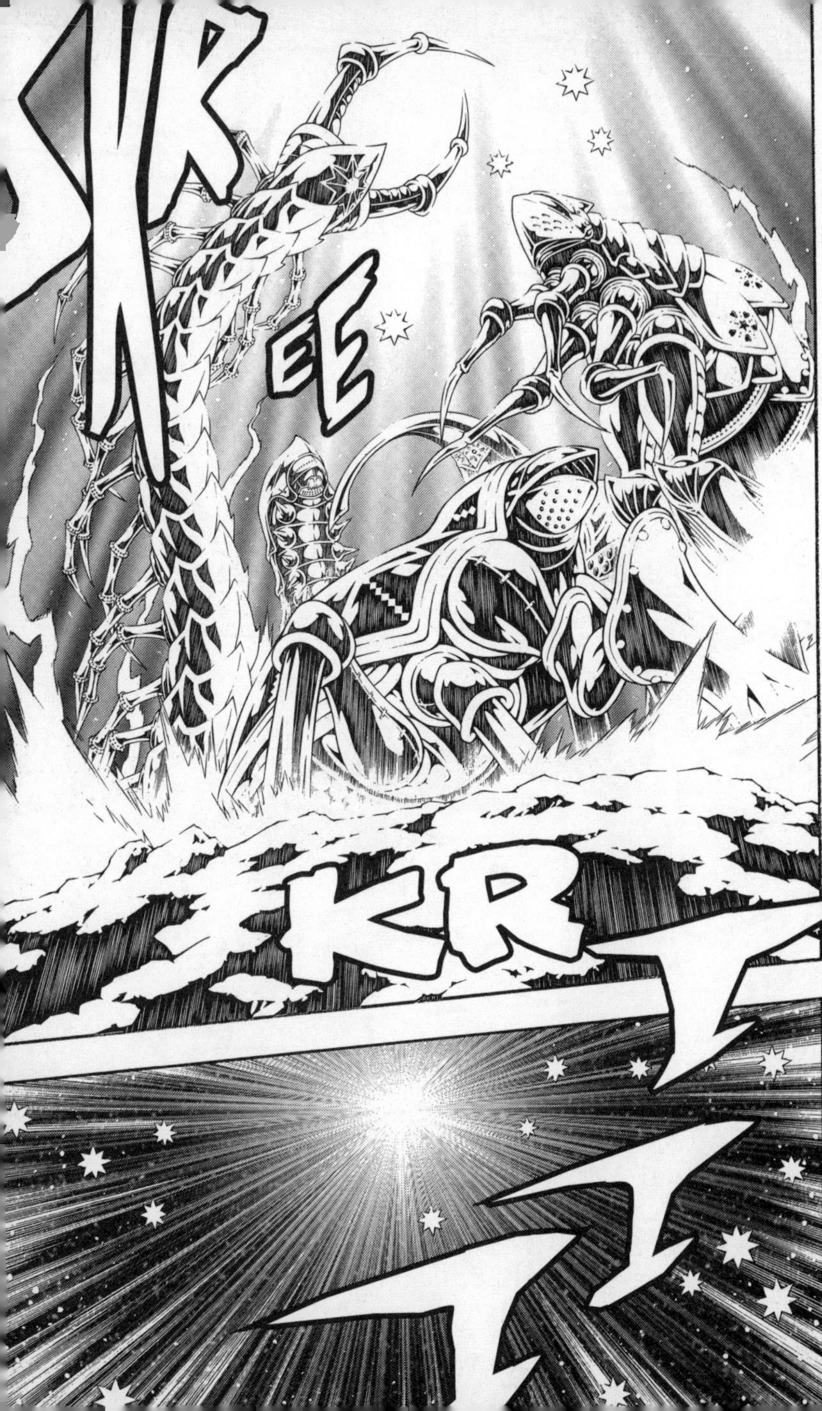
EE
KR

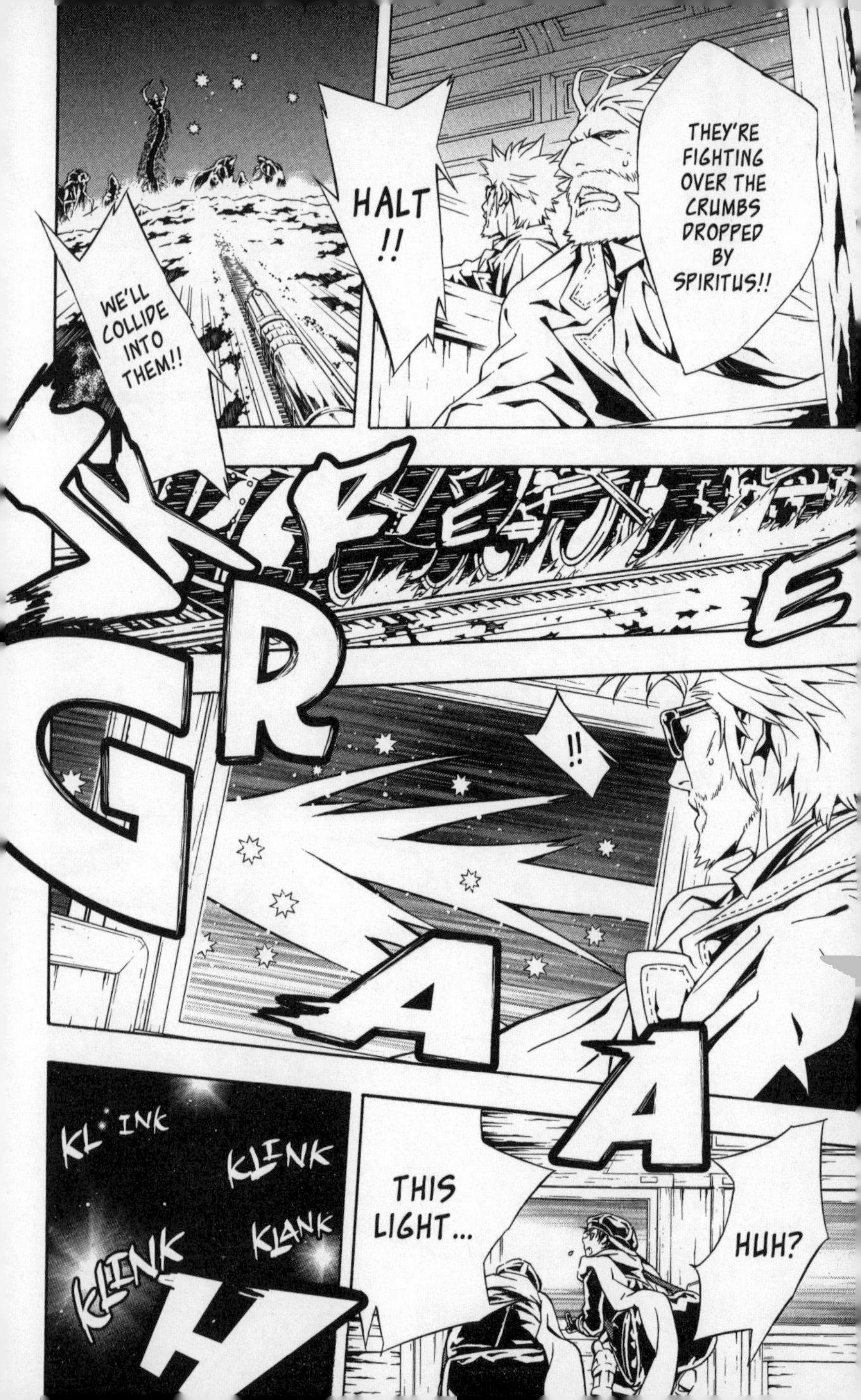

THEY'RE FIGHTING OVER THE CRUMBS DROPPED BY SPIRITUS!!
HALT!!
WE'LL COLLIDE INTO THEM!!
GRAAAH
!!
HUH?
THIS LIGHT...
KL INK
KLINK
KLANK
KLINK

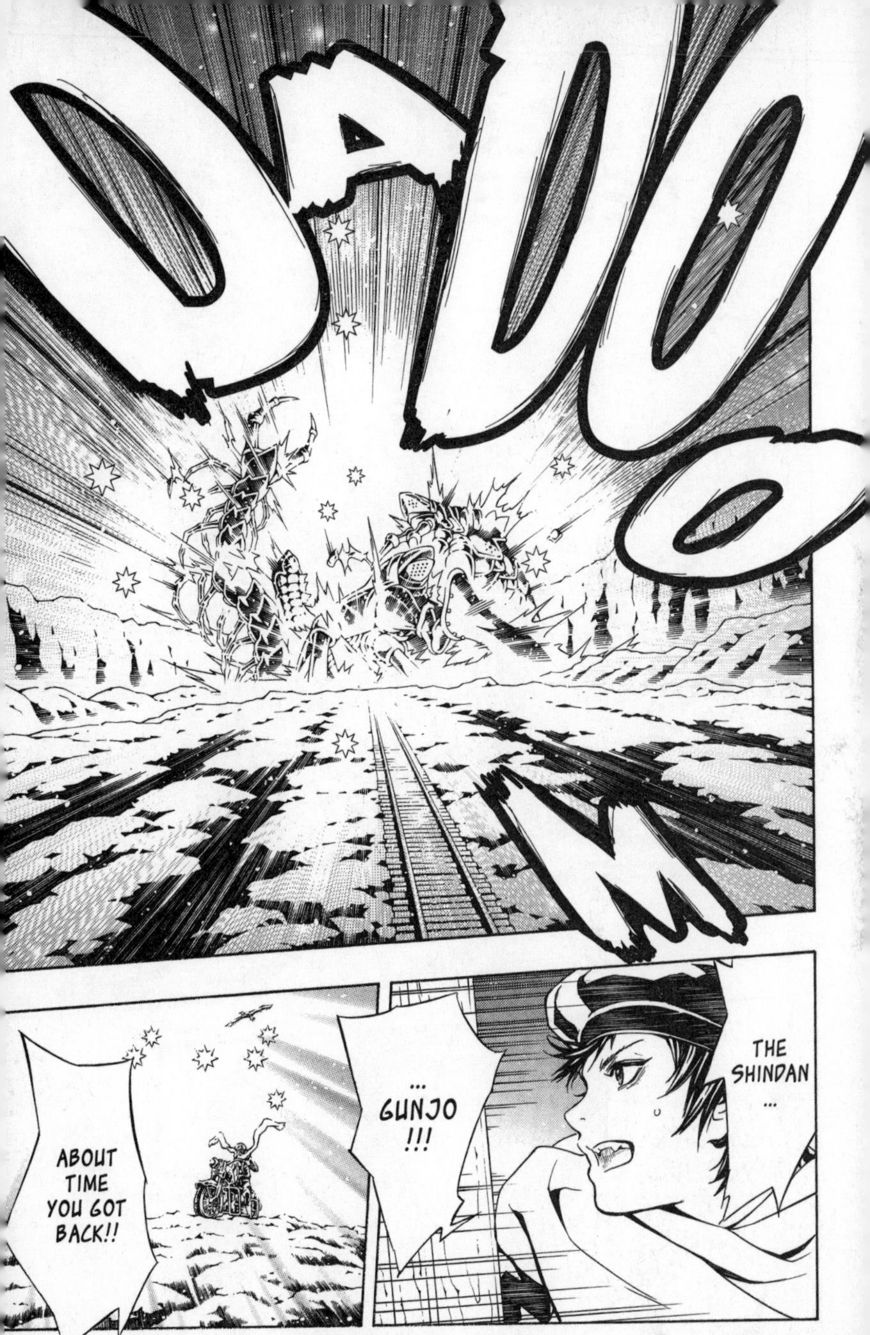
THE SHINDAN ...
... GUNJO !!!
ABOUT TIME YOU GOT BACK!!

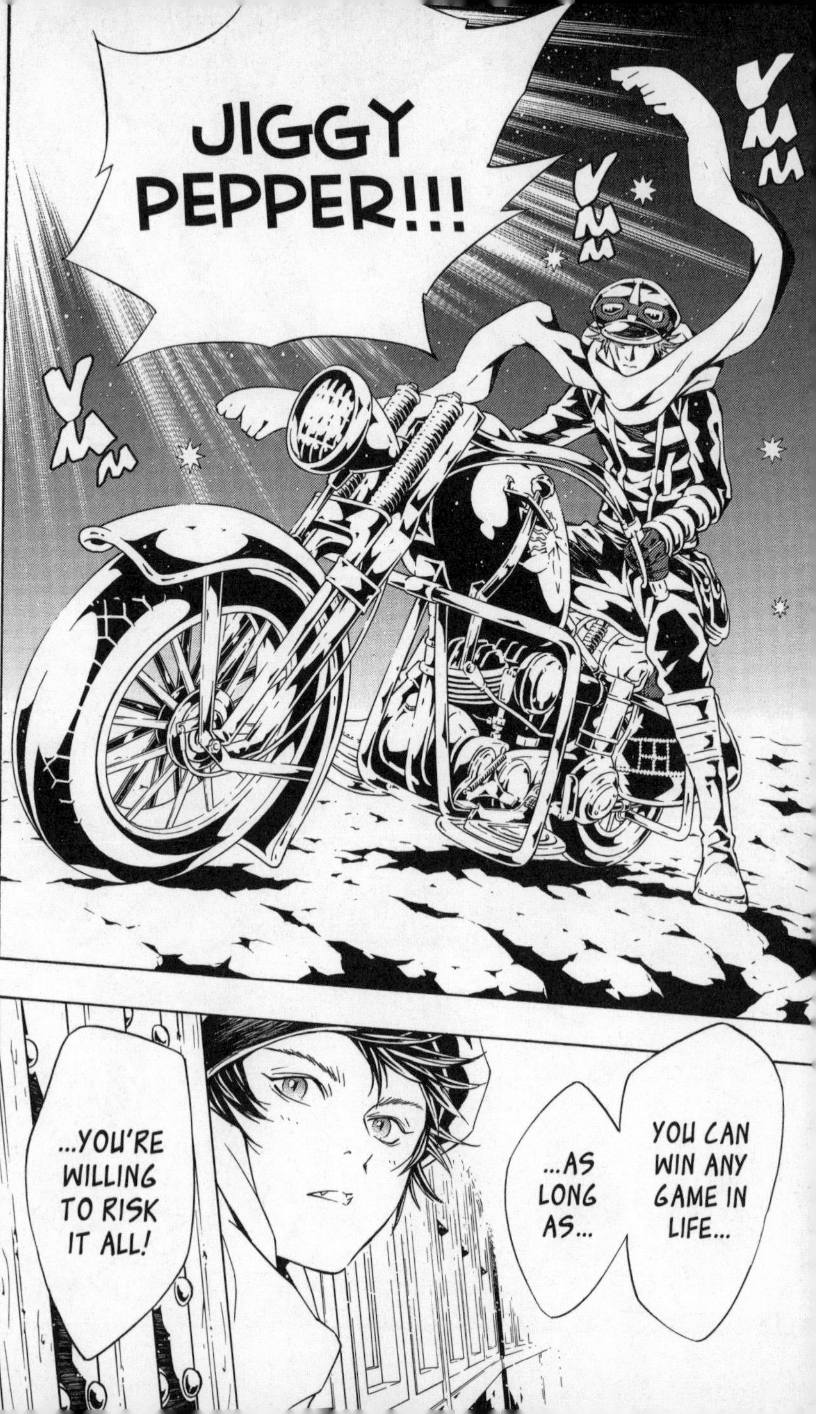
JIGGY PEPPER!!!
VMM
VMM
VMM
YOU CAN WIN ANY GAME IN LIFE...
...AS LONG AS...
...YOU'RE WILLING TO RISK IT ALL!

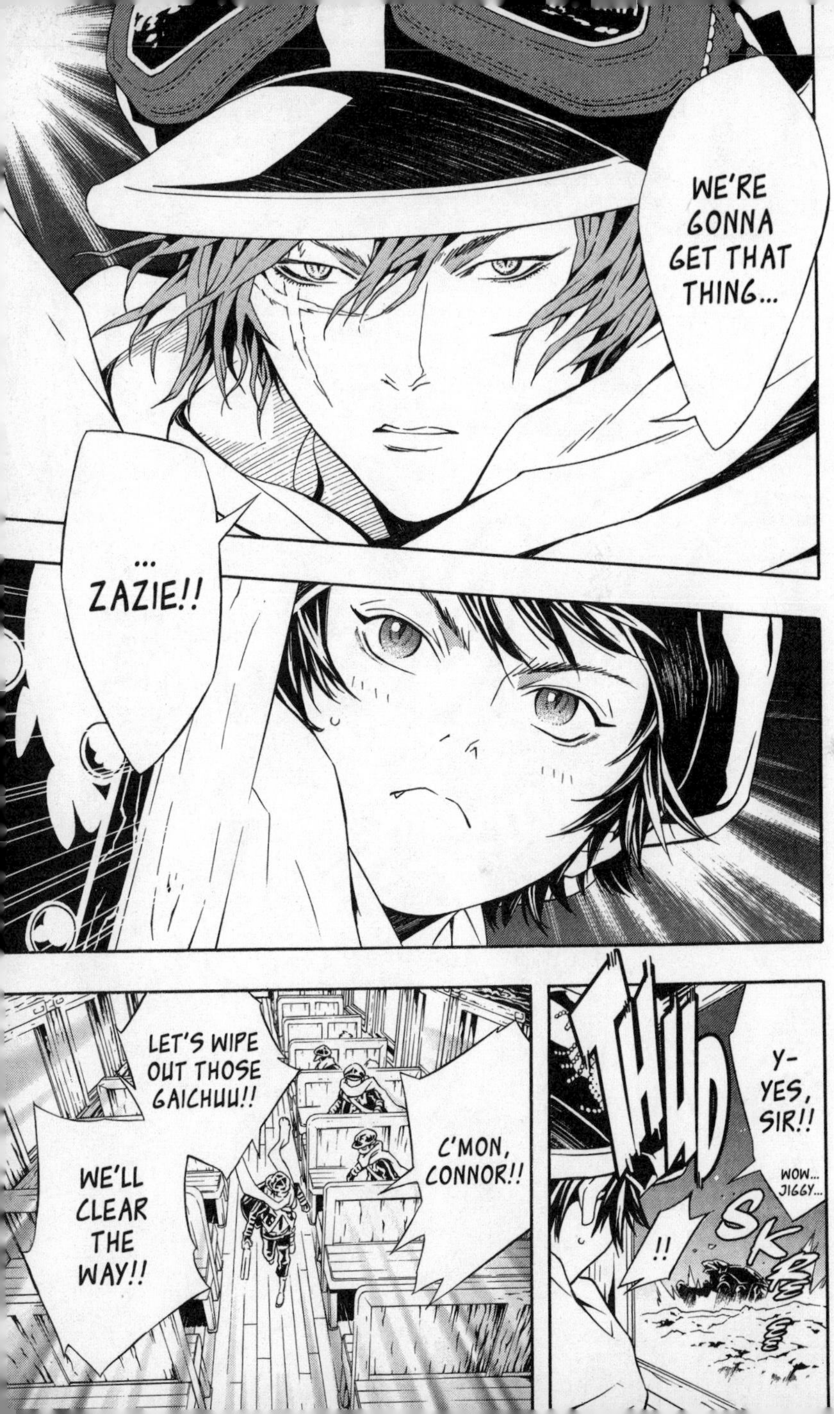
WE'RE GONNA GET THAT THING...
... ZAZIE!!
Y-YES, SIR!!
THUD
WOW... JIGGY...
!!
LET'S WIPE OUT THOSE GAICHUU!!
C'MON, CONNOR!!
WE'LL CLEAR THE WAY!!

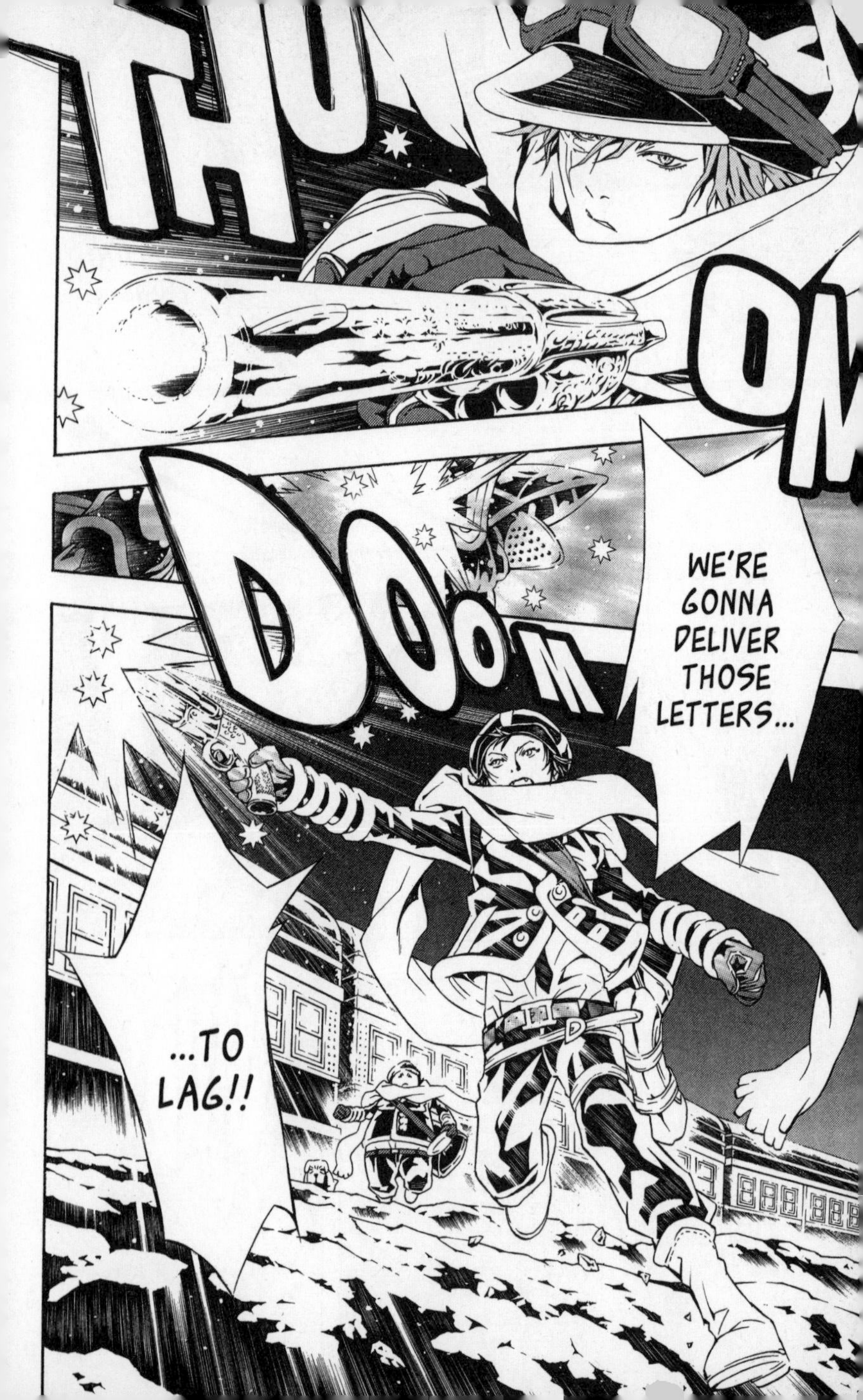
DOOOM
WE'RE GONNA DELIVER THOSE LETTERS...
...TO LAG!!

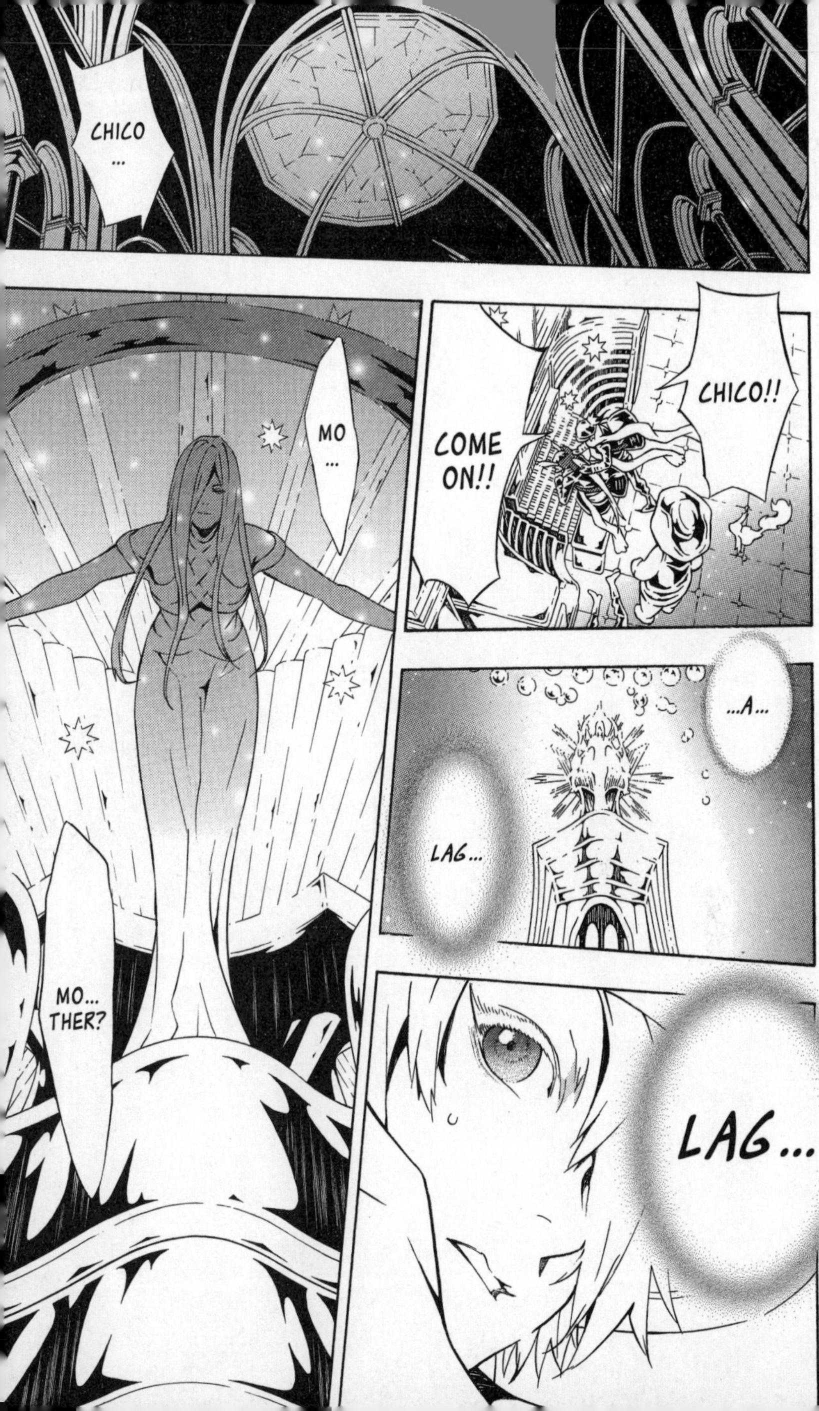
CHICO ...
CHICO!!
COME ON!!
...A...
LAG...
LAG...
MO ...
MO... THER?

Dr. Thunderland's Reference Desk

Oh no, Chico! This is terrible, Lag and Empress!! What's going to happen next?
Do I have to keep posting these notes through the final volume? Yes!!

Hello! I am Dr. Thunderland! But…this is really…this is no time for small talk…
Boo hoo hoo!! [bawling]

[Wiping away tears] Get ready for my final report on this world. I'll be waiting at
the end of the book…

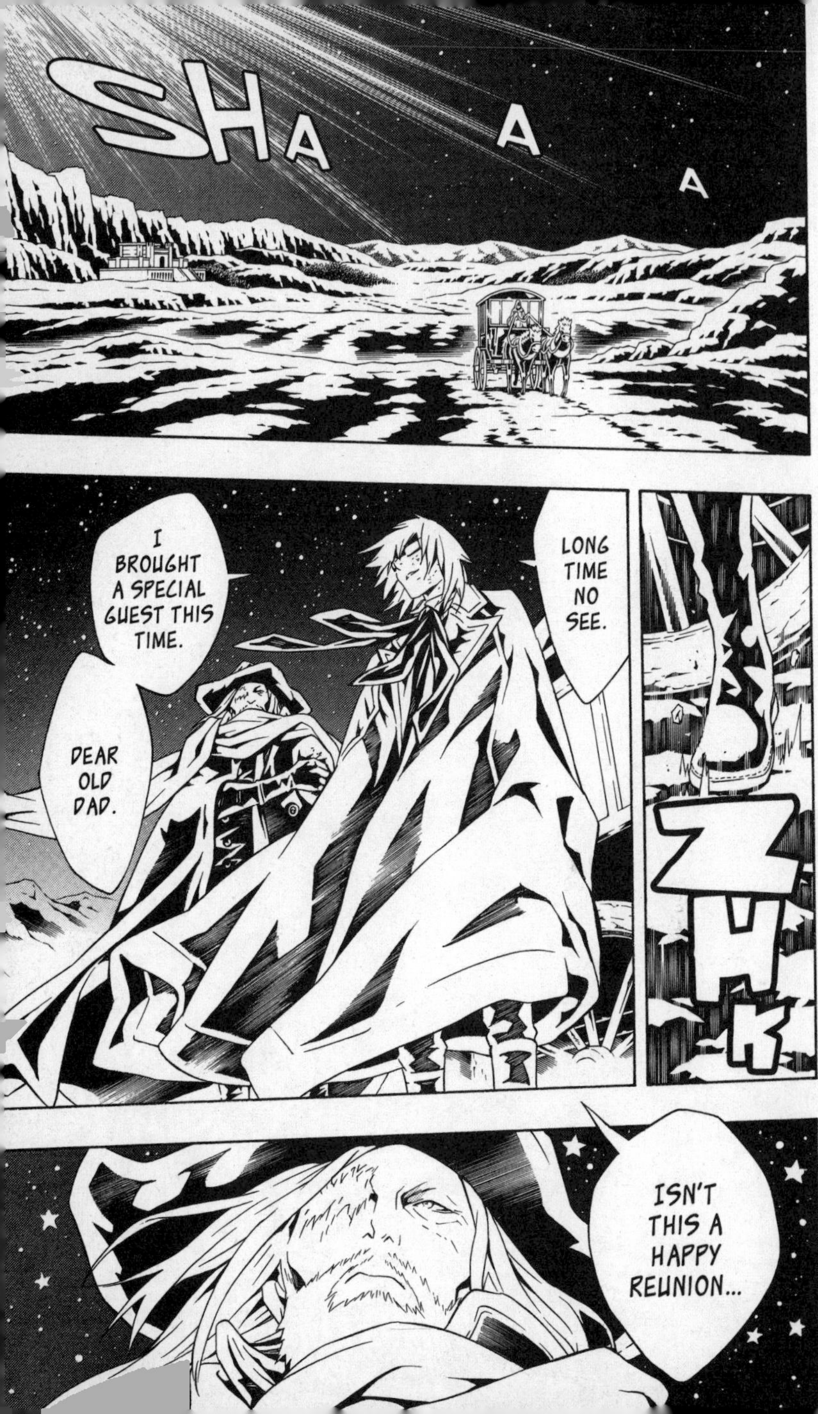
SHAAA
ZUK
LONG TIME NO SEE.
I BROUGHT A SPECIAL GUEST THIS TIME.
DEAR OLD DAD.
ISN'T THIS A HAPPY REUNION...

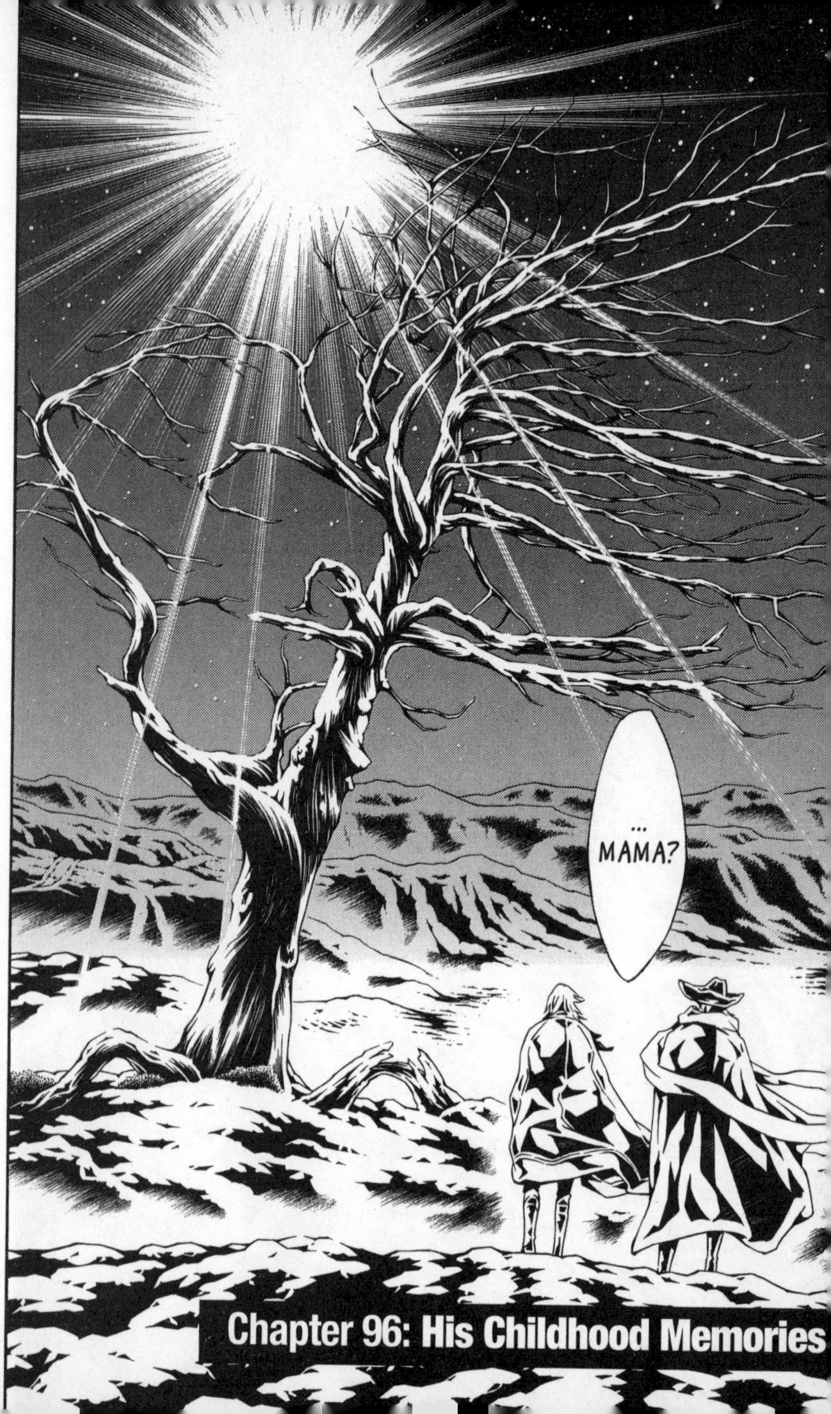
... MAMA?

Chapter 96: His Childhood Memories

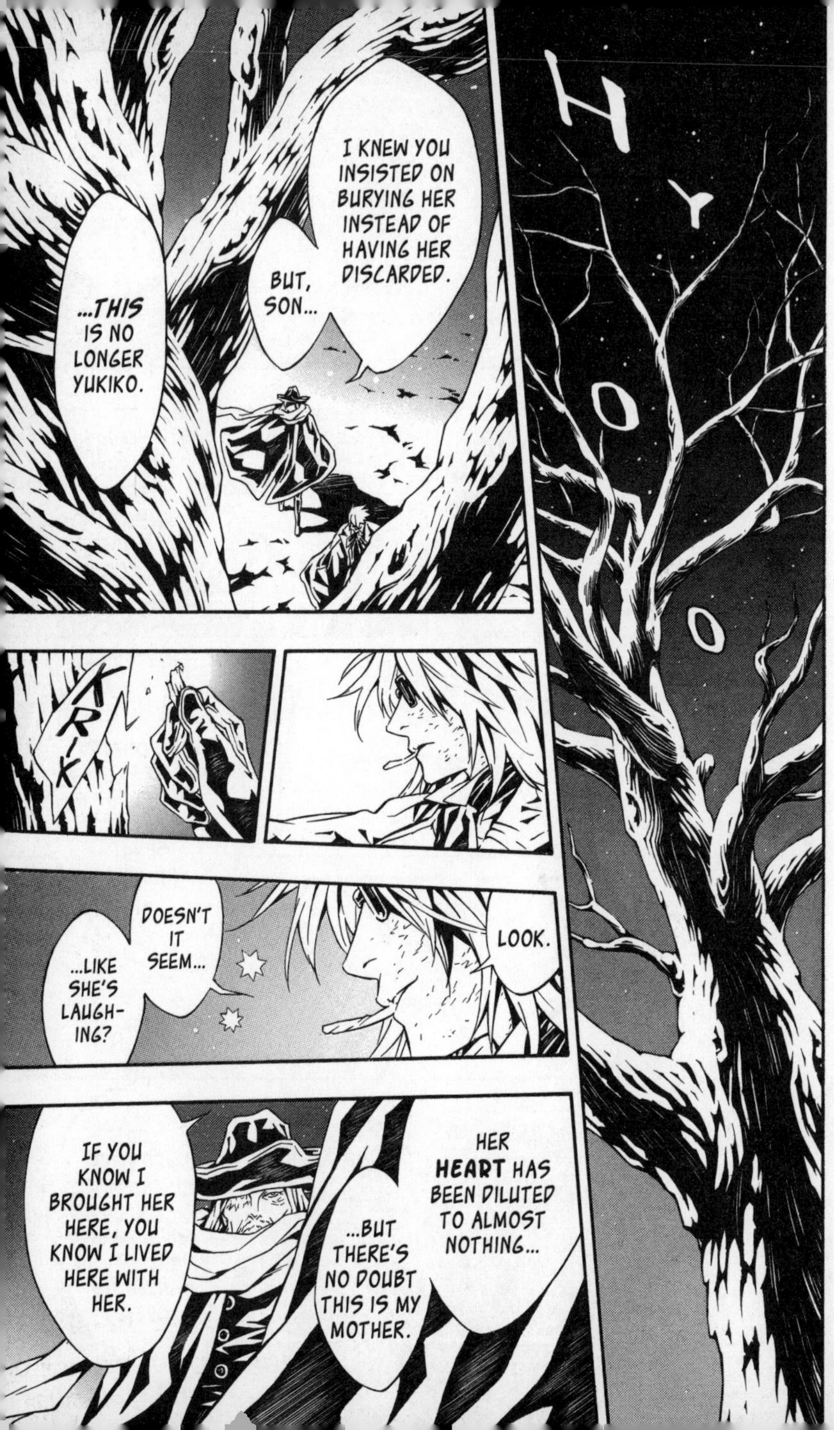
HYOO
I KNEW YOU INSISTED ON BURYING HER INSTEAD OF HAVING HER DISCARDED.
BUT, SON...
...THIS IS NO LONGER YUKIKO.
KRIK
LOOK.
DOESN'T IT SEEM...
...LIKE SHE'S LAUGHING?
HER HEART HAS BEEN DILUTED TO ALMOST NOTHING...
...BUT THERE'S NO DOUBT THIS IS MY MOTHER.
IF YOU KNOW I BROUGHT HER HERE, YOU KNOW I LIVED HERE WITH HER.

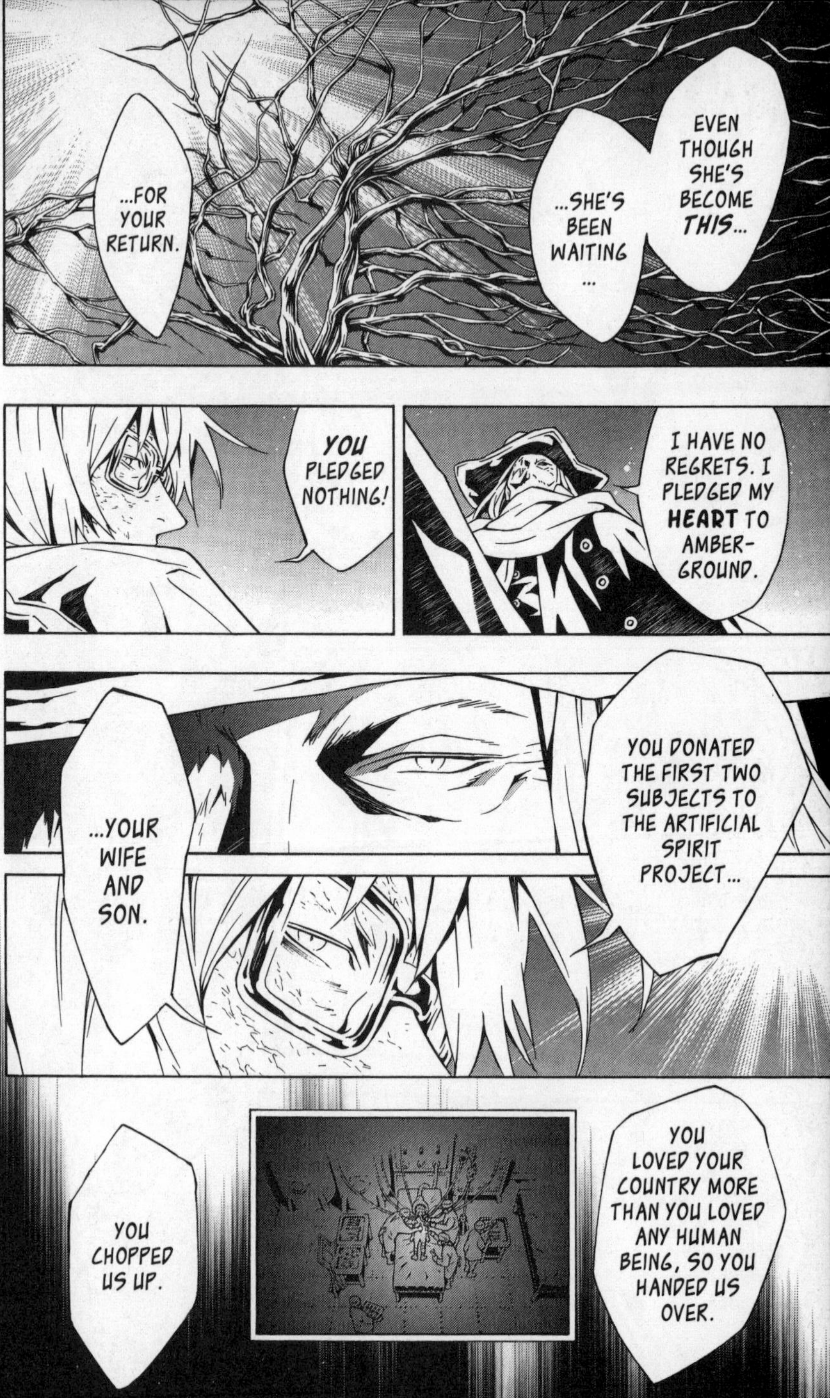
EVEN THOUGH SHE'S BECOME THIS...
...SHE'S BEEN WAITING ...
...FOR YOUR RETURN.
I HAVE NO REGRETS. I PLEDGED MY HEART TO AMBER-GROUND.
YOU PLEDGED NOTHING!
YOU DONATED THE FIRST TWO SUBJECTS TO THE ARTIFICIAL SPIRIT PROJECT...
...YOUR WIFE AND SON.
YOU LOVED YOUR COUNTRY MORE THAN YOU LOVED ANY HUMAN BEING, SO YOU HANDED US OVER.
YOU CHOPPED US UP.

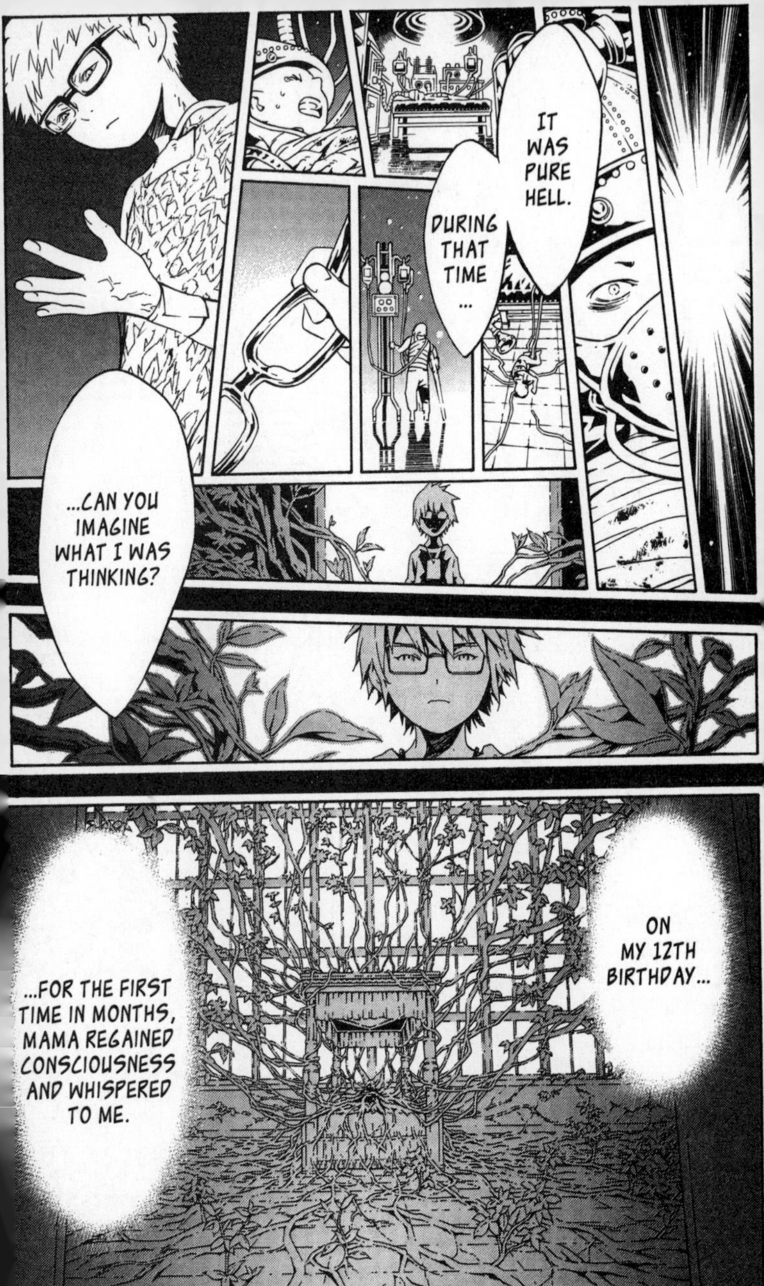
IT WAS PURE HELL.
DURING THAT TIME ...
...CAN YOU IMAGINE WHAT I WAS THINKING?
ON MY 12TH BIRTHDAY...
...FOR THE FIRST TIME IN MONTHS, MAMA REGAINED CONSCIOUSNESS AND WHISPERED TO ME.

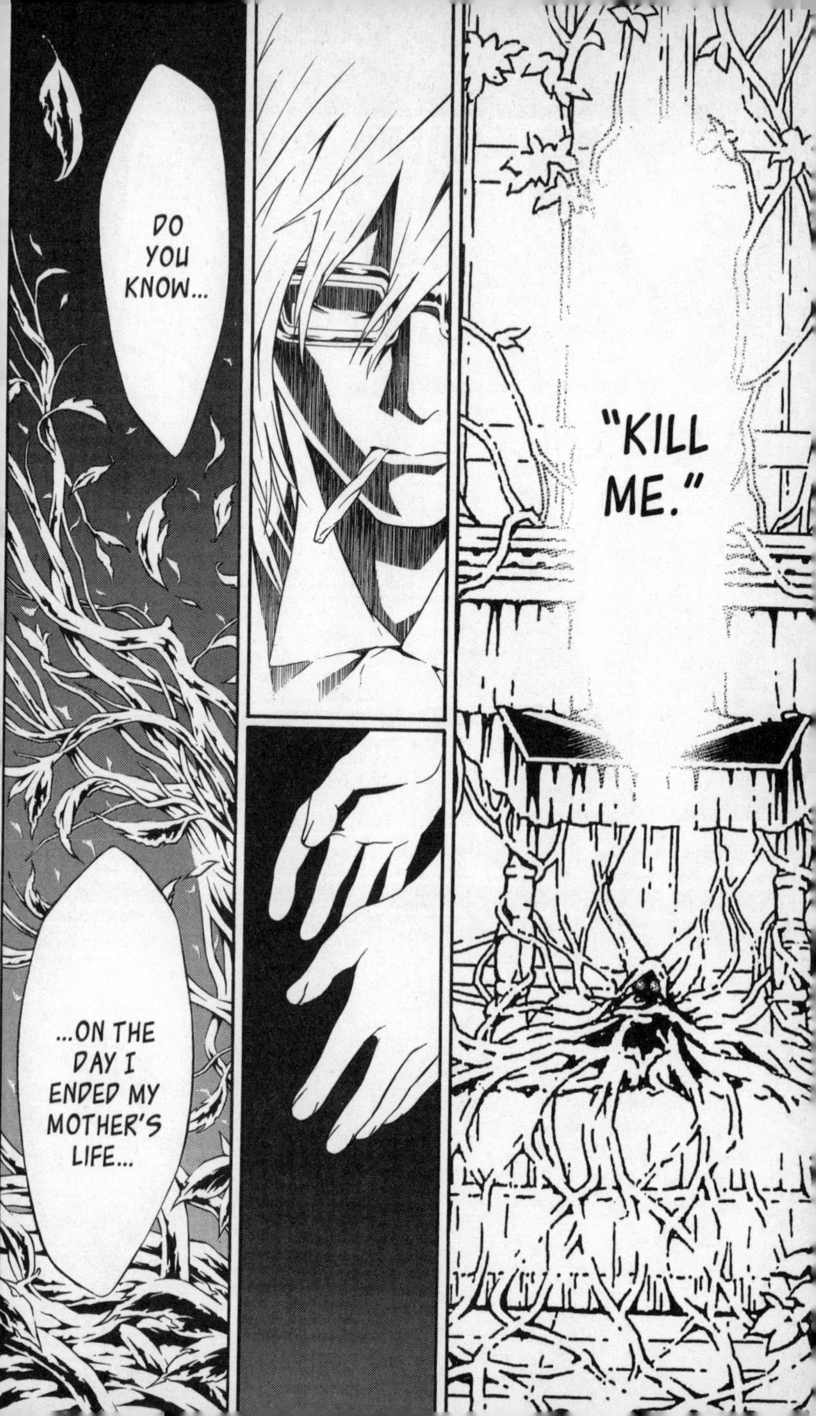
"KILL ME."
DO YOU KNOW...
...ON THE DAY I ENDED MY MOTHER'S LIFE...

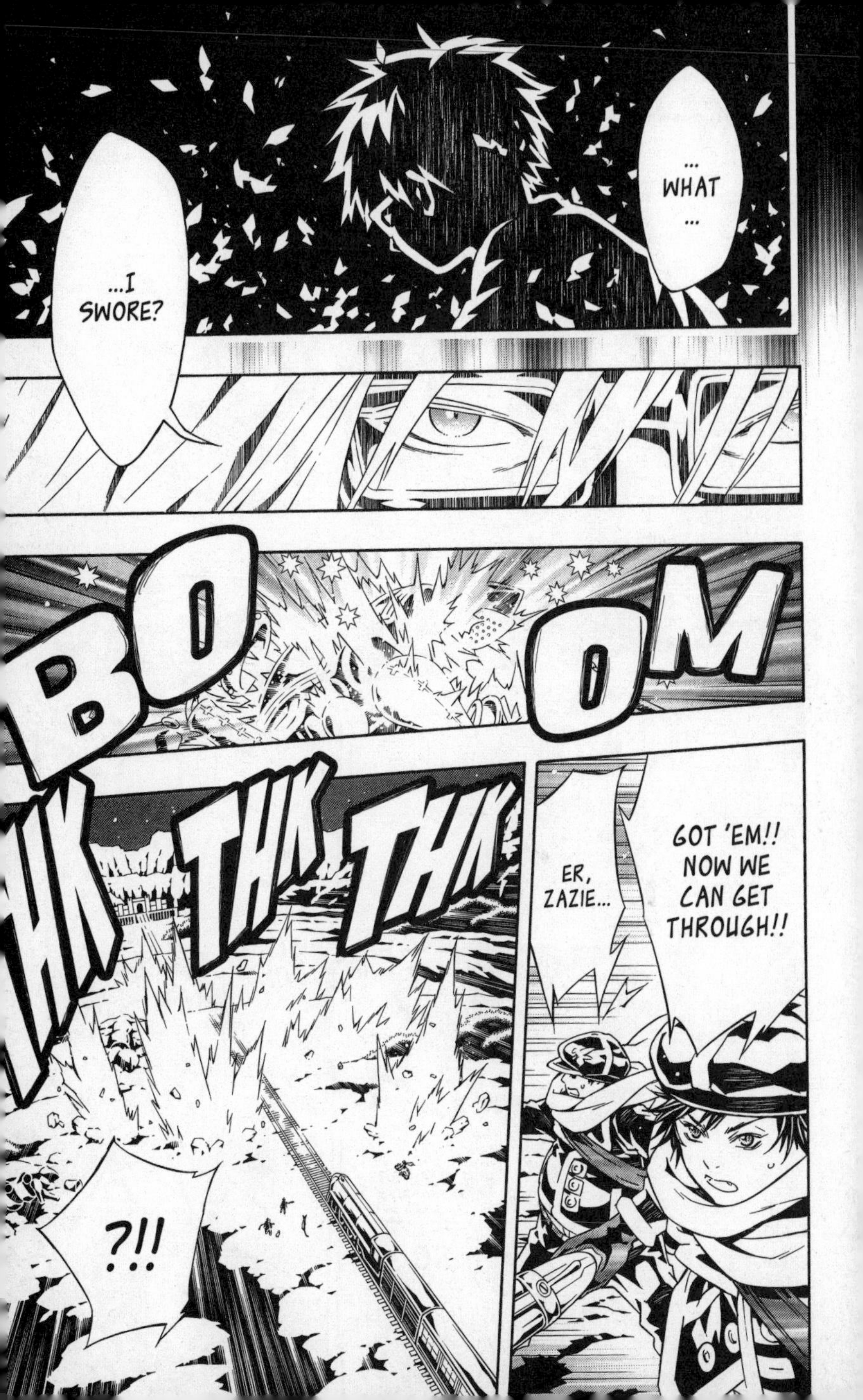
...WHAT...
...I SWORE?
BOOM
GOT 'EM!! NOW WE CAN GET THROUGH!!
ER, ZAZIE...
THK THK THK
?!!

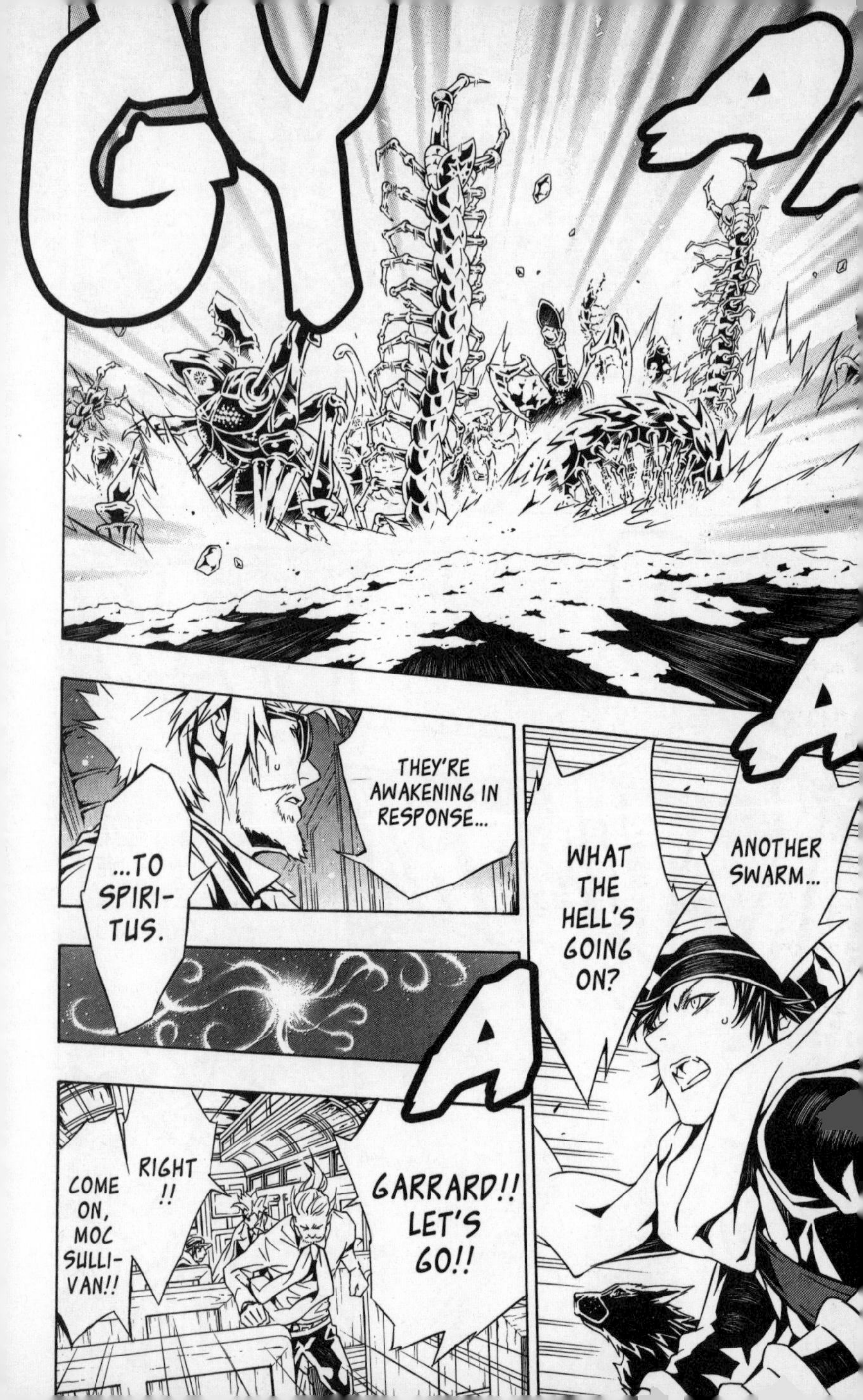
GYAAA
ANOTHER SWARM...
WHAT THE HELL'S GOING ON?
THEY'RE AWAKENING IN RESPONSE...
...TO SPIRITUS.
GARRARD!! LET'S GO!!
RIGHT!!
COME ON, MOC SULLIVAN!!

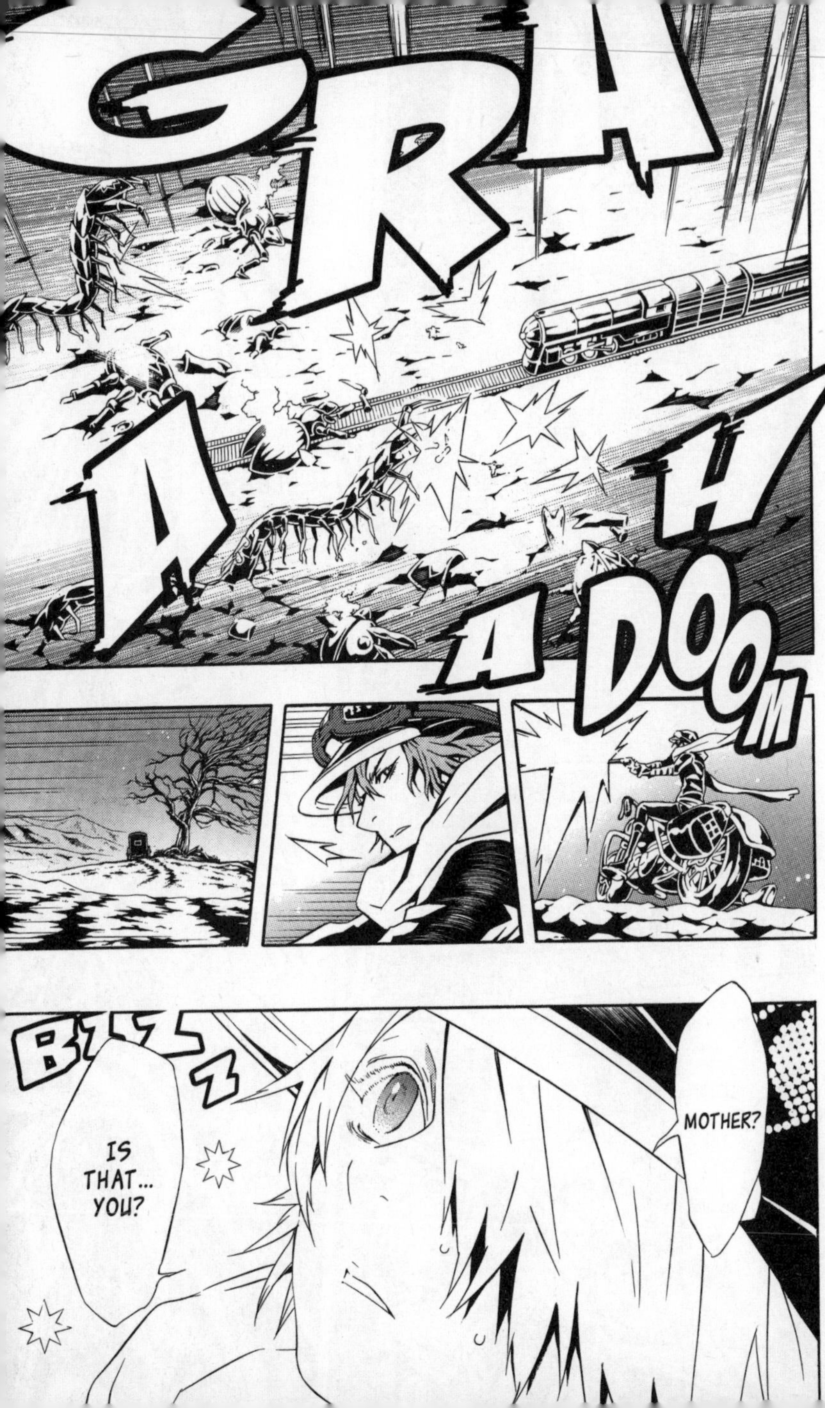
GRAAH
A DOOM
MOTHER?
IS THAT... YOU?

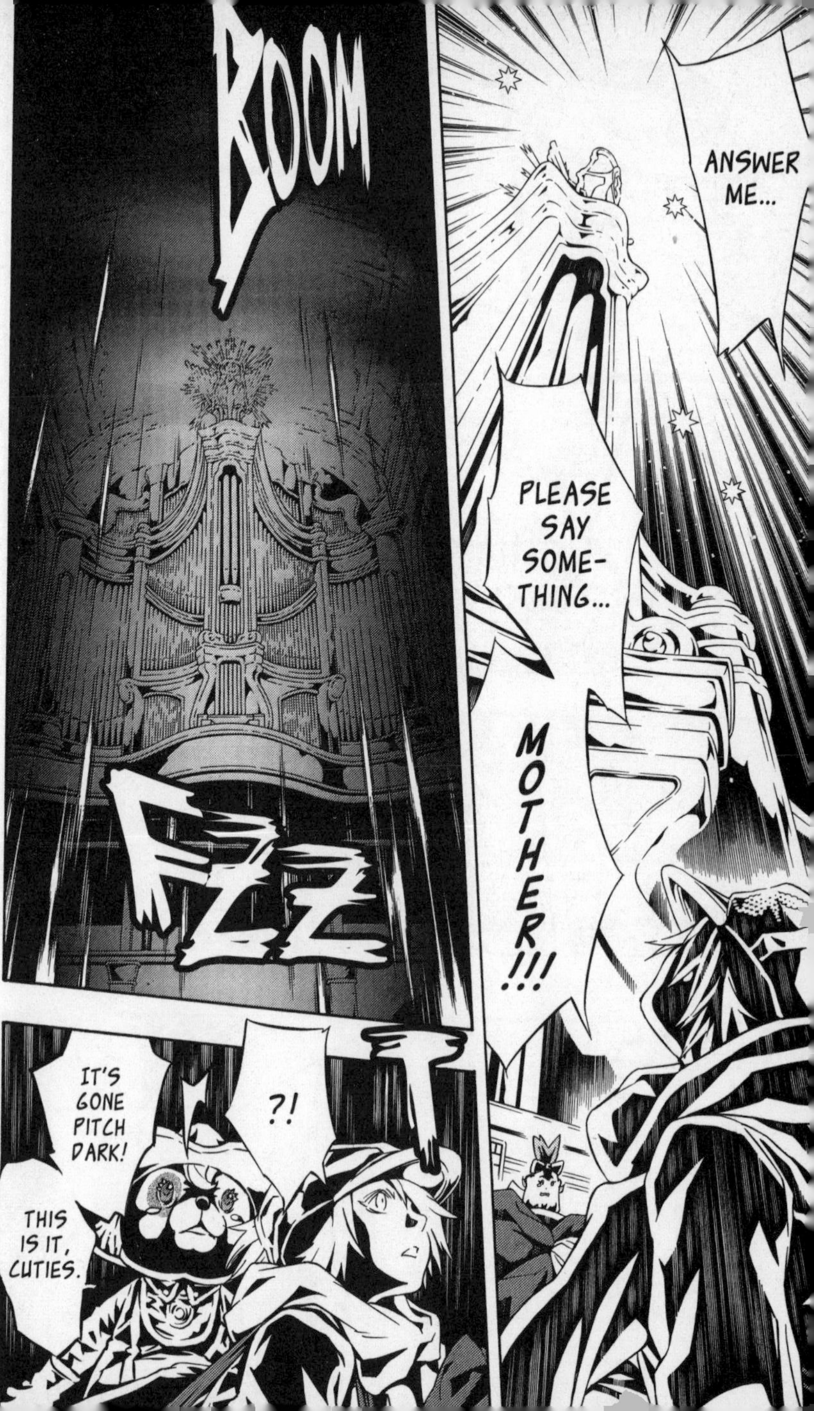
ANSWER ME...
PLEASE SAY SOMETHING...
MOTHER!!!
BOOM
FZZ
?!
IT'S GONE PITCH DARK!
THIS IS IT, CUTIES.

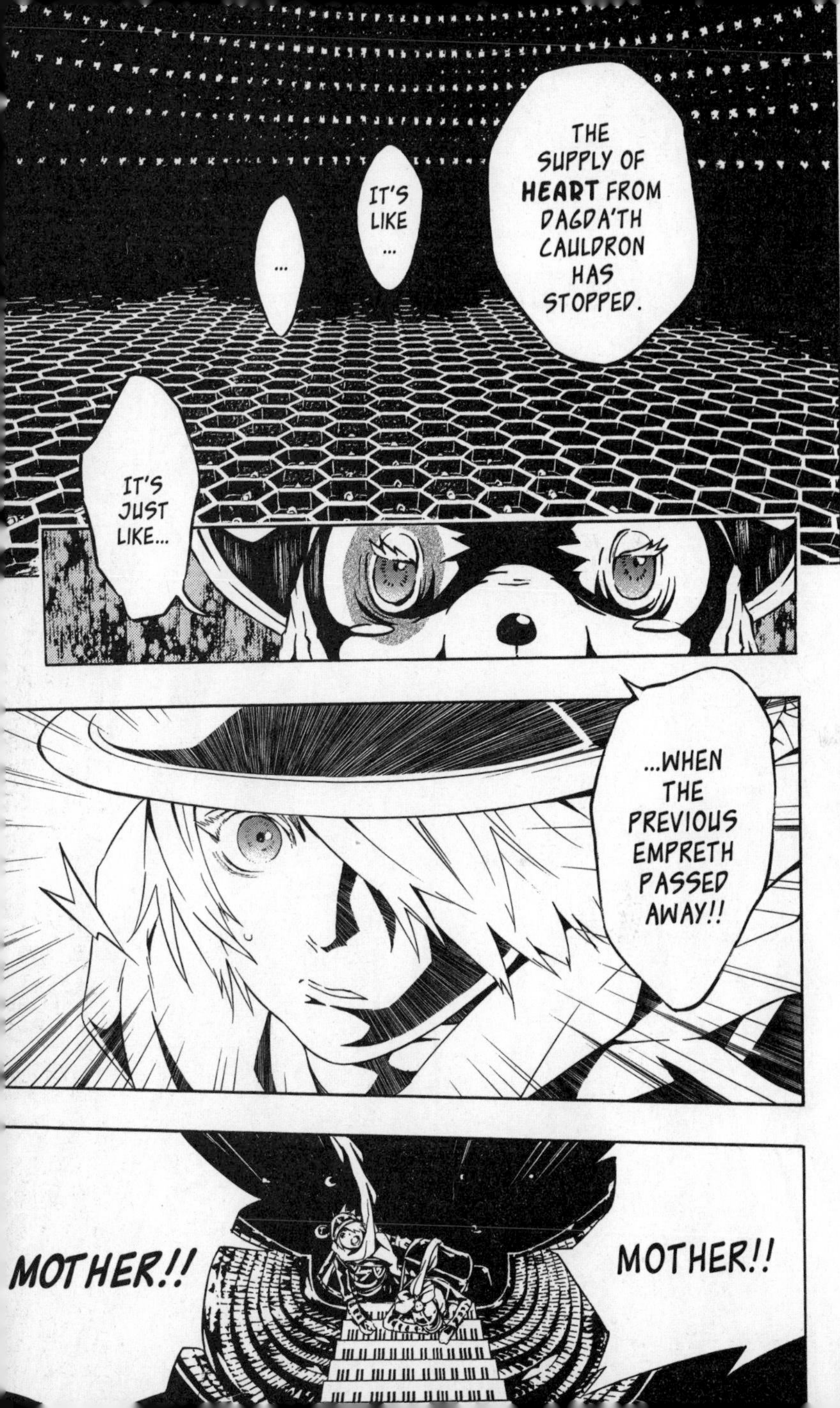
THE SUPPLY OF HEART FROM DAGDA'TH CAULDRON HAS STOPPED.
IT'S LIKE ...
...
IT'S JUST LIKE...
...WHEN THE PREVIOUS EMPRETH PASSED AWAY!!
MOTHER!!
MOTHER!!

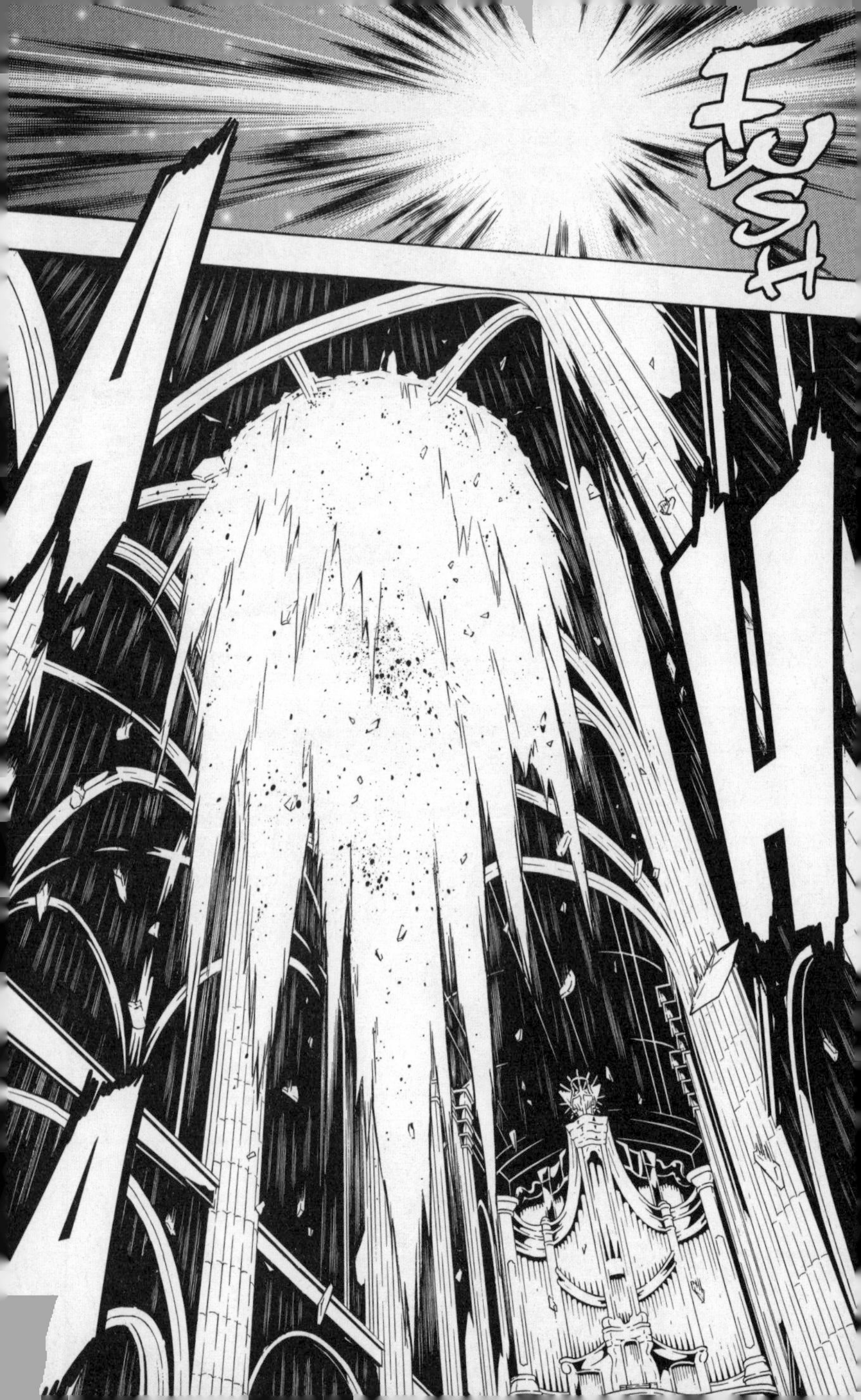
FUSH
AAH

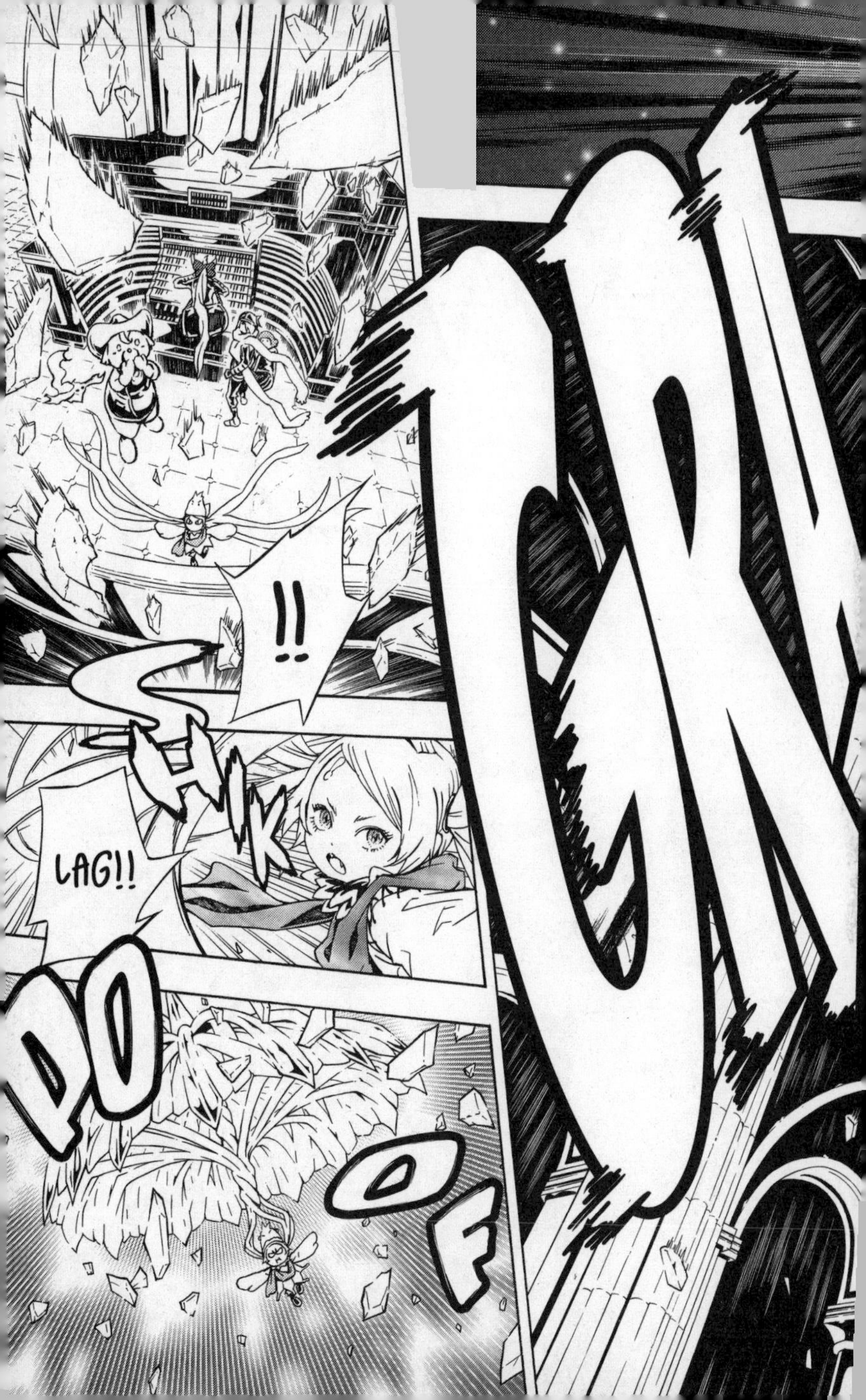
CRA
!!
SHK
LAG!!
DOOF

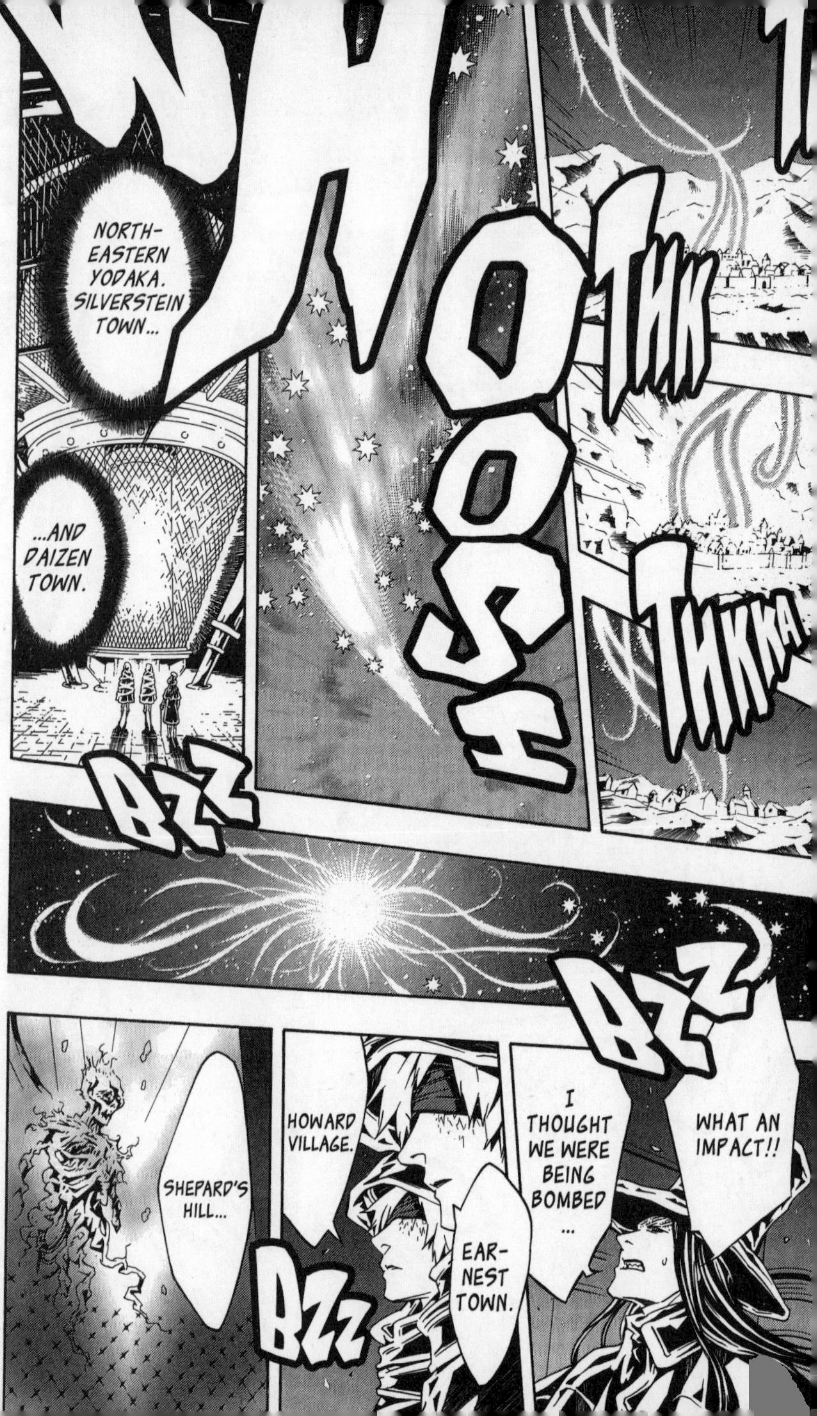
THK
THKKA
WHOOSH
NORTH-EASTERN YODAKA. SILVERSTEIN TOWN...
...AND DAIZEN TOWN.
BZZ
BZZ
WHAT AN IMPACT!!
I THOUGHT WE WERE BEING BOMBED...
EAR-NEST TOWN.
HOWARD VILLAGE.
BZZ
SHEPARD'S HILL...

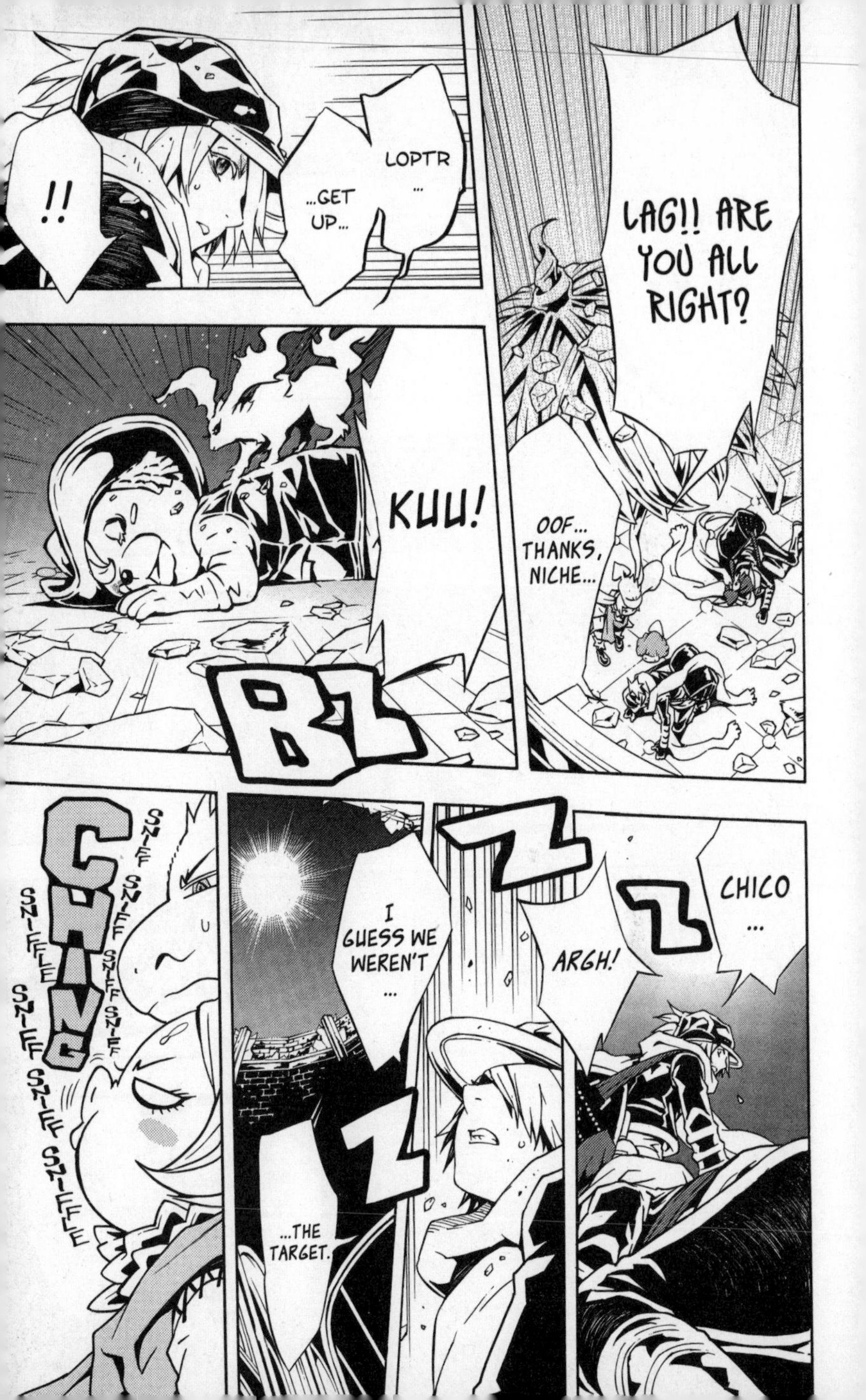
LAG!! ARE YOU ALL RIGHT?
OOF... THANKS, NICHE...
LOPTR ...
...GET UP...
!!
KUU!
BZ
CHICO ...
ZZ
ARGH!
I GUESS WE WEREN'T ...
...THE TARGET.
Z
CHING
SNIFF SNIFF SNIFF SNIFF SNIFF
SNIFFLE
SNIFF SNIFF SNIFF SNIFFLE

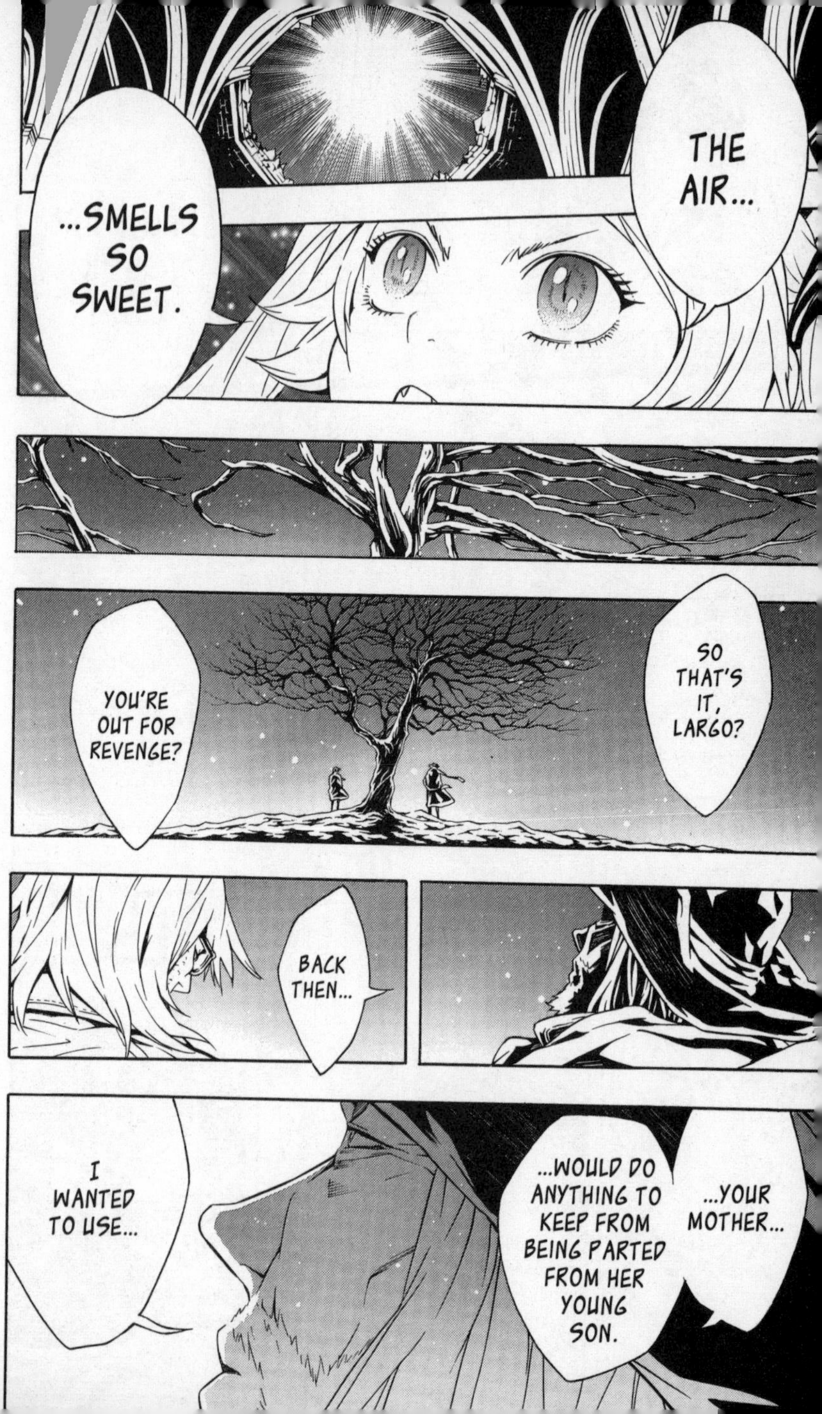
THE AIR...
...SMELLS SO SWEET.
SO THAT'S IT, LARGO?
YOU'RE OUT FOR REVENGE?
BACK THEN...
...YOUR MOTHER...
...WOULD DO ANYTHING TO KEEP FROM BEING PARTED FROM HER YOUNG SON.
I WANTED TO USE...

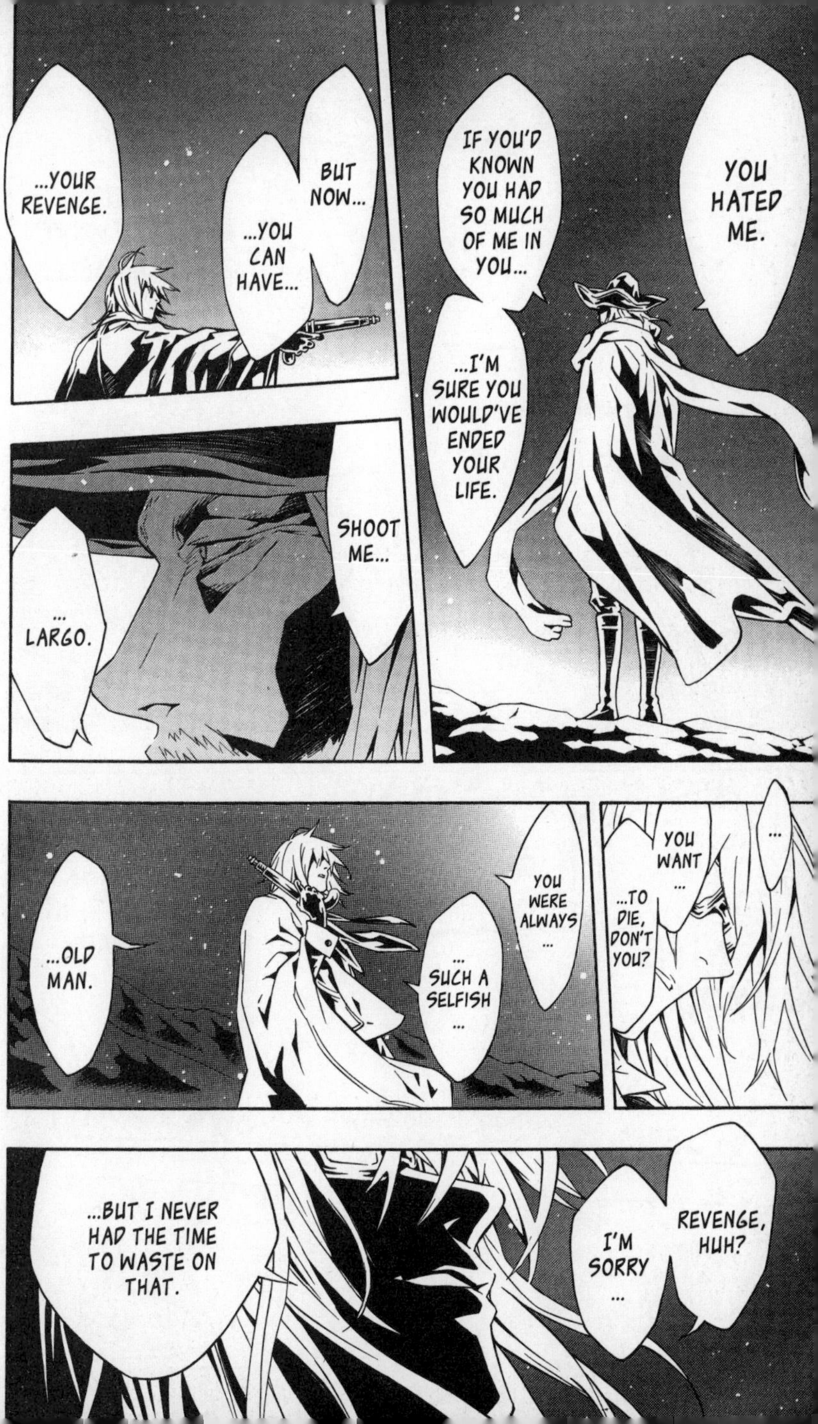
YOU HATED ME.
IF YOU'D KNOWN YOU HAD SO MUCH OF ME IN YOU...
...I'M SURE YOU WOULD'VE ENDED YOUR LIFE.
BUT NOW...
...YOU CAN HAVE...
...YOUR REVENGE.
SHOOT ME...
...LARGO.
...
YOU WANT...
...TO DIE, DON'T YOU?
YOU WERE ALWAYS...
...SUCH A SELFISH...
...OLD MAN.
REVENGE, HUH?
I'M SORRY...
...BUT I NEVER HAD THE TIME TO WASTE ON THAT.

BUT *MINE* WERE AVAILABLE.

LARGO...

...I SHARED EVERYTHING I HAD...

...WITH YOU.

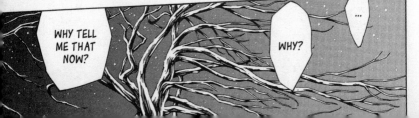

WHY TELL ME THAT NOW?

WHY?

...

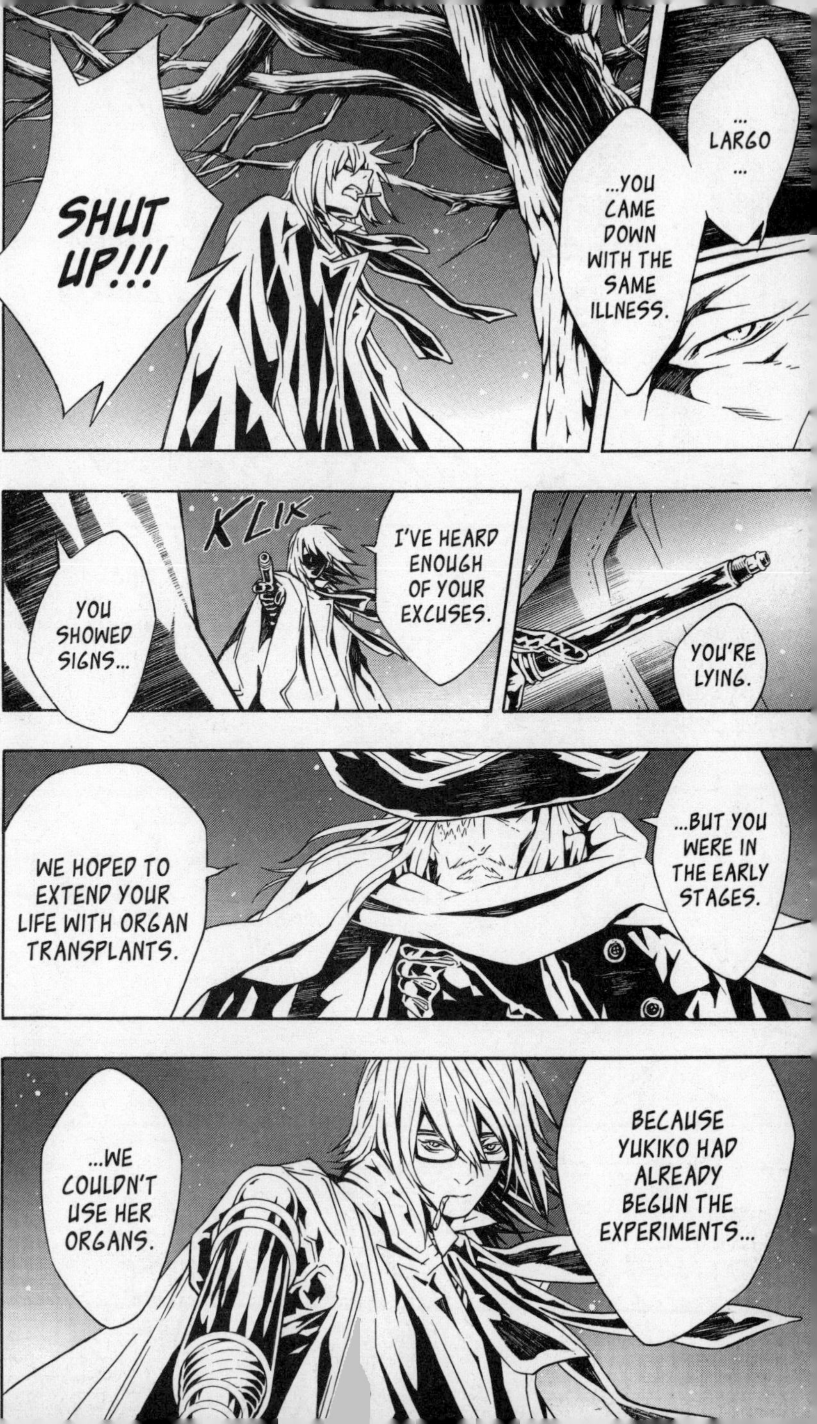
...LARGO...
...YOU CAME DOWN WITH THE SAME ILLNESS.
SHUT UP!!!
YOU'RE LYING.
KLIK
I'VE HEARD ENOUGH OF YOUR EXCUSES.
YOU SHOWED SIGNS...
...BUT YOU WERE IN THE EARLY STAGES.
WE HOPED TO EXTEND YOUR LIFE WITH ORGAN TRANSPLANTS.
BECAUSE YUKIKO HAD ALREADY BEGUN THE EXPERIMENTS...
...WE COULDN'T USE HER ORGANS.

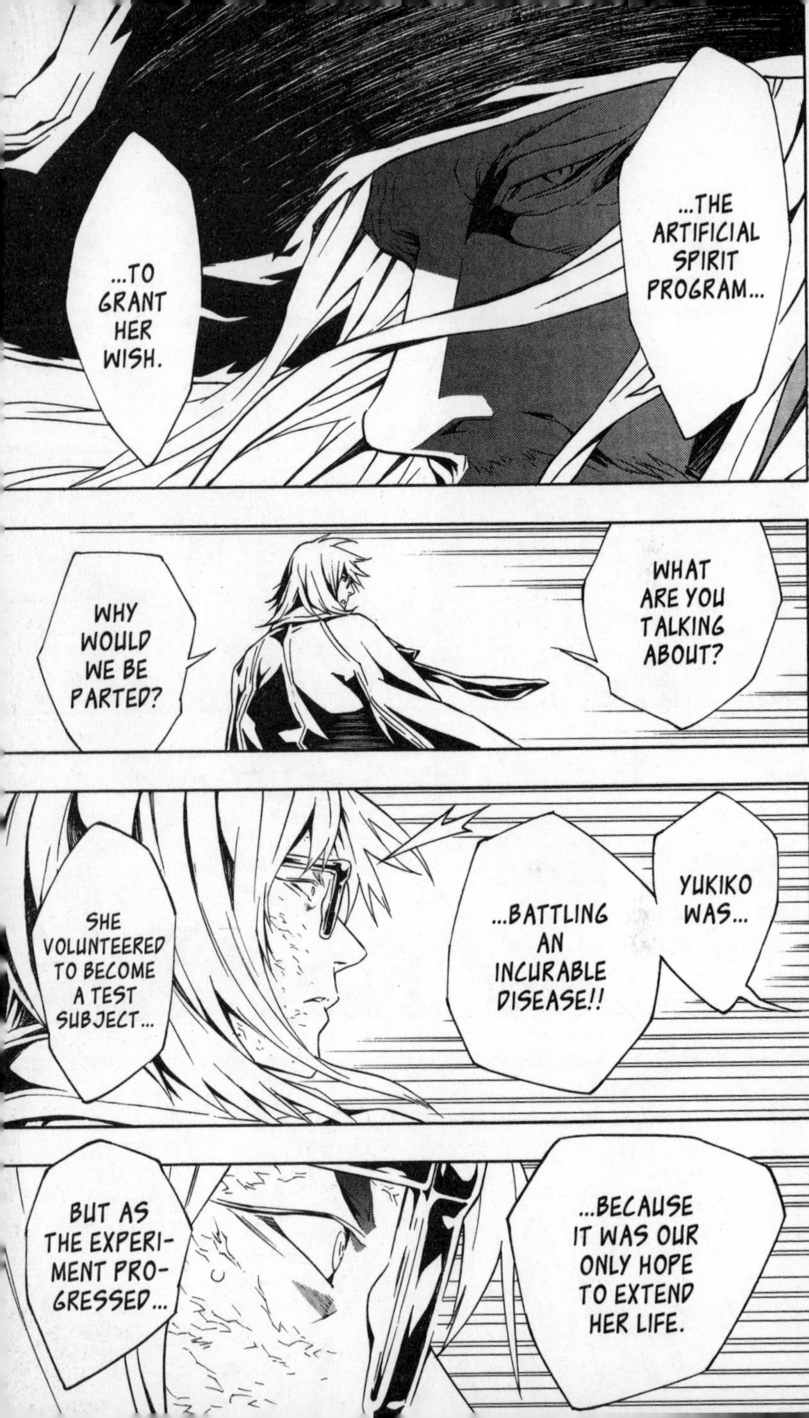
...THE ARTIFICIAL SPIRIT PROGRAM...
...TO GRANT HER WISH.
WHAT ARE YOU TALKING ABOUT?
WHY WOULD WE BE PARTED?
YUKIKO WAS...
...BATTLING AN INCURABLE DISEASE!!
SHE VOLUNTEERED TO BECOME A TEST SUBJECT...
...BECAUSE IT WAS OUR ONLY HOPE TO EXTEND HER LIFE.
BUT AS THE EXPERIMENT PROGRESSED...

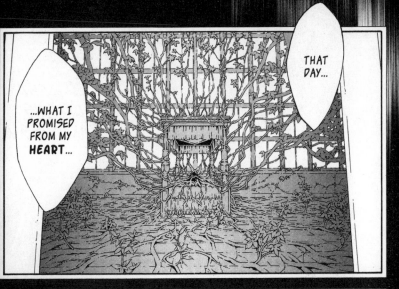

THAT DAY...

...WHAT I PROMISED FROM MY **HEART**...

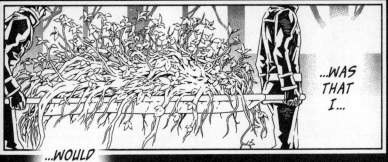

...WAS THAT I...

...WOULD BRING THE WORLD LIGHT.

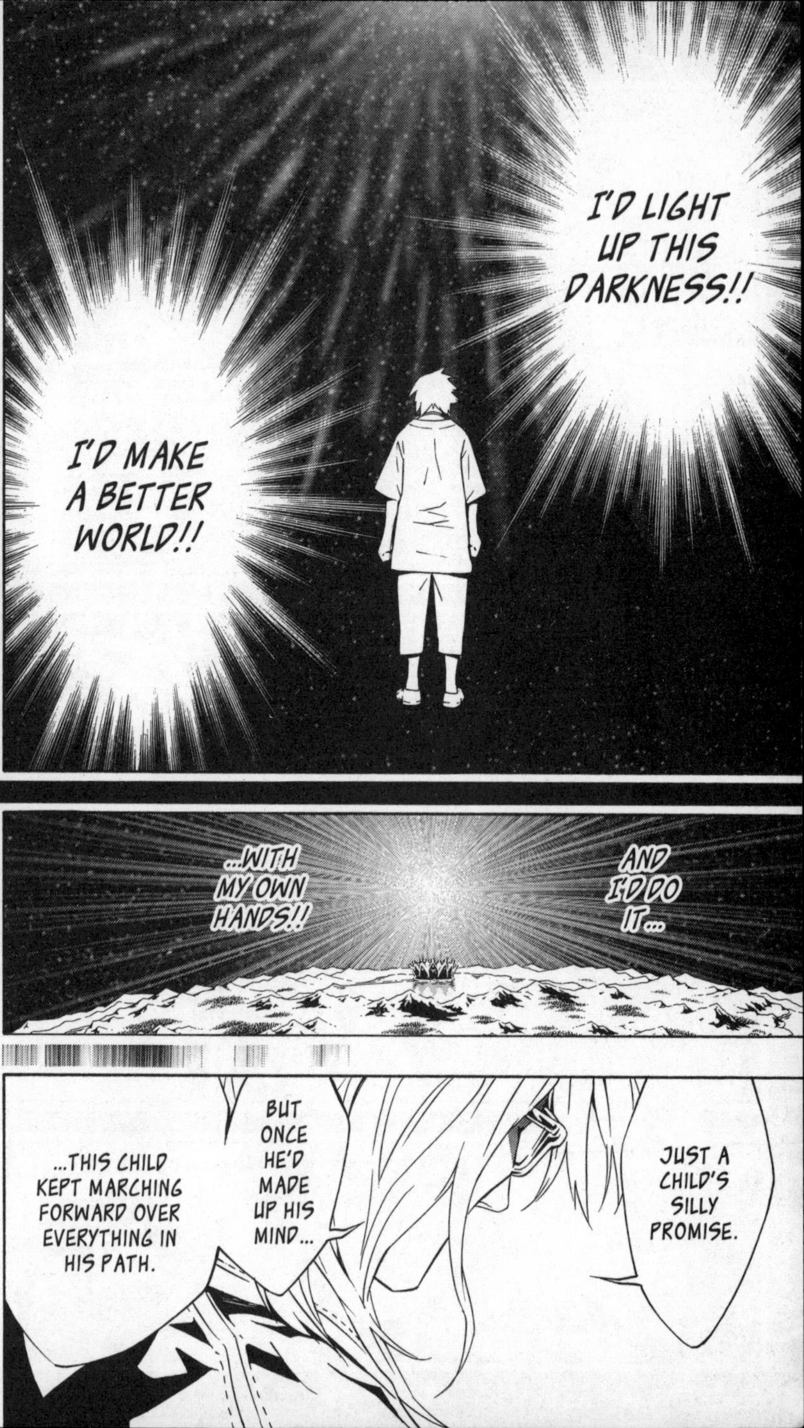
I'D LIGHT UP THIS DARKNESS!!
I'D MAKE A BETTER WORLD!!
AND I'D DO IT...
...WITH MY OWN HANDS!!
JUST A CHILD'S SILLY PROMISE.
BUT ONCE HE'D MADE UP HIS MIND...
...THIS CHILD KEPT MARCHING FORWARD OVER EVERYTHING IN HIS PATH.

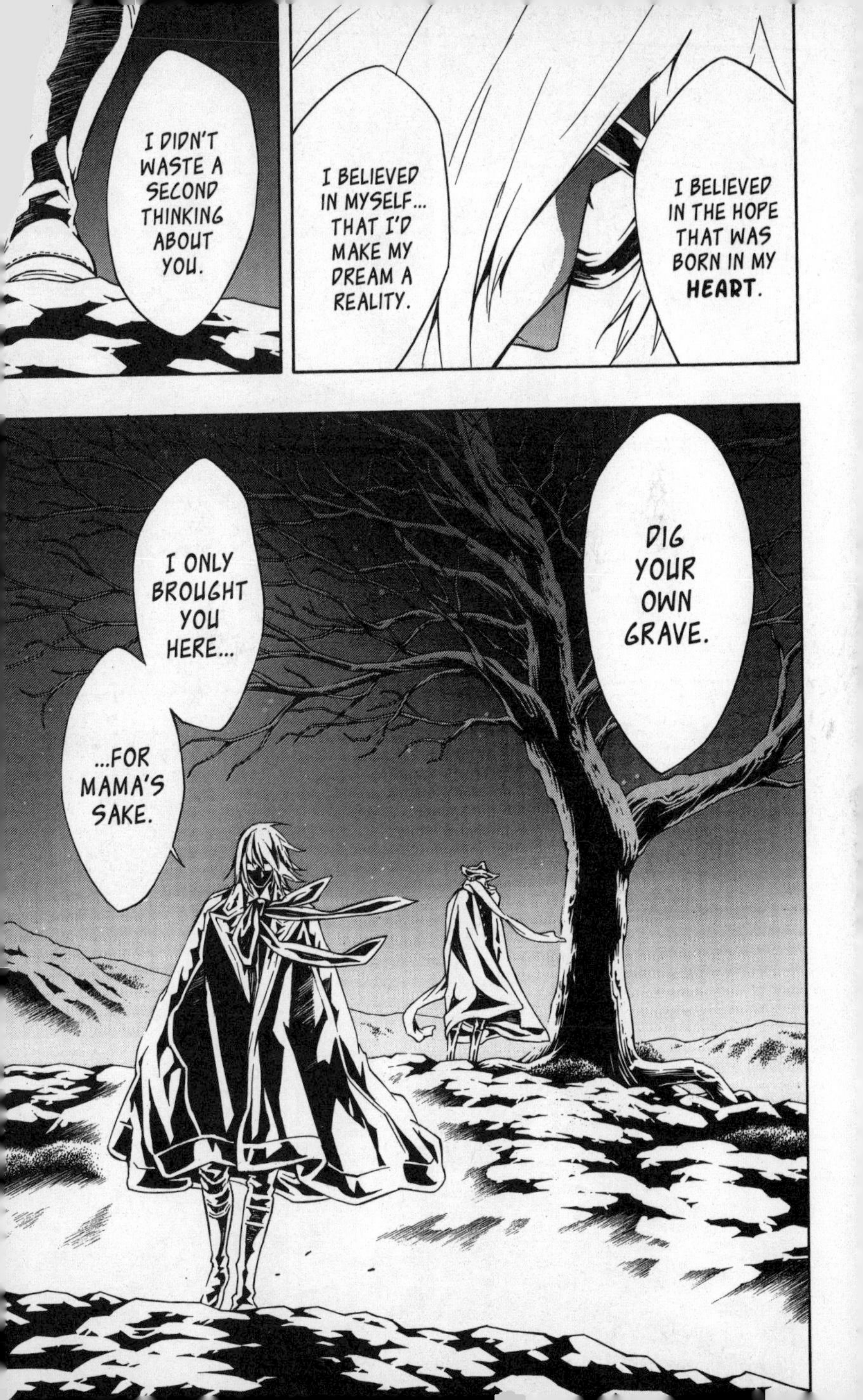
I BELIEVED IN THE HOPE THAT WAS BORN IN MY **HEART**.
I BELIEVED IN MYSELF... THAT I'D MAKE MY DREAM A REALITY.
I DIDN'T WASTE A SECOND THINKING ABOUT YOU.
DIG YOUR OWN GRAVE.
I ONLY BROUGHT YOU HERE...
...FOR MAMA'S SAKE.

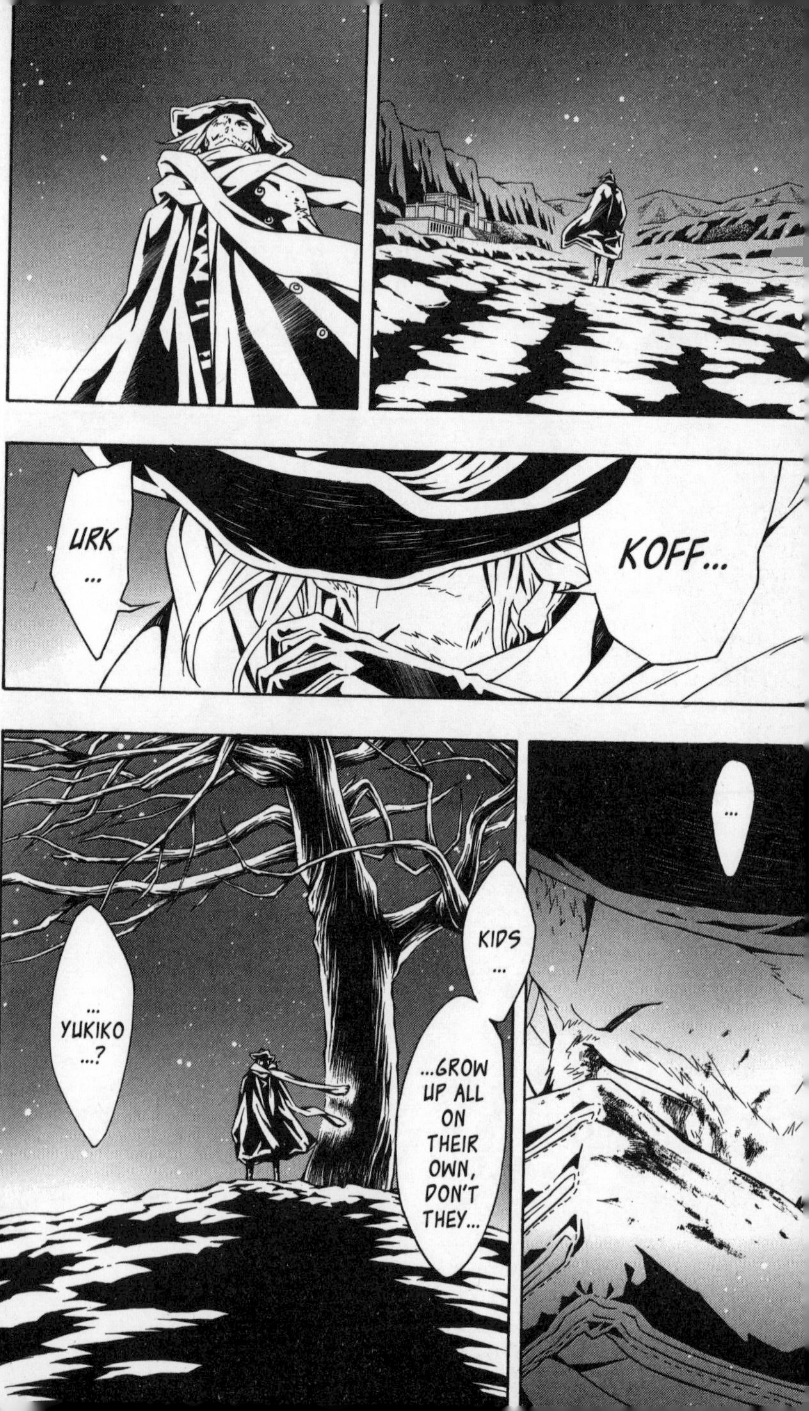
KOFF...
URK ...
...
KIDS ...
...GROW UP ALL ON THEIR OWN, DON'T THEY...
... YUKIKO ...?

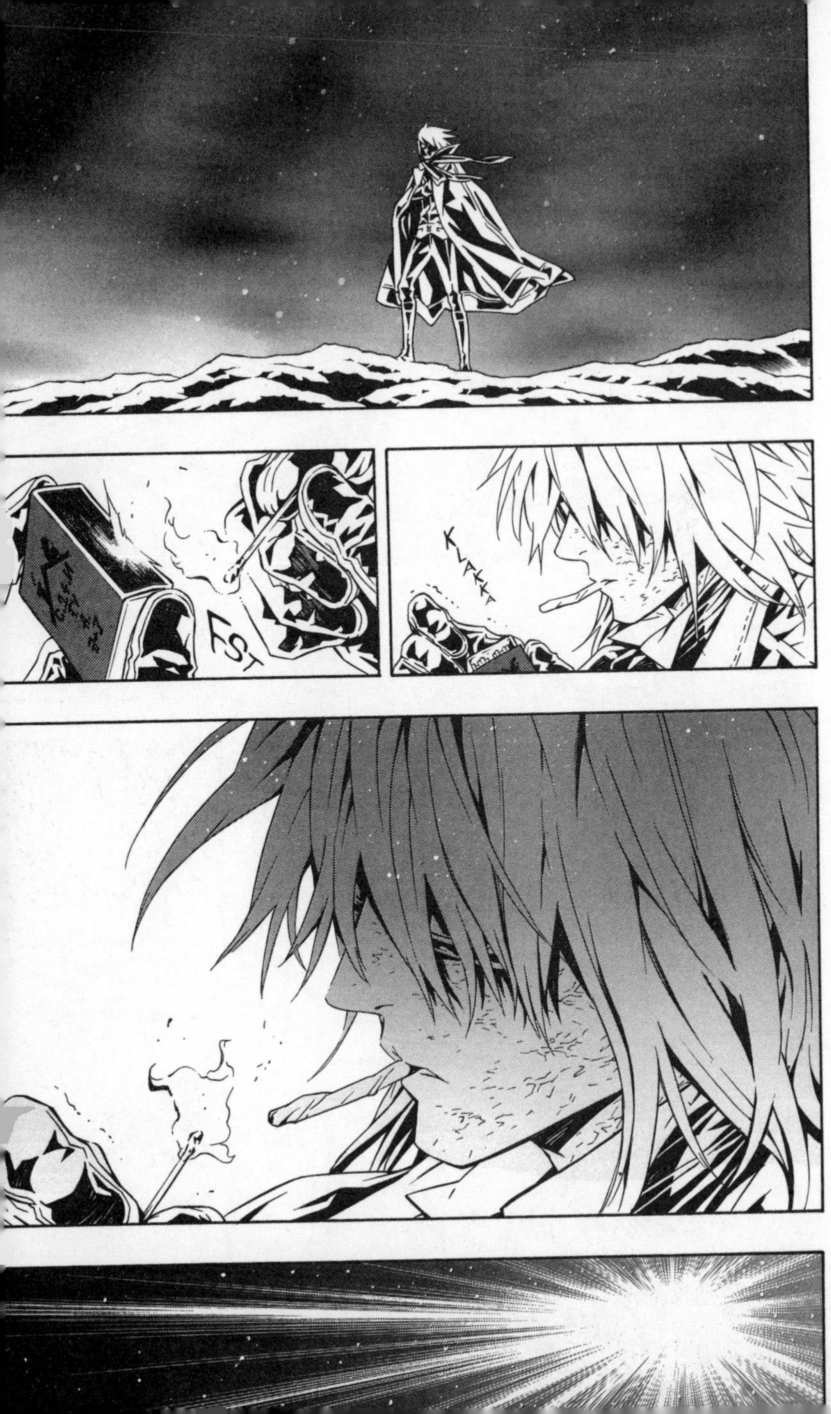
KLAKKA
FST

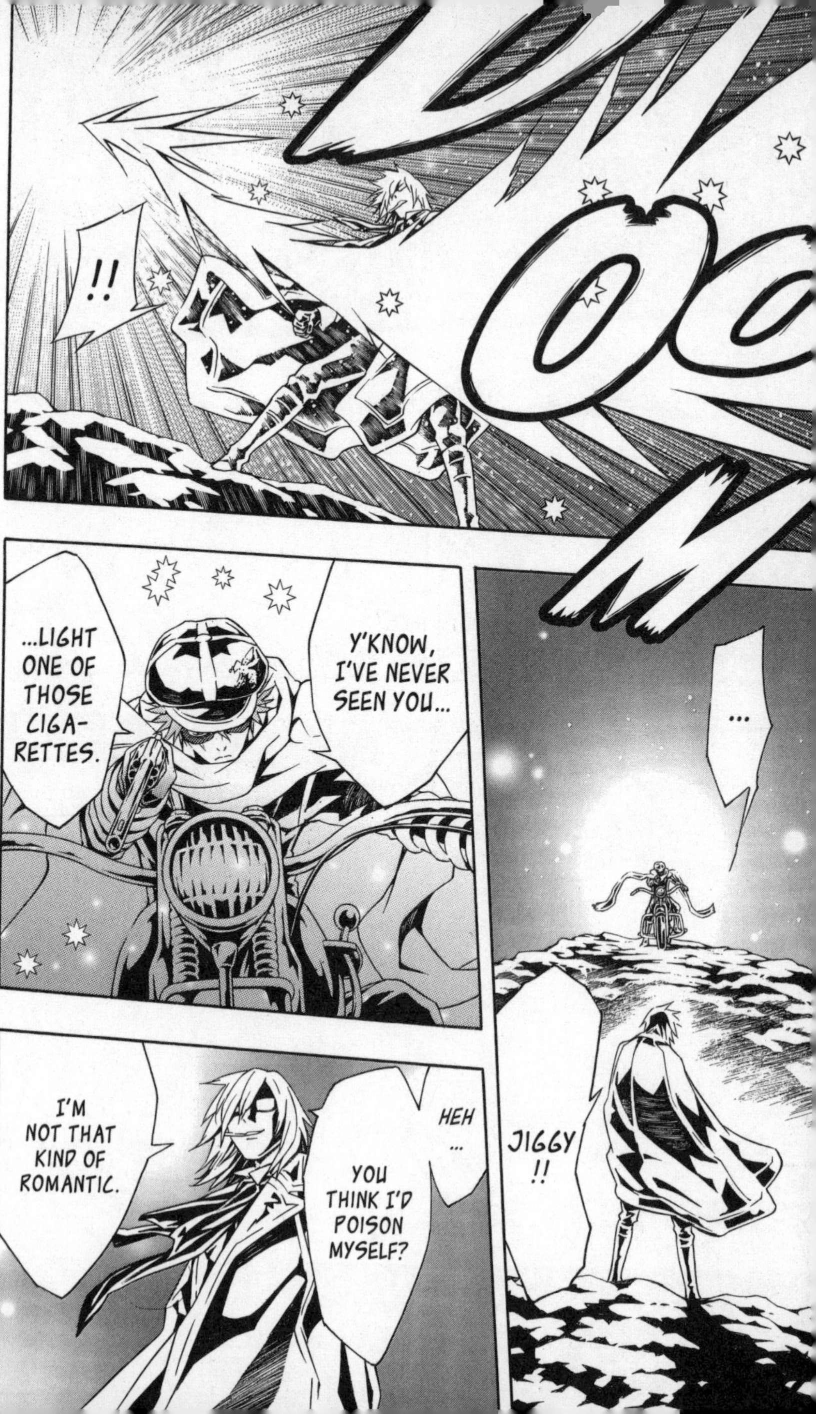
!!
...
JIGGY!!
Y'KNOW, I'VE NEVER SEEN YOU...
...LIGHT ONE OF THOSE CIGA-RETTES.
HEH ...
YOU THINK I'D POISON MYSELF?
I'M NOT THAT KIND OF ROMANTIC.

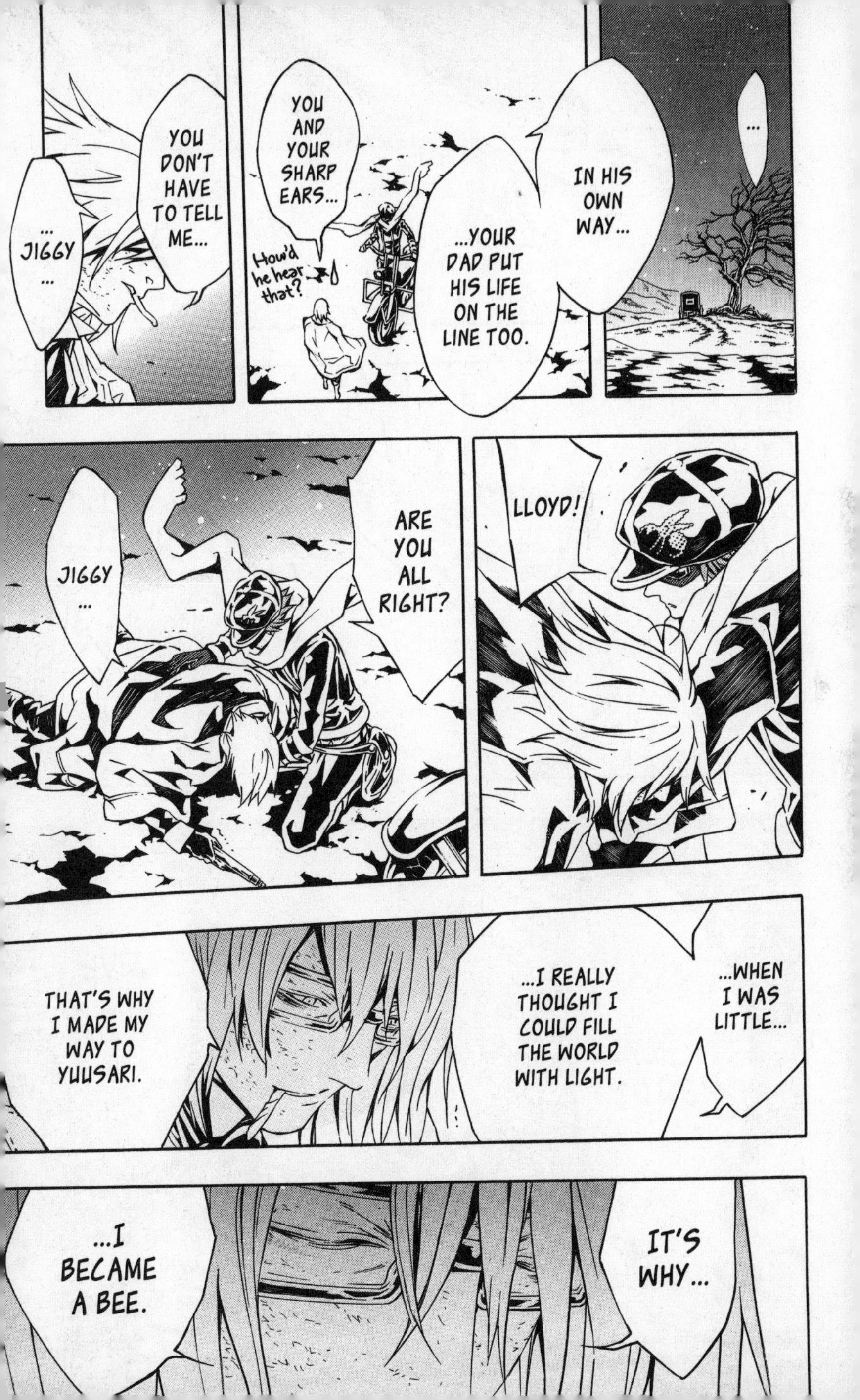
...
IN HIS OWN WAY...
...YOUR DAD PUT HIS LIFE ON THE LINE TOO.
YOU AND YOUR SHARP EARS...
How'd he hear that?
YOU DON'T HAVE TO TELL ME...
... JIGGY ...
LLOYD!
ARE YOU ALL RIGHT?
JIGGY ...
...WHEN I WAS LITTLE...
...I REALLY THOUGHT I COULD FILL THE WORLD WITH LIGHT.
THAT'S WHY I MADE MY WAY TO YUUSARI.
IT'S WHY...
...I BECAME A BEE.

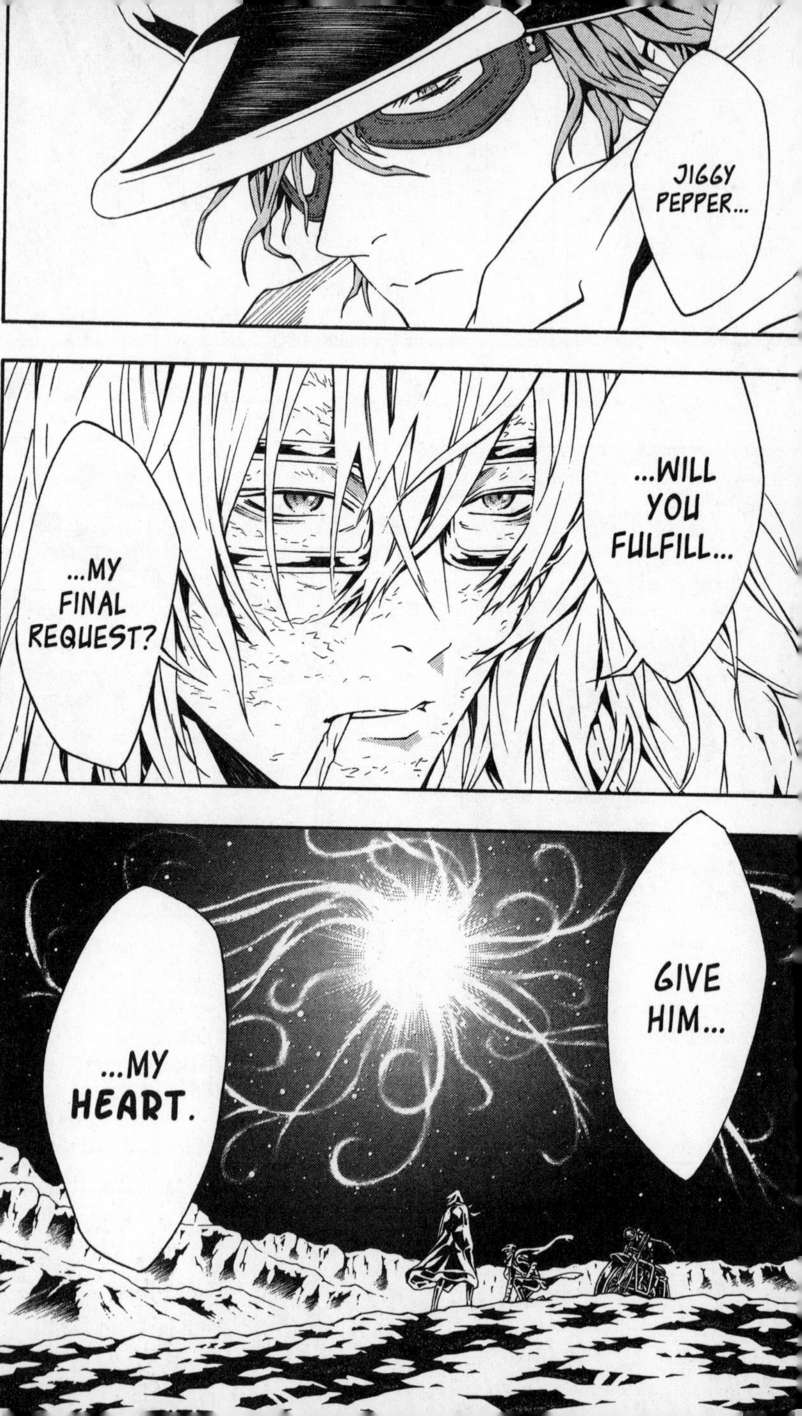
JIGGY PEPPER...
...WILL YOU FULFILL...
...MY FINAL REQUEST?
GIVE HIM...
...MY HEART.

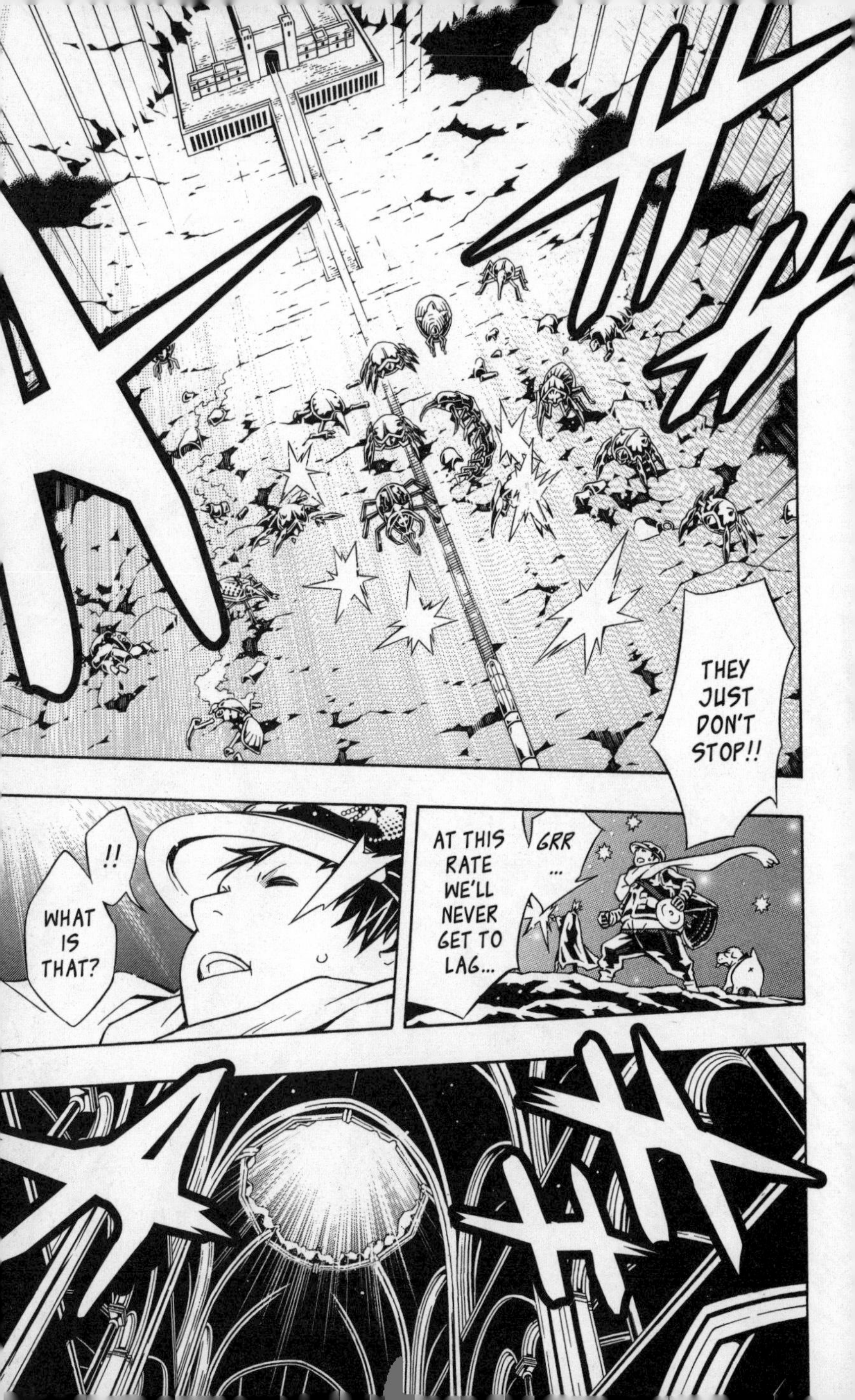
THEY JUST DON'T STOP!!
GRR ...
AT THIS RATE WE'LL NEVER GET TO LAG...
!!
WHAT IS THAT?

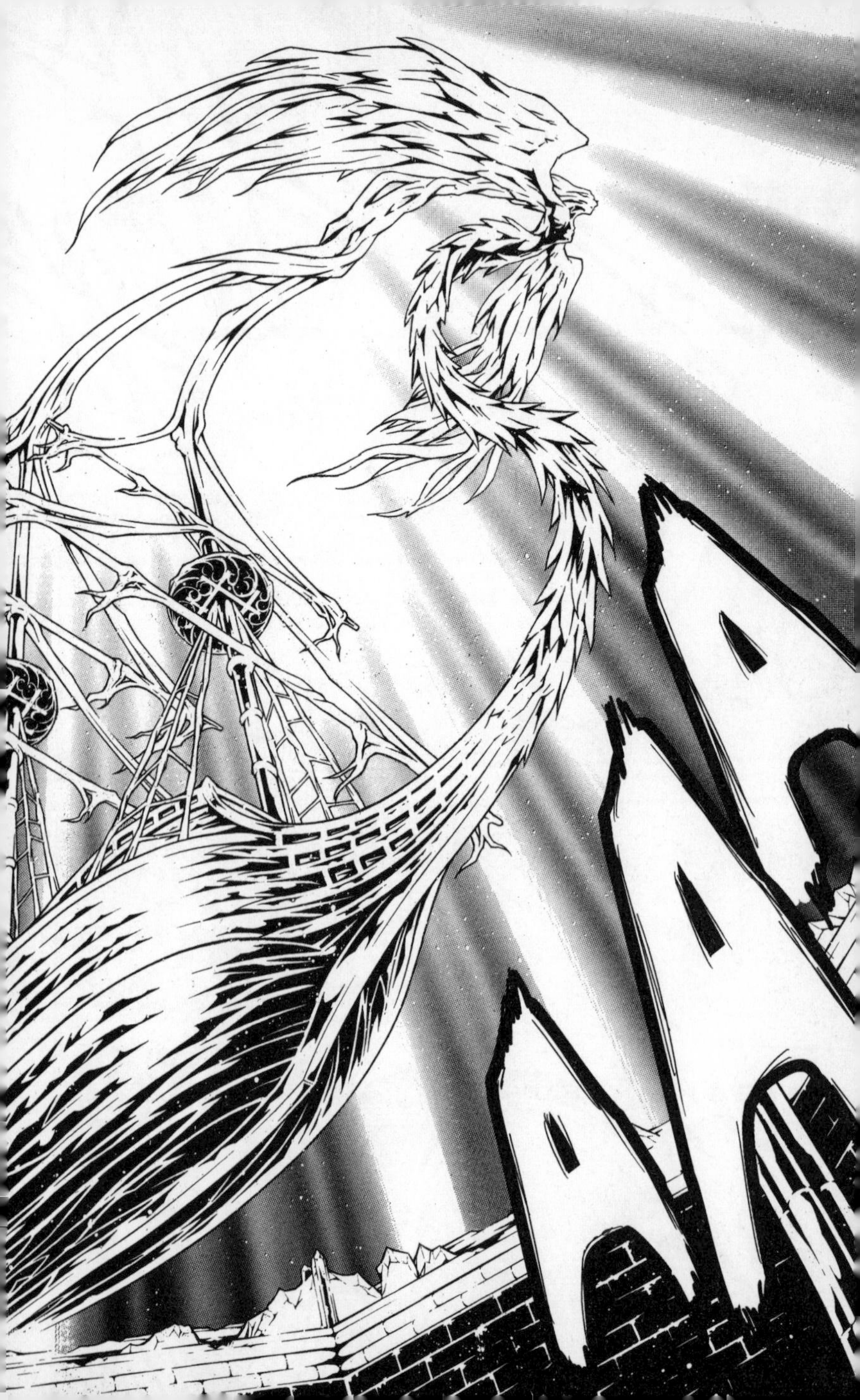
AAA

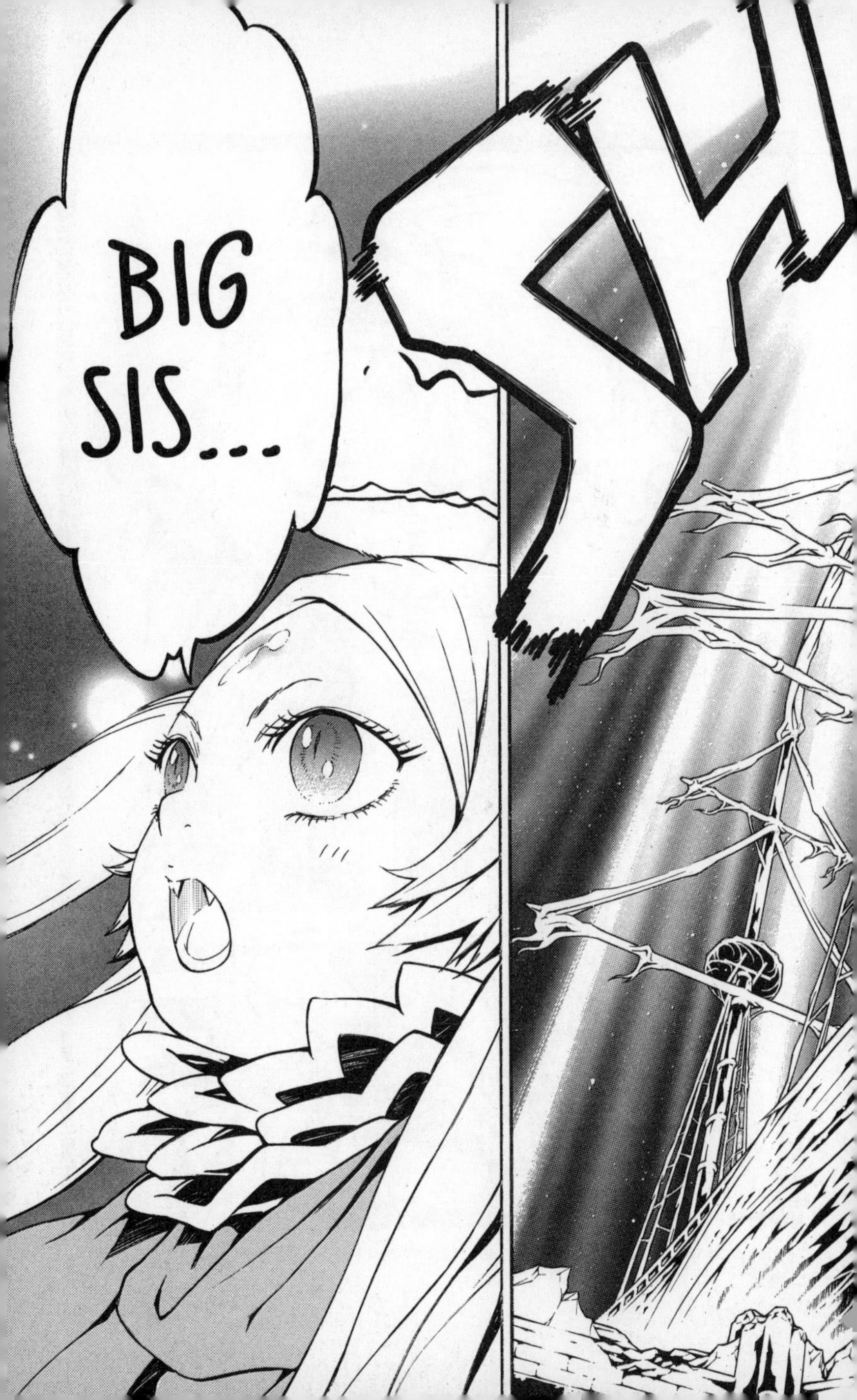
BIG SIS...

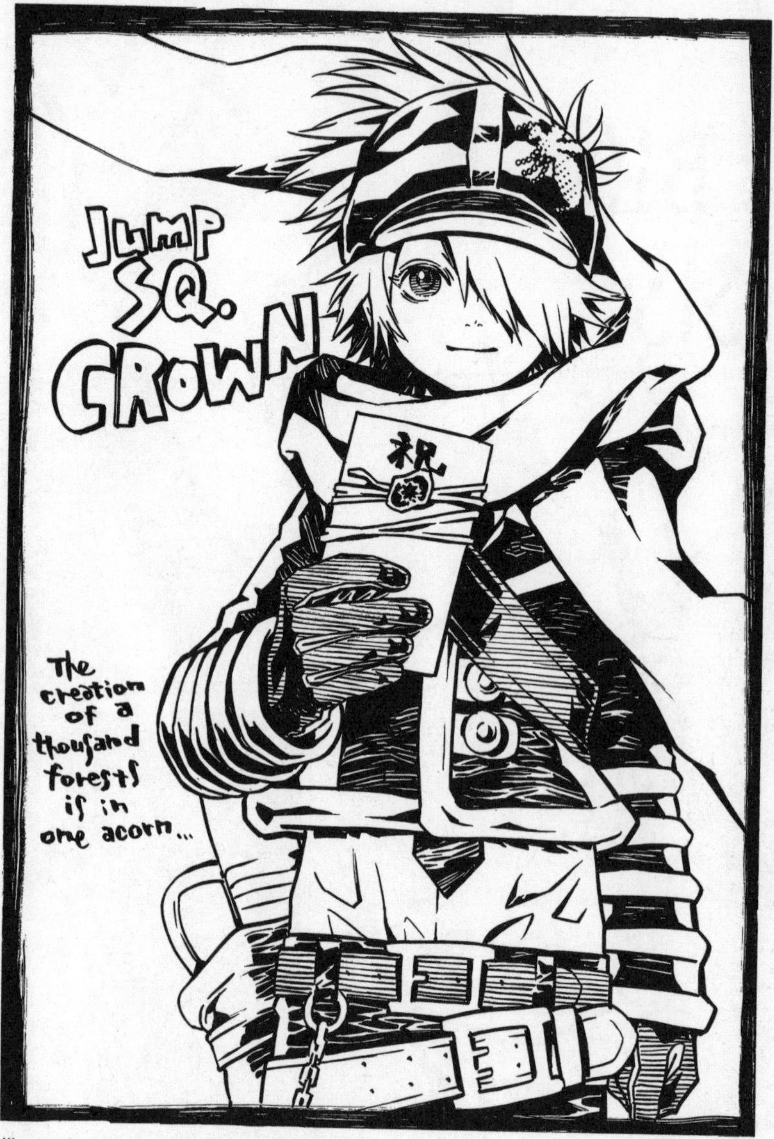
Jump SQ. CROWN
祝
The creation of a thousand forests is in one acorn...

Illustration for a *Jump Square Crown* special issue.

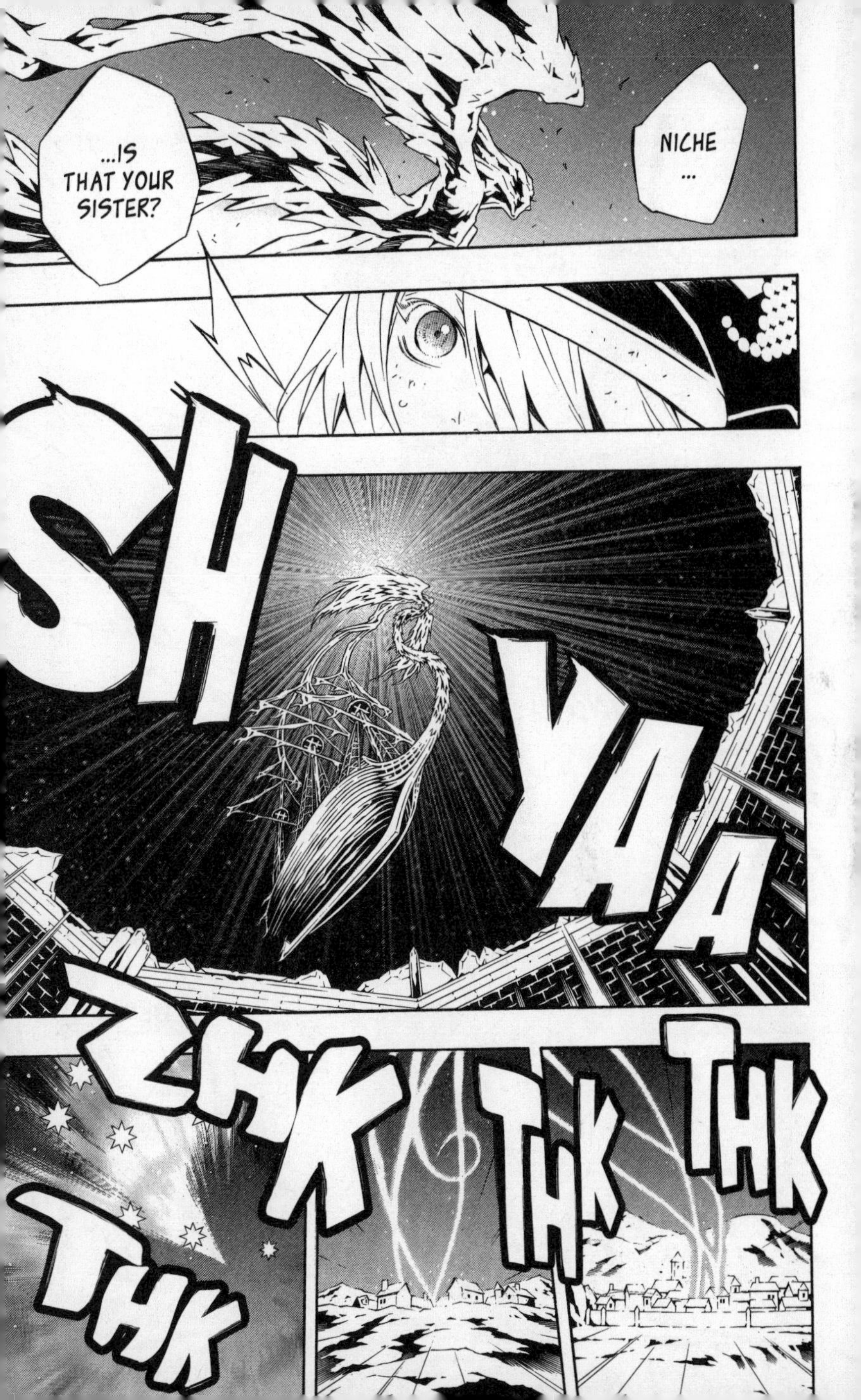
NICHE ...
...IS THAT YOUR SISTER?
SHYAA
THK
THK
ZHK
THK

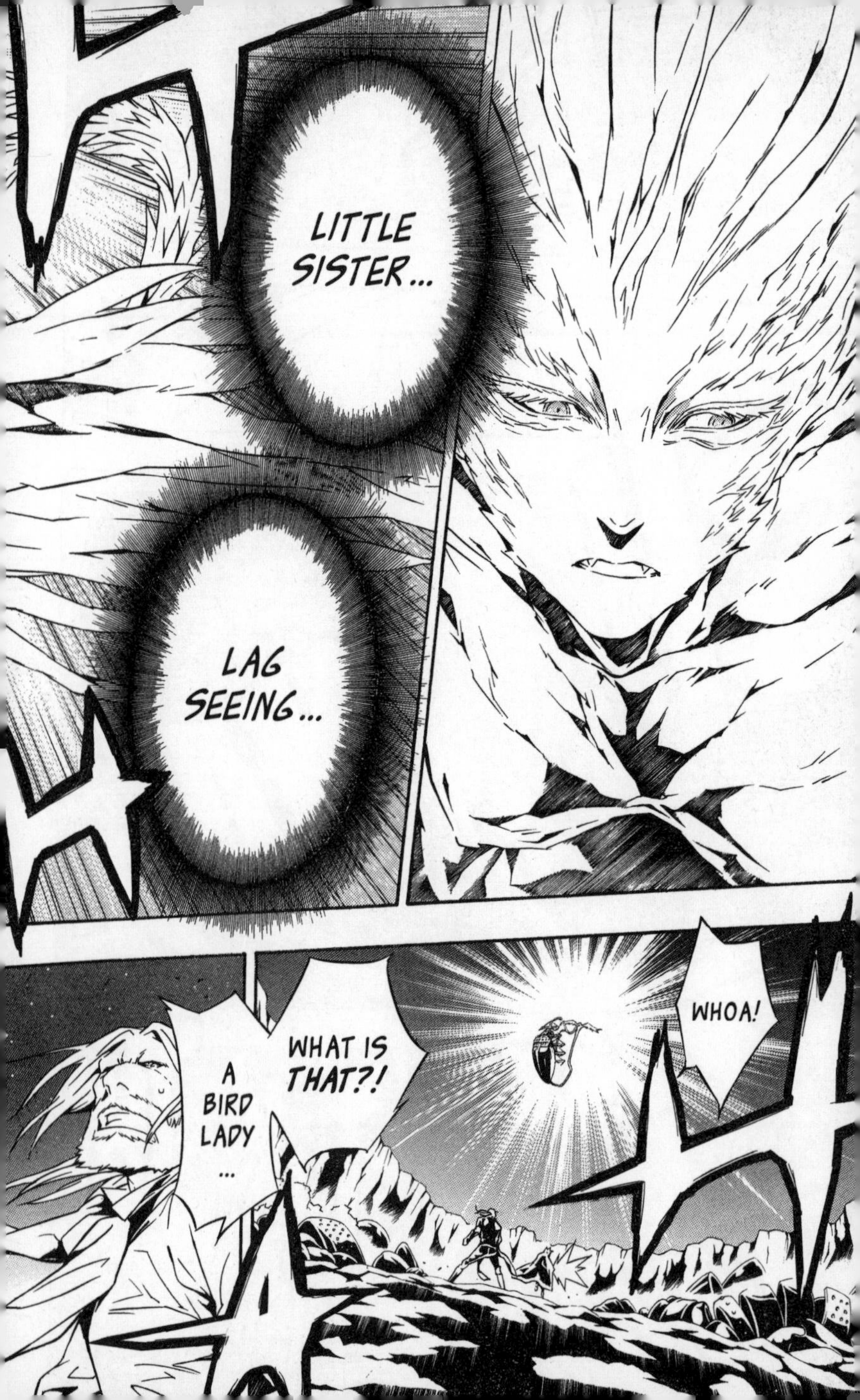
LITTLE SISTER...
LAG SEEING...
WHOA!
WHAT IS THAT?!
A BIRD LADY ...

Chapter 97: Hikaribari

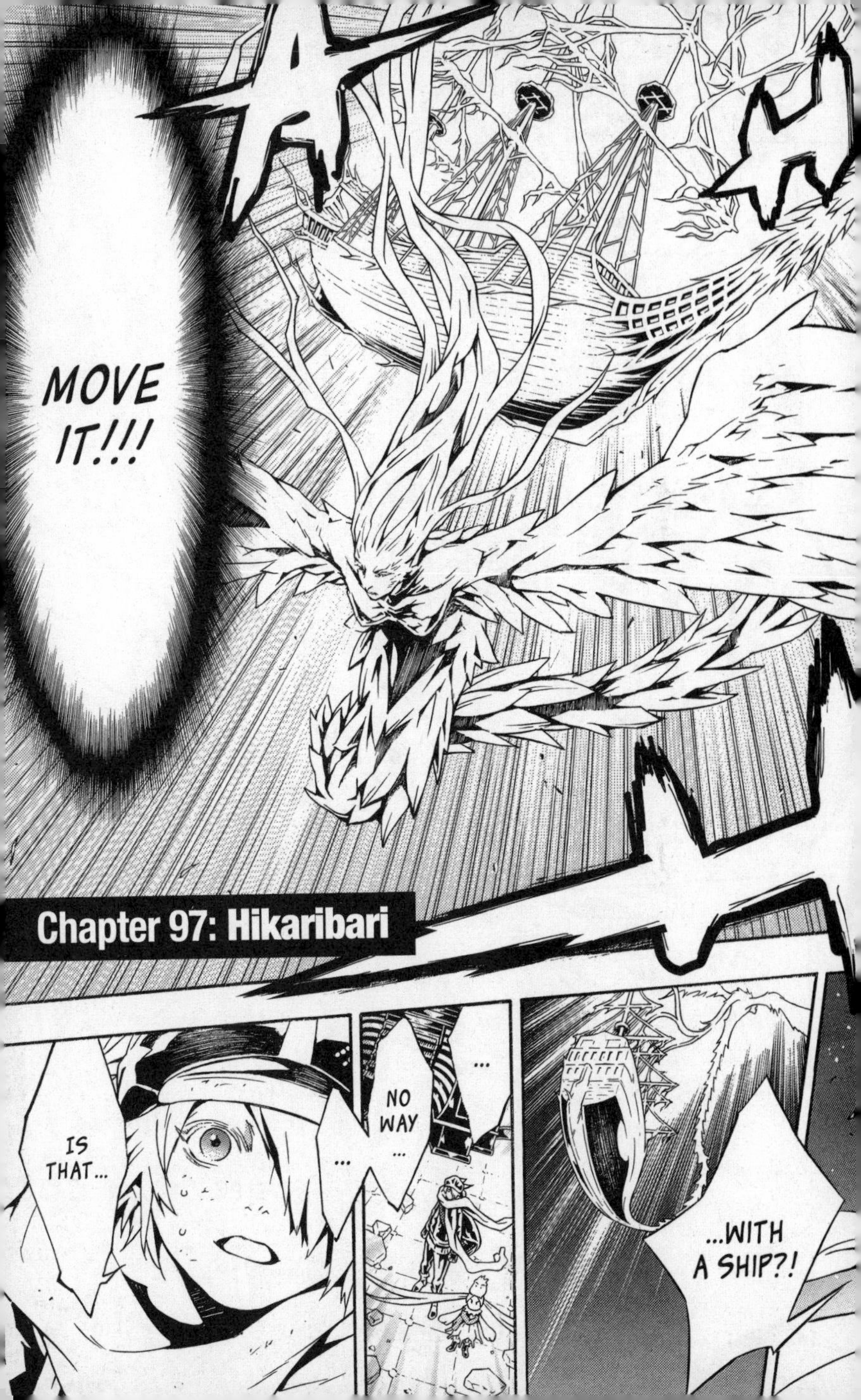
MOVE IT!!!
...WITH A SHIP?!
...
NO WAY ...
...
IS THAT...

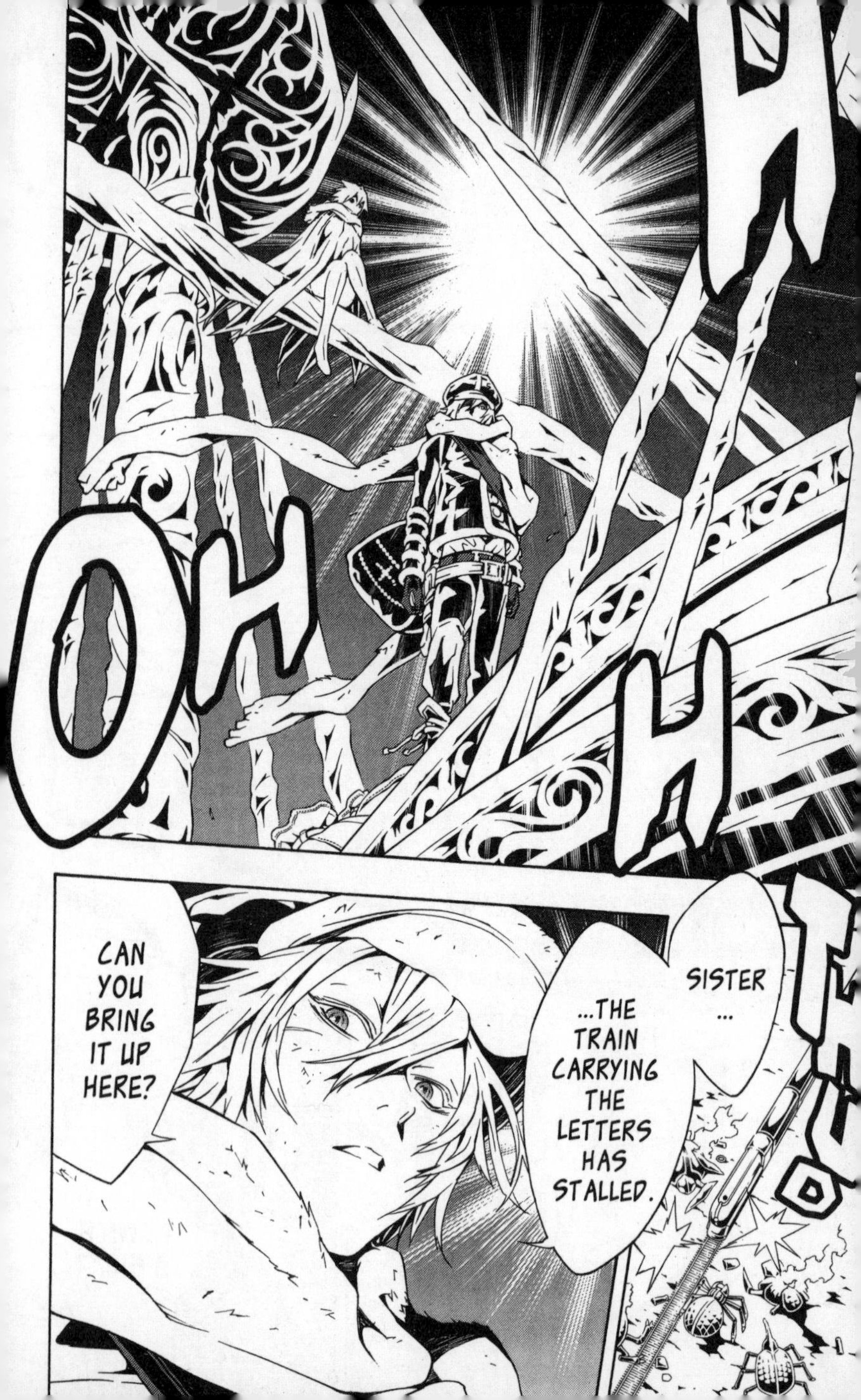
SISTER ...
...THE TRAIN CARRYING THE LETTERS HAS STALLED.
CAN YOU BRING IT UP HERE?

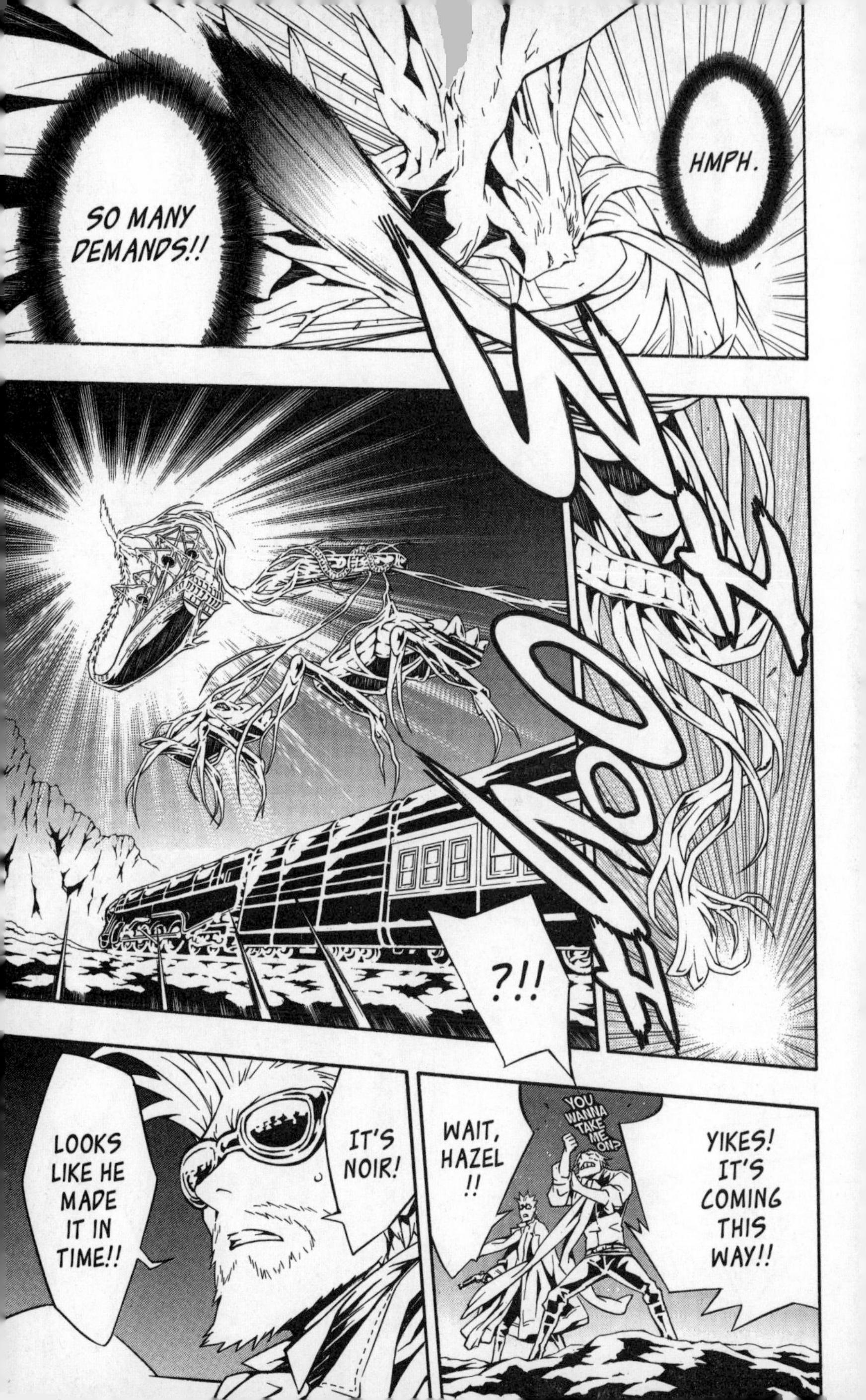
HMPH.
SO MANY DEMANDS!!
?!!
YIKES! IT'S COMING THIS WAY!!
YOU WANNA TAKE ME ON?
WAIT, HAZEL!!
IT'S NOIR!
LOOKS LIKE HE MADE IT IN TIME!!

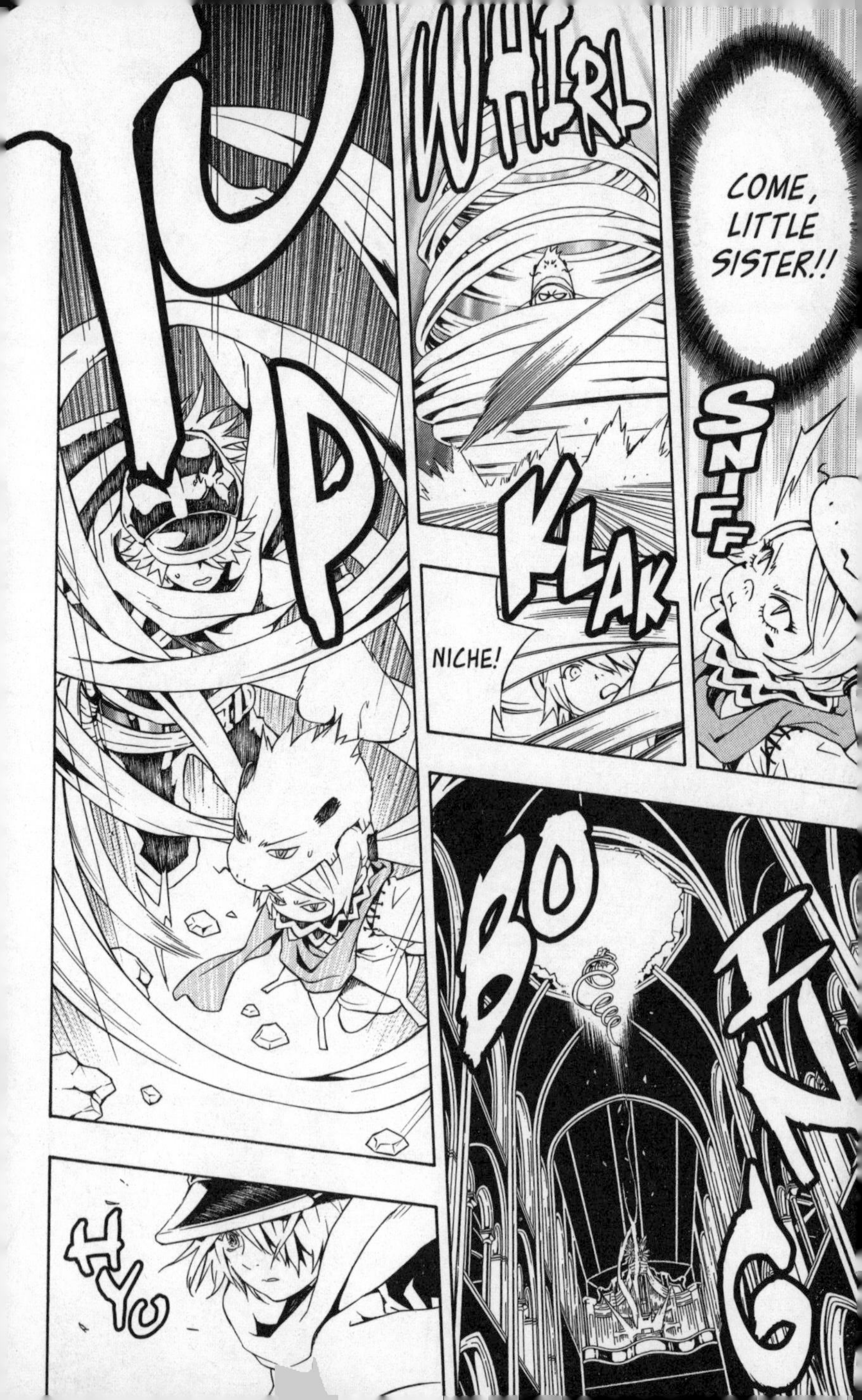
COME, LITTLE SISTER!!
SNIFF
WHIRL
KLAK
NICHE!

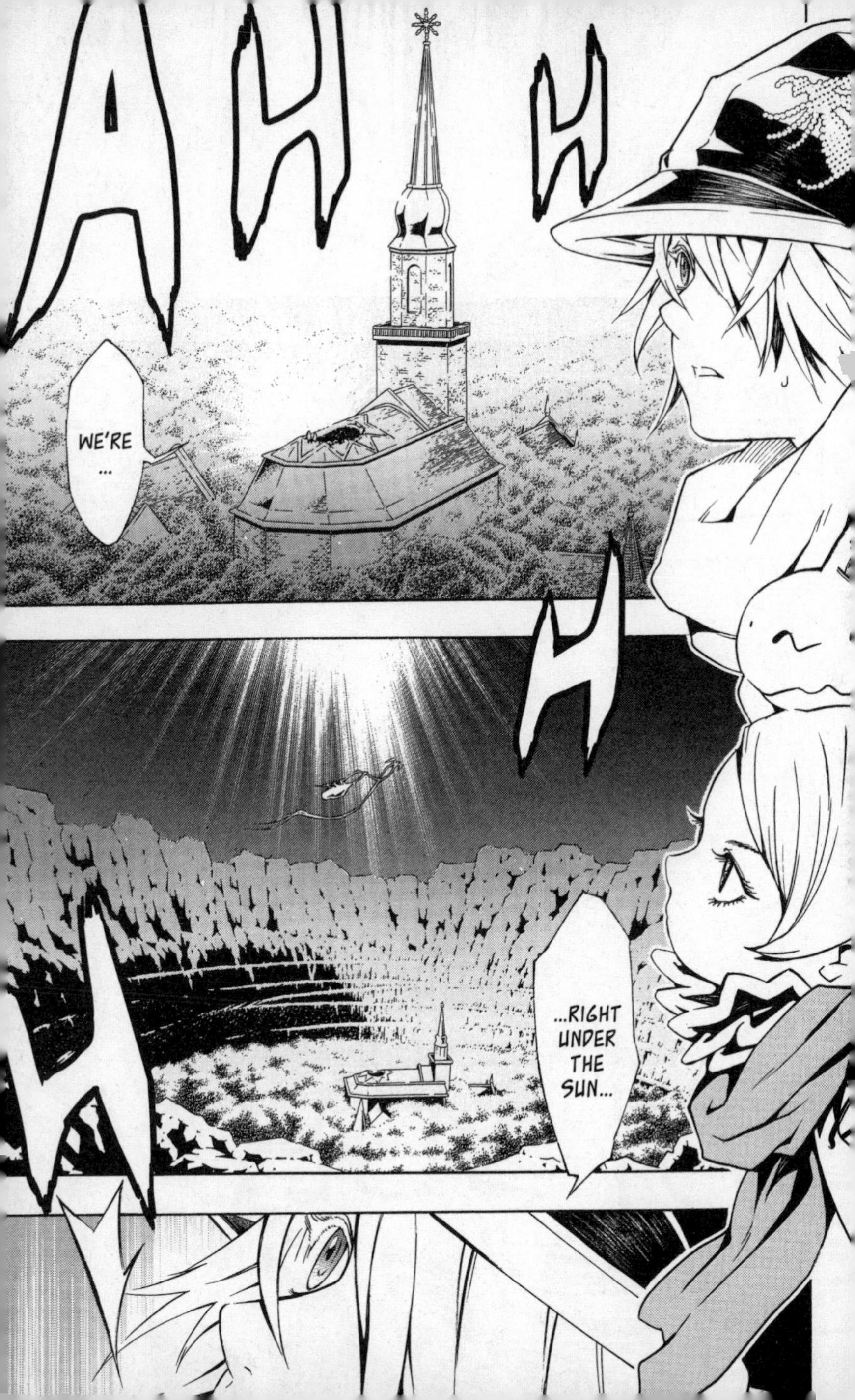
AHHHH
WE'RE ...
...RIGHT UNDER THE SUN...

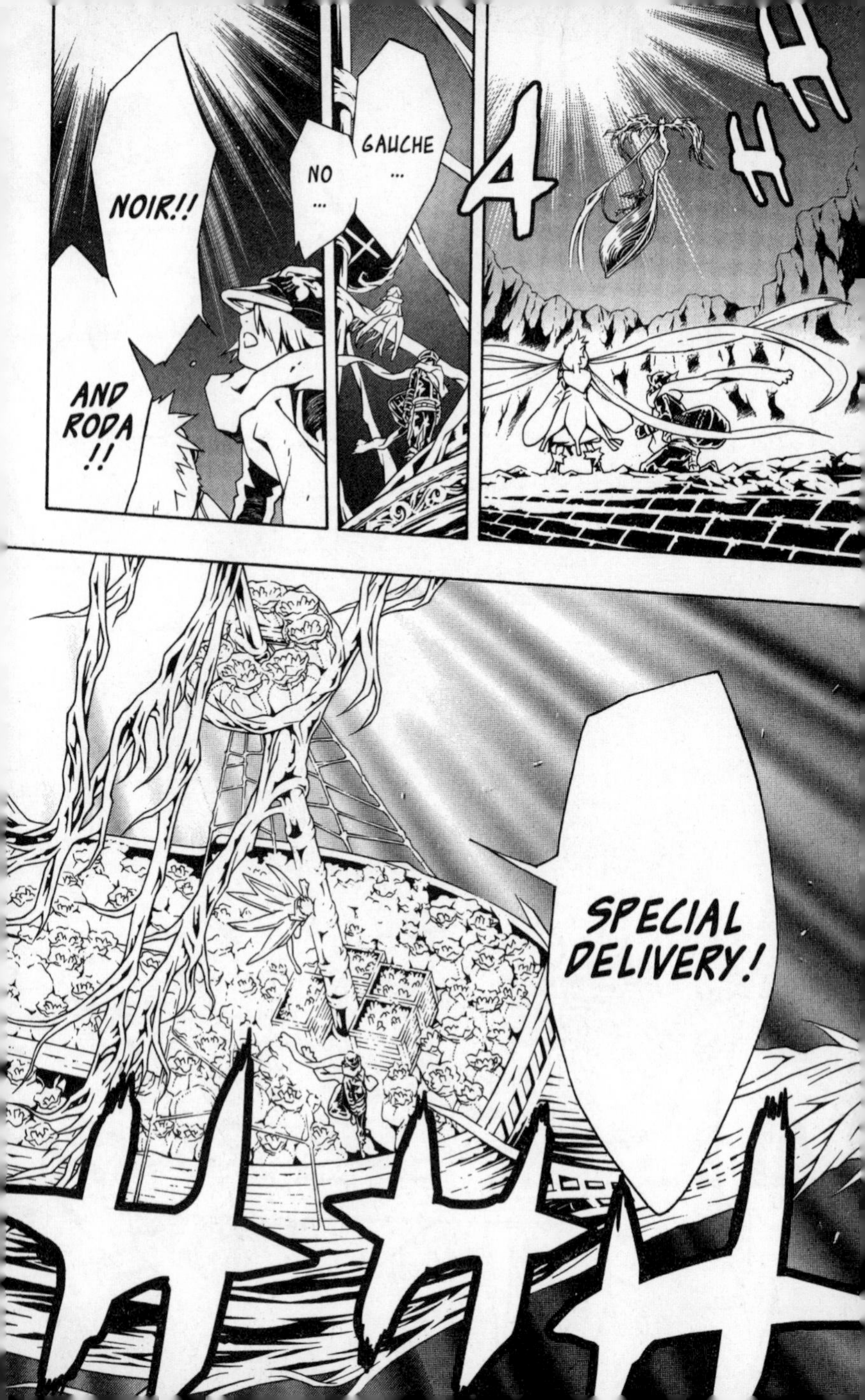

GAUCHE ... NO ...
NOIR!!
AND RODA !!
SPECIAL DELIVERY!

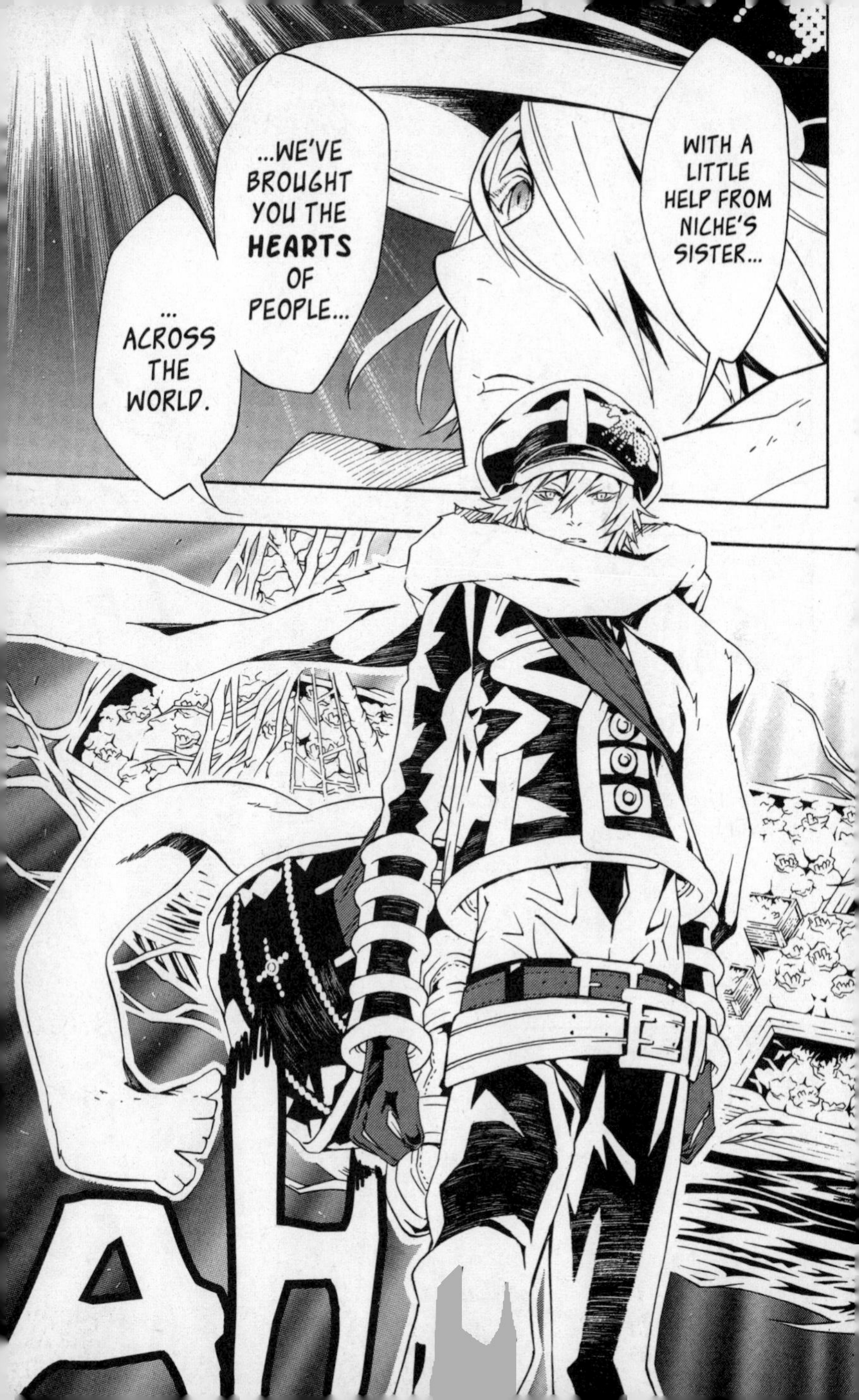
WITH A LITTLE HELP FROM NICHE'S SISTER...
...WE'VE BROUGHT YOU THE **HEARTS** OF PEOPLE...
... ACROSS THE WORLD.
AH

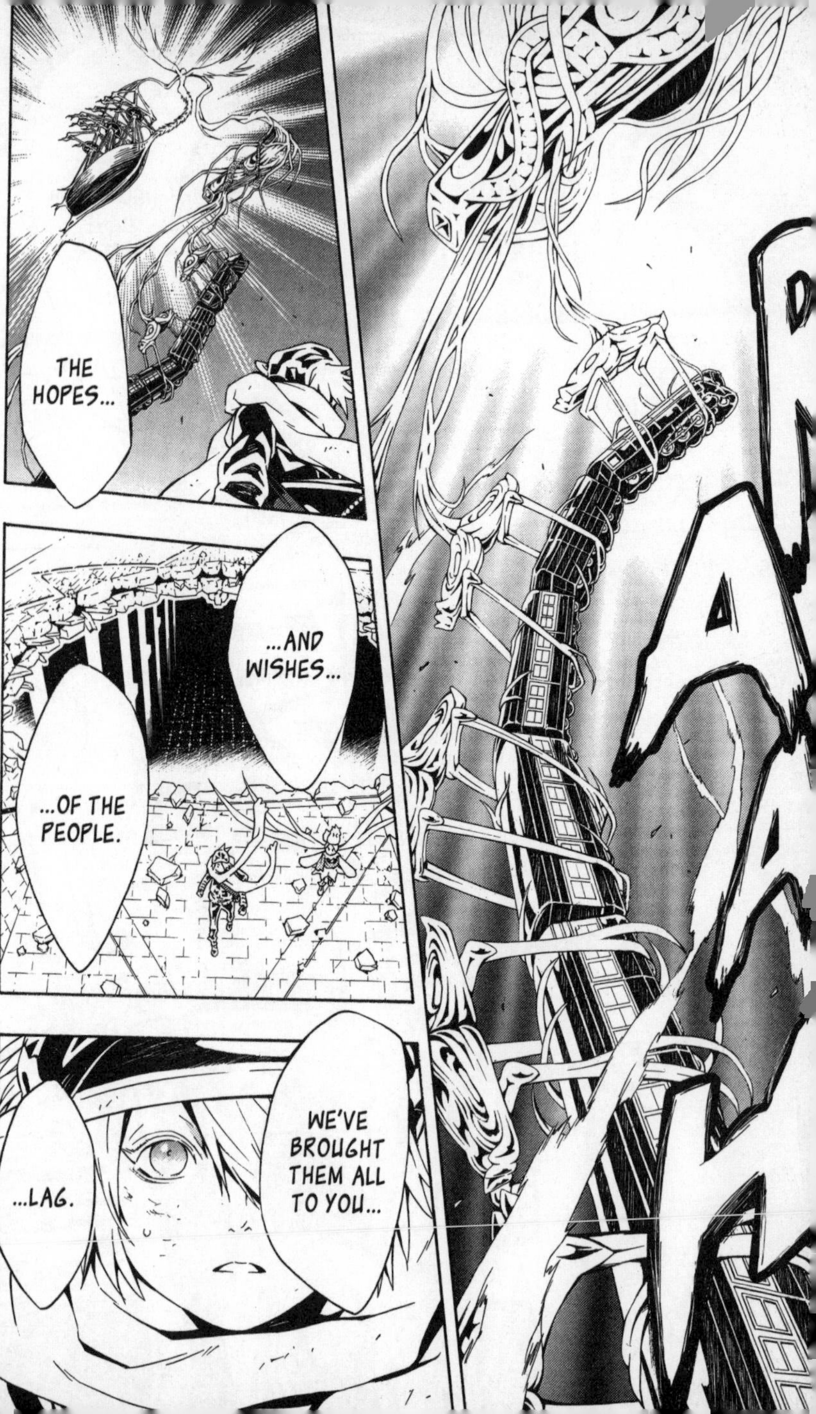
THE HOPES...
...AND WISHES...
...OF THE PEOPLE.
WE'VE BROUGHT THEM ALL TO YOU...
...LAG.

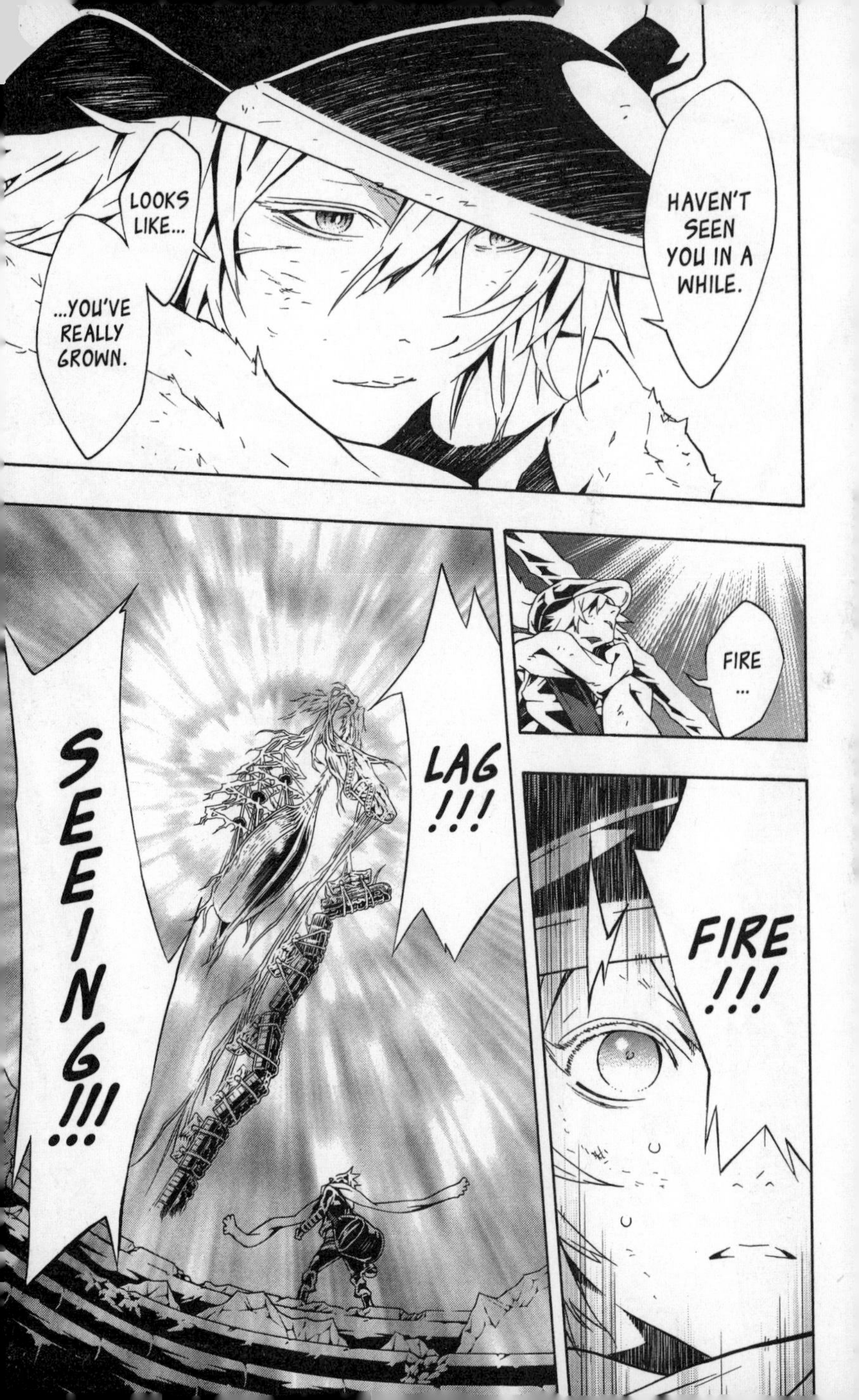
HAVEN'T SEEN YOU IN A WHILE.
LOOKS LIKE...
...YOU'VE REALLY GROWN.
FIRE ...
FIRE !!!
LAG !!!
SEEING!!!

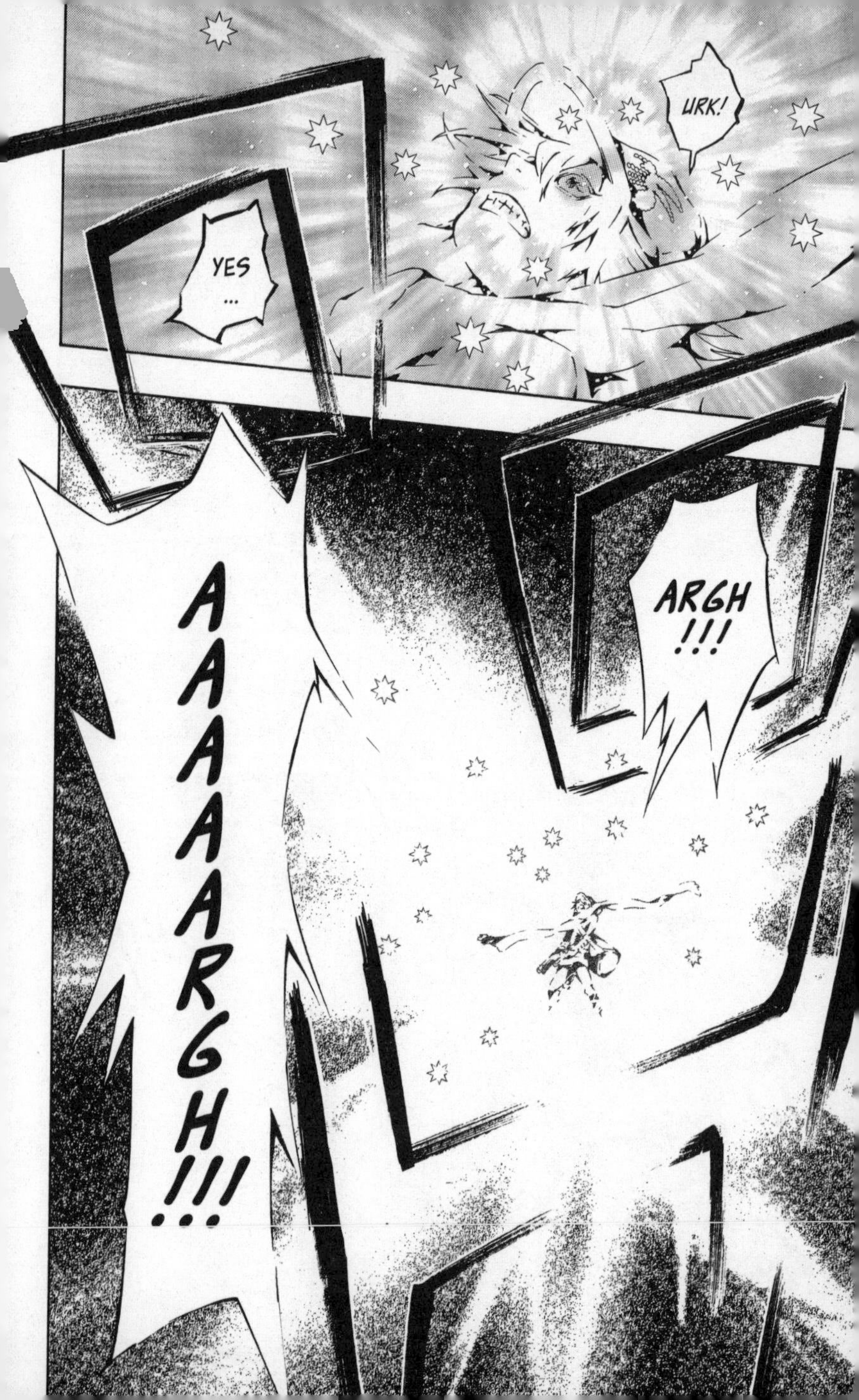
URK!
YES...
ARGH!!!
AAAAARGH!!!

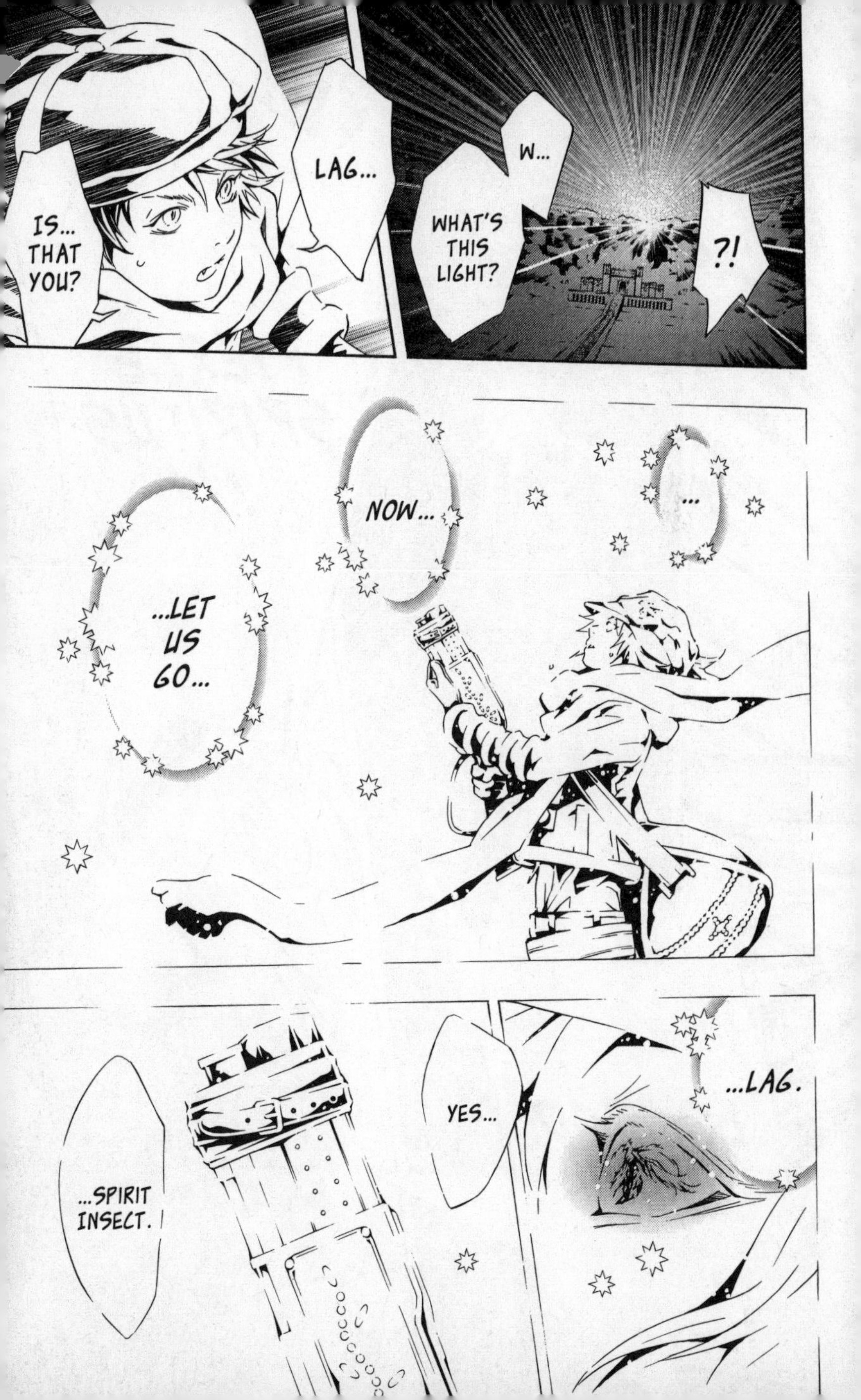
?!
W...
WHAT'S THIS LIGHT?
LAG...
IS... THAT YOU?
...
NOW...
...LET US GO...
...LAG.
YES...
...SPIRIT INSECT.

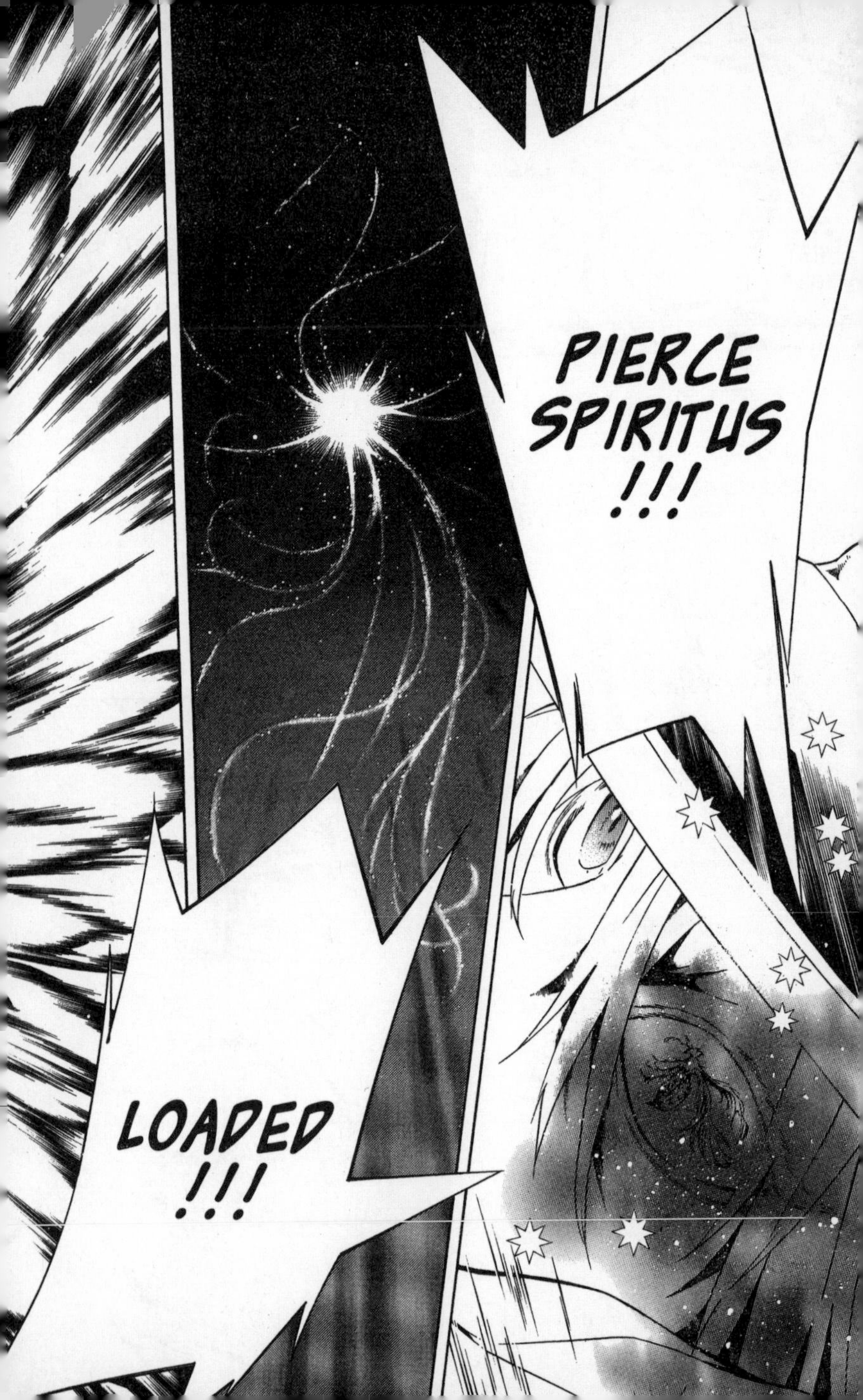
PIERCE SPIRITUS!!!
LOADED!!!

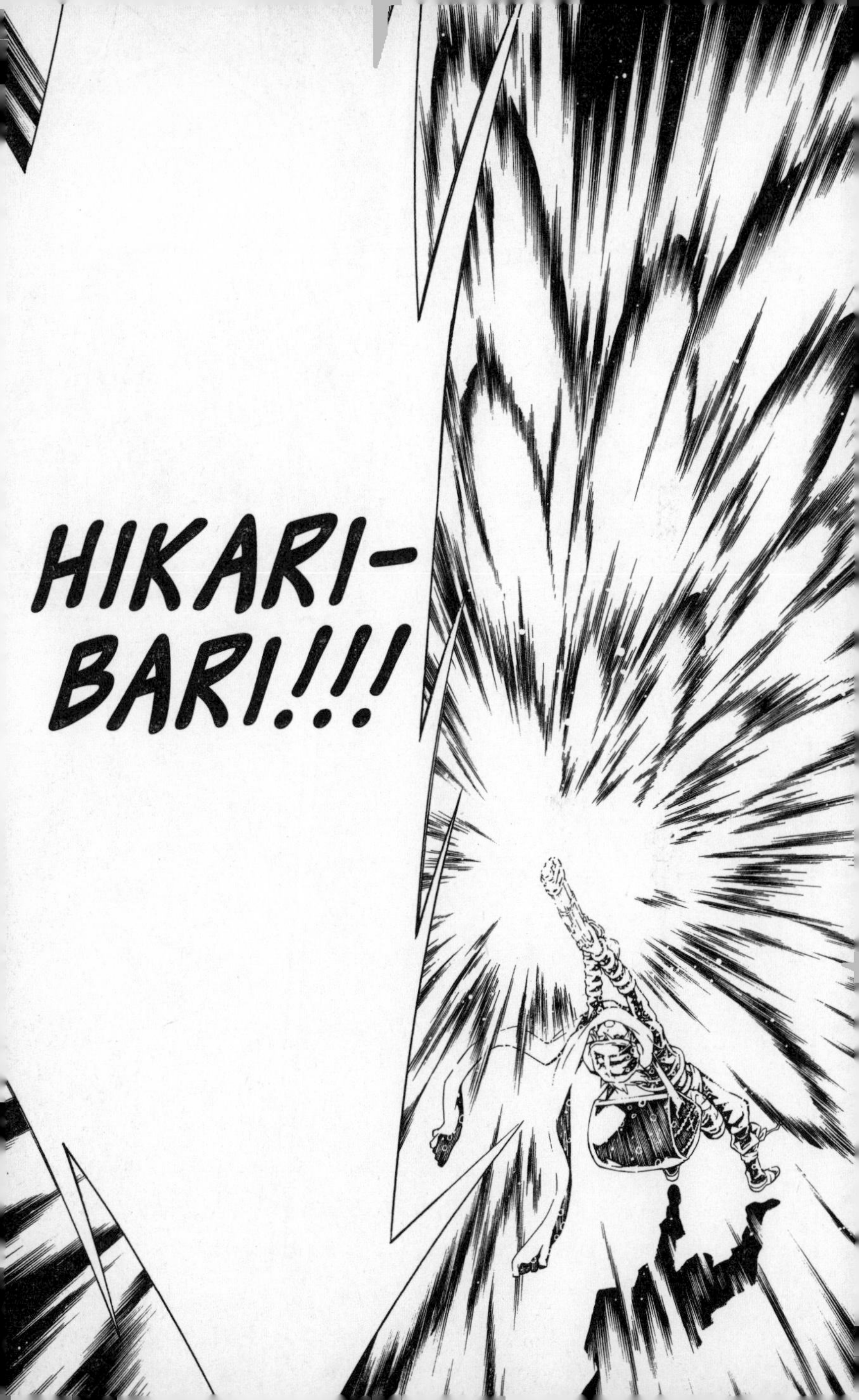
HIKARI-
BARI!!!

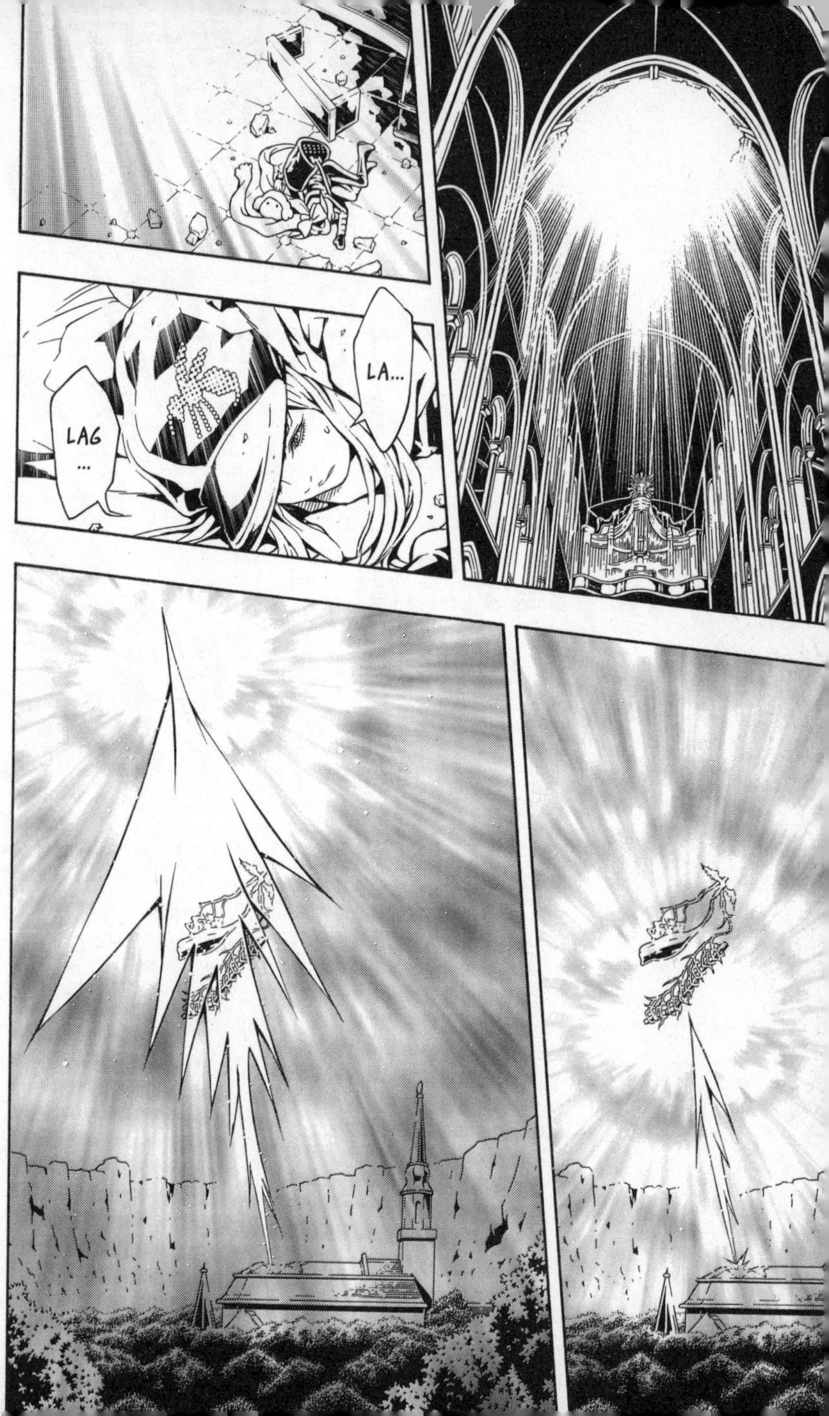
LA...
LAG ...

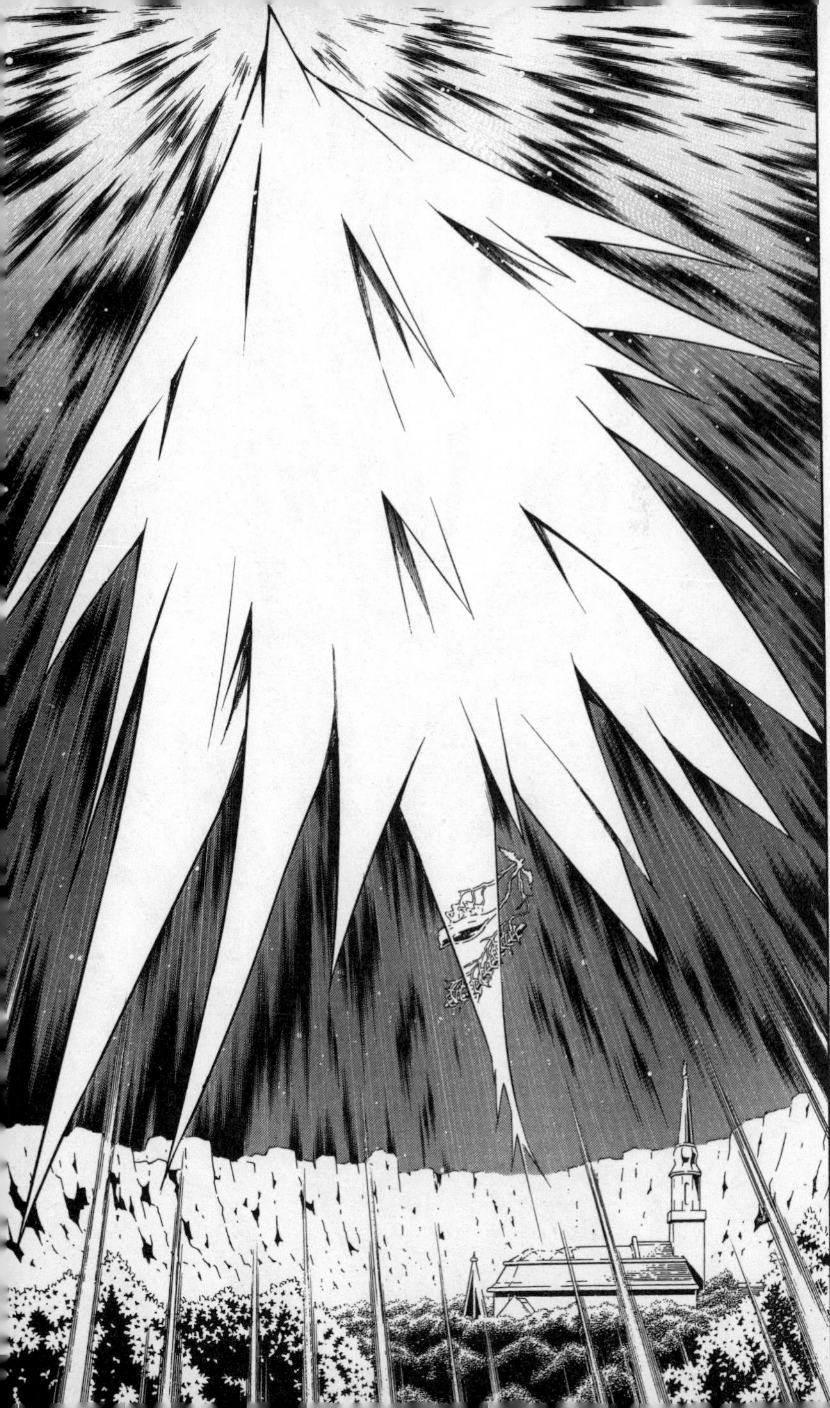

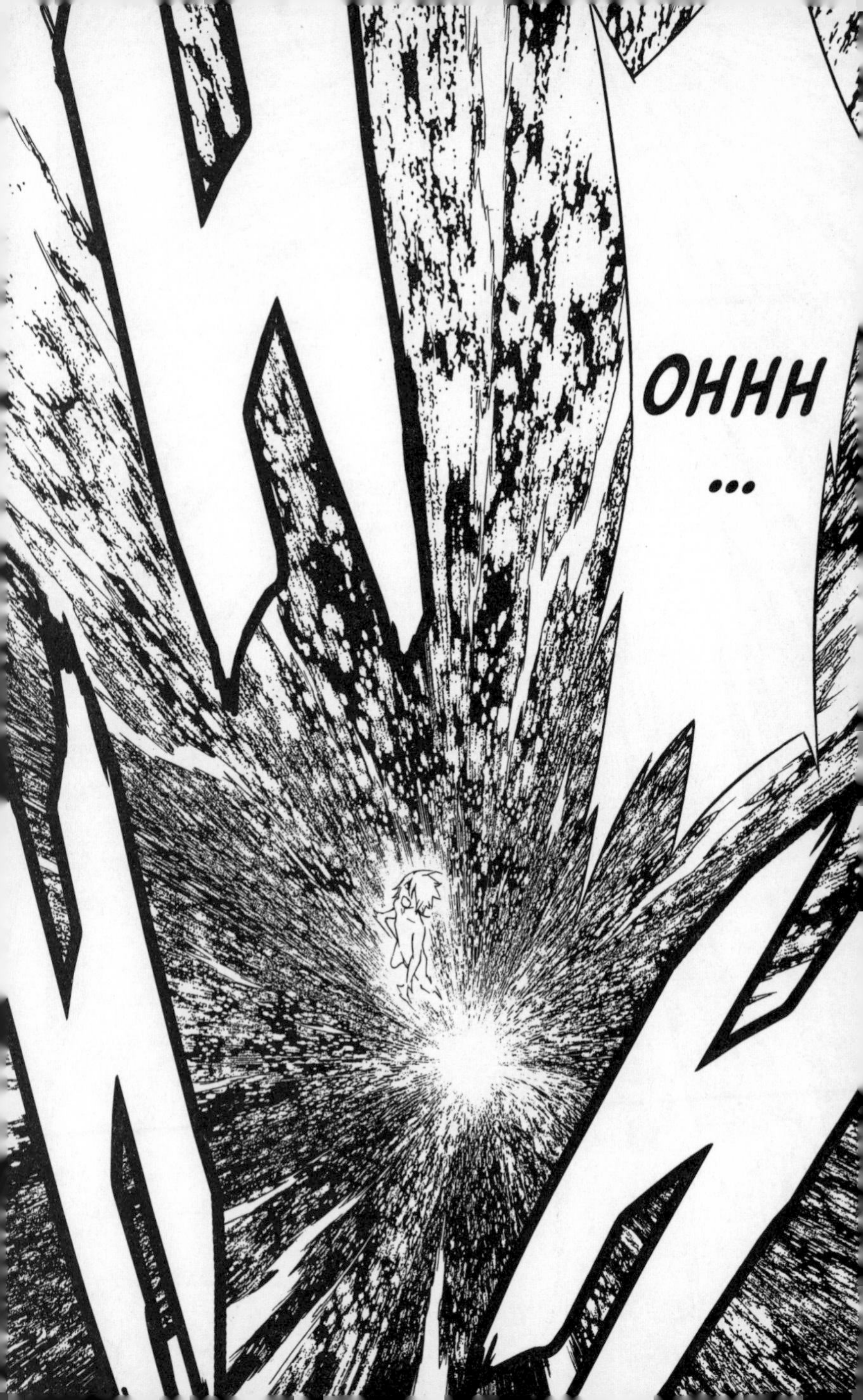
OHHH
...

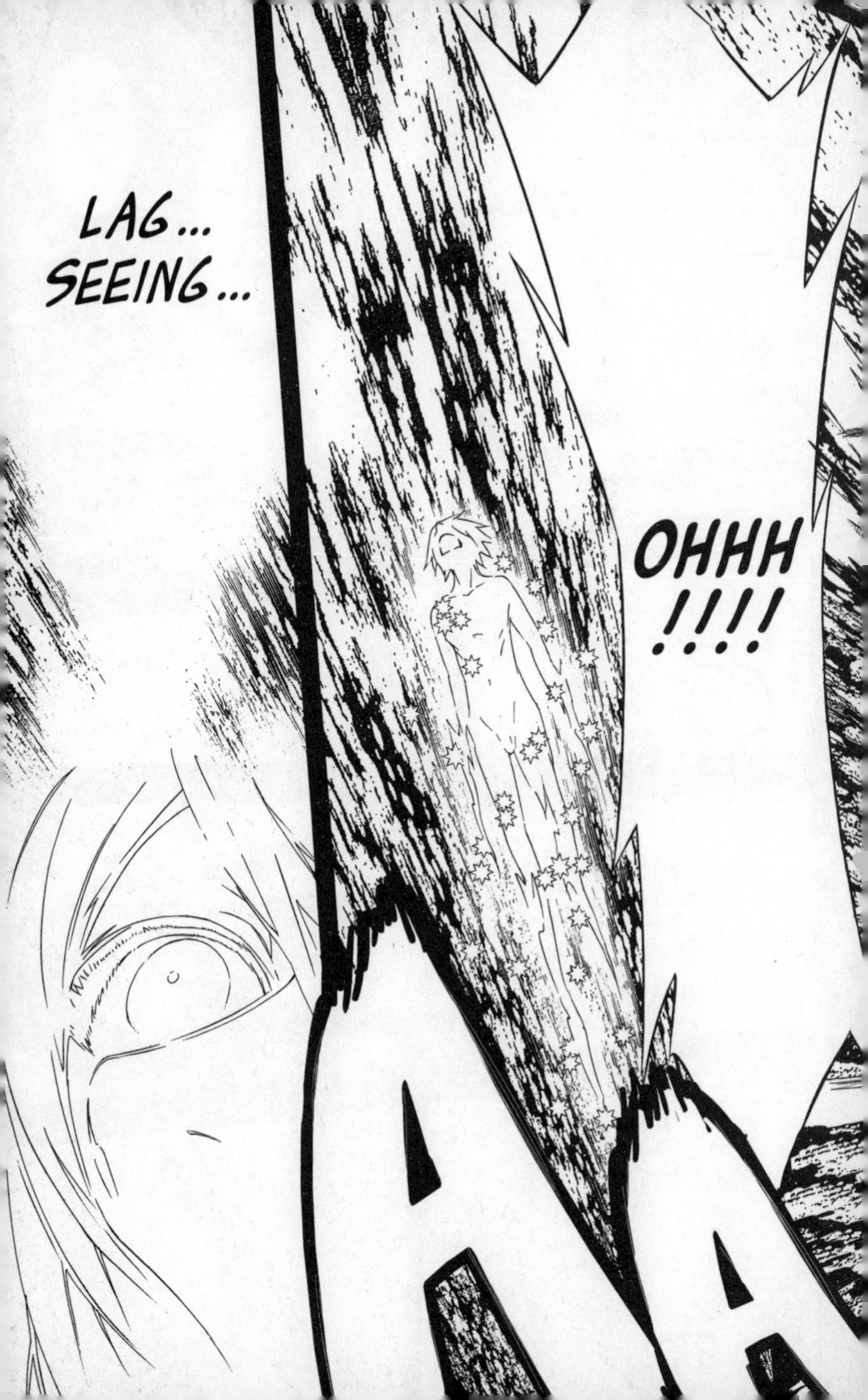
OHHH
!!!!
LAG...
SEEING...

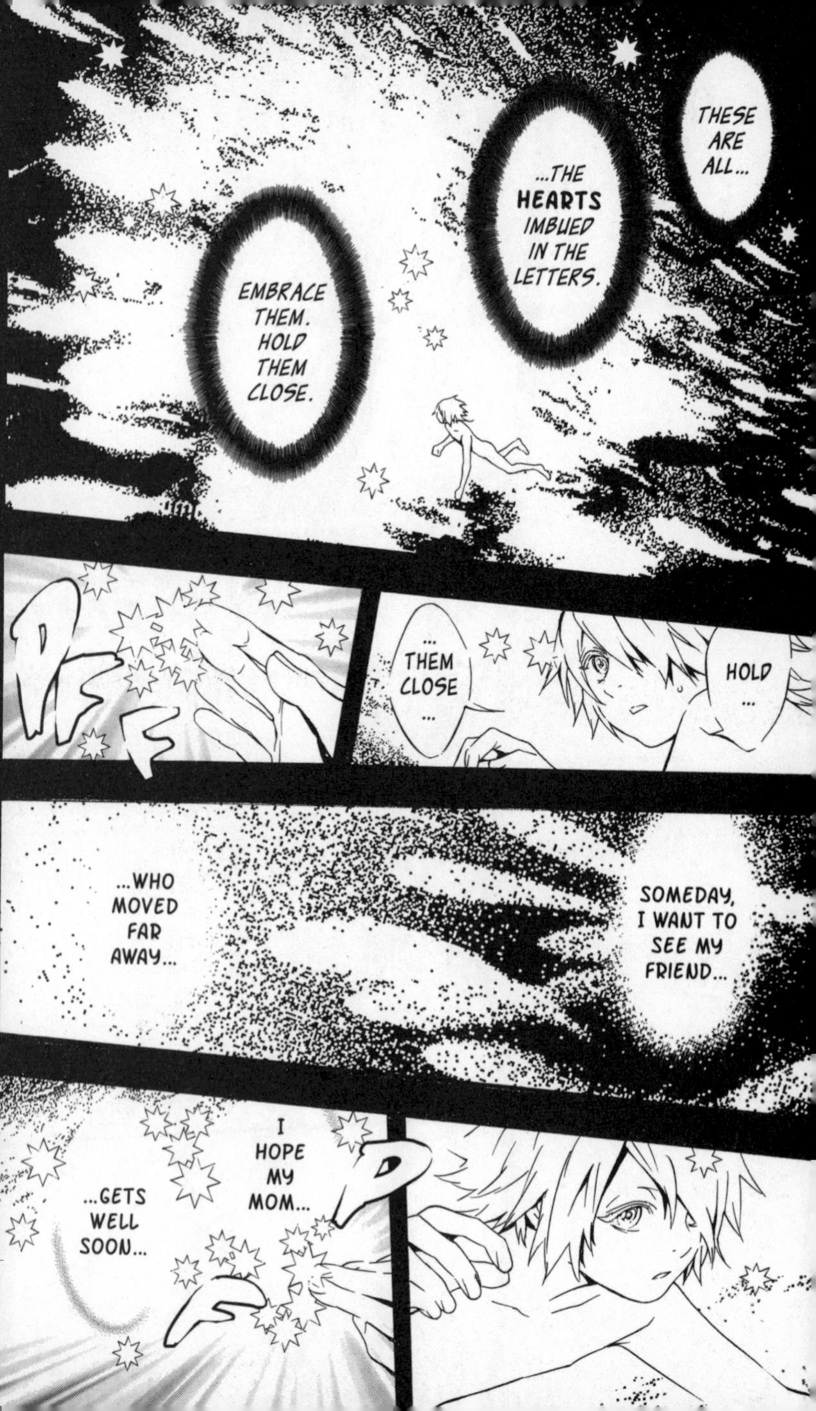
THESE ARE ALL...
...THE HEARTS IMBUED IN THE LETTERS.
EMBRACE THEM. HOLD THEM CLOSE.
HOLD...
...THEM CLOSE...
SOMEDAY, I WANT TO SEE MY FRIEND...
...WHO MOVED FAR AWAY...
I HOPE MY MOM...
...GETS WELL SOON...

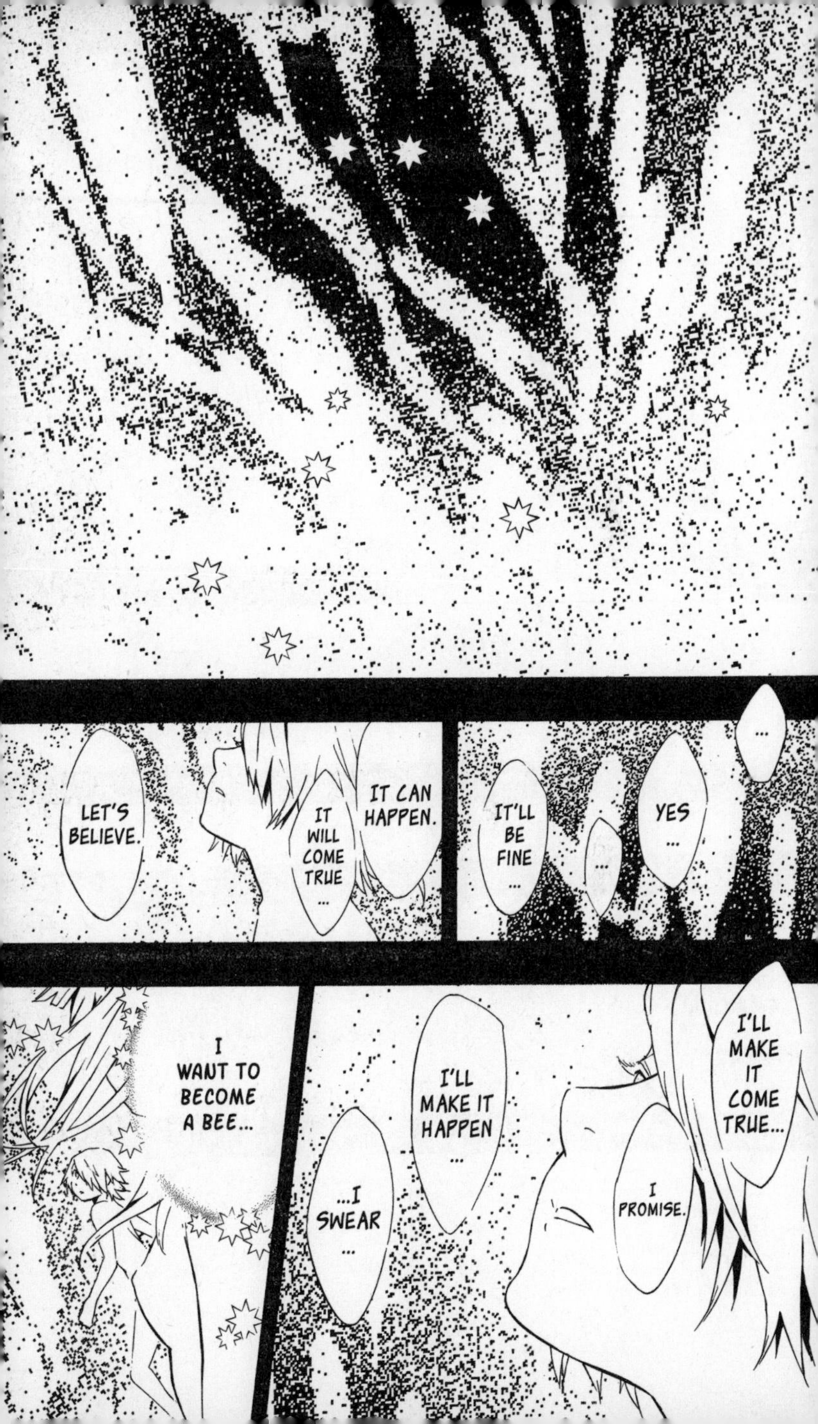
...
YES ...
...
IT'LL BE FINE ...
IT CAN HAPPEN.
IT WILL COME TRUE ...
LET'S BELIEVE.
I'LL MAKE IT COME TRUE...
I PROMISE.
I'LL MAKE IT HAPPEN ...
...I SWEAR ...
I WANT TO BECOME A BEE...

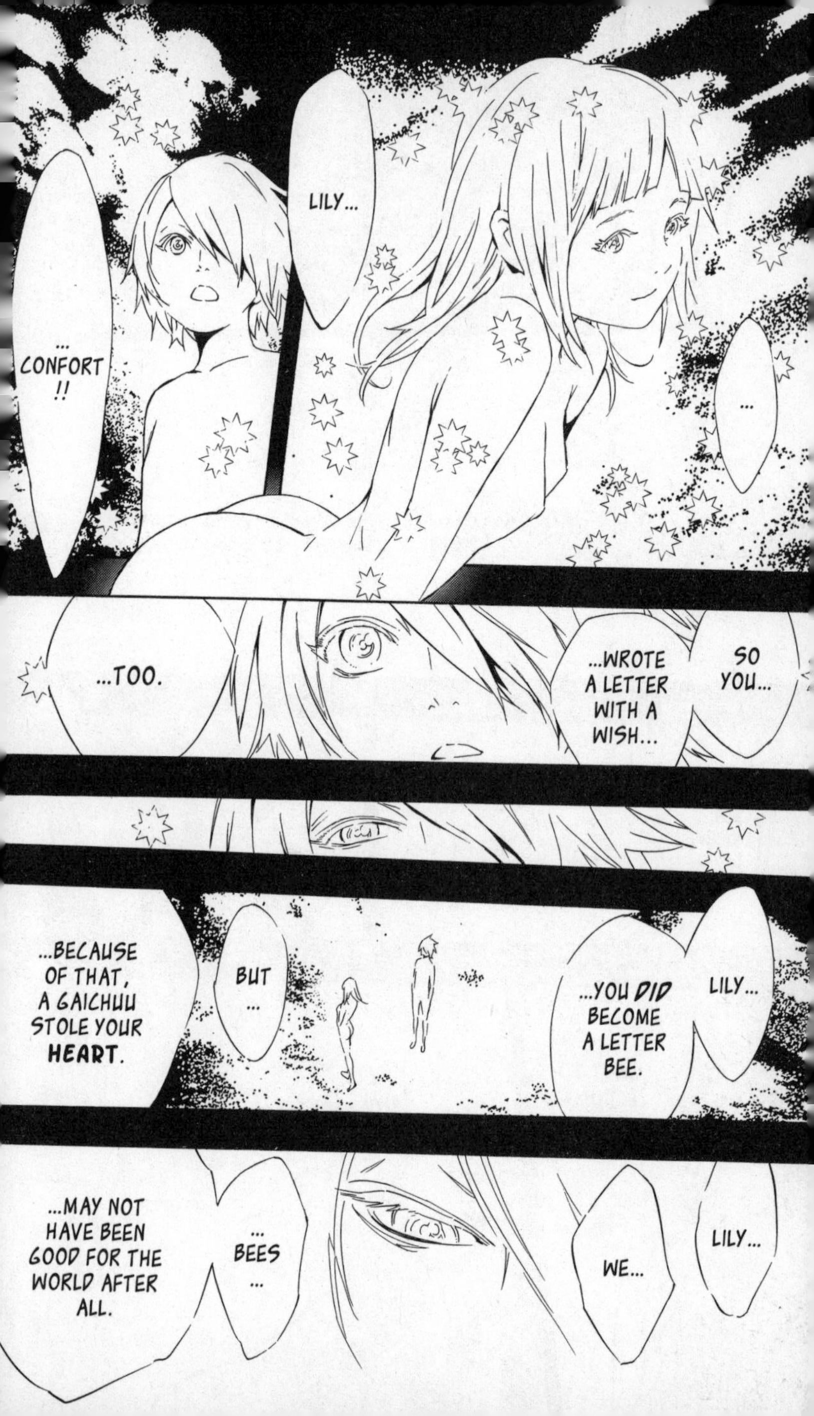
...
LILY...
... CONFORT !!
SO YOU...
...WROTE A LETTER WITH A WISH...
...TOO.
LILY...
...YOU *DID* BECOME A LETTER BEE.
BUT ...
...BECAUSE OF THAT, A GAICHUU STOLE YOUR **HEART**.
LILY...
WE...
... BEES ...
...MAY NOT HAVE BEEN GOOD FOR THE WORLD AFTER ALL.

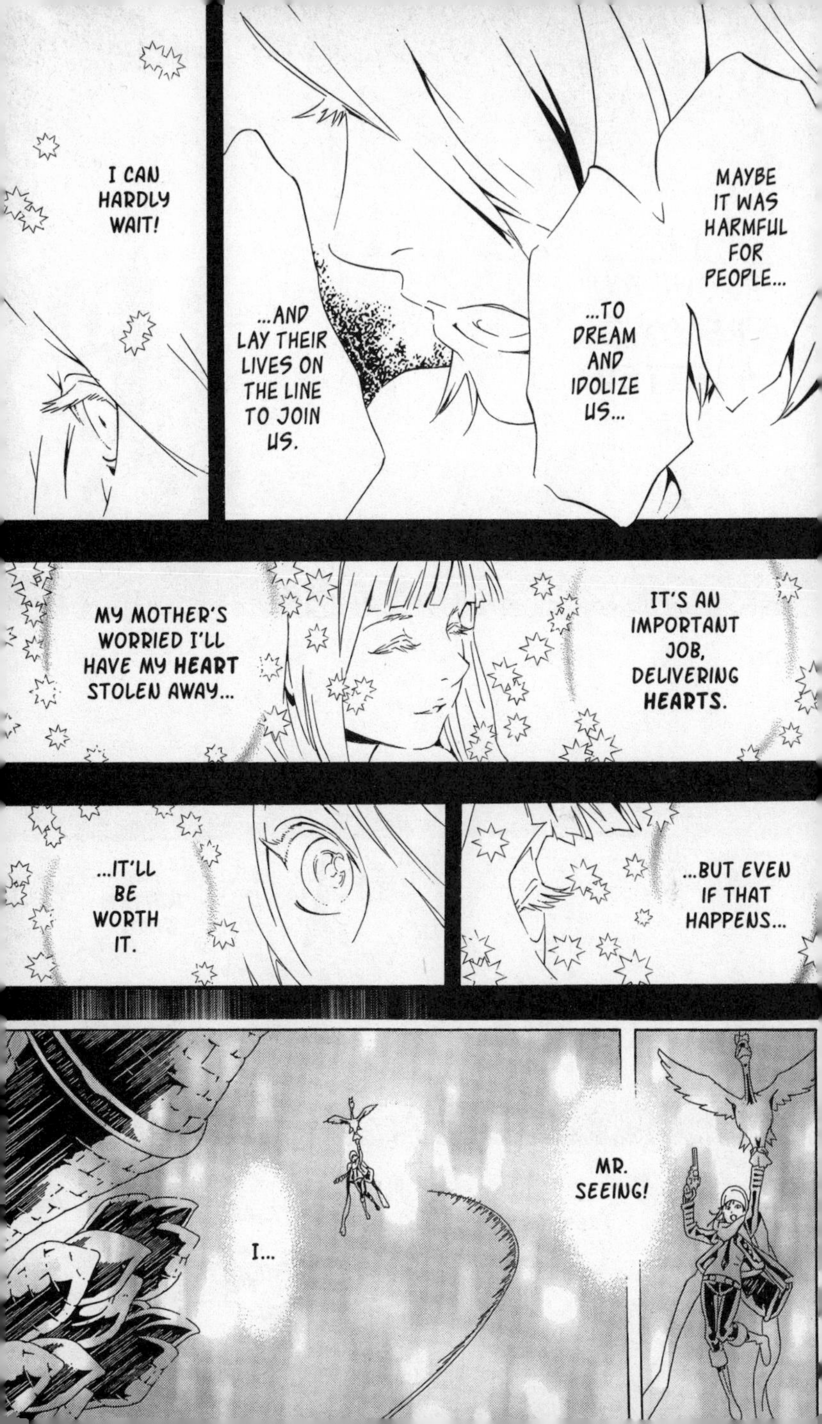
MAYBE IT WAS HARMFUL FOR PEOPLE...
...TO DREAM AND IDOLIZE US...
...AND LAY THEIR LIVES ON THE LINE TO JOIN US.
I CAN HARDLY WAIT!
IT'S AN IMPORTANT JOB, DELIVERING HEARTS.
MY MOTHER'S WORRIED I'LL HAVE MY HEART STOLEN AWAY...
...BUT EVEN IF THAT HAPPENS...
...IT'LL BE WORTH IT.
MR. SEEING!
I...

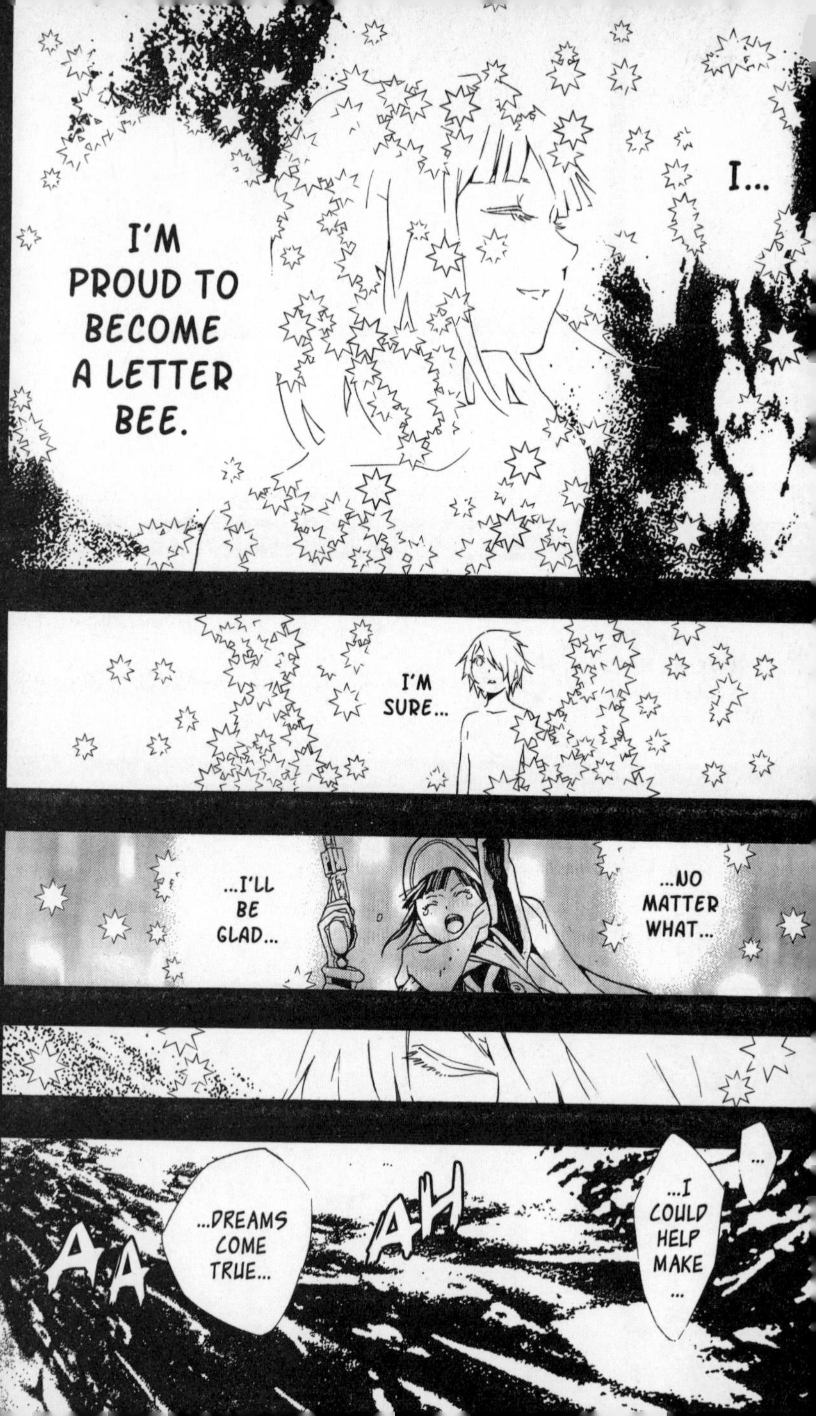
I...
I'M PROUD TO BECOME A LETTER BEE.
I'M SURE...
...NO MATTER WHAT...
...I'LL BE GLAD...
...
...I COULD HELP MAKE ...
AH
...DREAMS COME TRUE...
AA

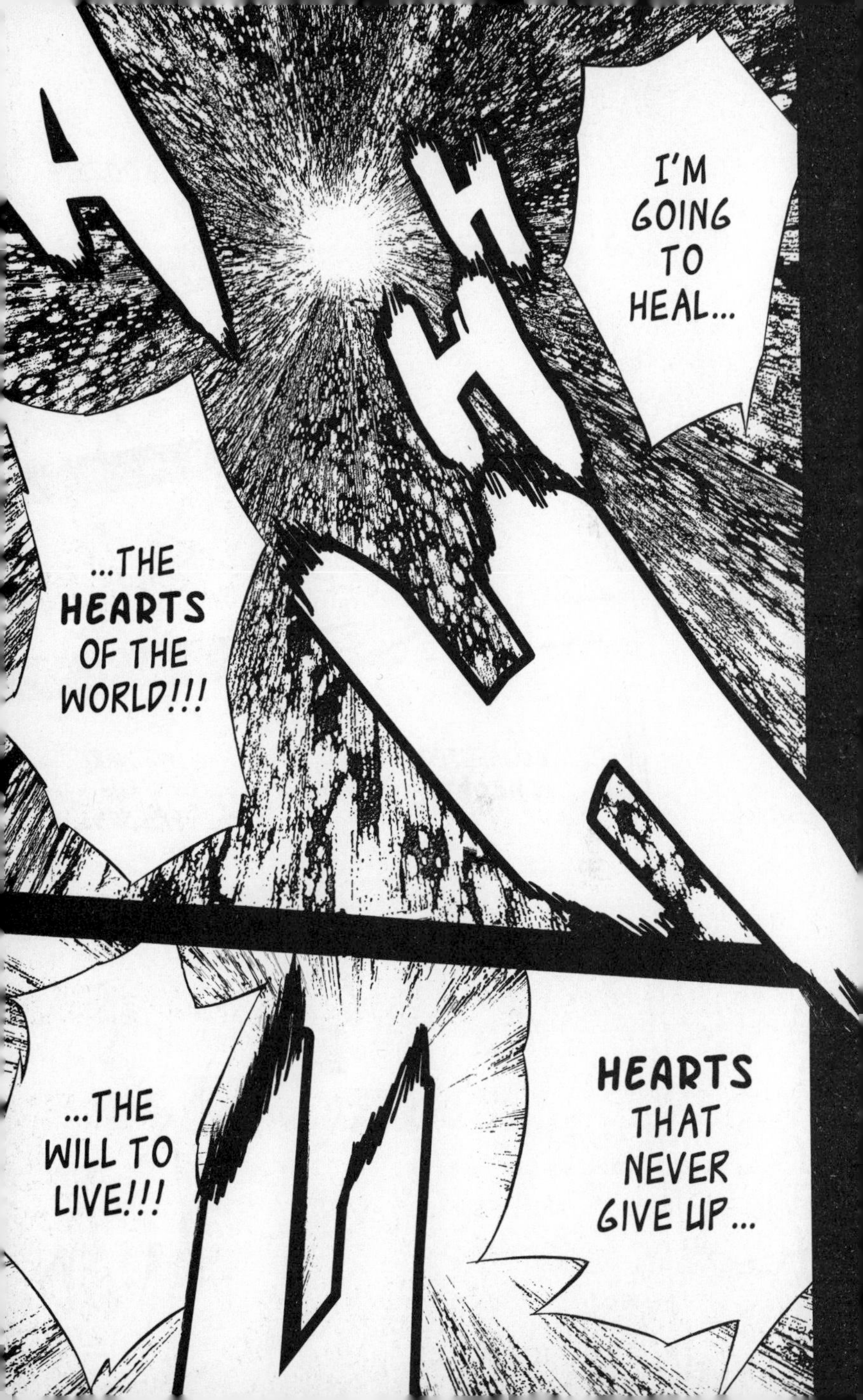
I'M GOING TO HEAL...
...THE **HEARTS** OF THE WORLD!!!
HEARTS THAT NEVER GIVE UP...
...THE WILL TO LIVE!!!

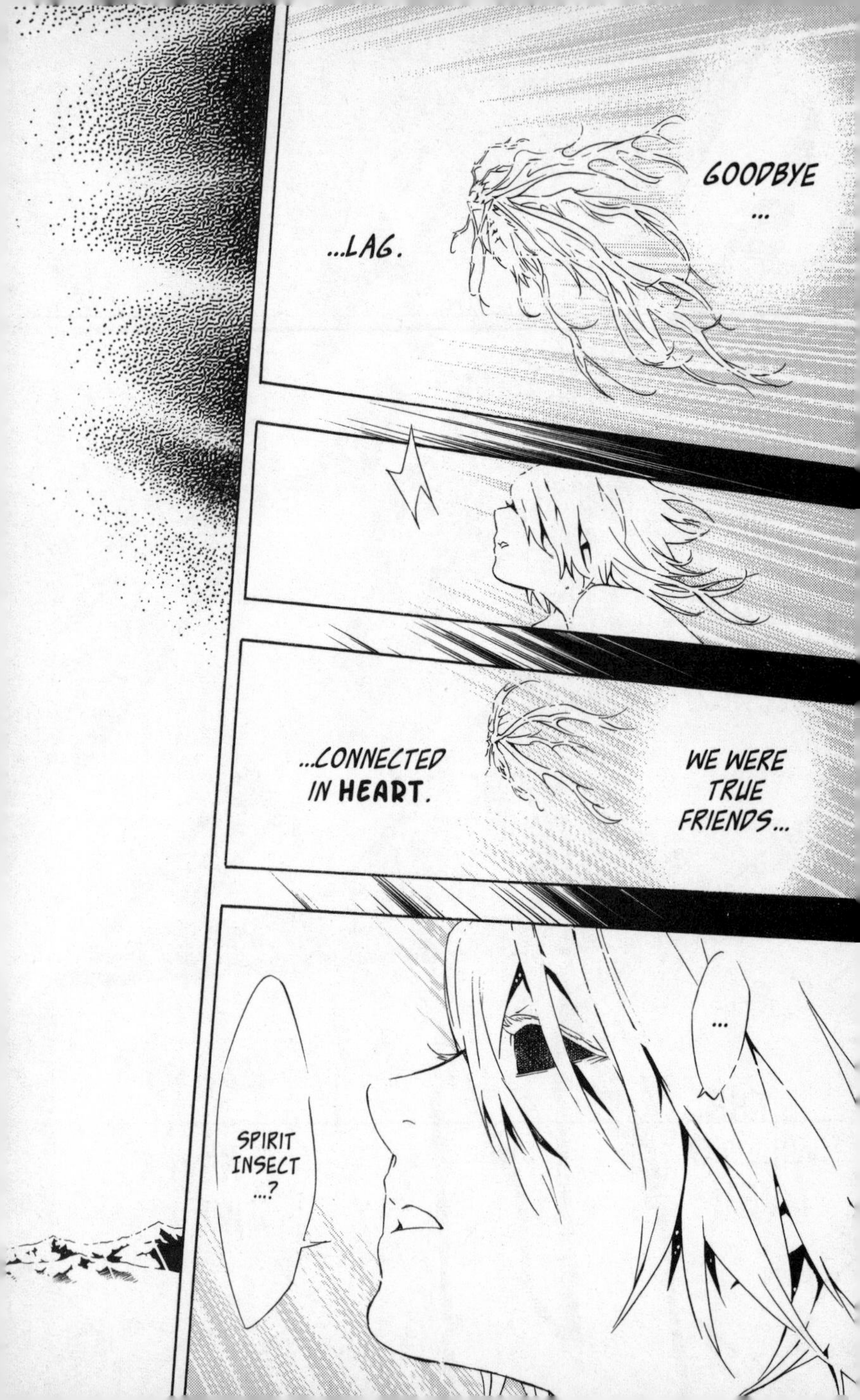
GOODBYE ...
...LAG.
WE WERE TRUE FRIENDS...
...CONNECTED IN HEART.
...
SPIRIT INSECT ...?

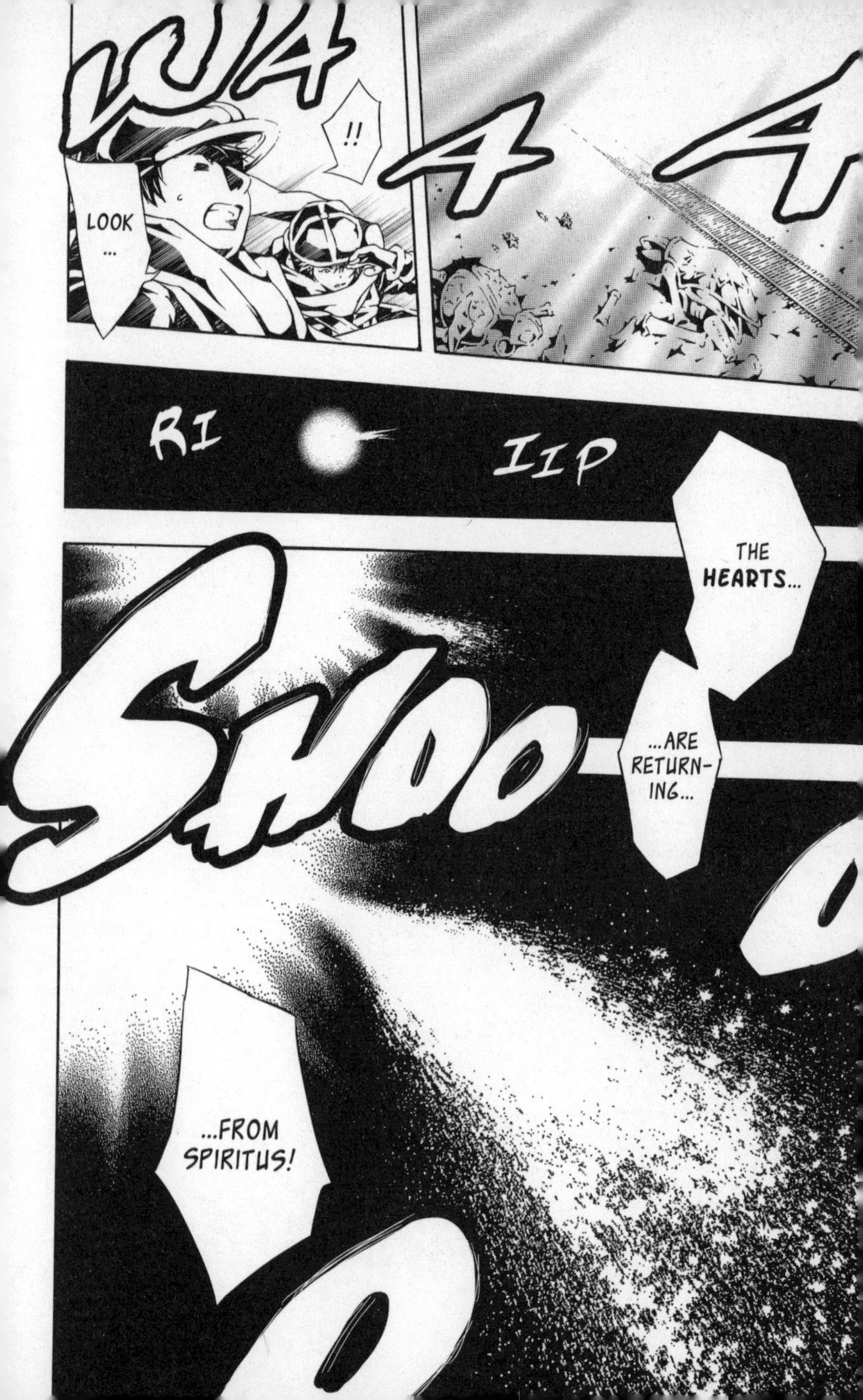
WAAA
!!
LOOK...
RIIIP
THE HEARTS...
...ARE RETURNING...
...FROM SPIRITUS!
SHOOOO

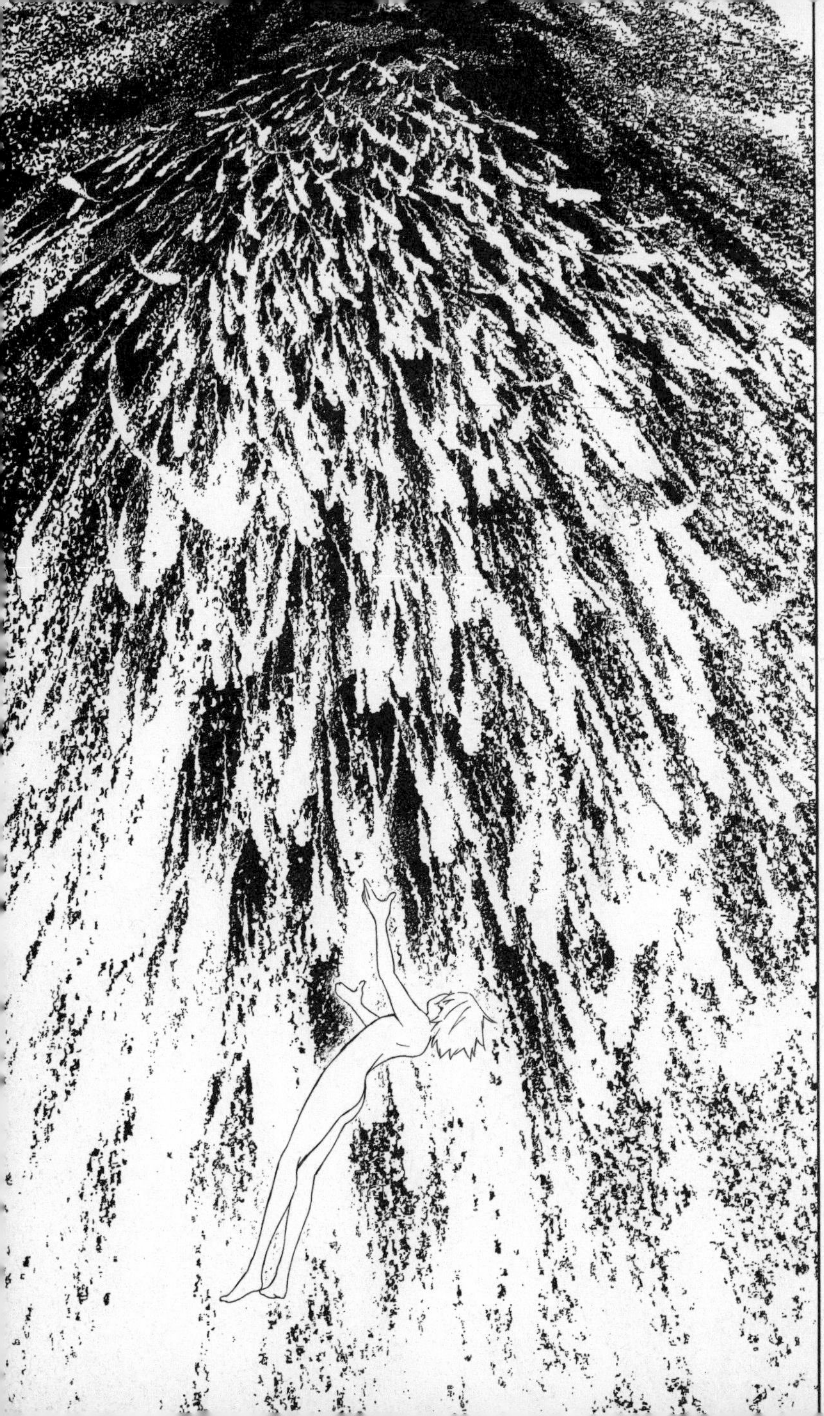

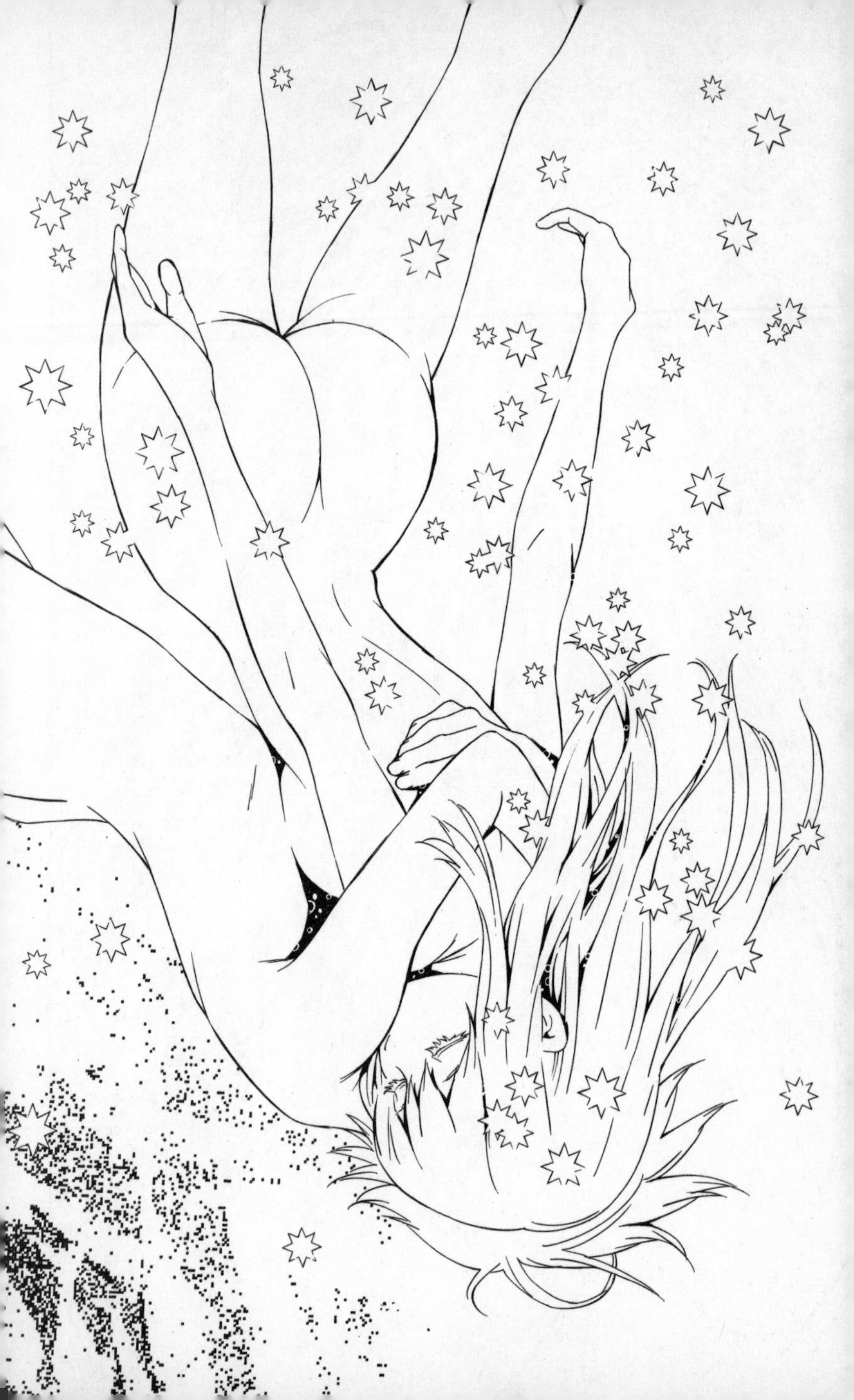

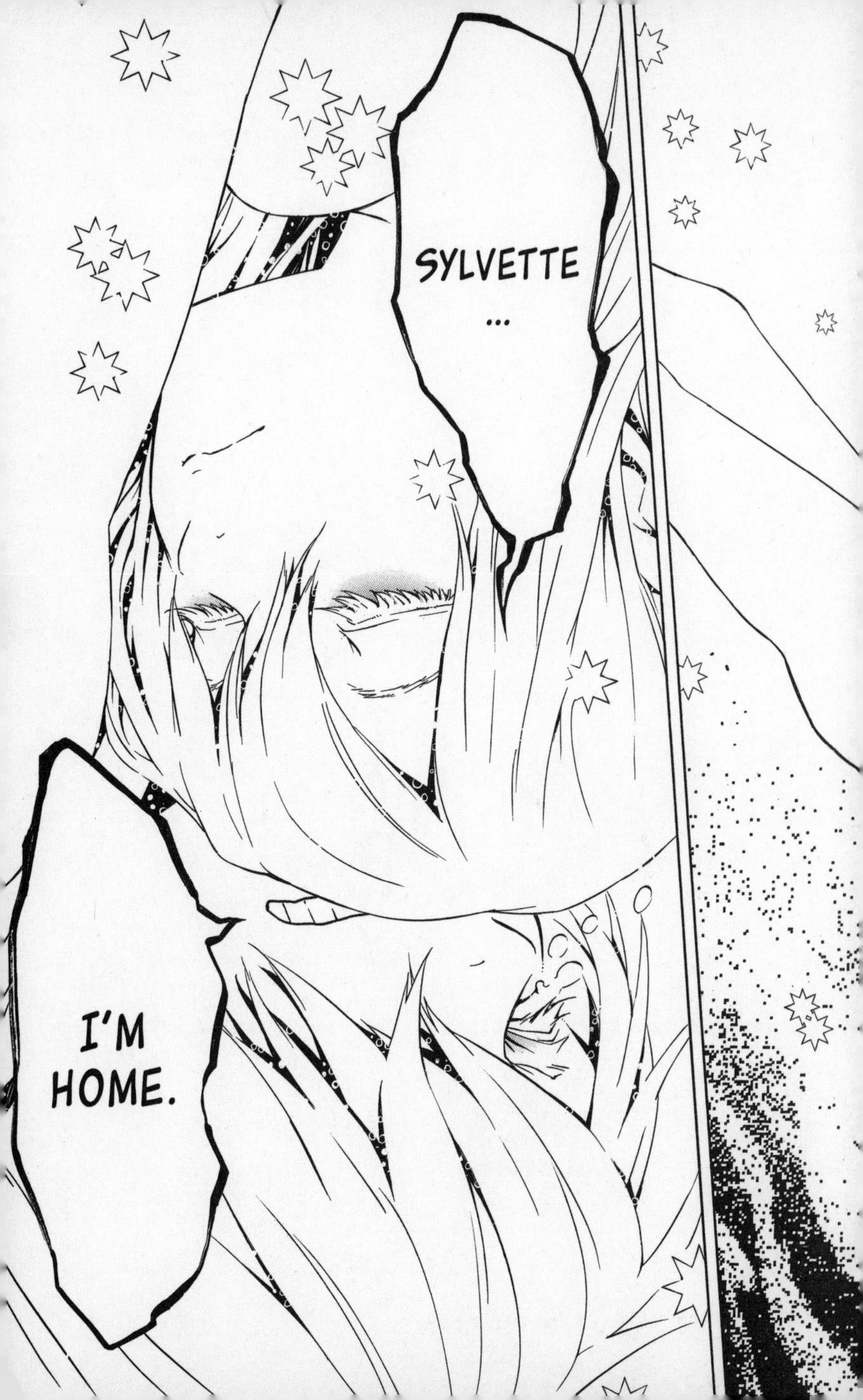
SYLVETTE ...
I'M HOME.

Rough sketch for the volume 18 title page.

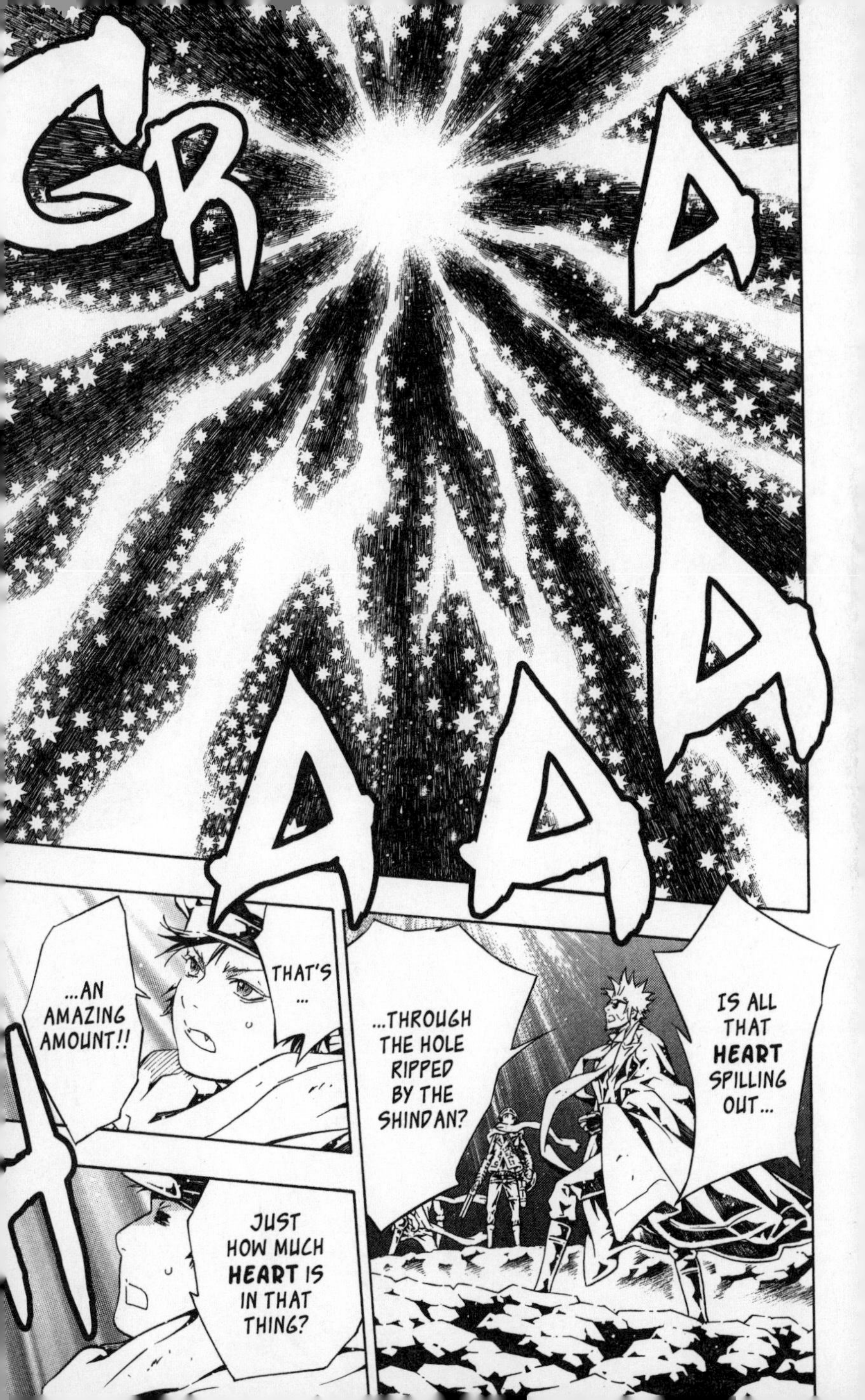
GRAAAA
IS ALL THAT **HEART** SPILLING OUT...
...THROUGH THE HOLE RIPPED BY THE SHINDAN?
THAT'S...
...AN AMAZING AMOUNT!!
JUST HOW MUCH **HEART** IS IN THAT THING?

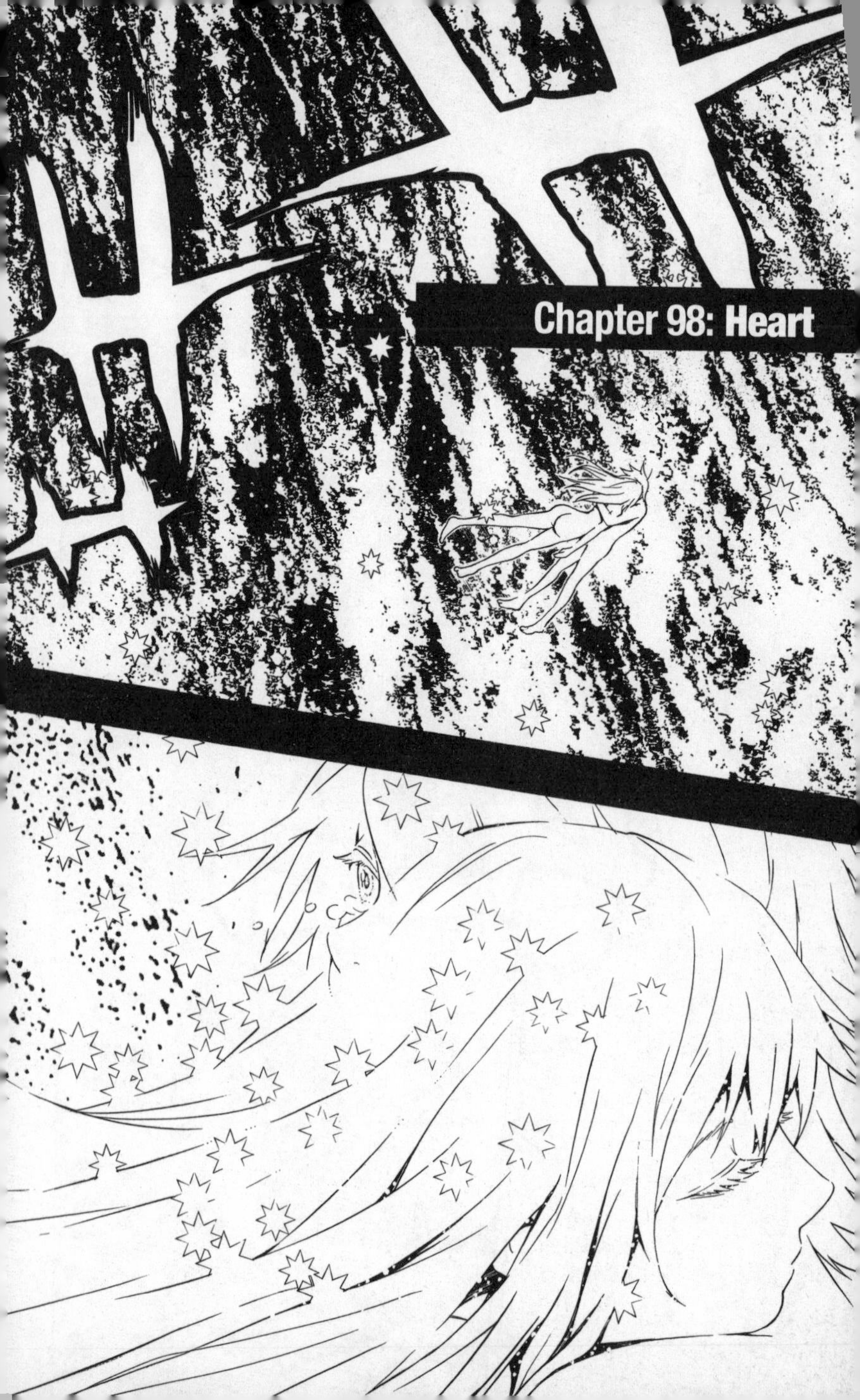
Chapter 98: Heart

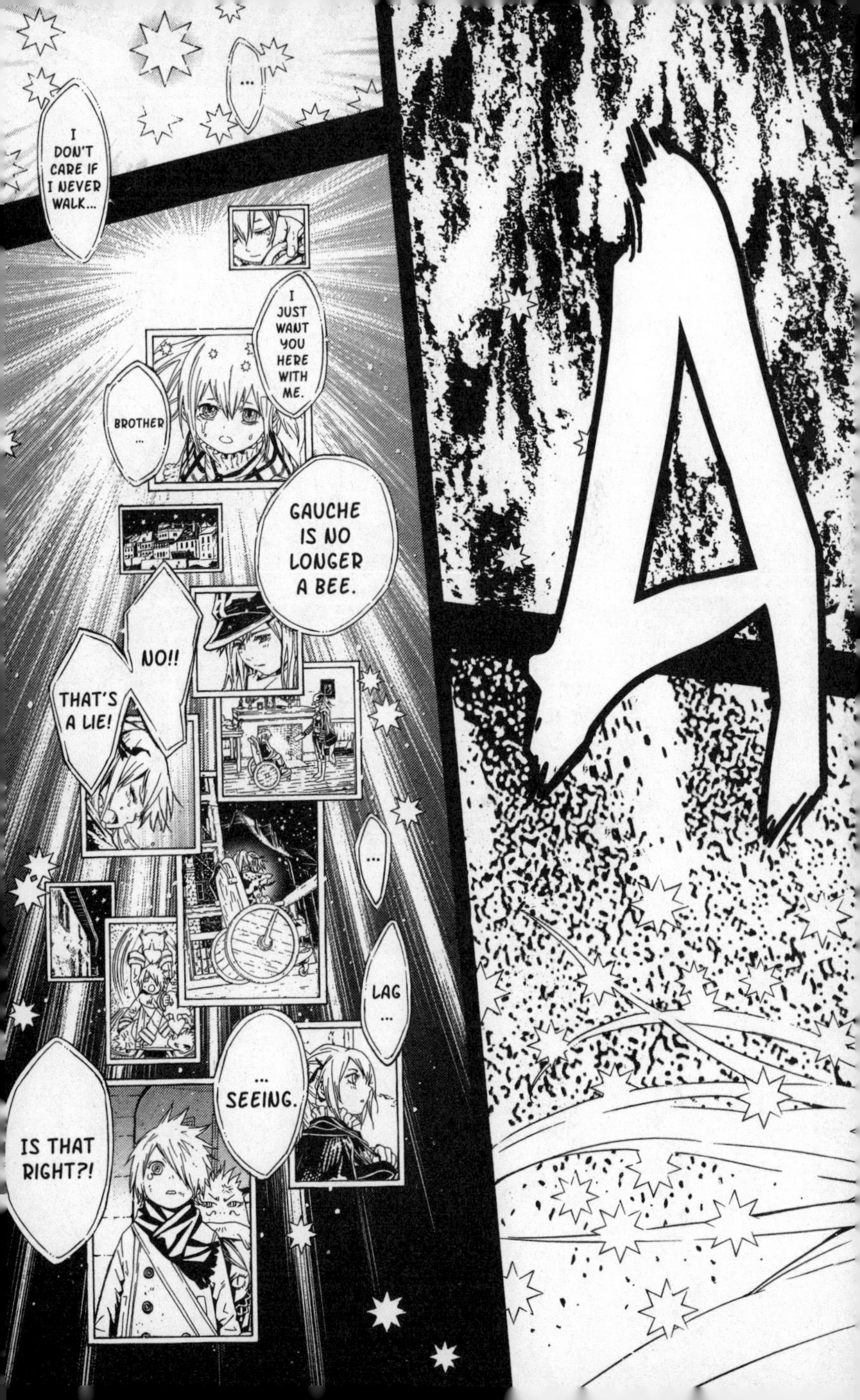
...
I DON'T CARE IF I NEVER WALK...
I JUST WANT YOU HERE WITH ME.
BROTHER...
GAUCHE IS NO LONGER A BEE.
NO!! THAT'S A LIE!
...
LAG...
... SEEING.
IS THAT RIGHT?!

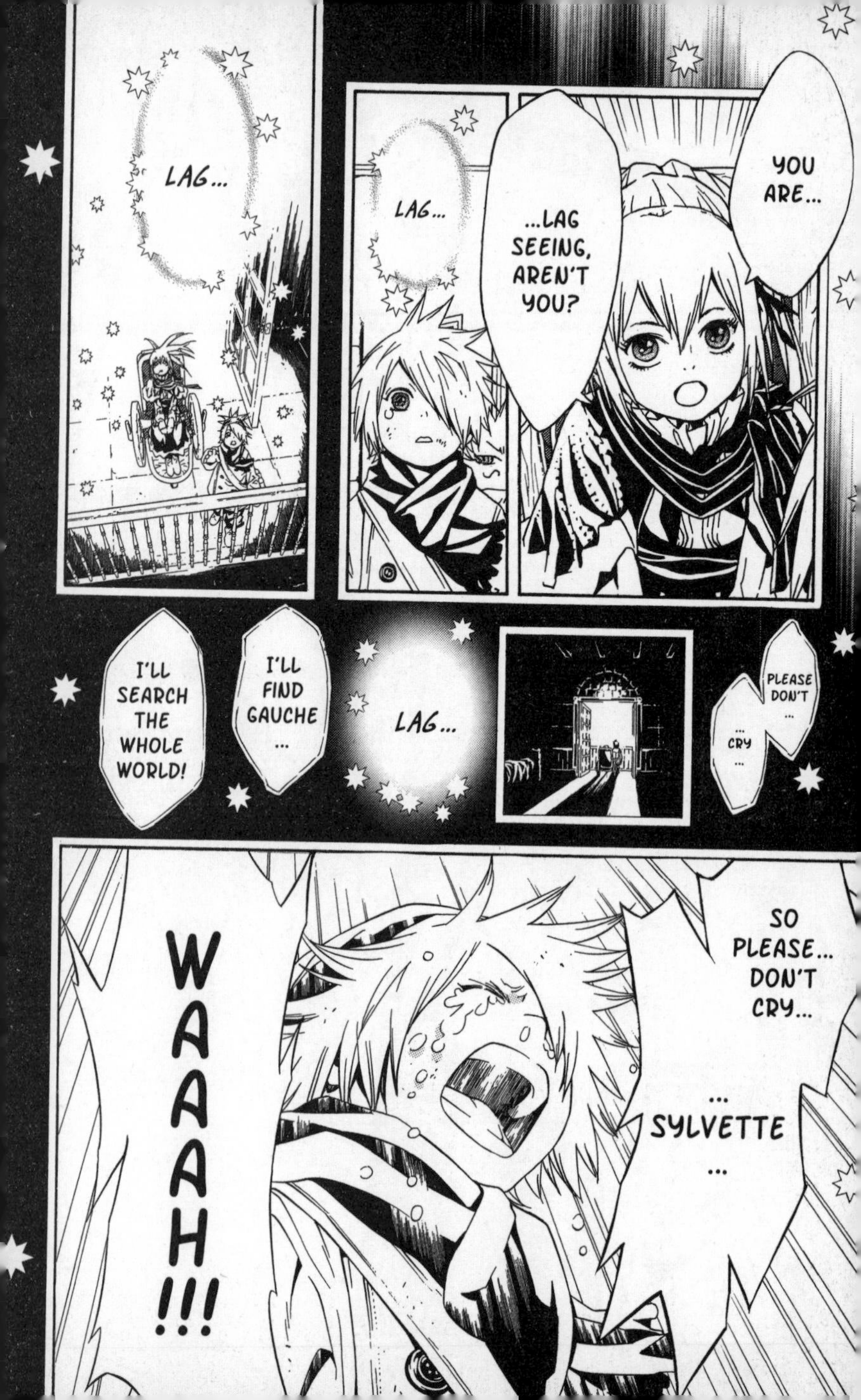
YOU ARE...
...LAG SEEING, AREN'T YOU?
LAG...
LAG...
PLEASE DON'T ... ... CRY ...
LAG...
I'LL FIND GAUCHE ...
I'LL SEARCH THE WHOLE WORLD!
SO PLEASE... DON'T CRY...
... SYLVETTE ...
WAAAAH!!!

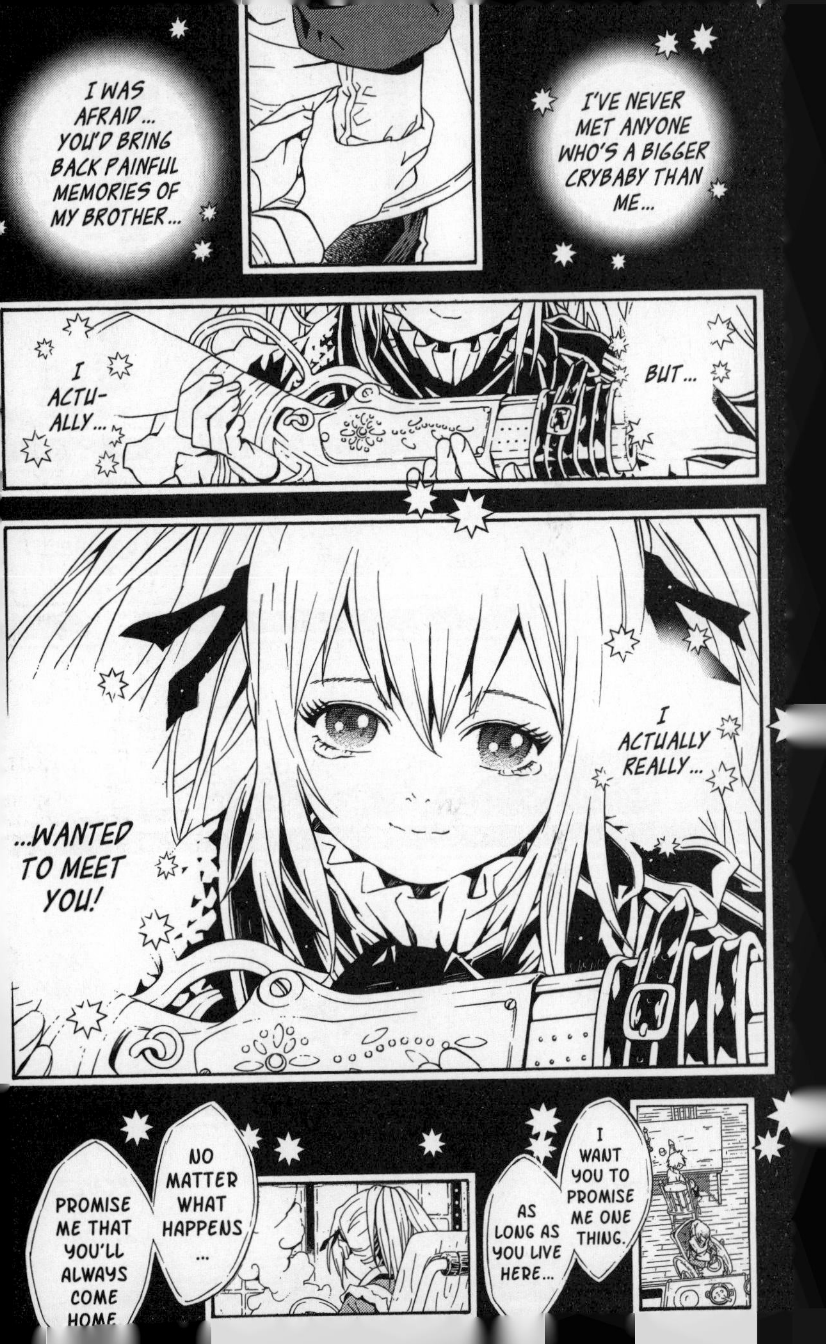
I'VE NEVER MET ANYONE WHO'S A BIGGER CRYBABY THAN ME...
I WAS AFRAID... YOU'D BRING BACK PAINFUL MEMORIES OF MY BROTHER...
BUT...
I ACTU-ALLY...
I ACTUALLY REALLY...
...WANTED TO MEET YOU!
I WANT YOU TO PROMISE ME ONE THING.
AS LONG AS YOU LIVE HERE...
NO MATTER WHAT HAPPENS...
PROMISE ME THAT YOU'LL ALWAYS COME HOME

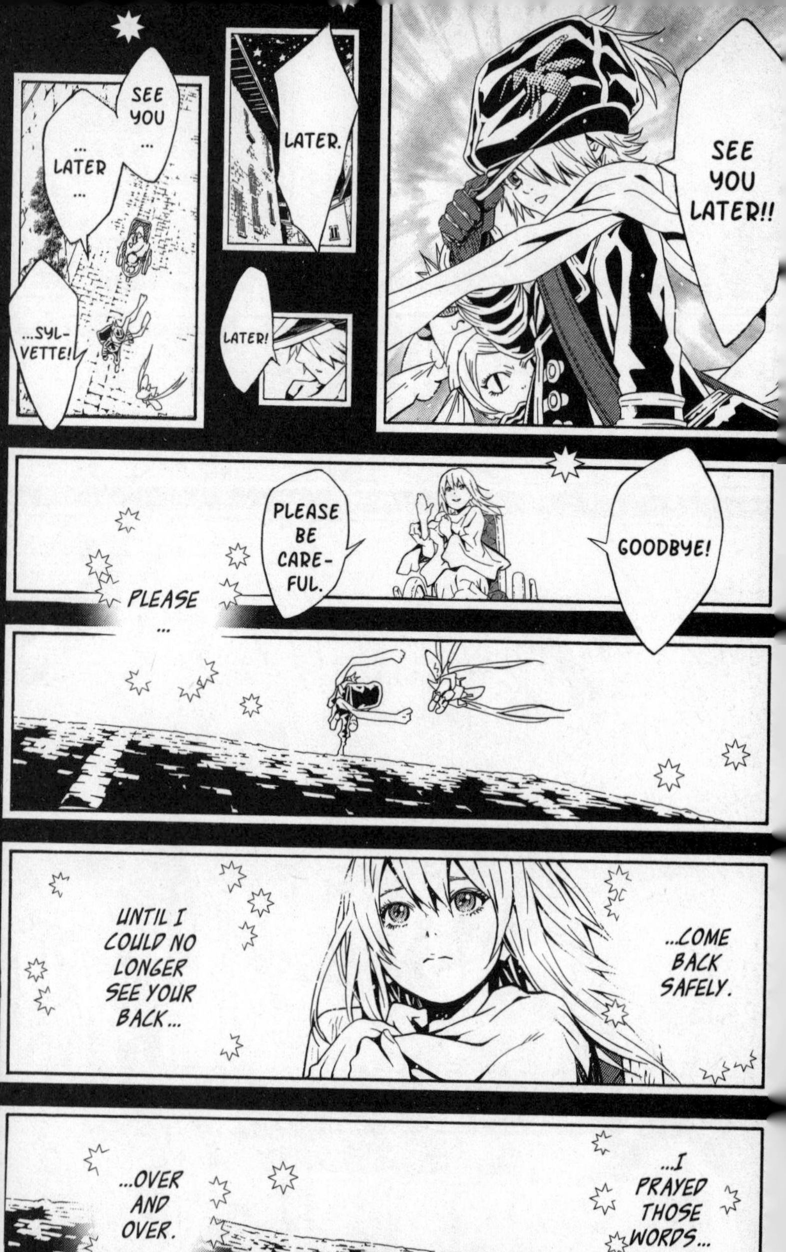
SEE YOU LATER!!
LATER.
LATER!
SEE YOU ...
... LATER ...
...SYL-VETTE!
GOODBYE!
PLEASE BE CARE-FUL.
PLEASE ...
...COME BACK SAFELY.
UNTIL I COULD NO LONGER SEE YOUR BACK...
...I PRAYED THOSE WORDS...
...OVER AND OVER.

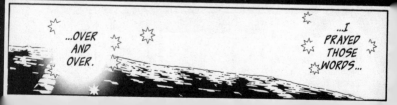

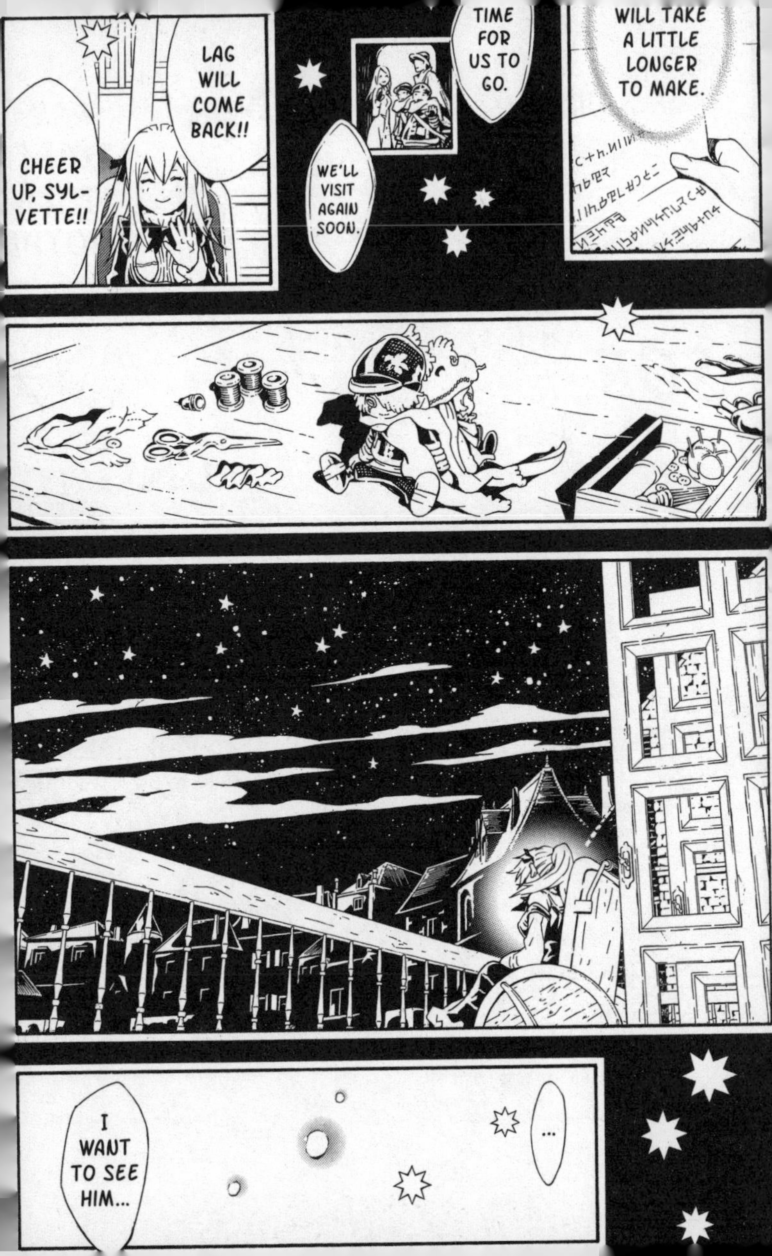
WILL TAKE A LITTLE LONGER TO MAKE.
TIME FOR US TO GO.
WE'LL VISIT AGAIN SOON.
LAG WILL COME BACK!!
CHEER UP, SYL-VETTE!!
...
I WANT TO SEE HIM...

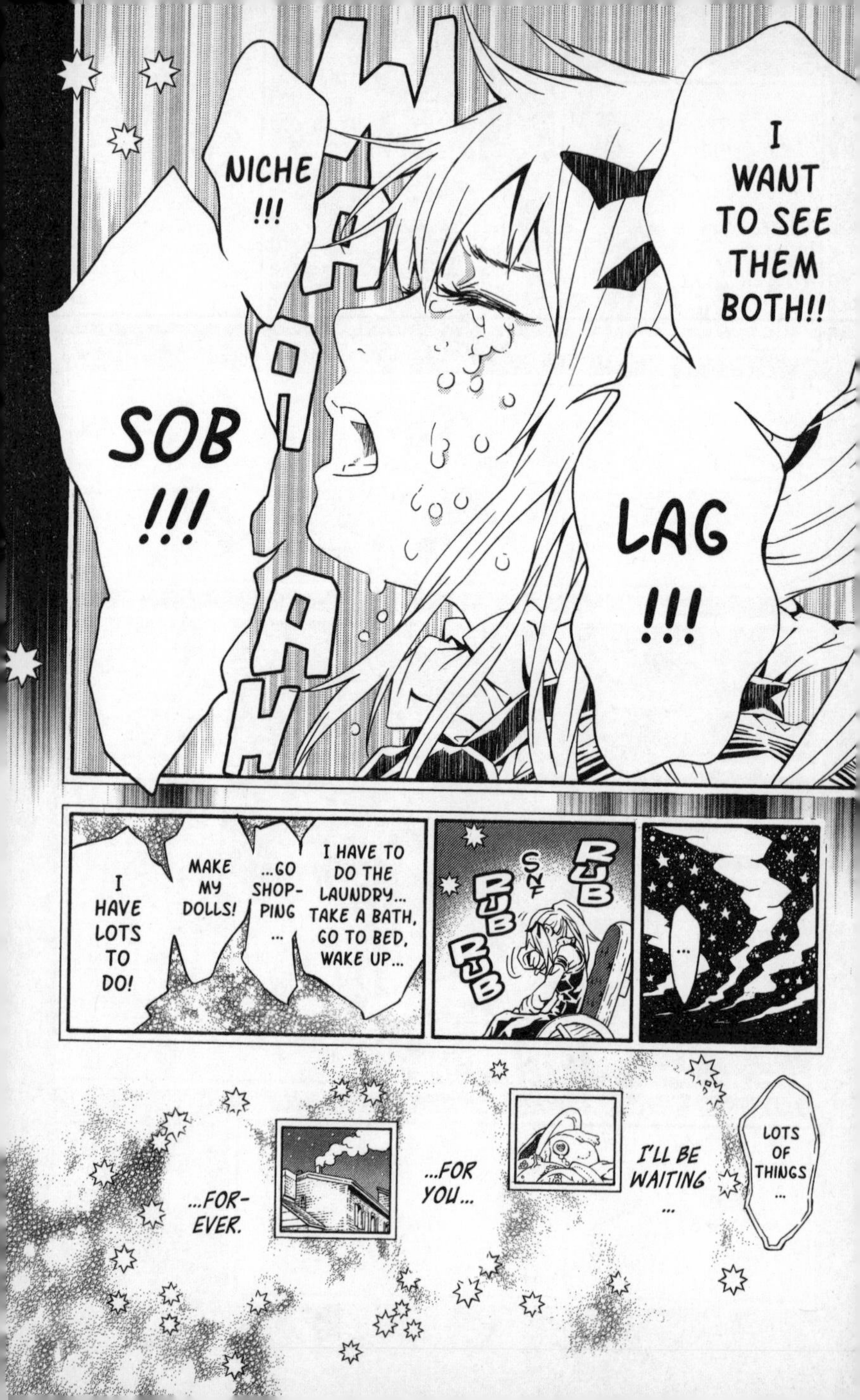
I WANT TO SEE THEM BOTH!!
NICHE!!!
LAG!!!
SOB!!!
...
RUB
RUB
SNF
RUB
RUB
I HAVE TO DO THE LAUNDRY... TAKE A BATH, GO TO BED, WAKE UP...
...GO SHOPPING...
MAKE MY DOLLS!
I HAVE LOTS TO DO!
LOTS OF THINGS...
I'LL BE WAITING...
...FOR YOU...
...FOREVER.

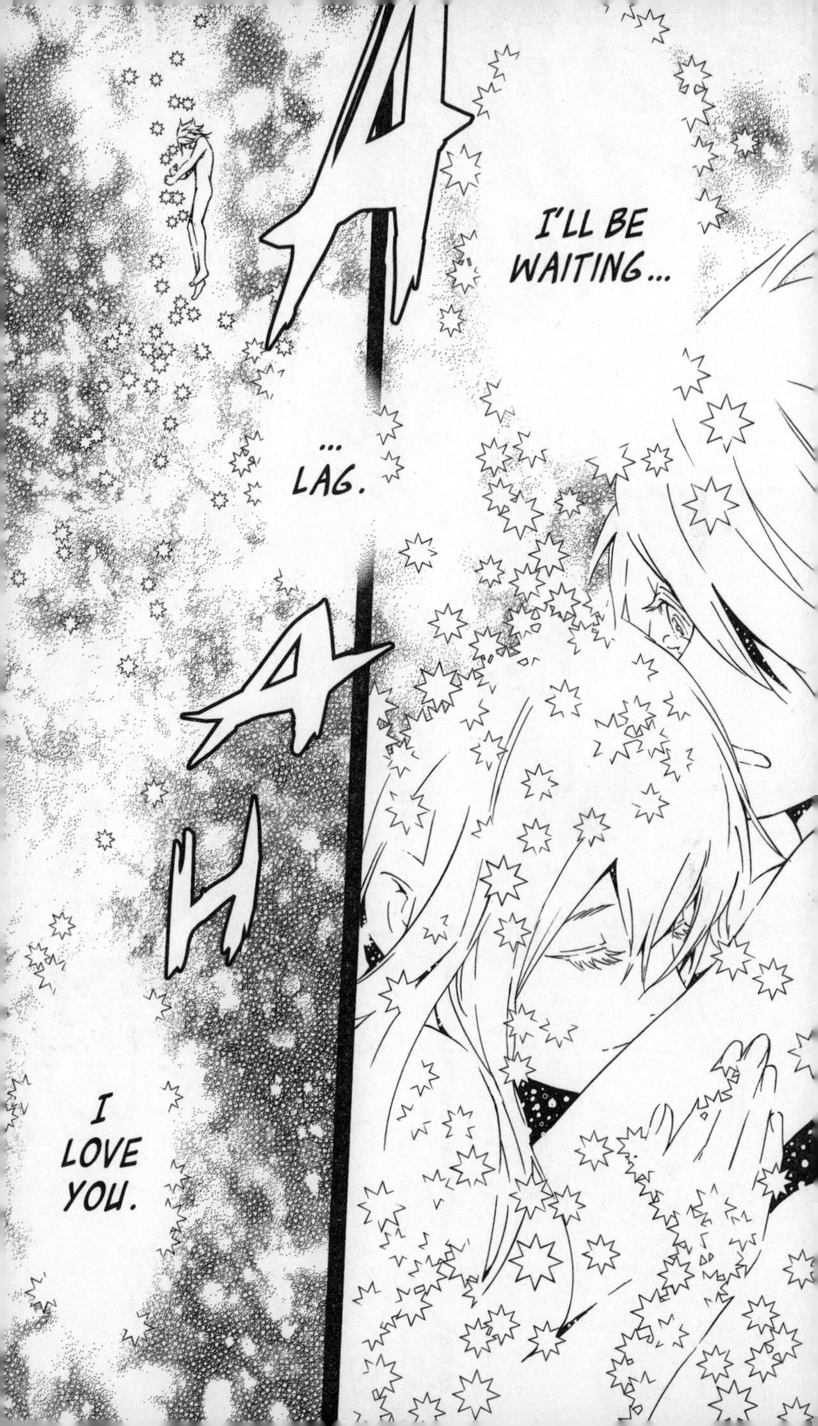
I'LL BE WAITING...
...LAG.
AAH
I LOVE YOU.

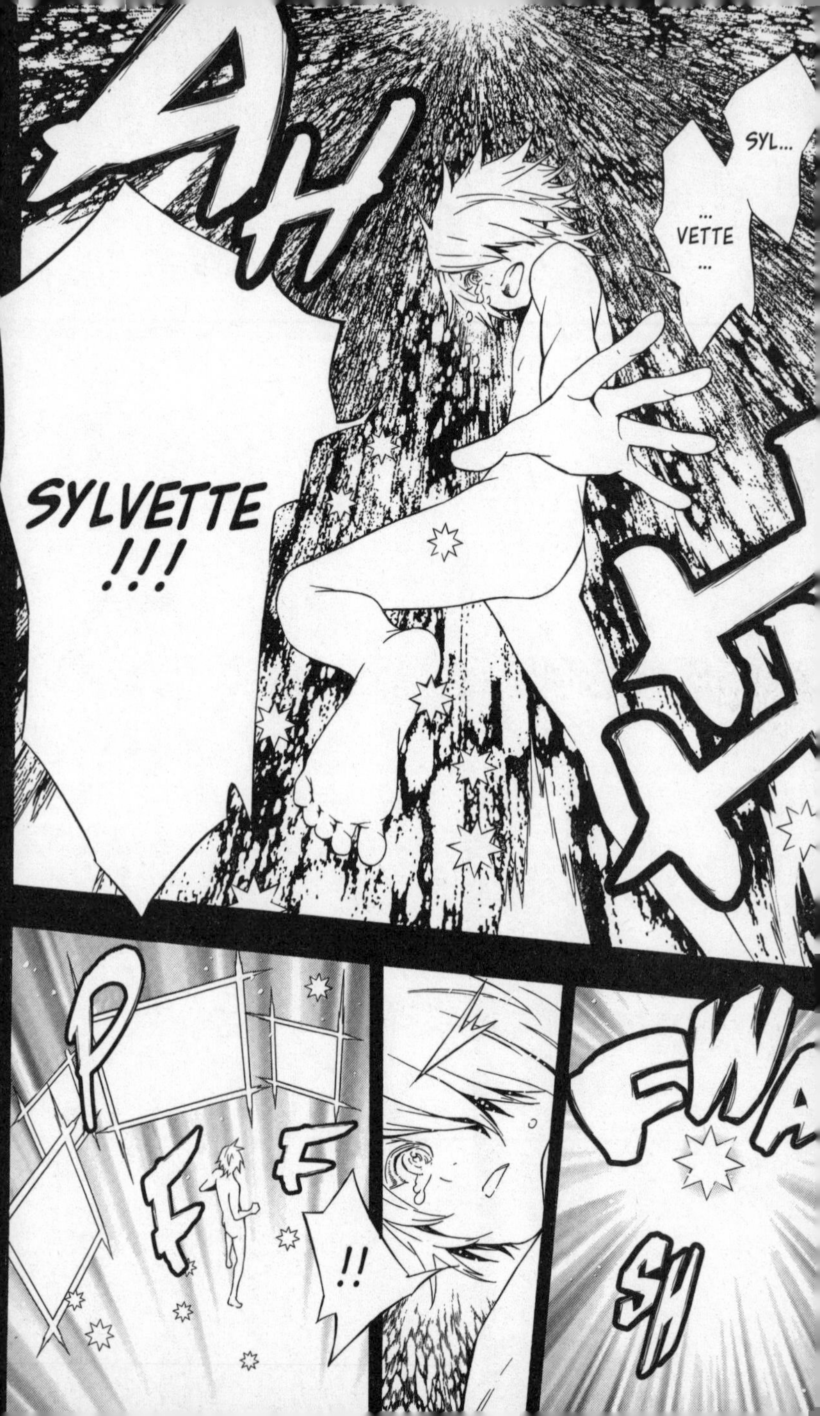
SYL...
... VETTE ...
AH
SYLVETTE !!!
FWA
SH
!!
P
F
F

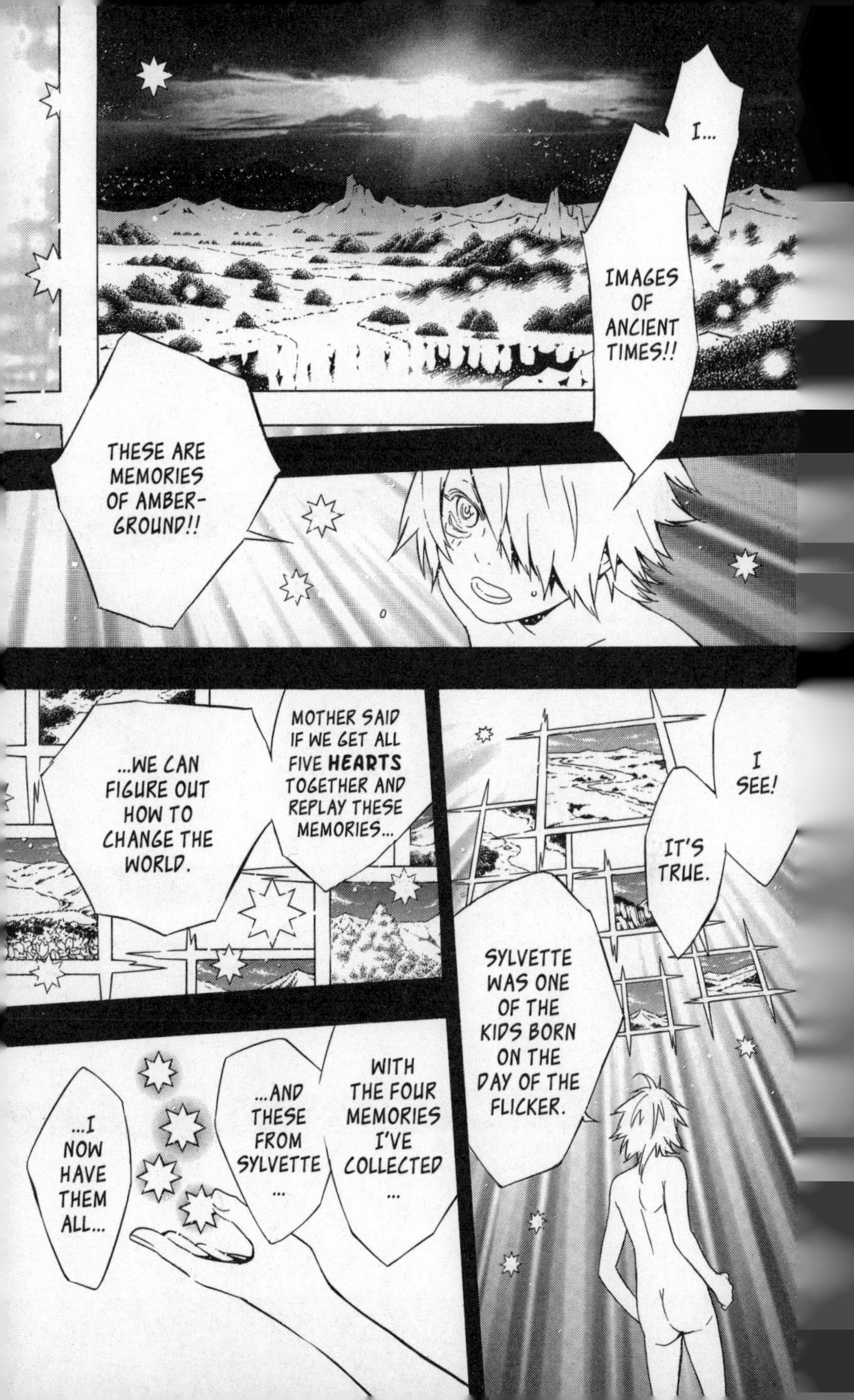
I...
IMAGES OF ANCIENT TIMES!!
THESE ARE MEMORIES OF AMBER-GROUND!!
I SEE!
IT'S TRUE.
SYLVETTE WAS ONE OF THE KIDS BORN ON THE DAY OF THE FLICKER.
MOTHER SAID IF WE GET ALL FIVE **HEARTS** TOGETHER AND REPLAY THESE MEMORIES...
...WE CAN FIGURE OUT HOW TO CHANGE THE WORLD.
WITH THE FOUR MEMORIES I'VE COLLECTED...
...AND THESE FROM SYLVETTE...
...I NOW HAVE THEM ALL...

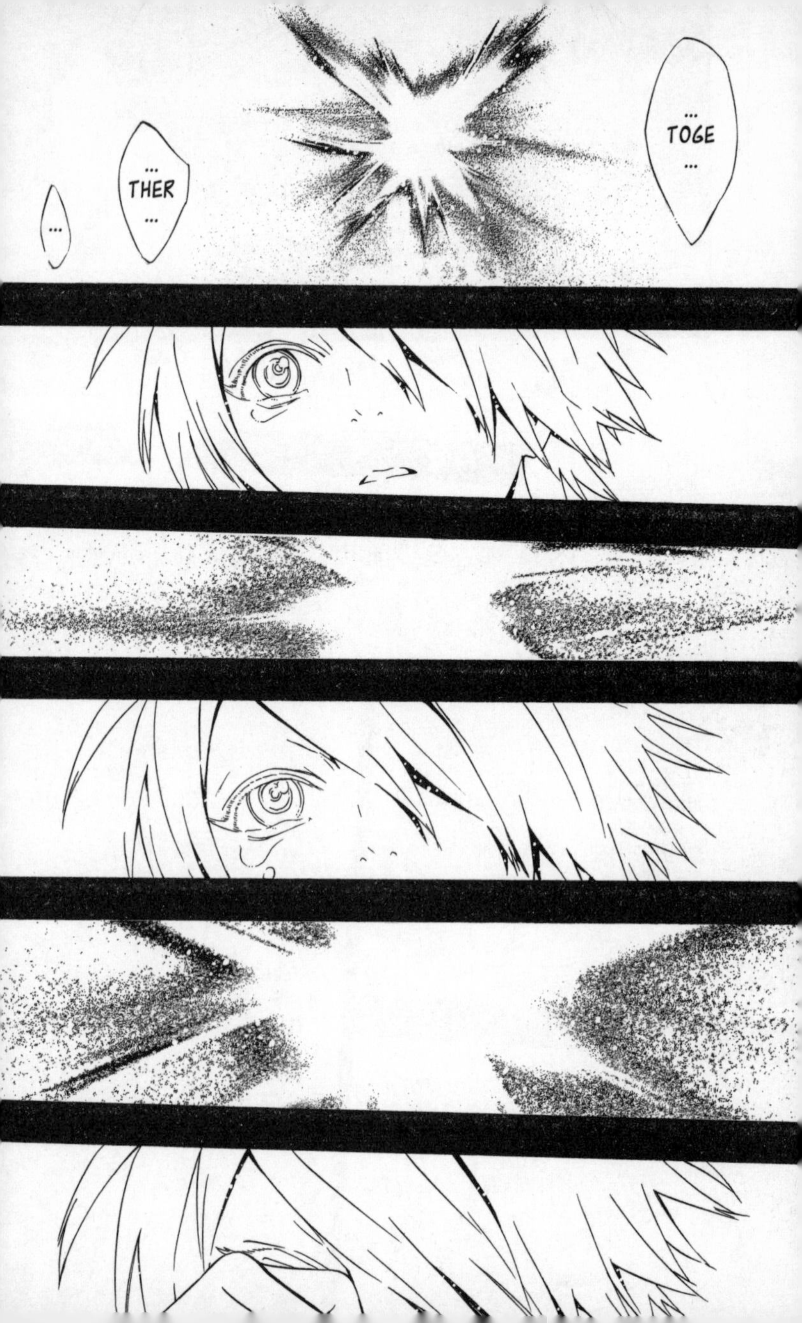
...TOGE...
...THER...
...

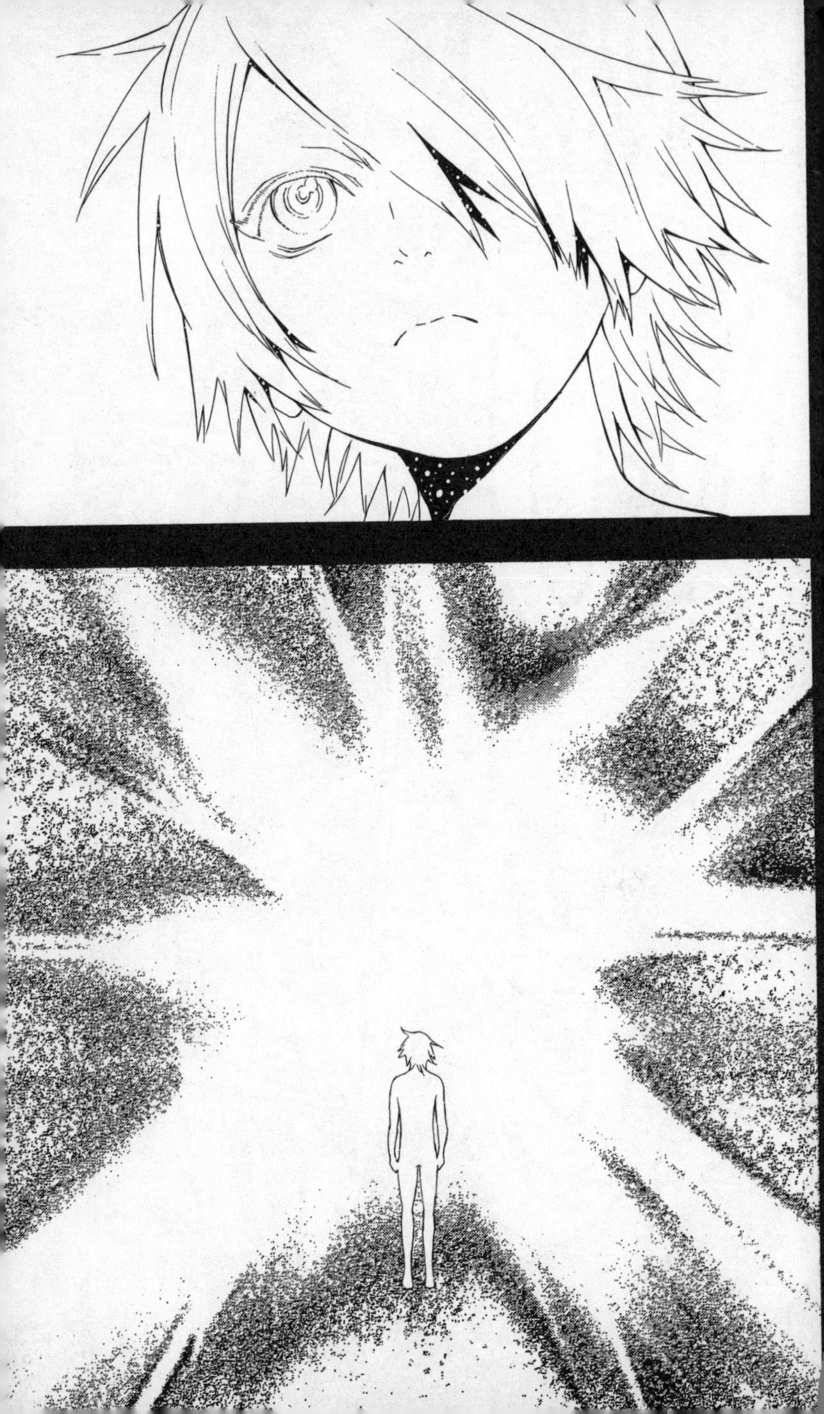

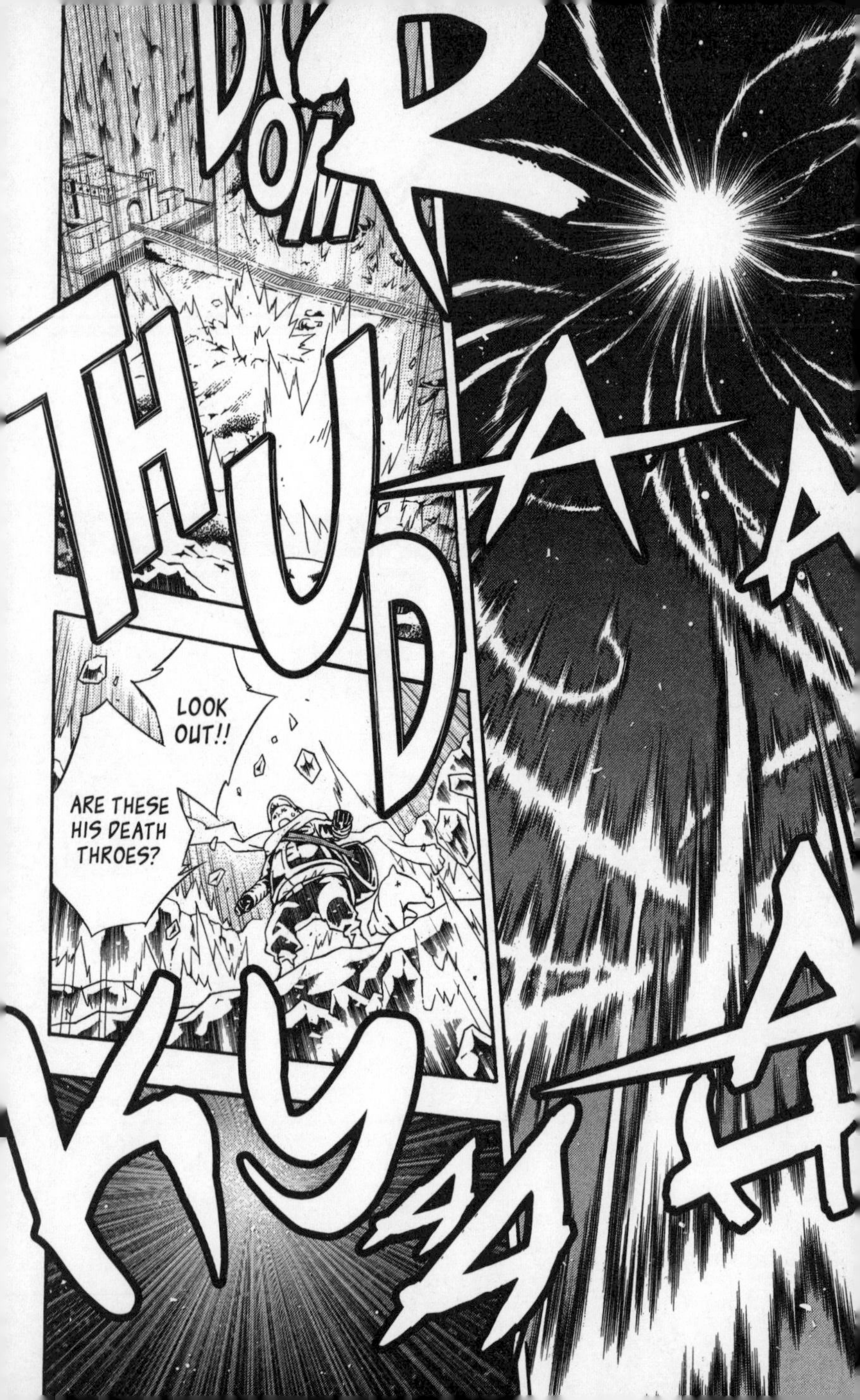
THUD
LOOK OUT!!
ARE THESE HIS DEATH THROES?

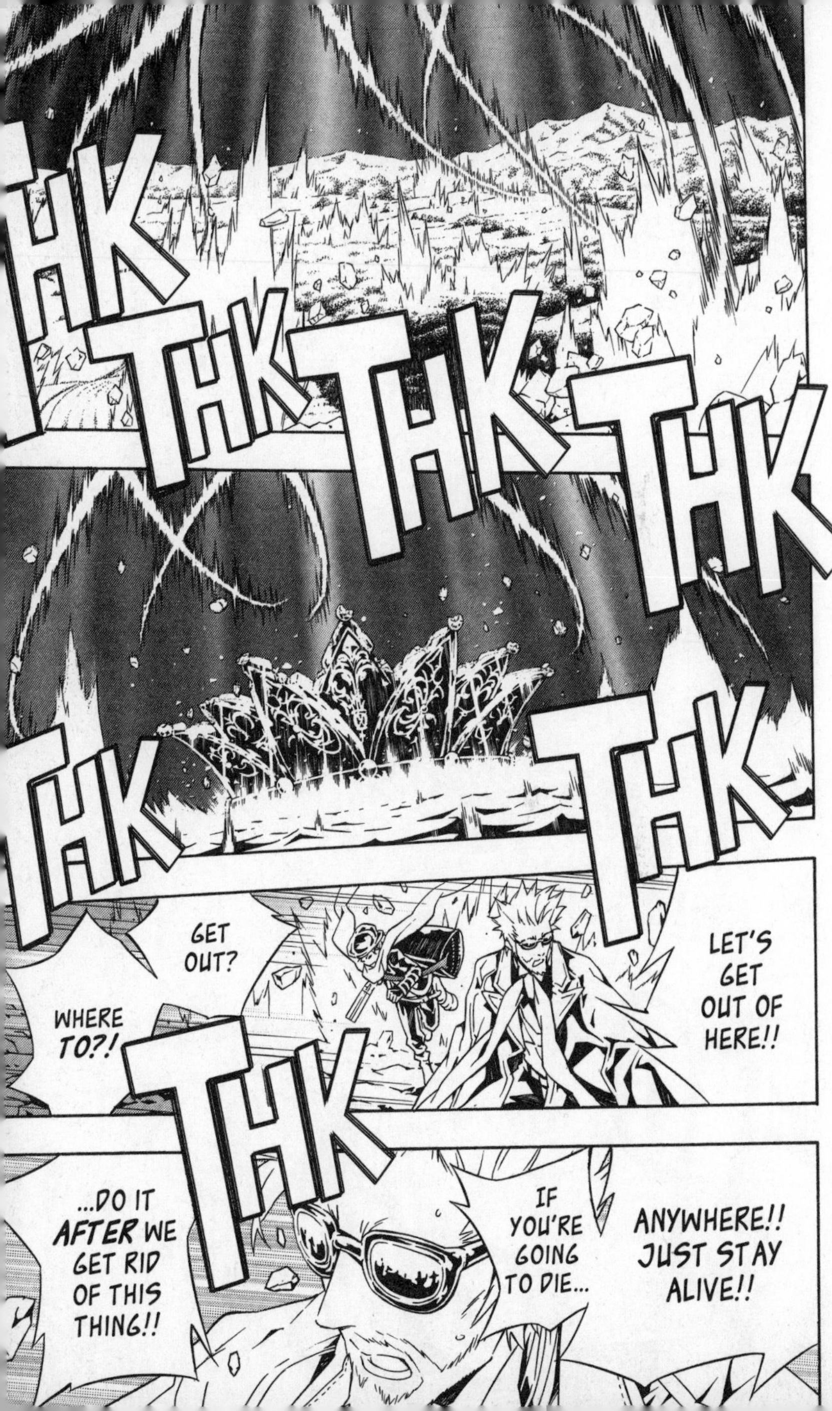
THK
THK
THK
THK
THK
THK
LET'S GET OUT OF HERE!!
GET OUT?
WHERE *TO?!*
THK
ANYWHERE!! JUST STAY ALIVE!!
IF YOU'RE GOING TO DIE...
...DO IT *AFTER* WE GET RID OF THIS THING!!

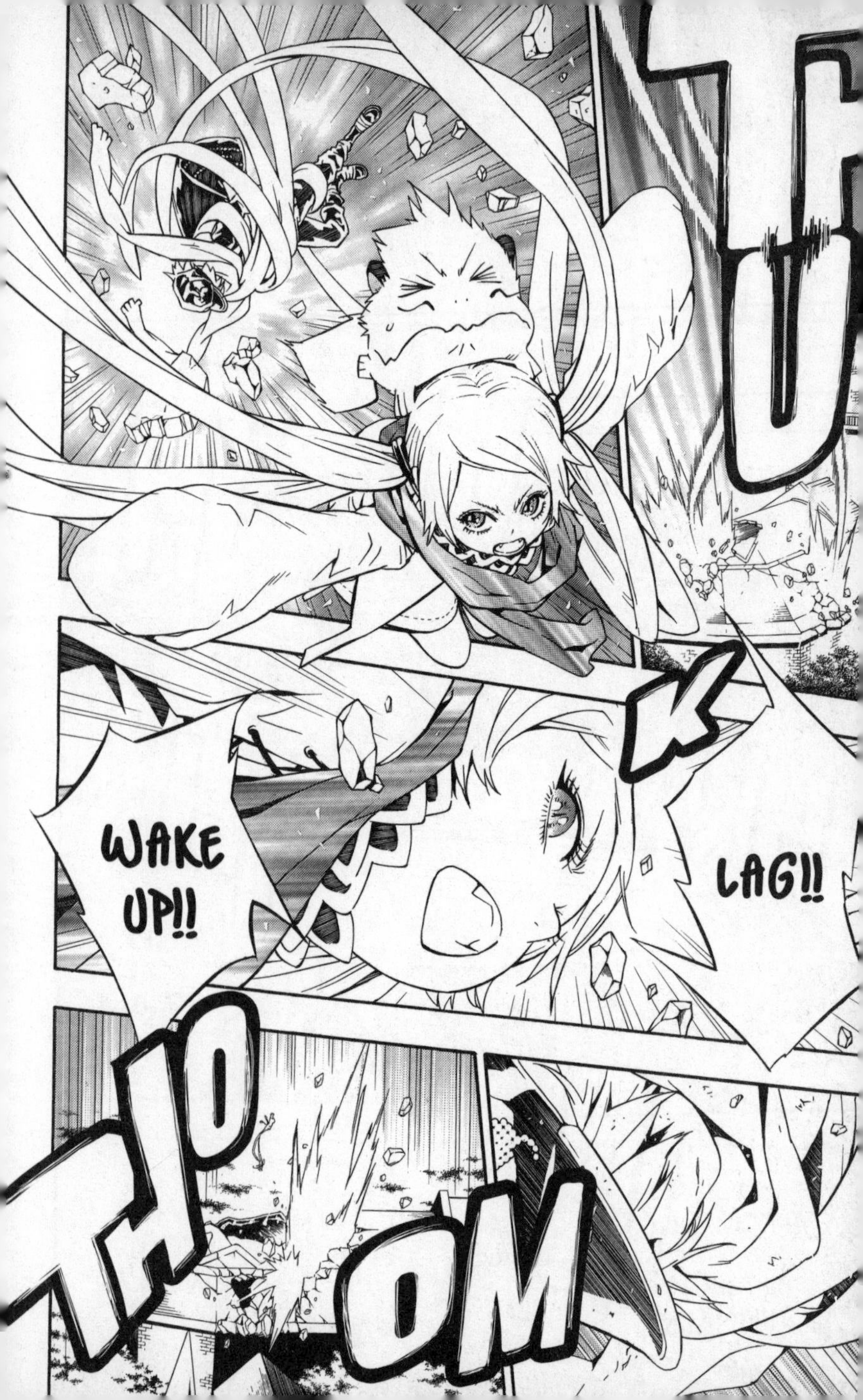
WAKE UP!! LAG!!
THOOM

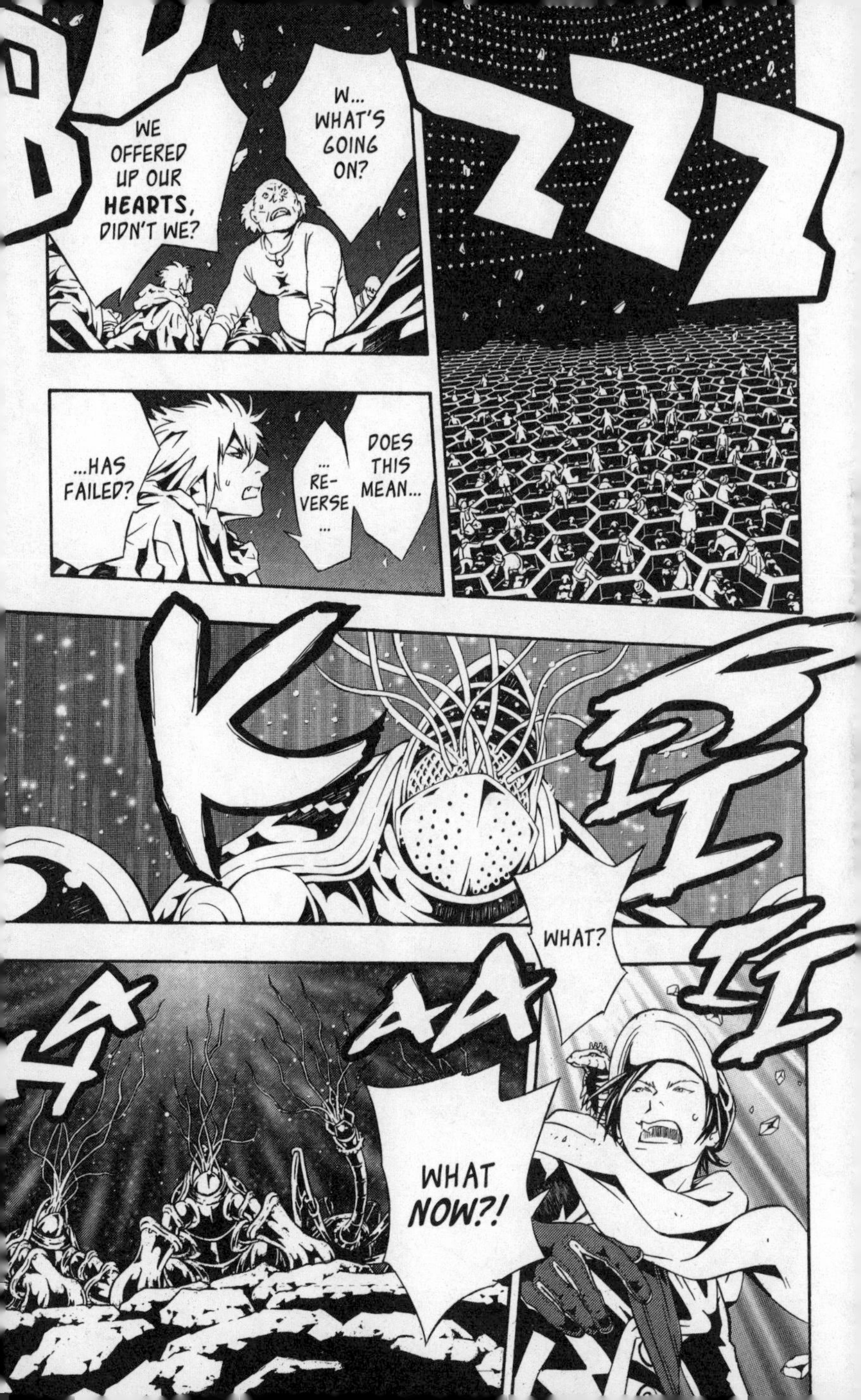
W... WHAT'S GOING ON?
WE OFFERED UP OUR **HEARTS**, DIDN'T WE?
DOES THIS MEAN...
...REVERSE...
...HAS FAILED?
WHAT?
WHAT **NOW?!**

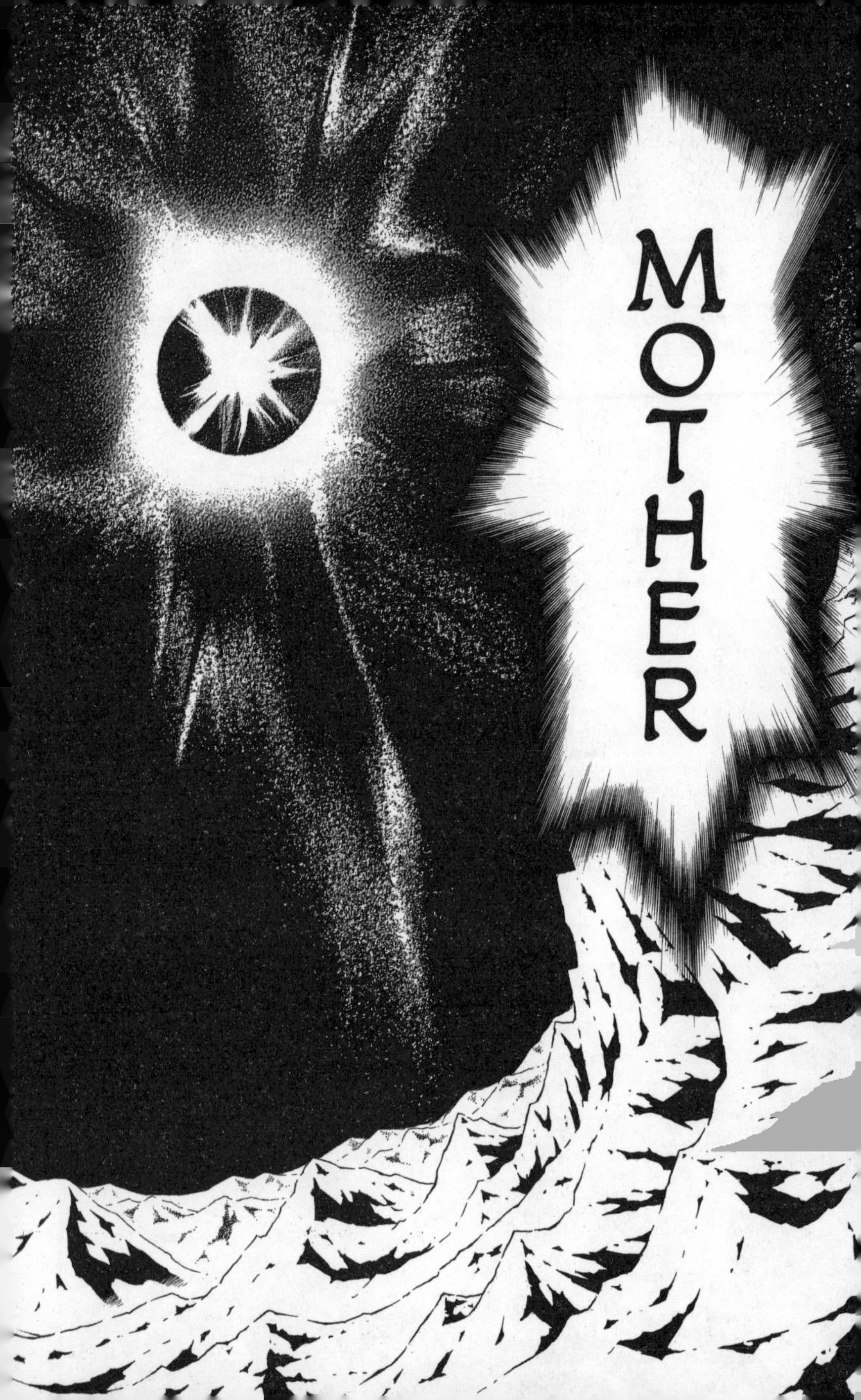
MOTHER

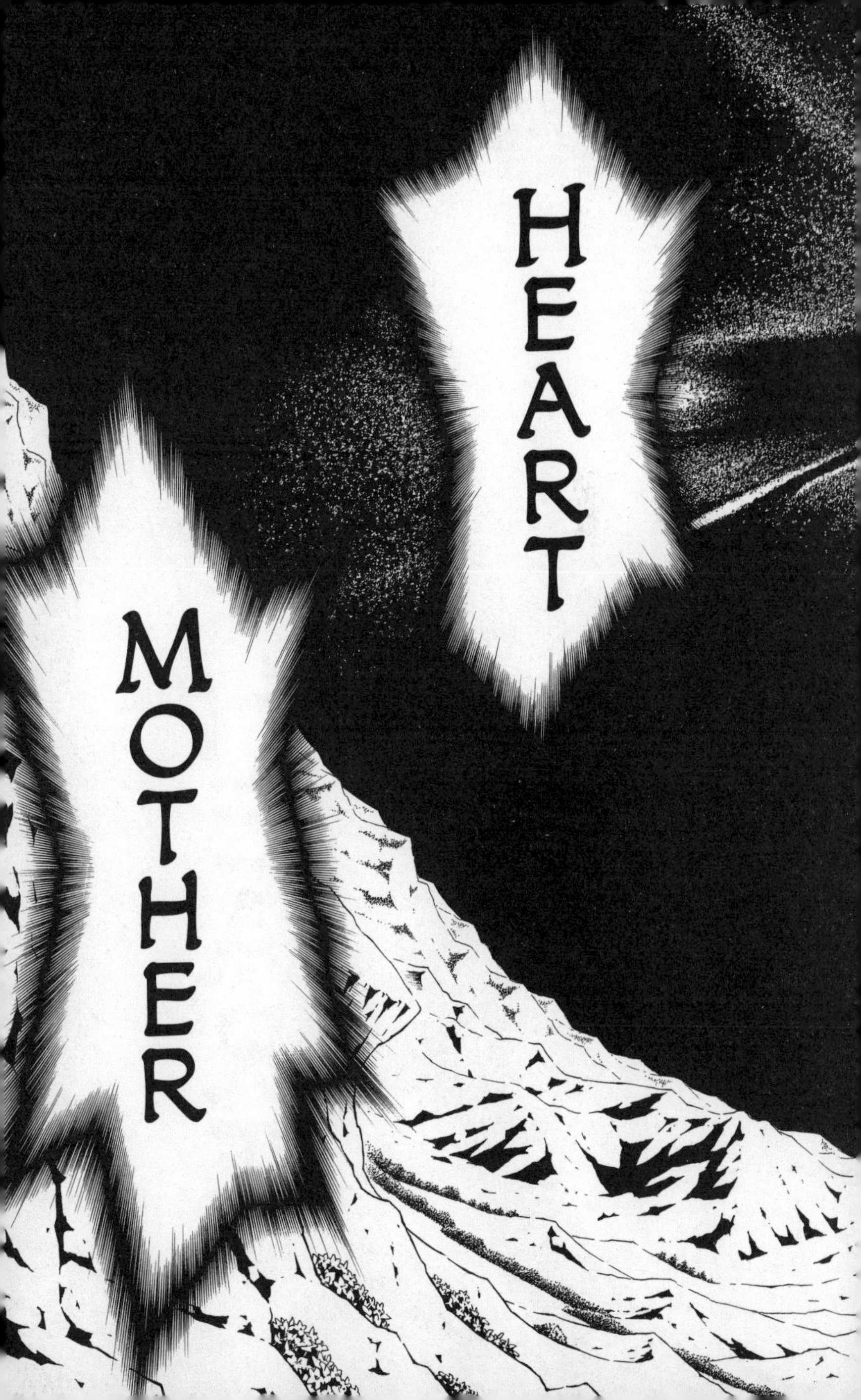
HEART
MOTHER

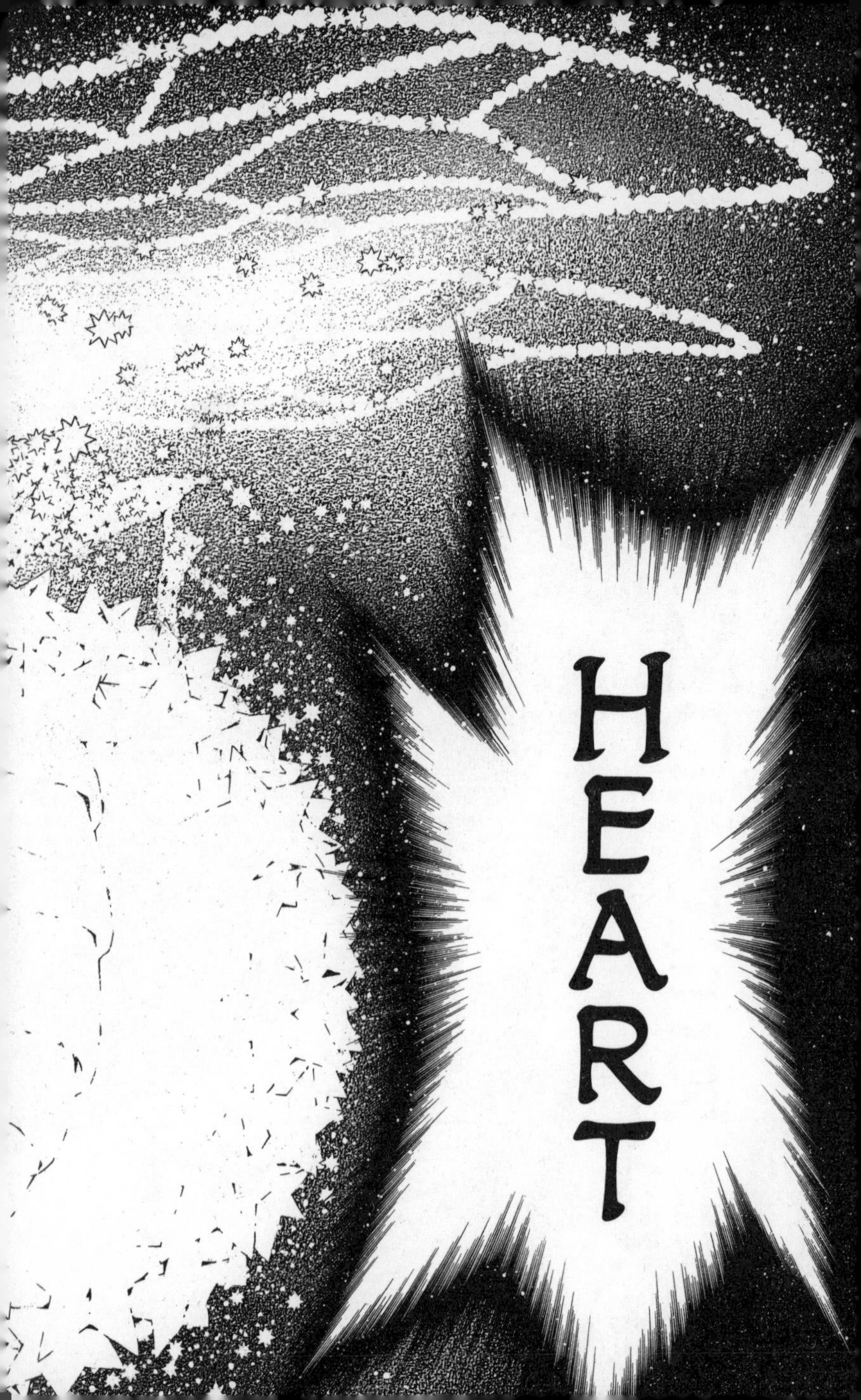
HEART

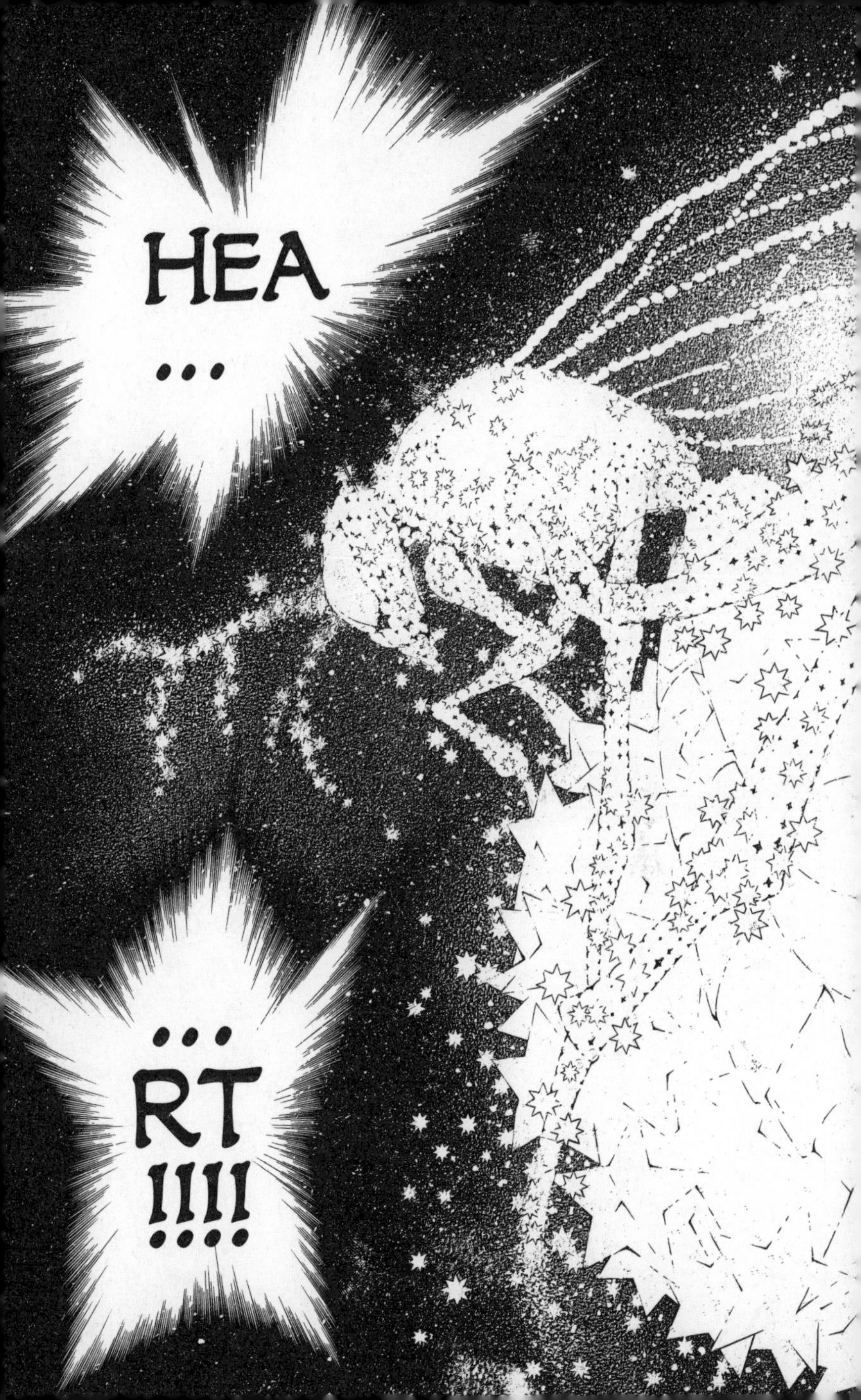
HEA
...
...
RT
!!!!

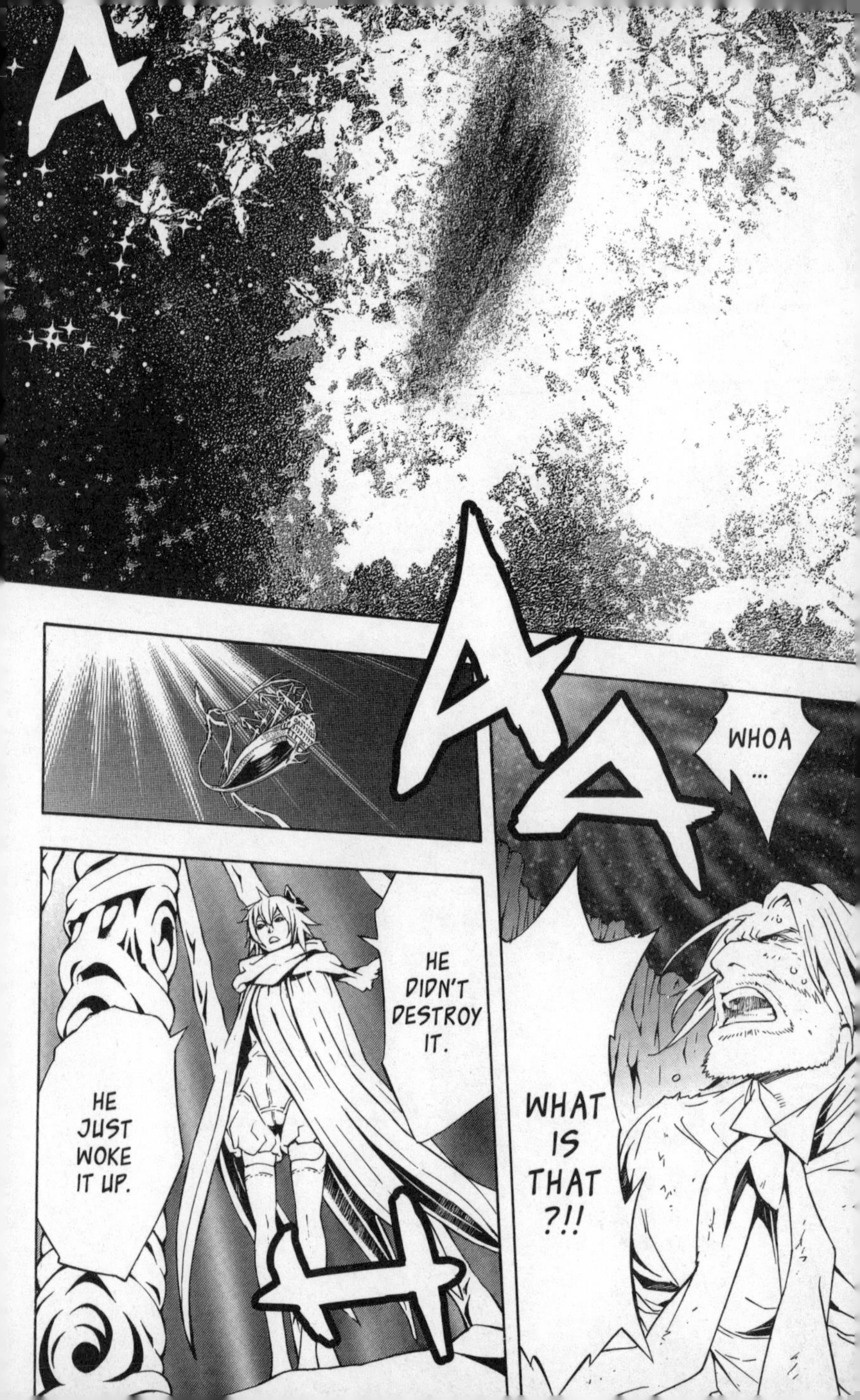
A
AA
WHOA ...
WHAT IS THAT?!!
HE DIDN'T DESTROY IT.
HE JUST WOKE IT UP.

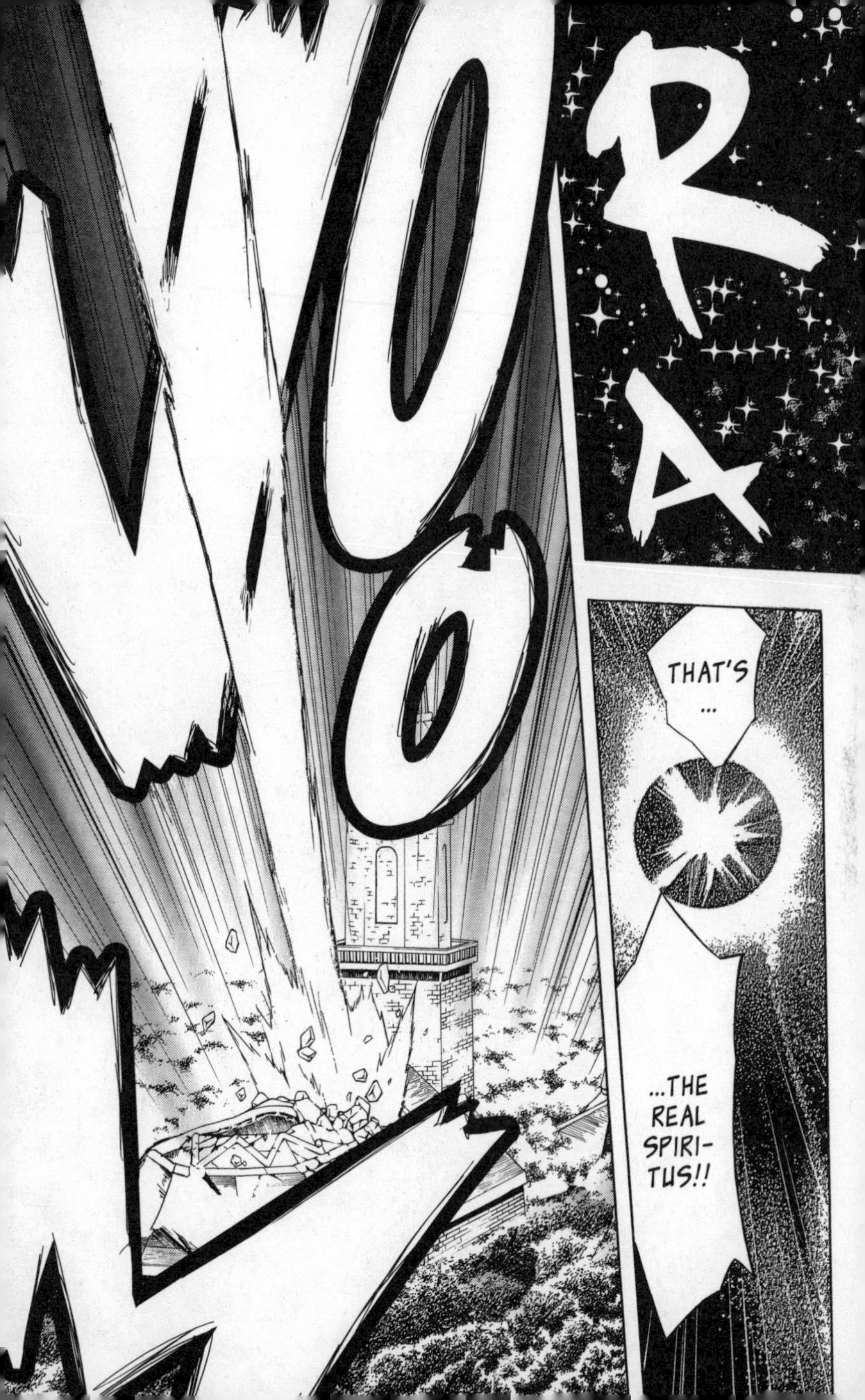
THAT'S ...
...THE REAL SPIRI-TUS!!

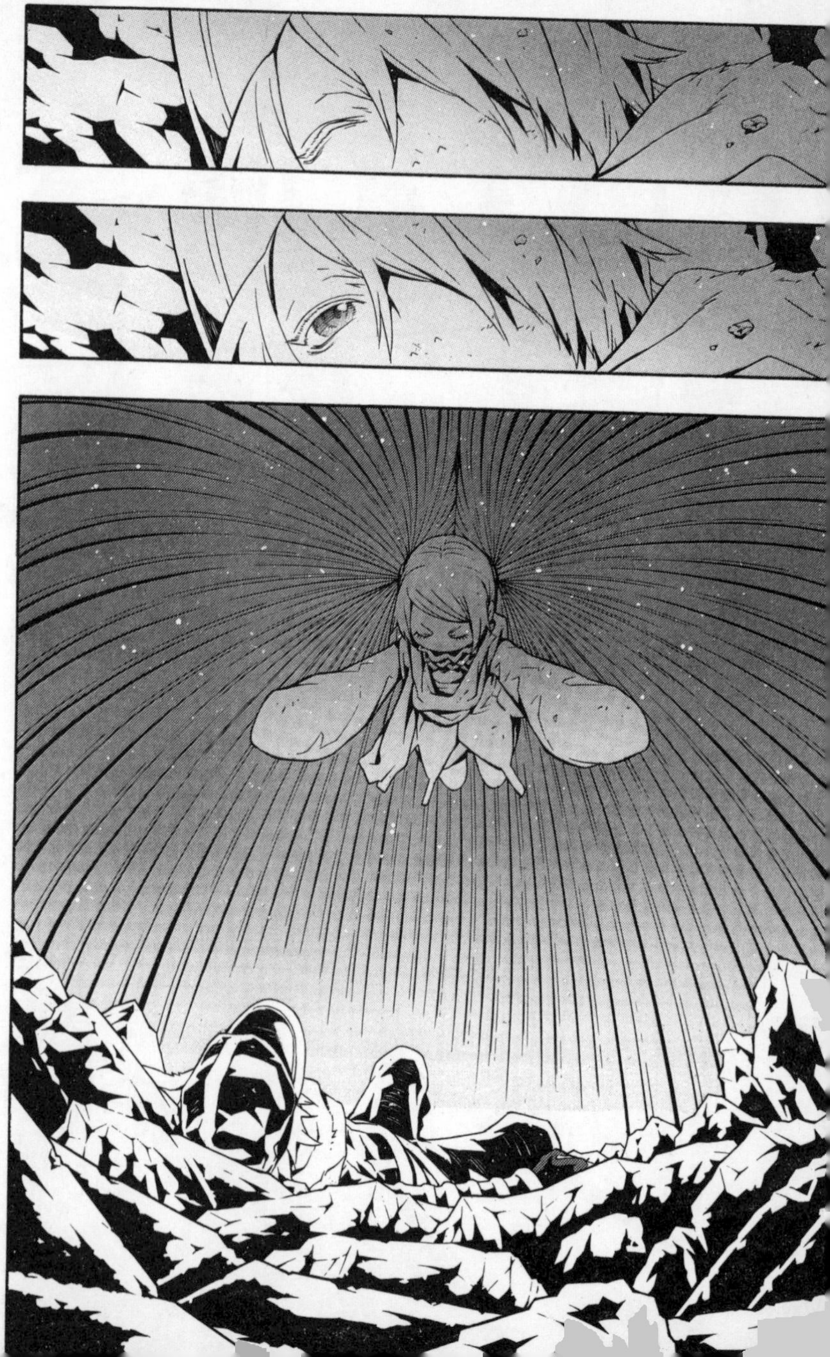

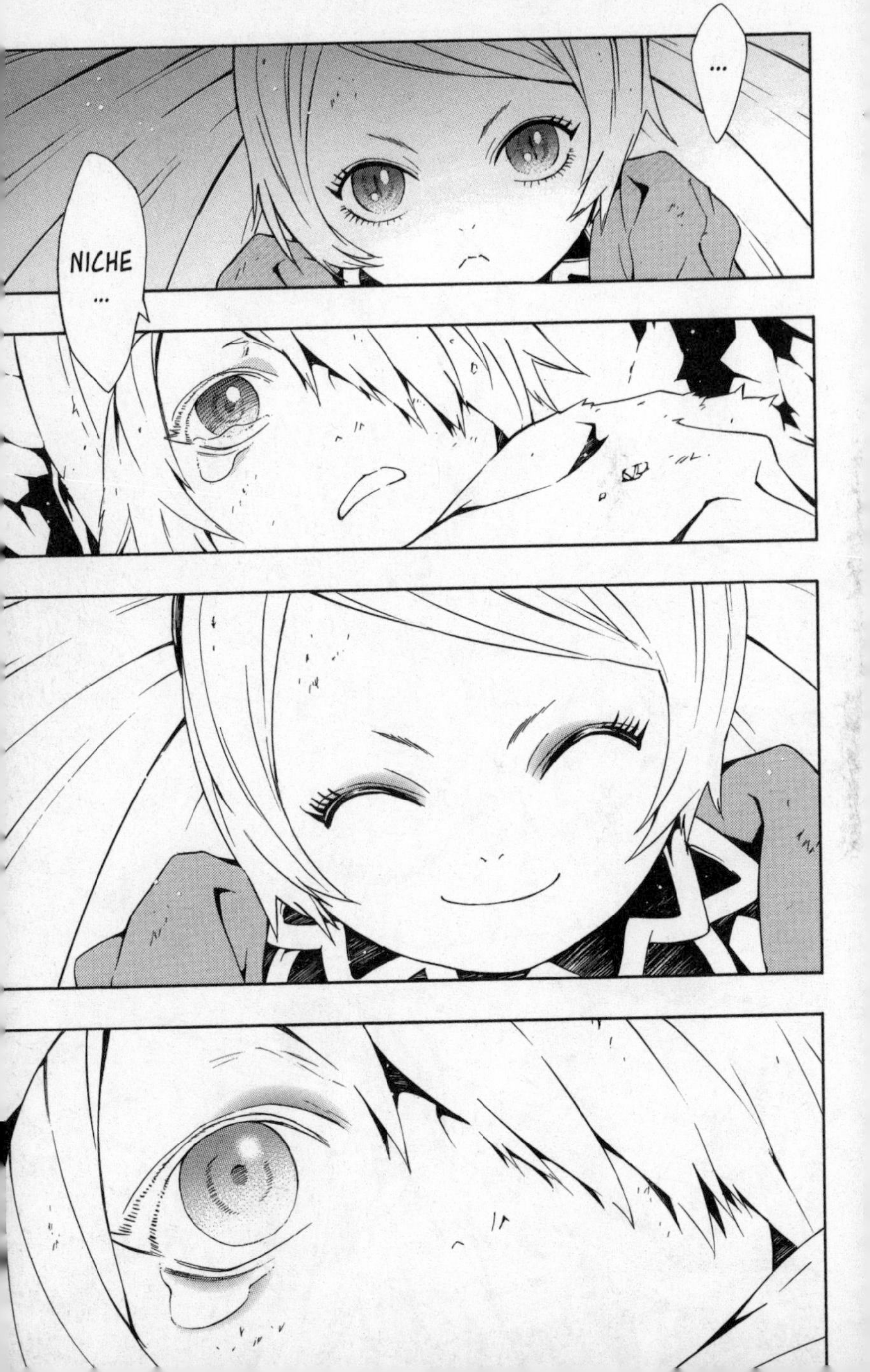
...
NICHE ...

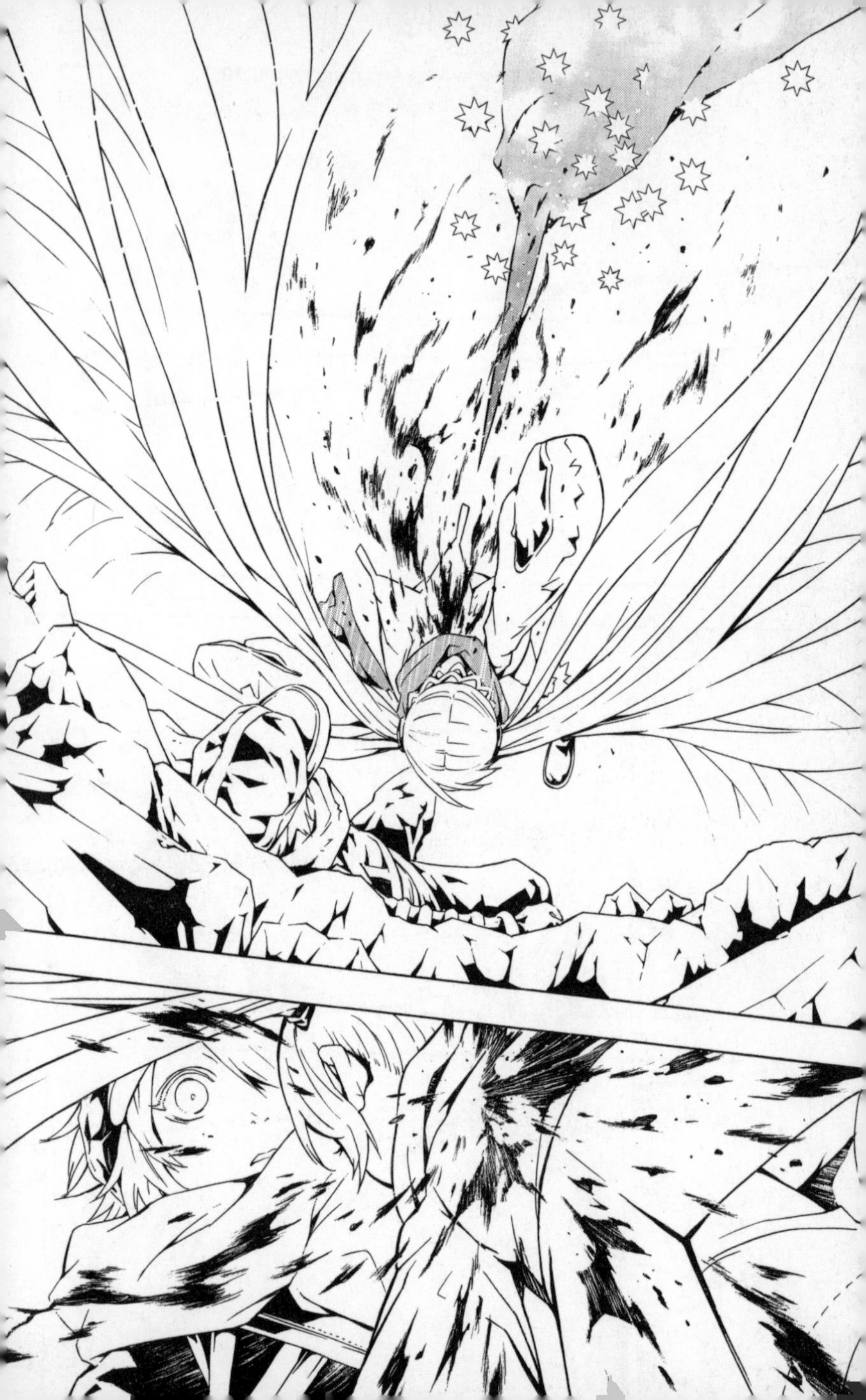

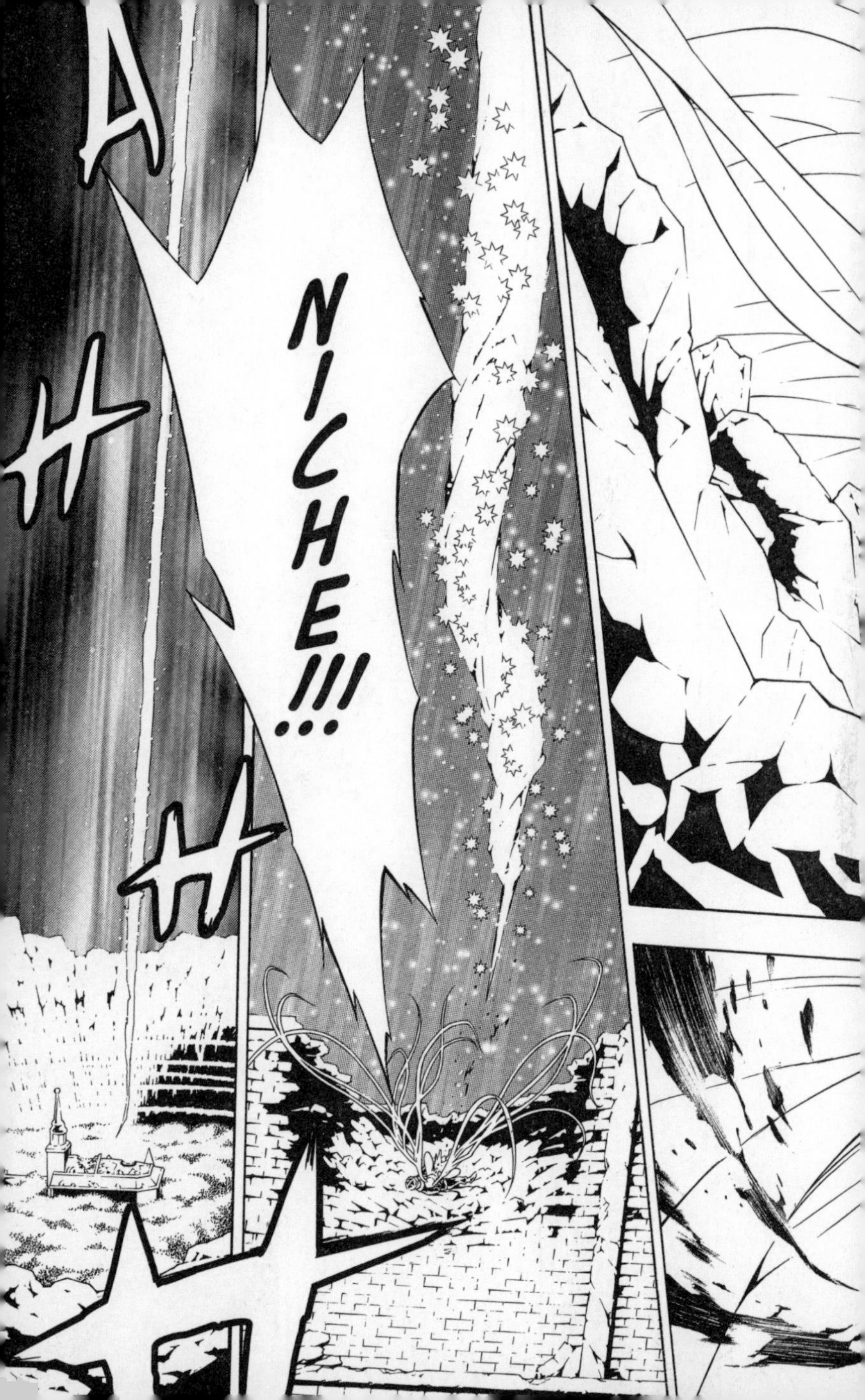
AHH
NICHE!!!

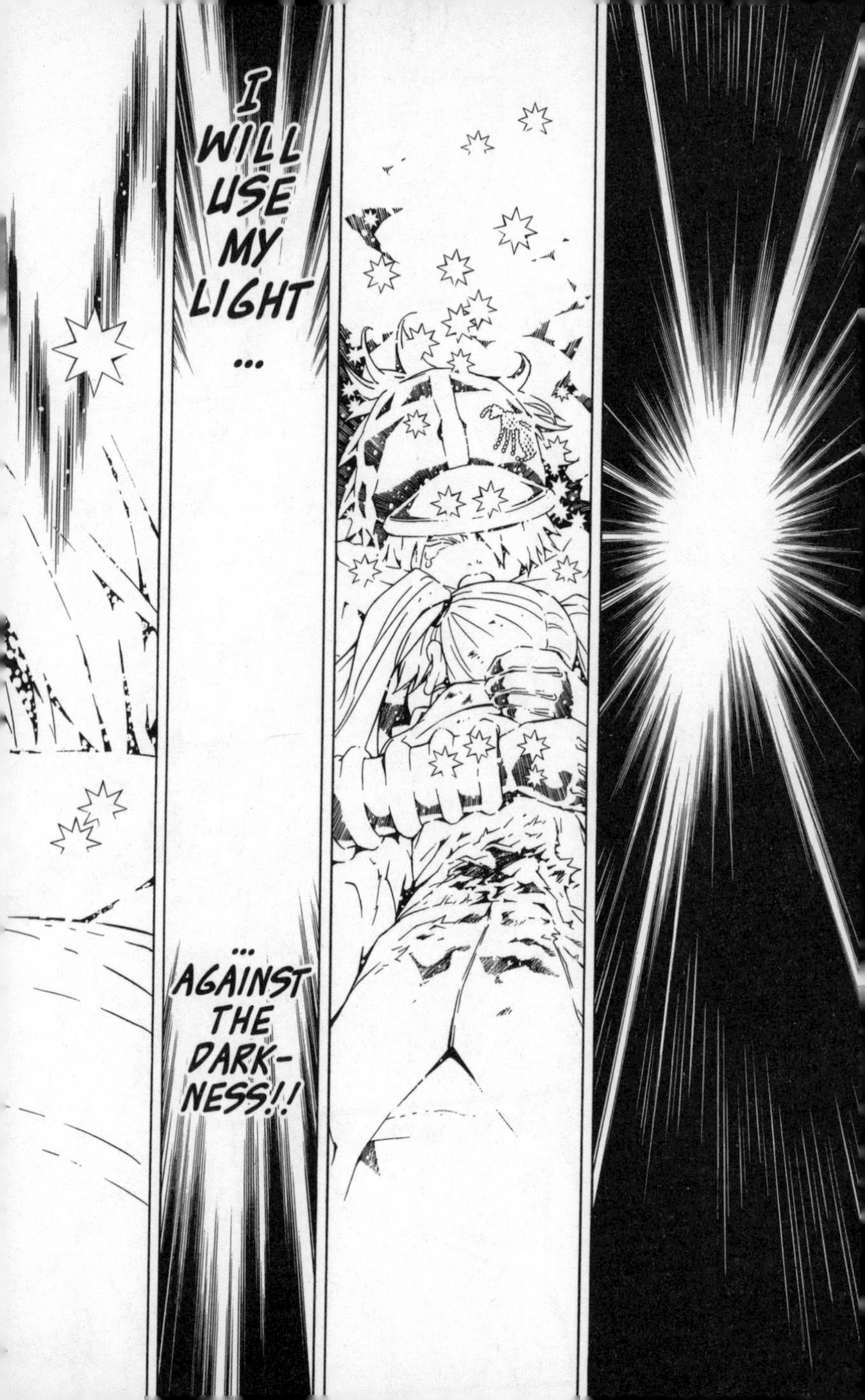
I WILL USE MY LIGHT ...
... AGAINST THE DARK-NESS!!

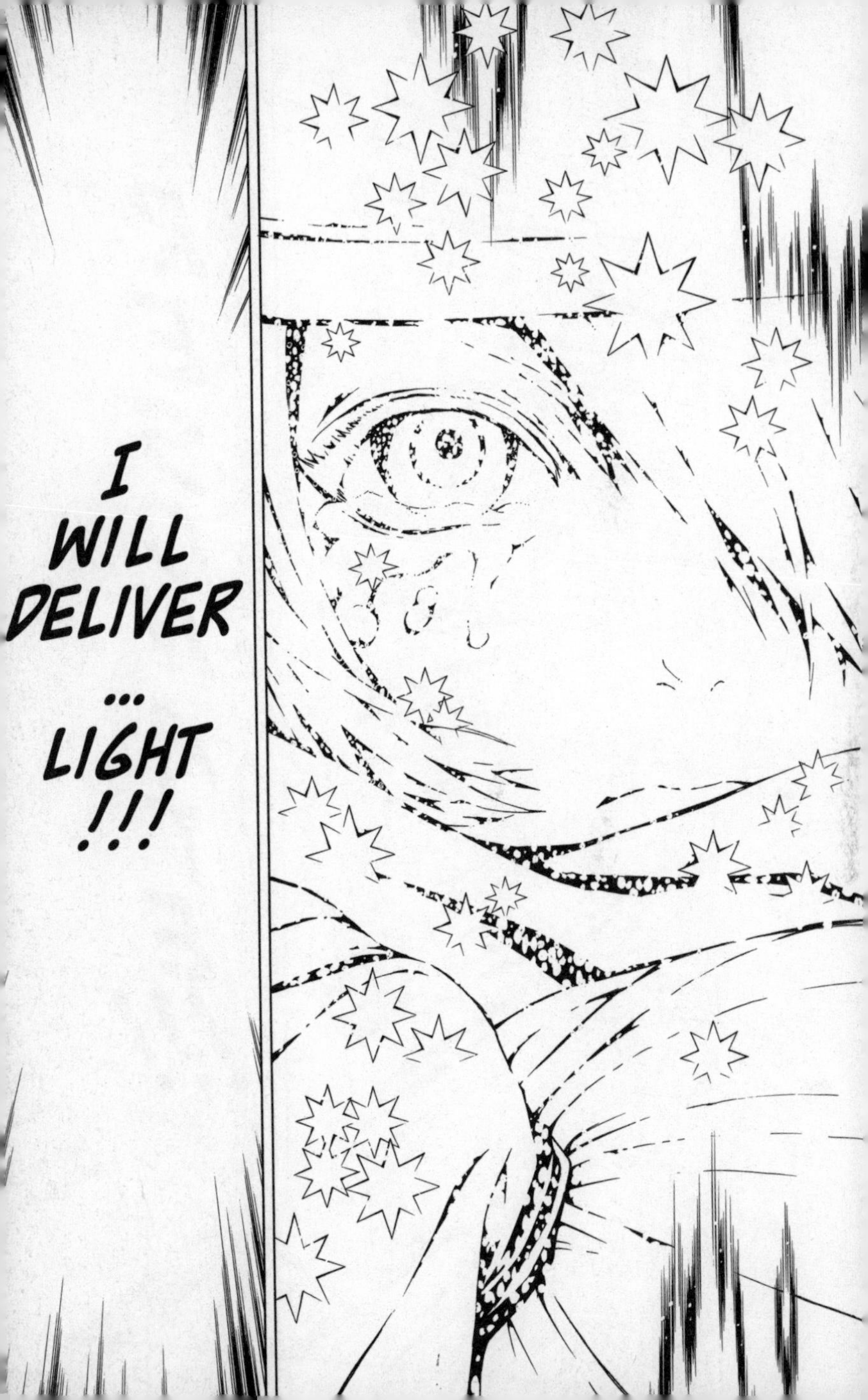
I WILL DELIVER ... LIGHT !!!

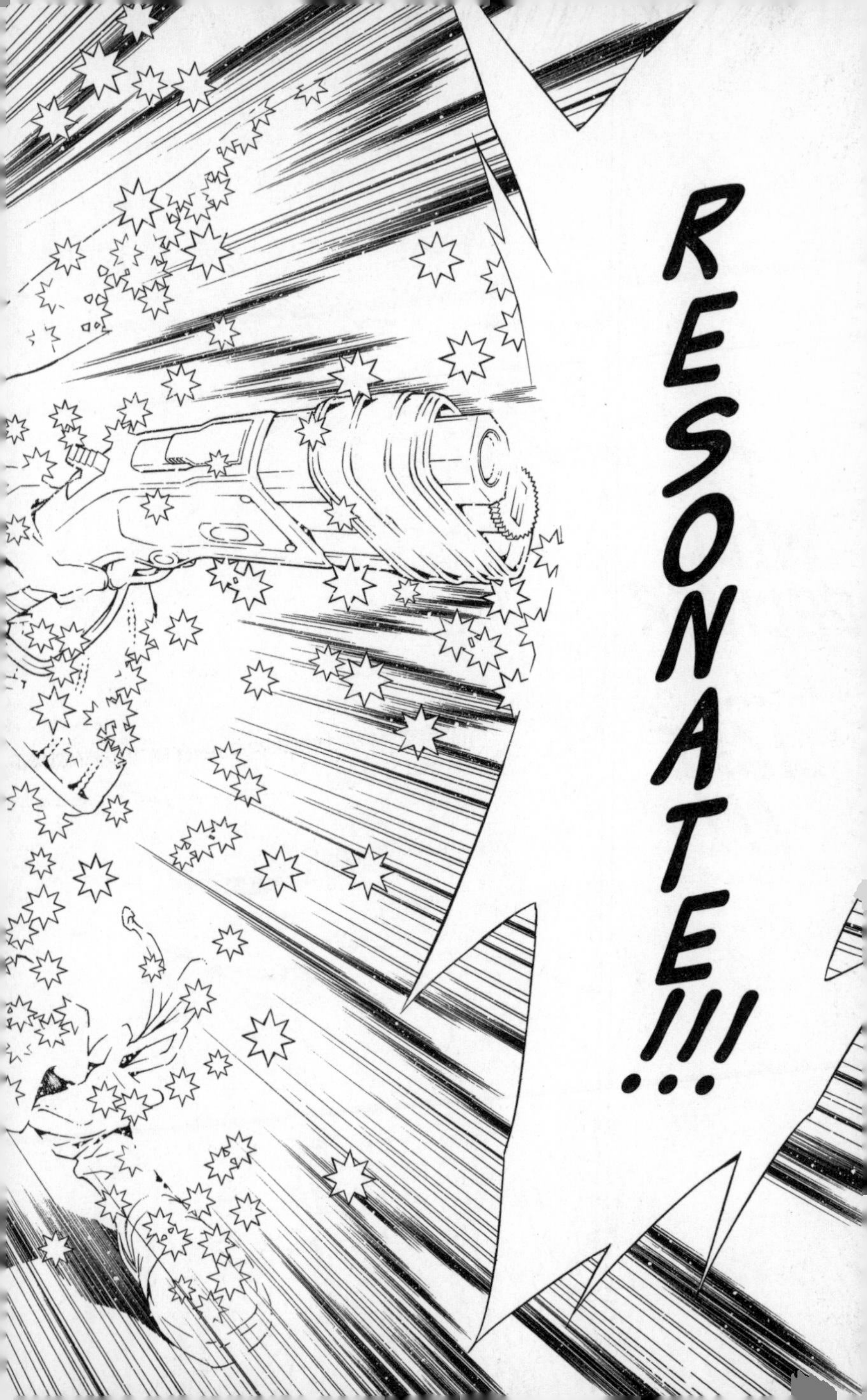
RESONATE!!!

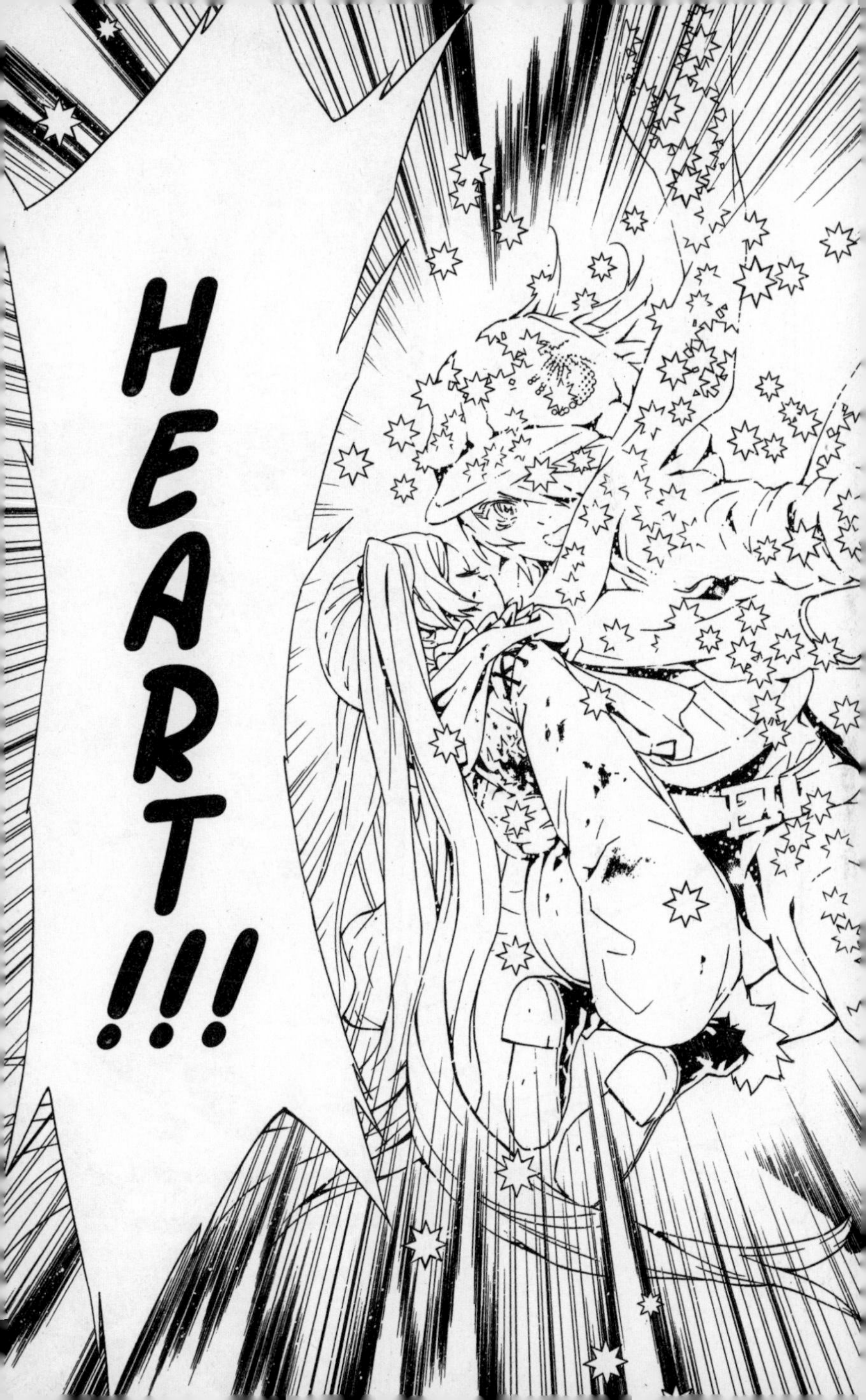
HEART!!!

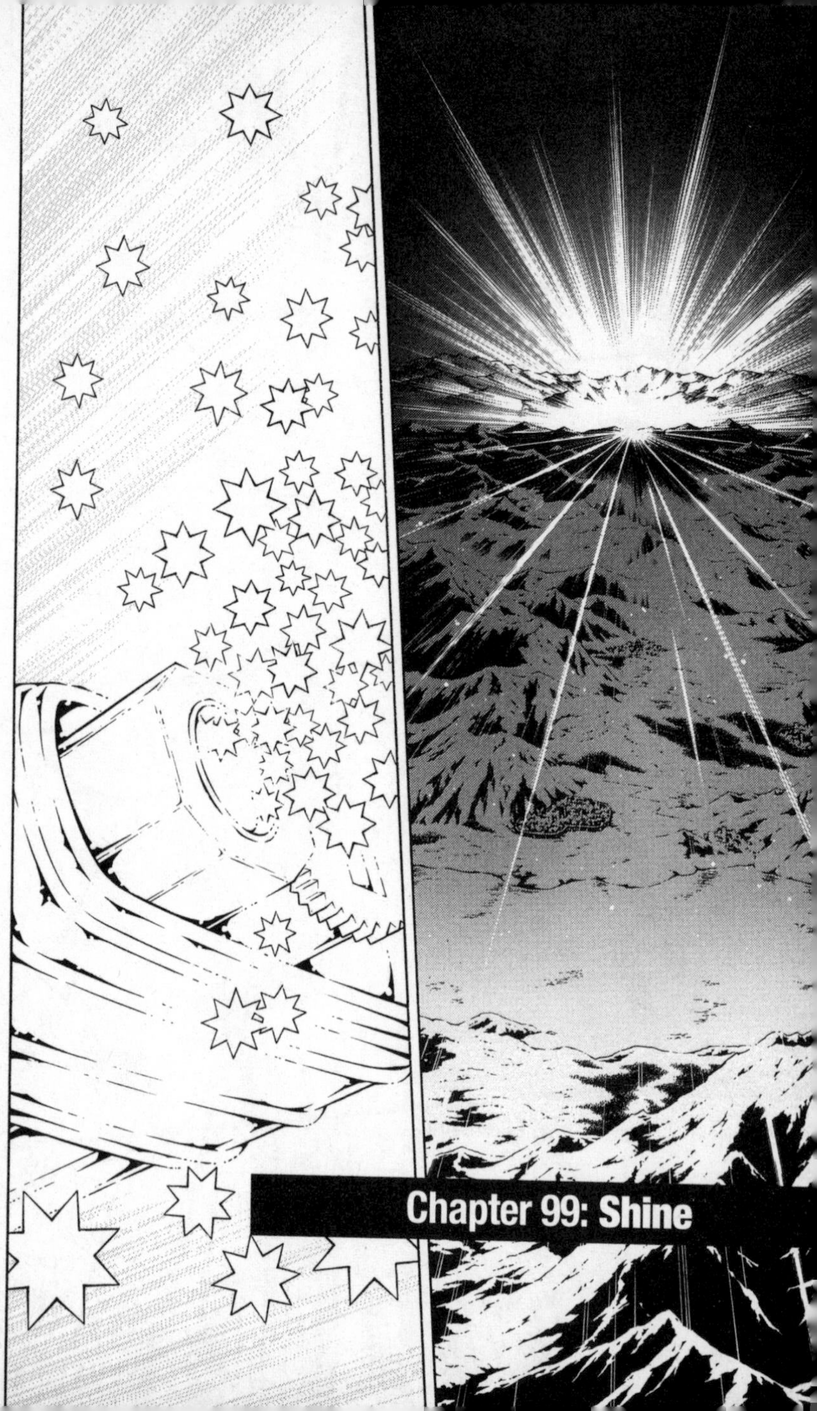

Chapter 99: Shine

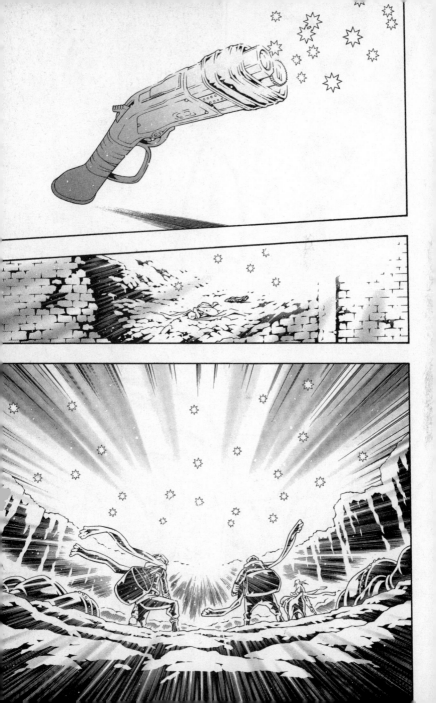

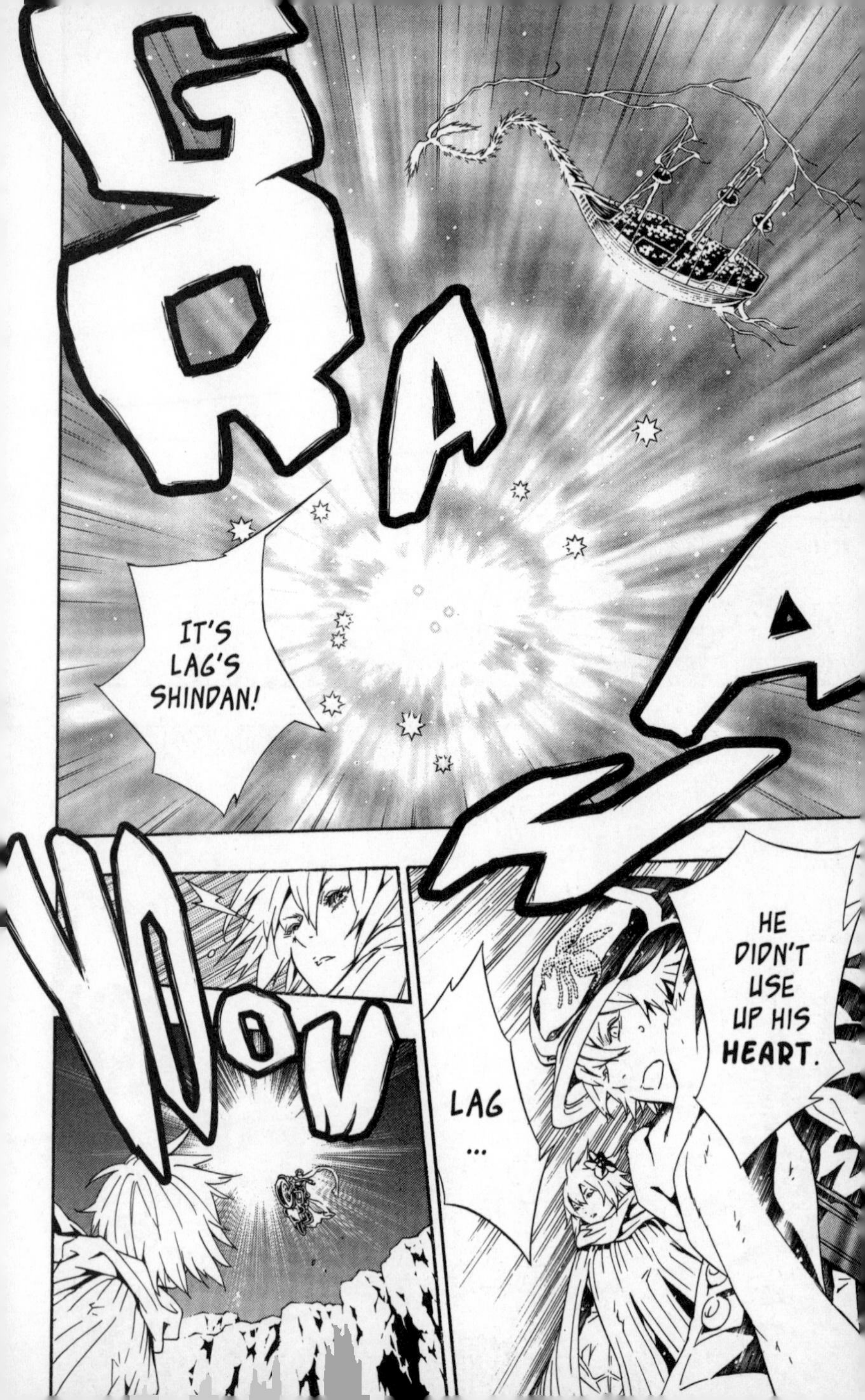
IT'S LAG'S SHINDAN!
HE DIDN'T USE UP HIS **HEART**.
LAG ...

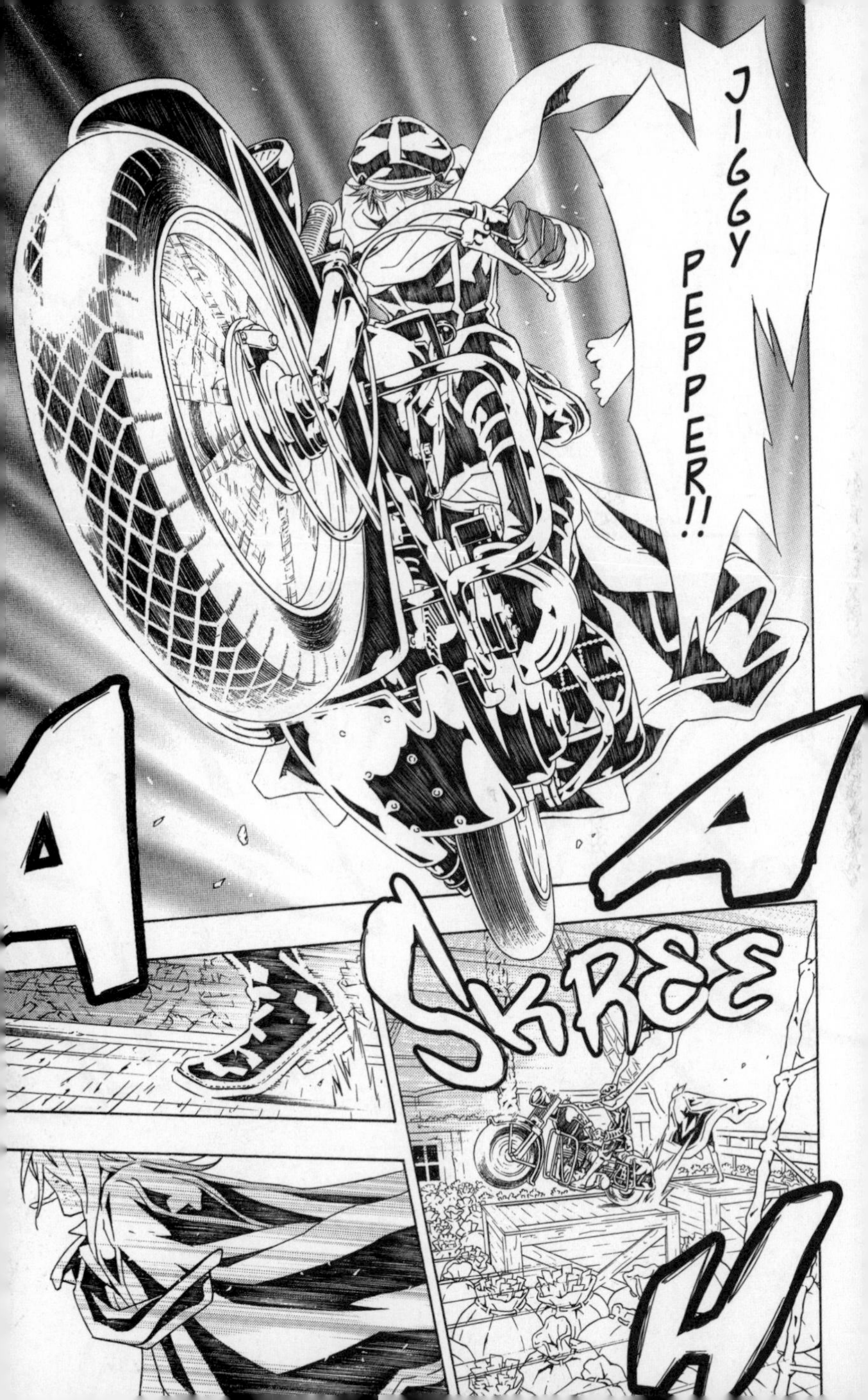
JIGGY PEPPER!!
SKREE

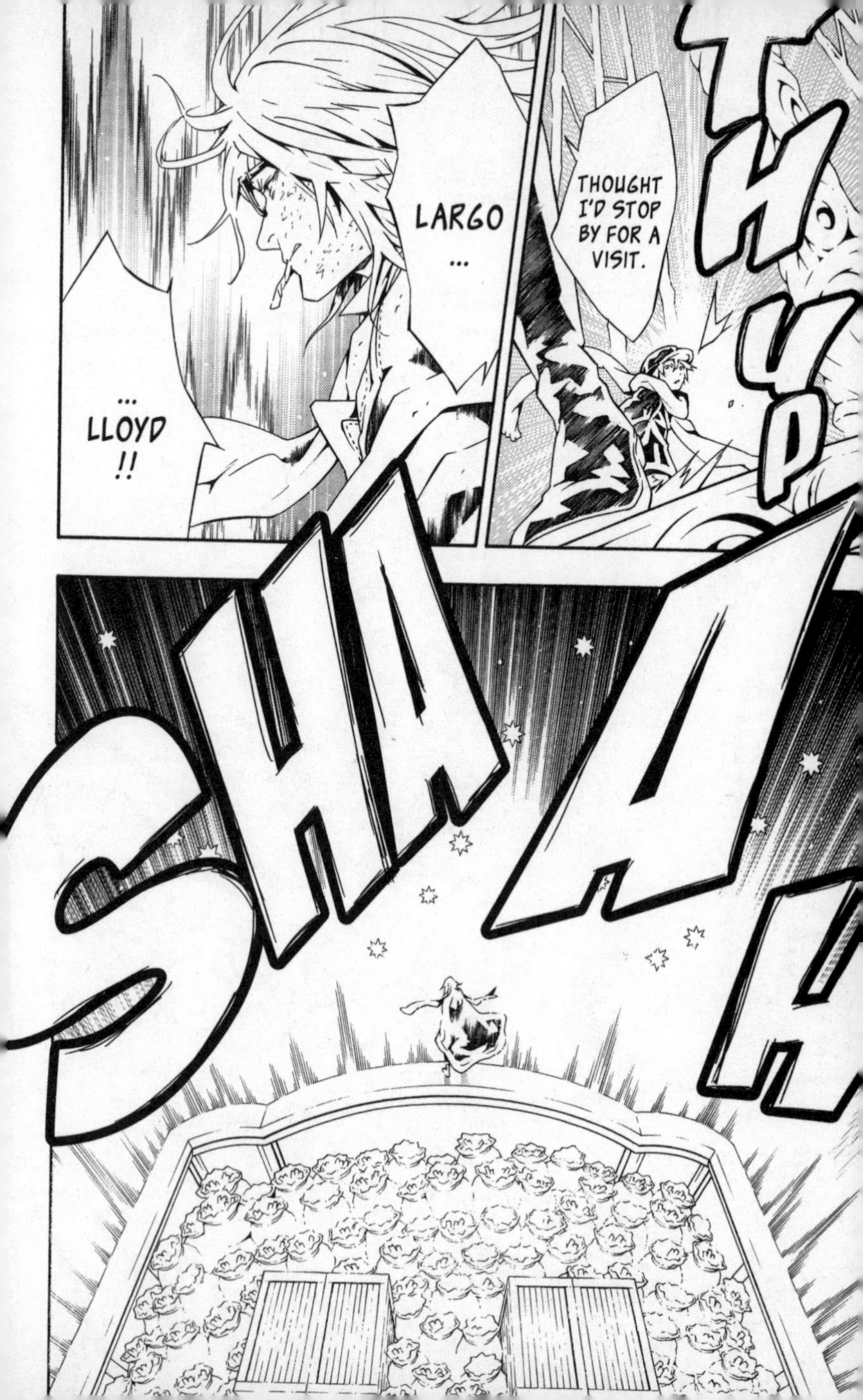
THUP
THOUGHT I'D STOP BY FOR A VISIT.
LARGO ...
... LLOYD !!
SHAAH

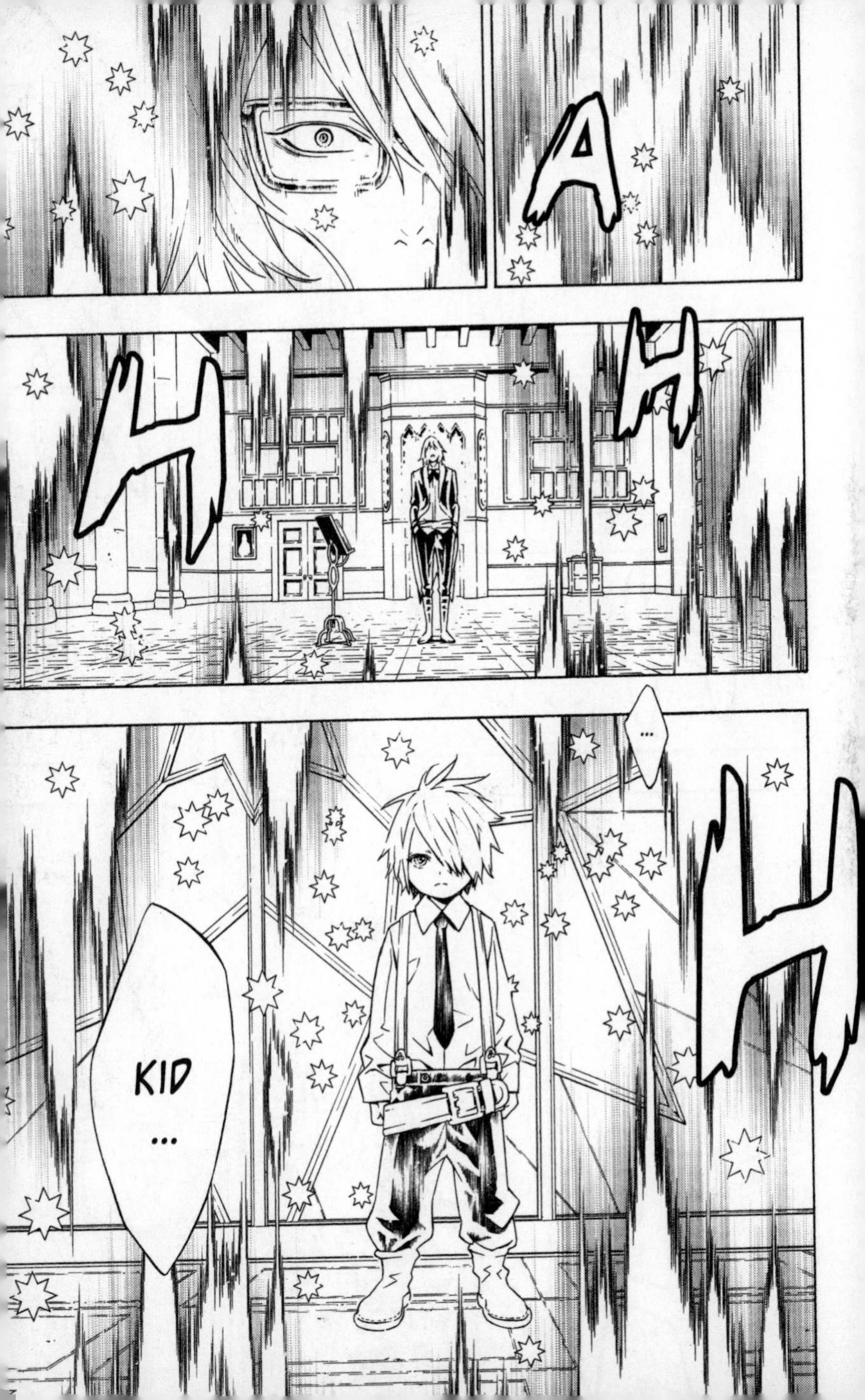
A
H
H
...
H
KID ...

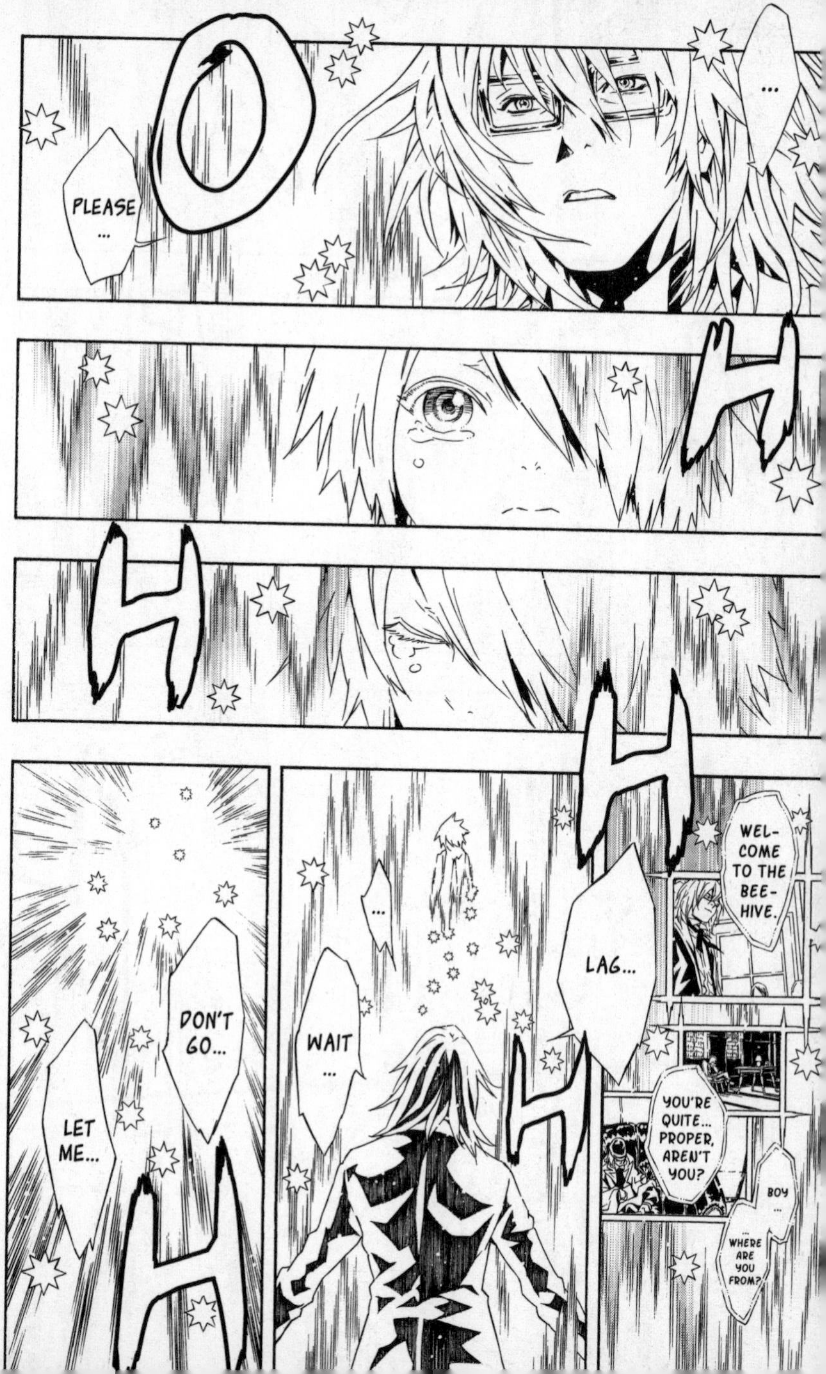
...
PLEASE ...
WEL-COME TO THE BEE-HIVE.
YOU'RE QUITE... PROPER, AREN'T YOU?
BOY ... ... WHERE ARE YOU FROM?
LAG...
...
WAIT ...
DON'T GO...
LET ME...

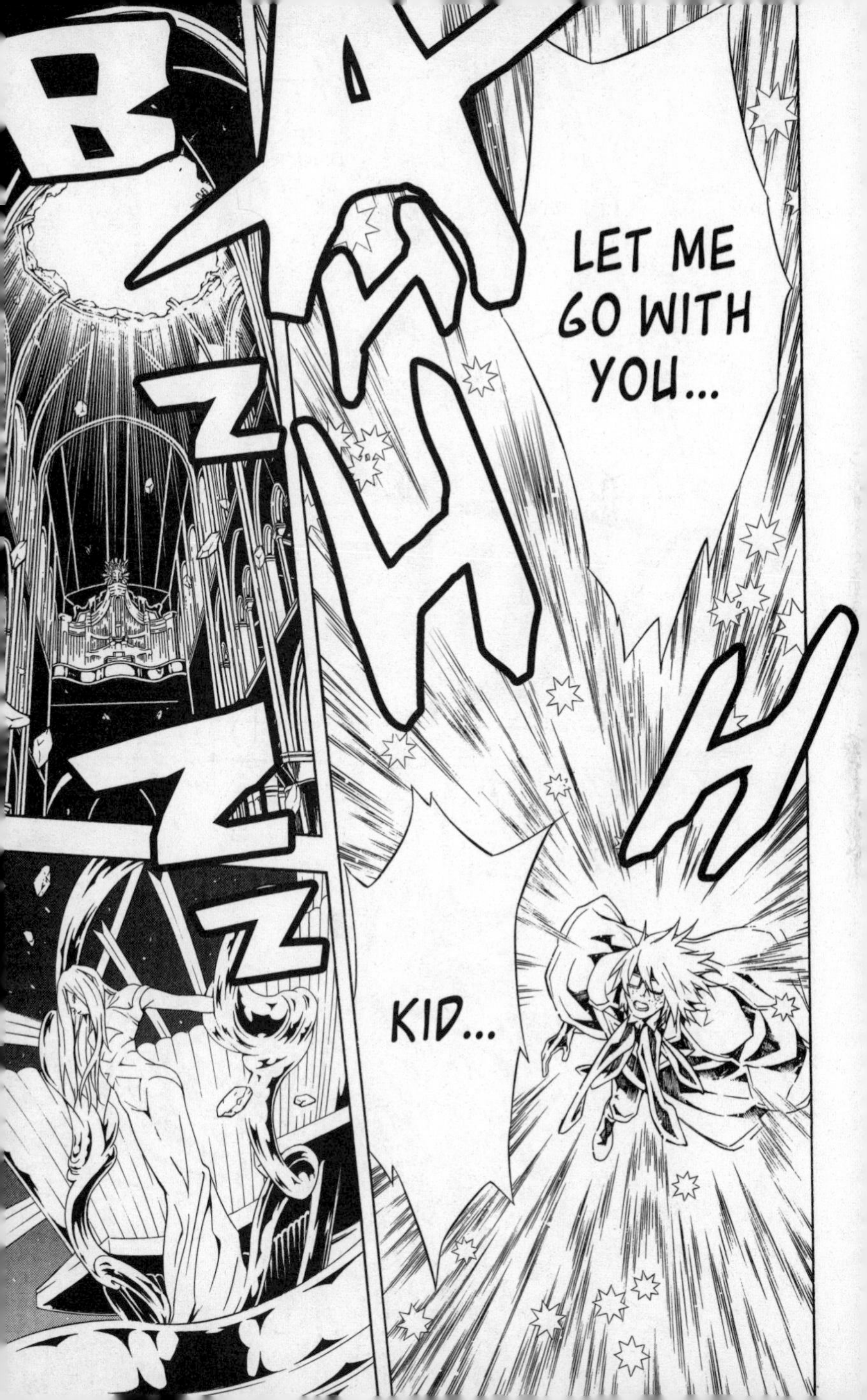
LET ME GO WITH YOU...
KID...

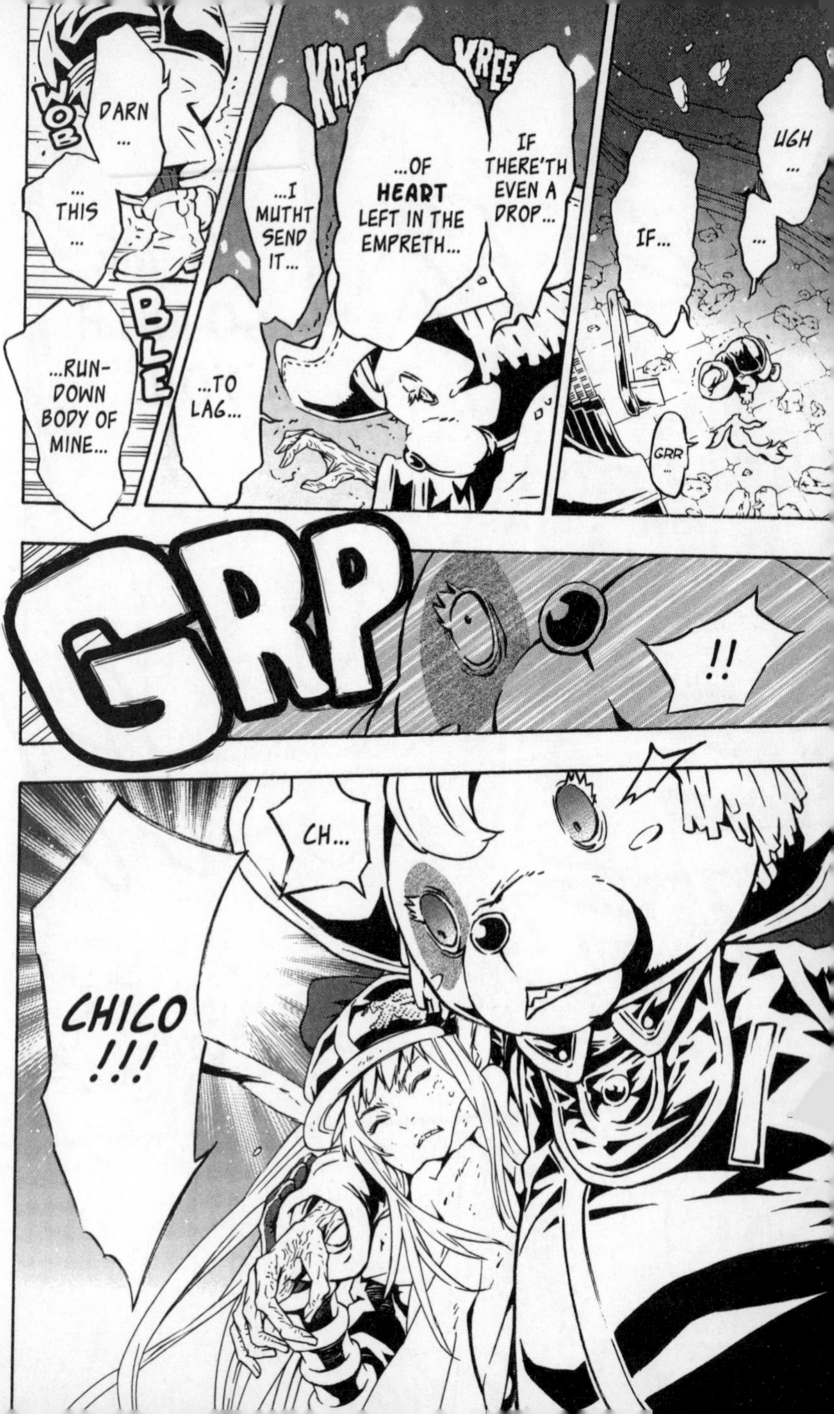
UGH ...
...
IF...
GRR ...
KREE
KREE
IF THERE'TH EVEN A DROP...
...OF HEART LEFT IN THE EMPRETH...
...I MUTHT SEND IT...
...TO LAG...
DARN ...
WOB
... THIS ...
BLE
...RUN-DOWN BODY OF MINE...
!!
GRP
CH...
CHICO !!!

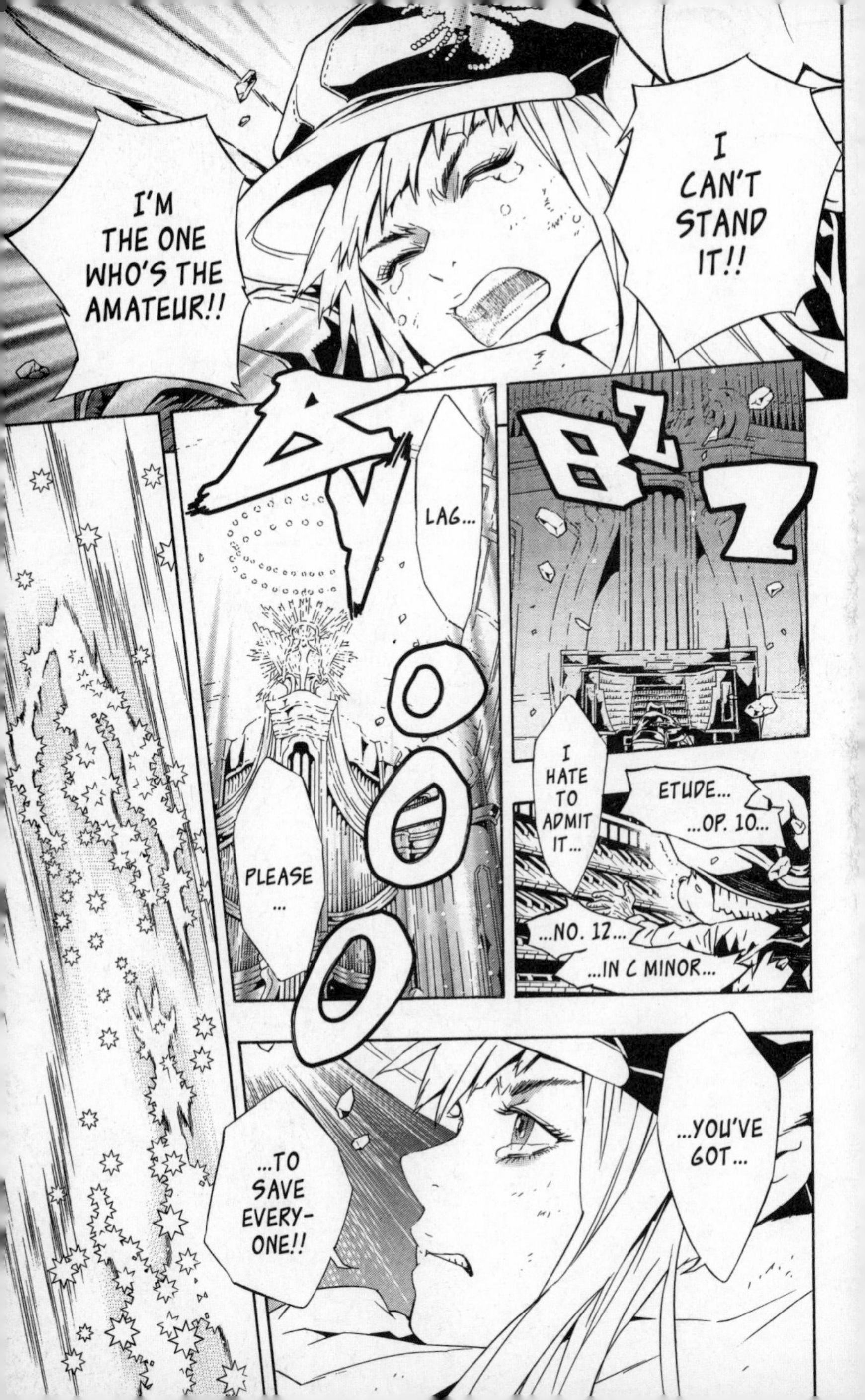
I CAN'T STAND IT!!
I'M THE ONE WHO'S THE AMATEUR!!
BZZ
I HATE TO ADMIT IT...
ETUDE...
...OP. 10...
...NO. 12...
...IN C MINOR...
BOOOO
LAG...
PLEASE ...
...YOU'VE GOT...
...TO SAVE EVERY-ONE!!

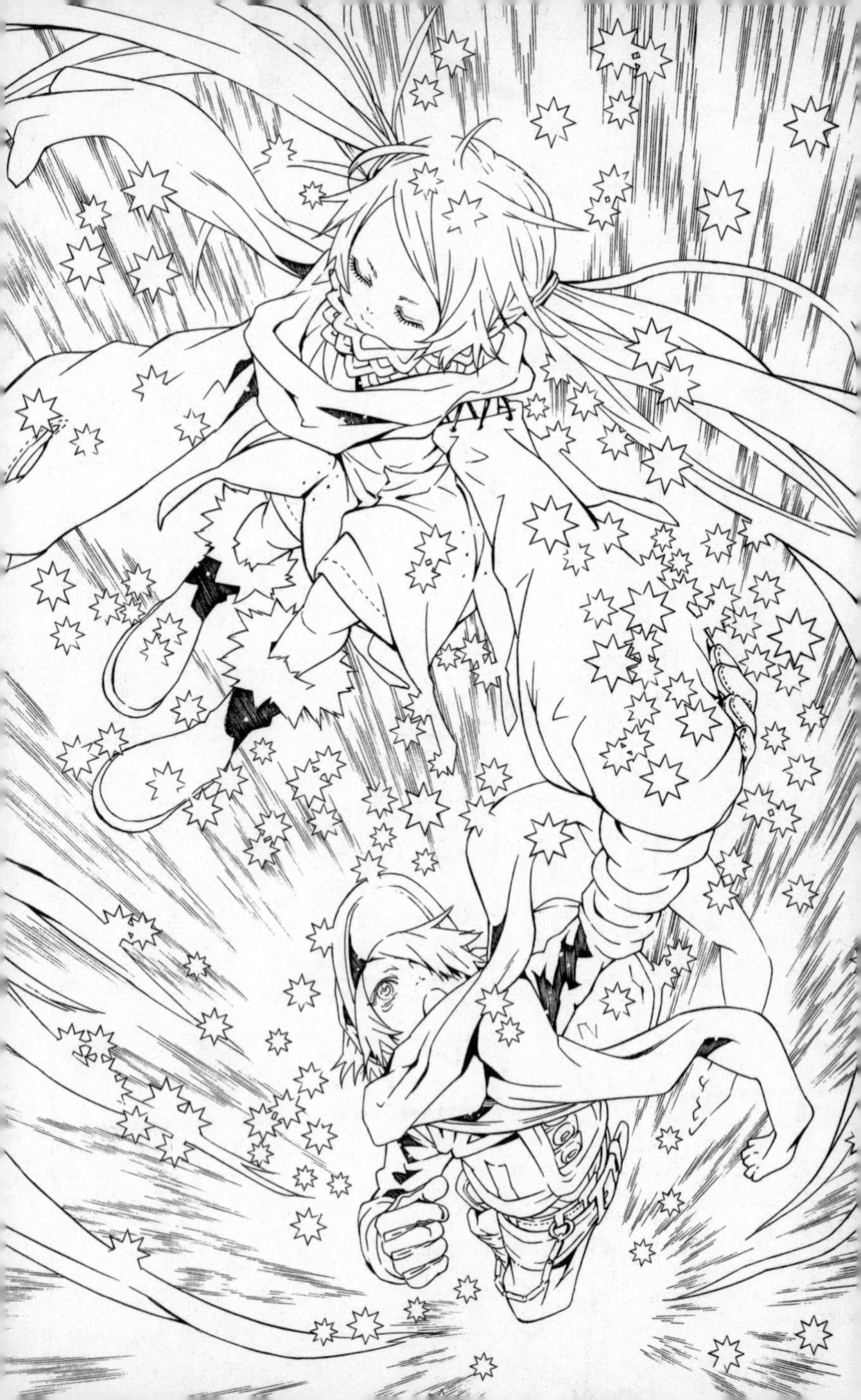

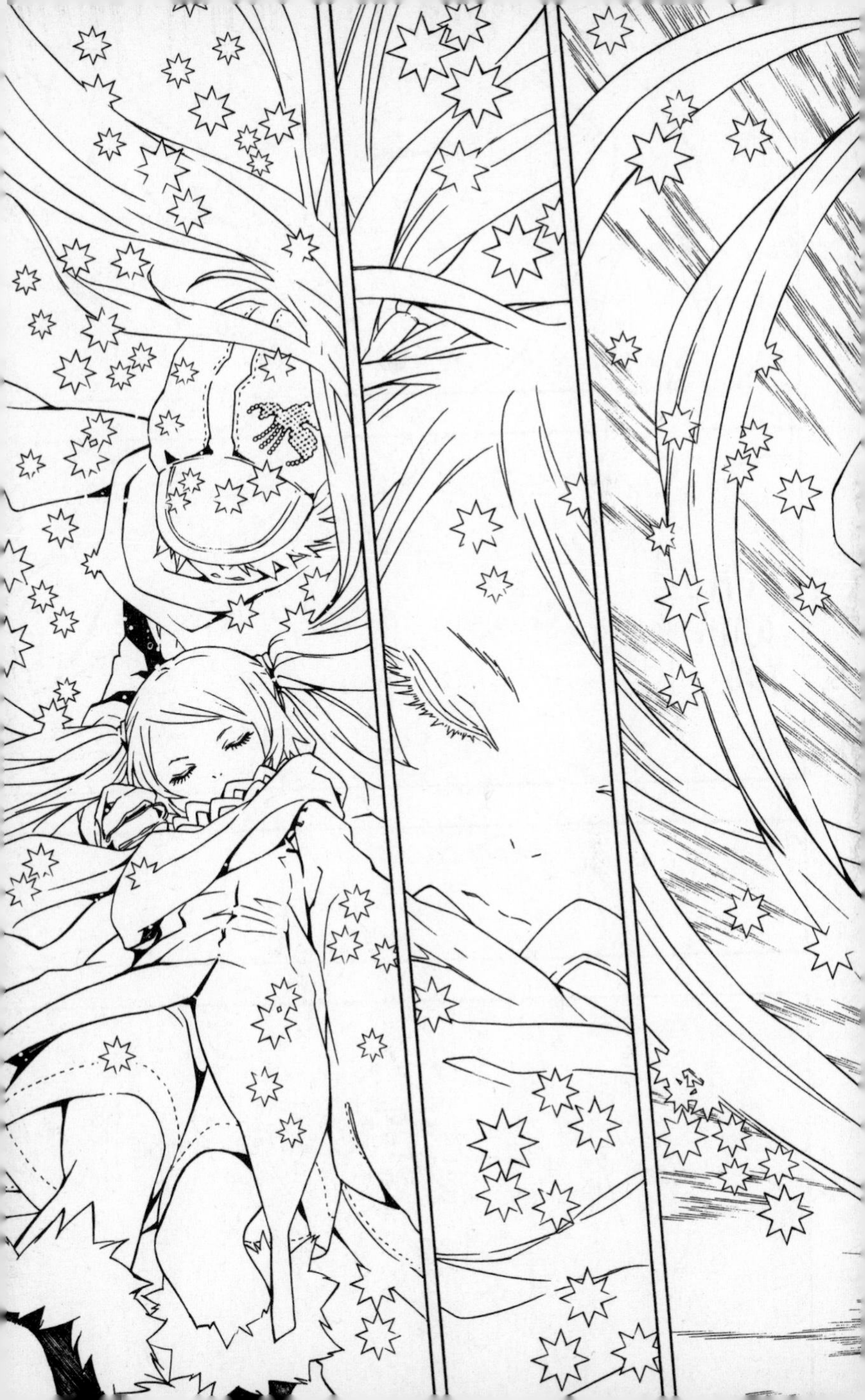

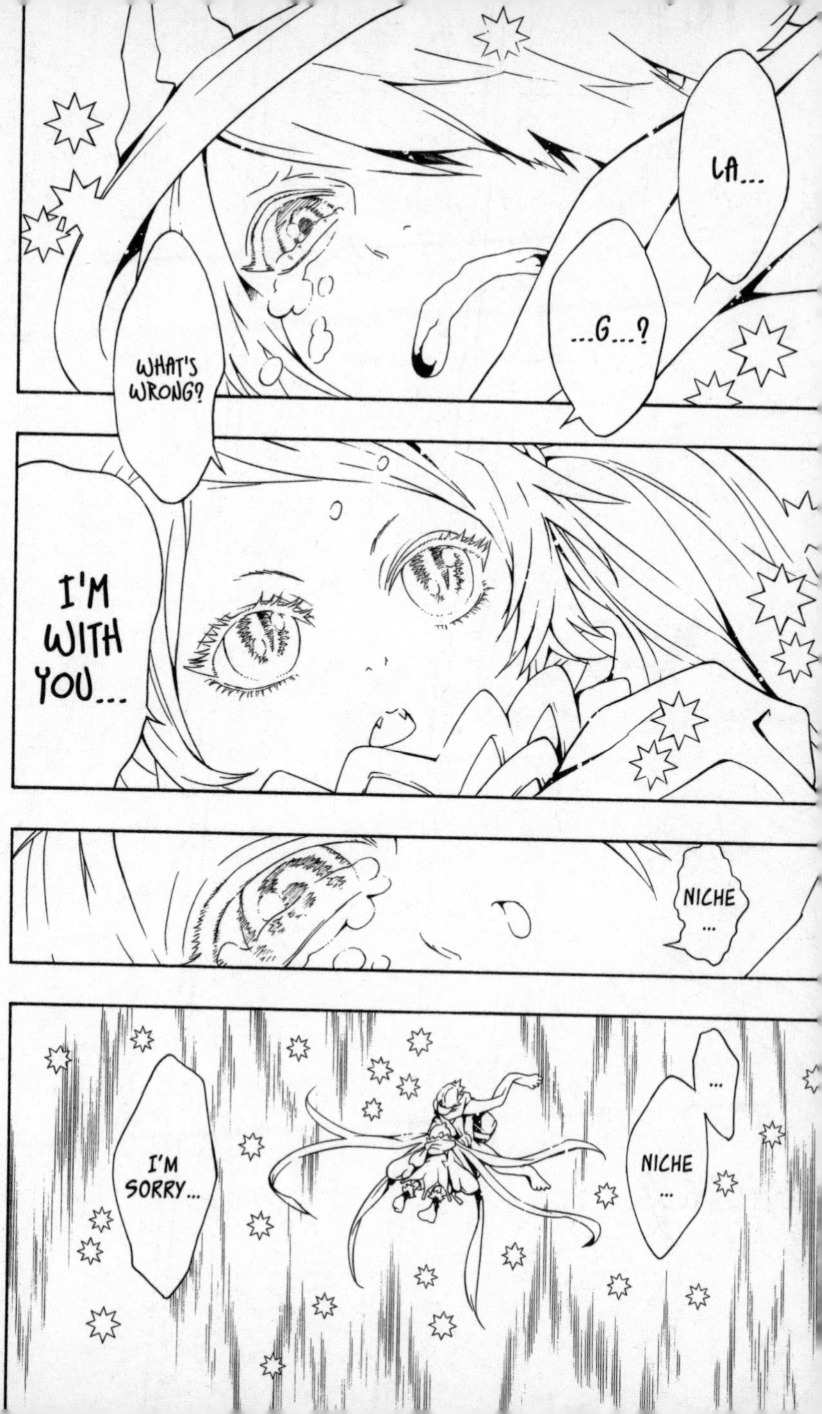
LA...
...G...?
WHAT'S WRONG?
I'M WITH YOU...
NICHE ...
... NICHE ...
I'M SORRY...

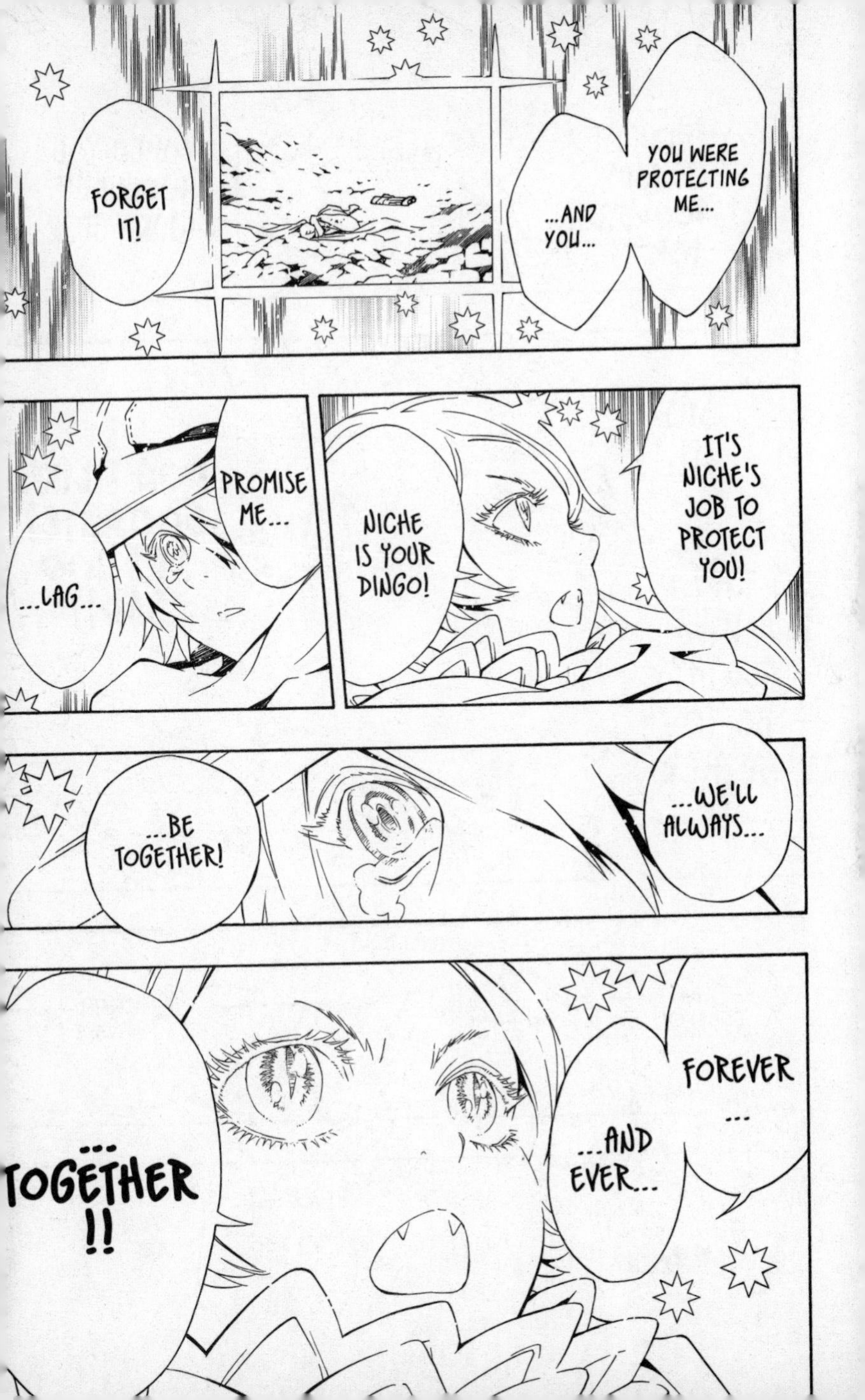
YOU WERE PROTECTING ME...
...AND YOU...
FORGET IT!
IT'S NICHE'S JOB TO PROTECT YOU!
NICHE IS YOUR DINGO!
PROMISE ME...
...LAG...
...WE'LL ALWAYS...
...BE TOGETHER!
FOREVER ...
...AND EVER...
...TOGETHER!!

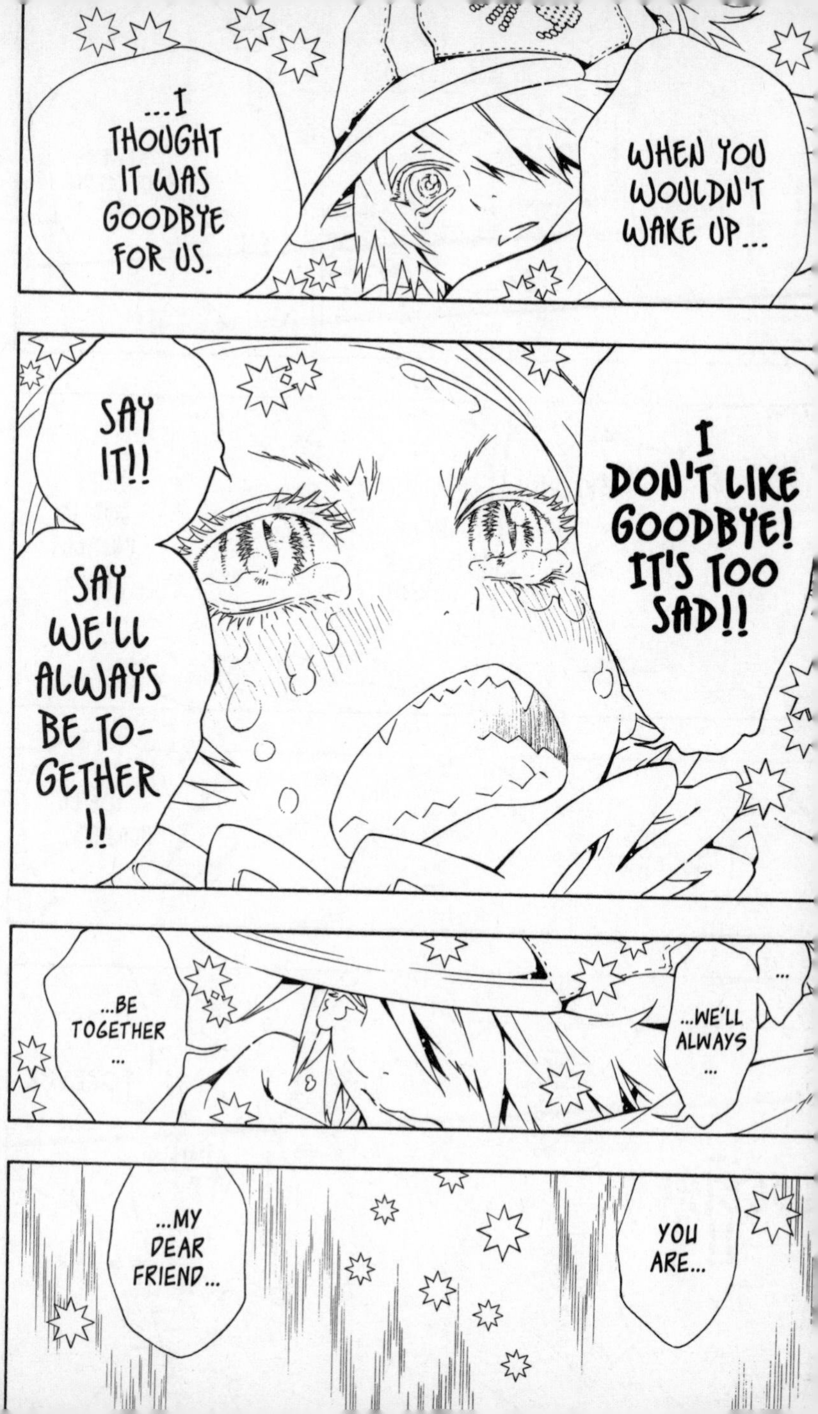
WHEN YOU WOULDN'T WAKE UP...
...I THOUGHT IT WAS GOODBYE FOR US.
I DON'T LIKE GOODBYE! IT'S TOO SAD!!
SAY IT!!
SAY WE'LL ALWAYS BE TO-GETHER!!
...
...WE'LL ALWAYS ...
...BE TOGETHER ...
YOU ARE...
...MY DEAR FRIEND...

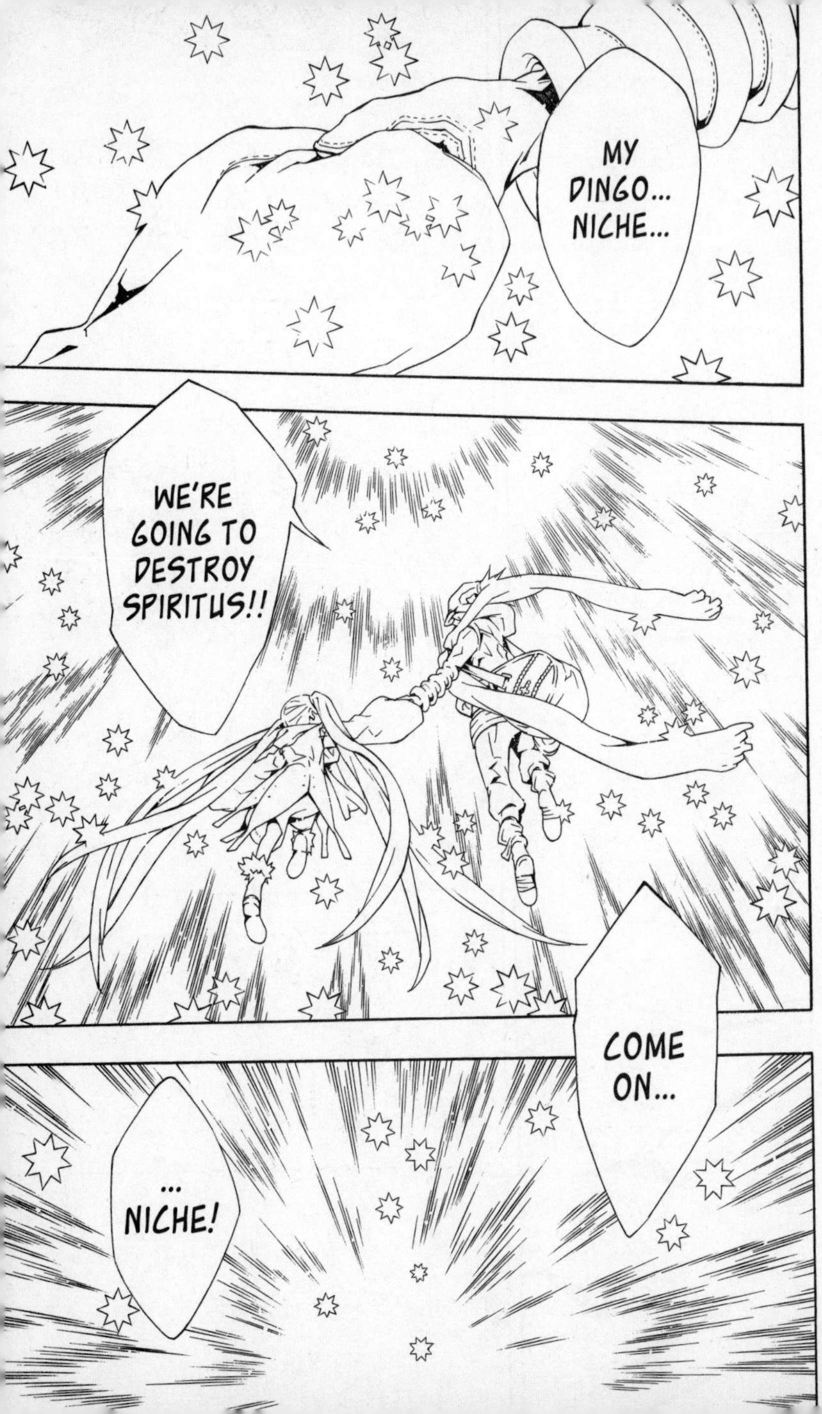
MY DINGO... NICHE...
WE'RE GOING TO DESTROY SPIRITUS!!
COME ON...
... NICHE!

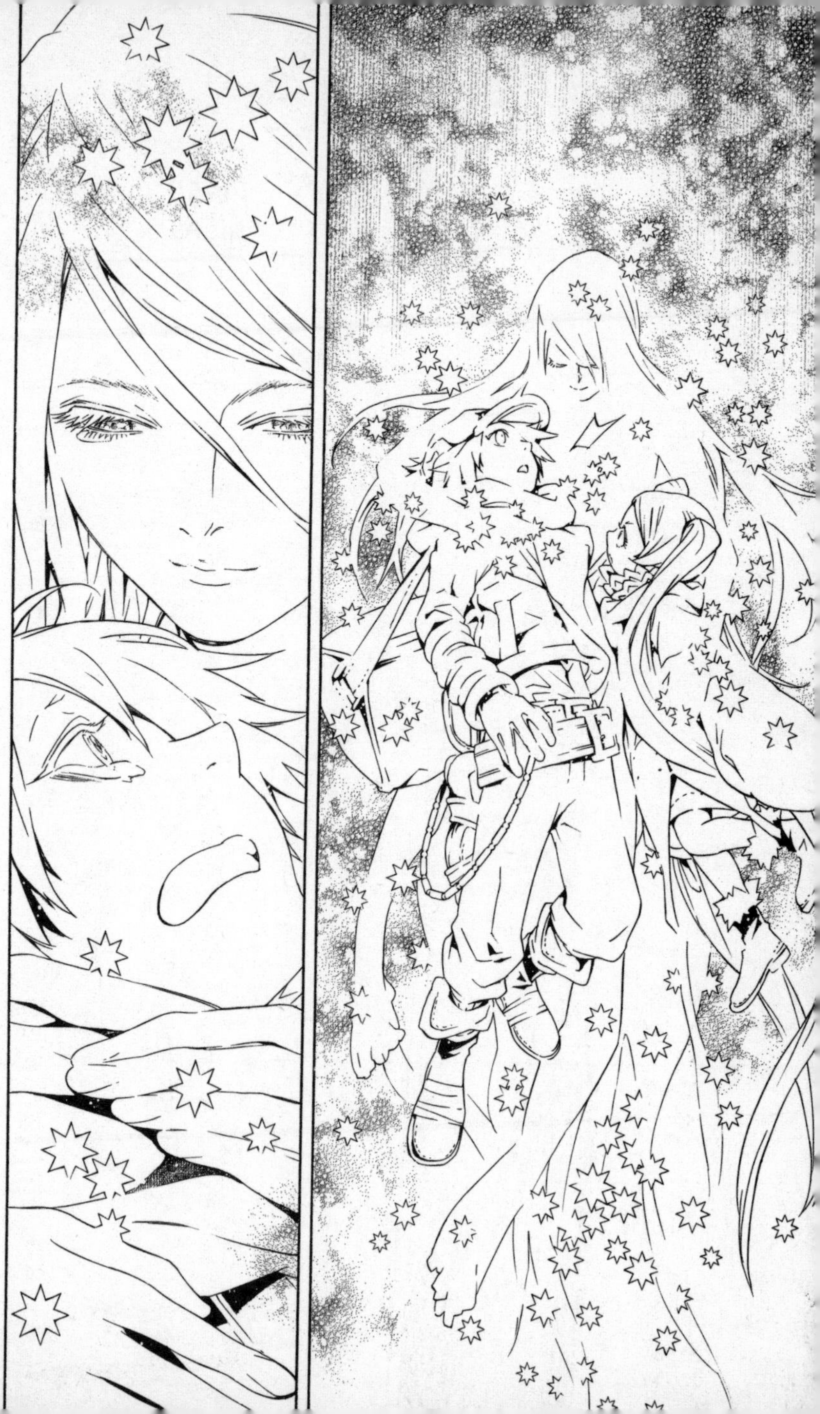

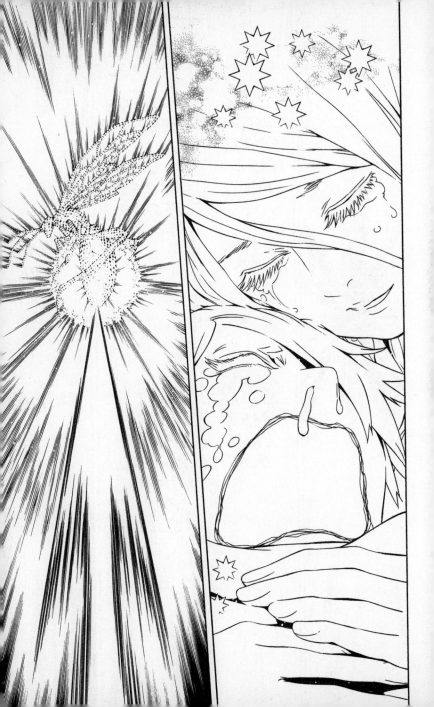

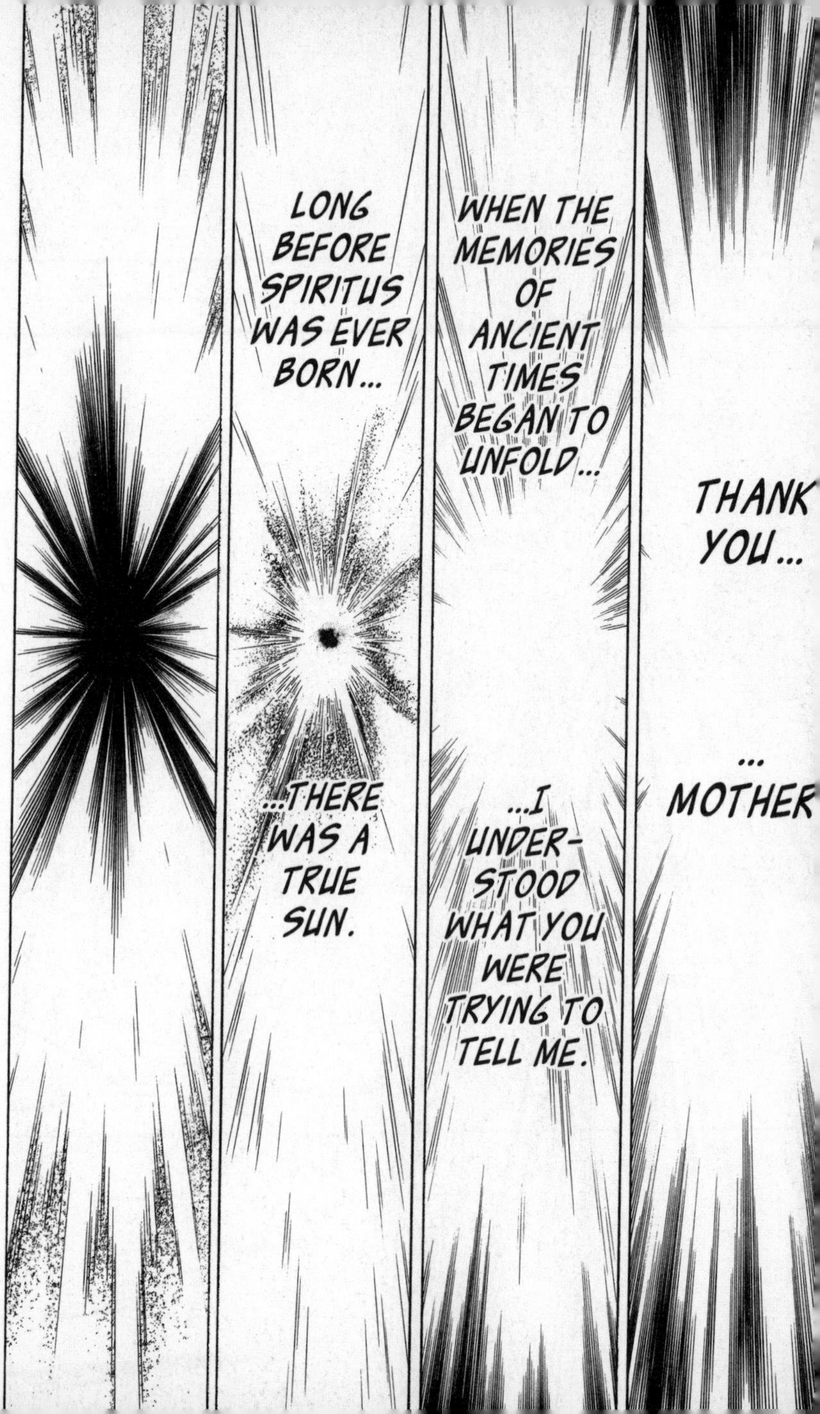
THANK YOU...
...MOTHER
WHEN THE MEMORIES OF ANCIENT TIMES BEGAN TO UNFOLD...
...I UNDERSTOOD WHAT YOU WERE TRYING TO TELL ME.
LONG BEFORE SPIRITUS WAS EVER BORN...
...THERE WAS A TRUE SUN.

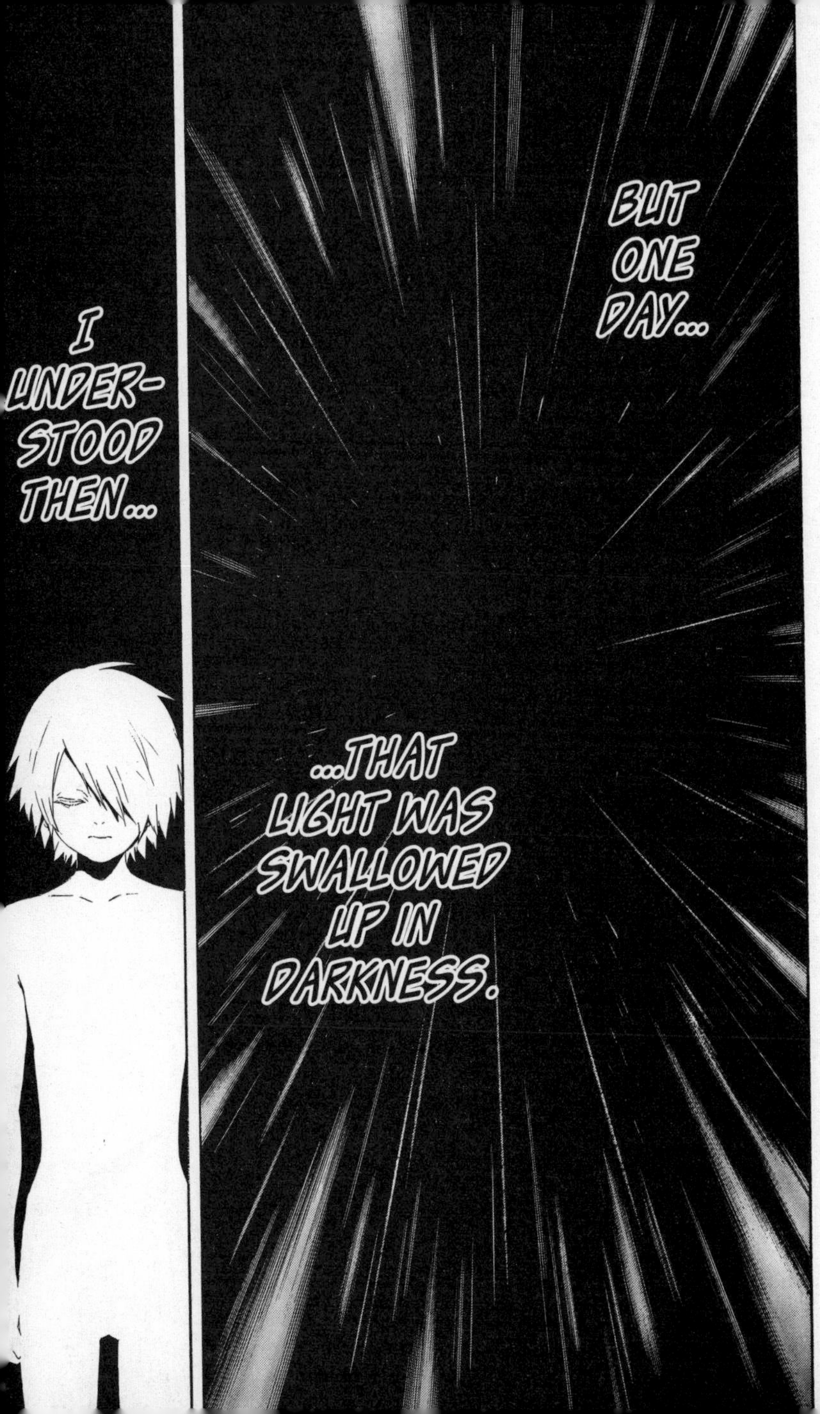
BUT ONE DAY...
...THAT LIGHT WAS SWALLOWED UP IN DARKNESS.
I UNDER-STOOD THEN...

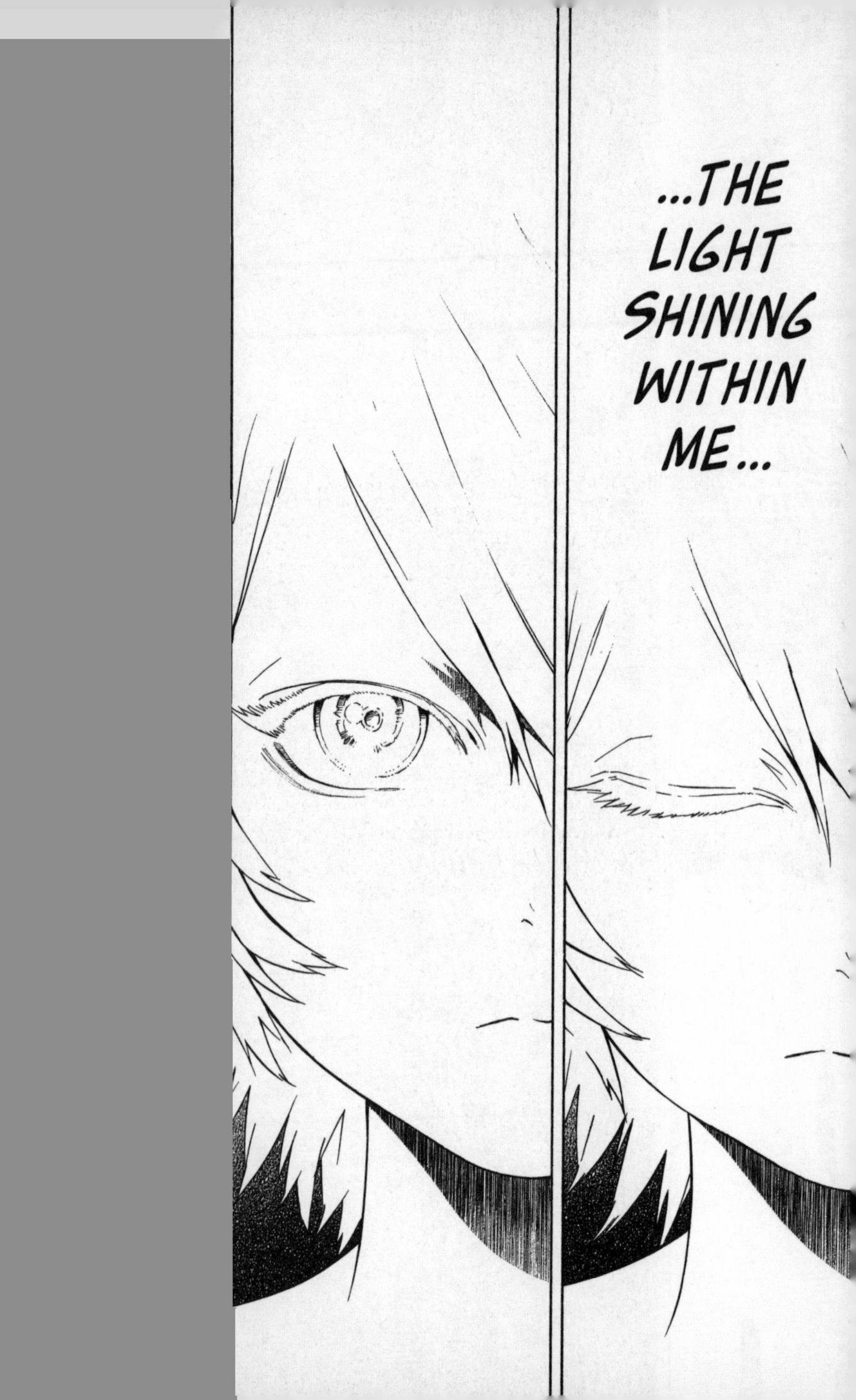
...THE LIGHT SHINING WITHIN ME...

THIS WARM...
...GENTLE...
...STRONG...
...HONEST AND STRAIGHT-FORWARD...
...LIGHT PIERC-ING THE DARK-NESS.

I...

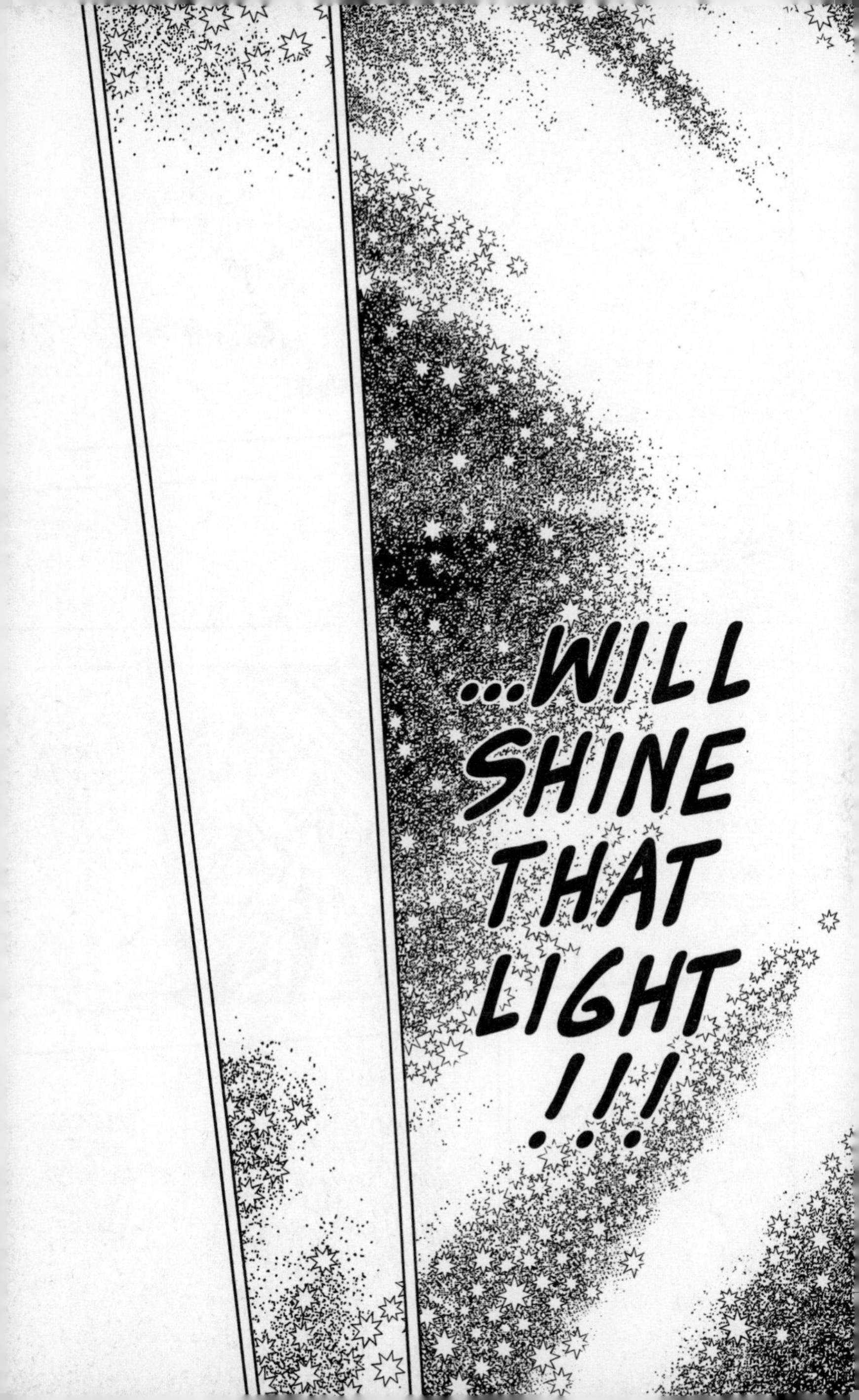
...WILL SHINE THAT LIGHT!!!

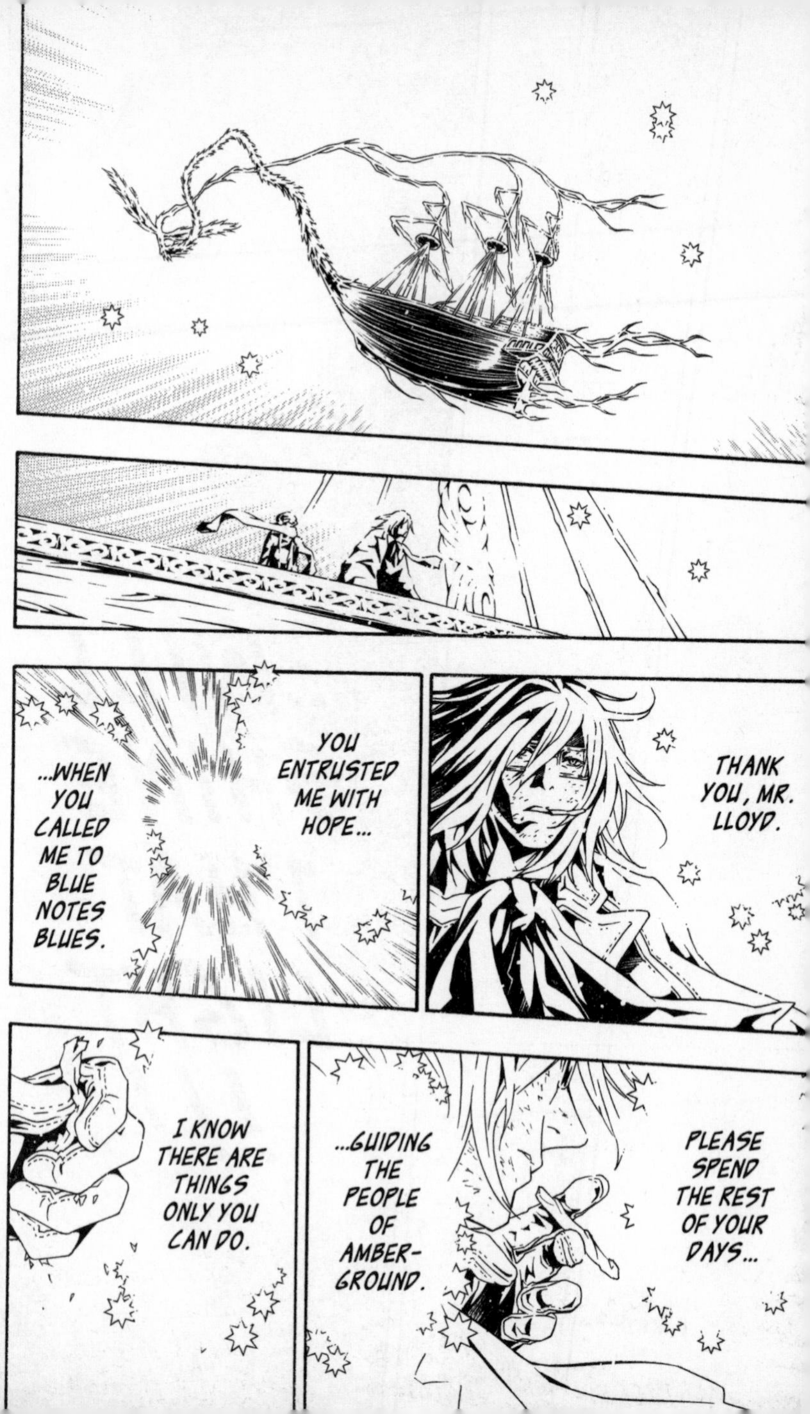
THANK YOU, MR. LLOYD.
YOU ENTRUSTED ME WITH HOPE...
...WHEN YOU CALLED ME TO BLUE NOTES BLUES.
PLEASE SPEND THE REST OF YOUR DAYS...
...GUIDING THE PEOPLE OF AMBER-GROUND.
I KNOW THERE ARE THINGS ONLY YOU CAN DO.

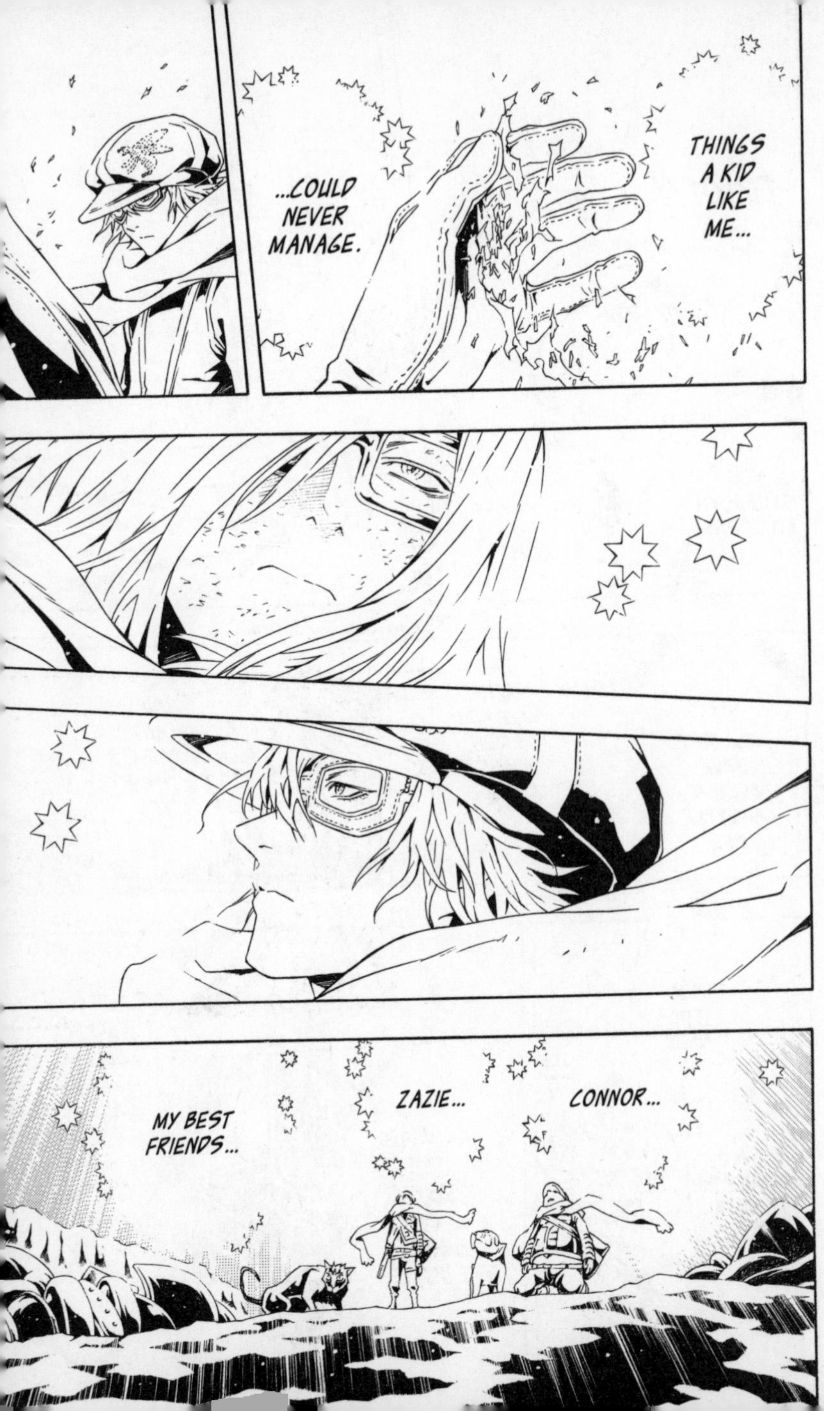
THINGS A KID LIKE ME...
...COULD NEVER MANAGE.
CONNOR...
ZAZIE...
MY BEST FRIENDS...

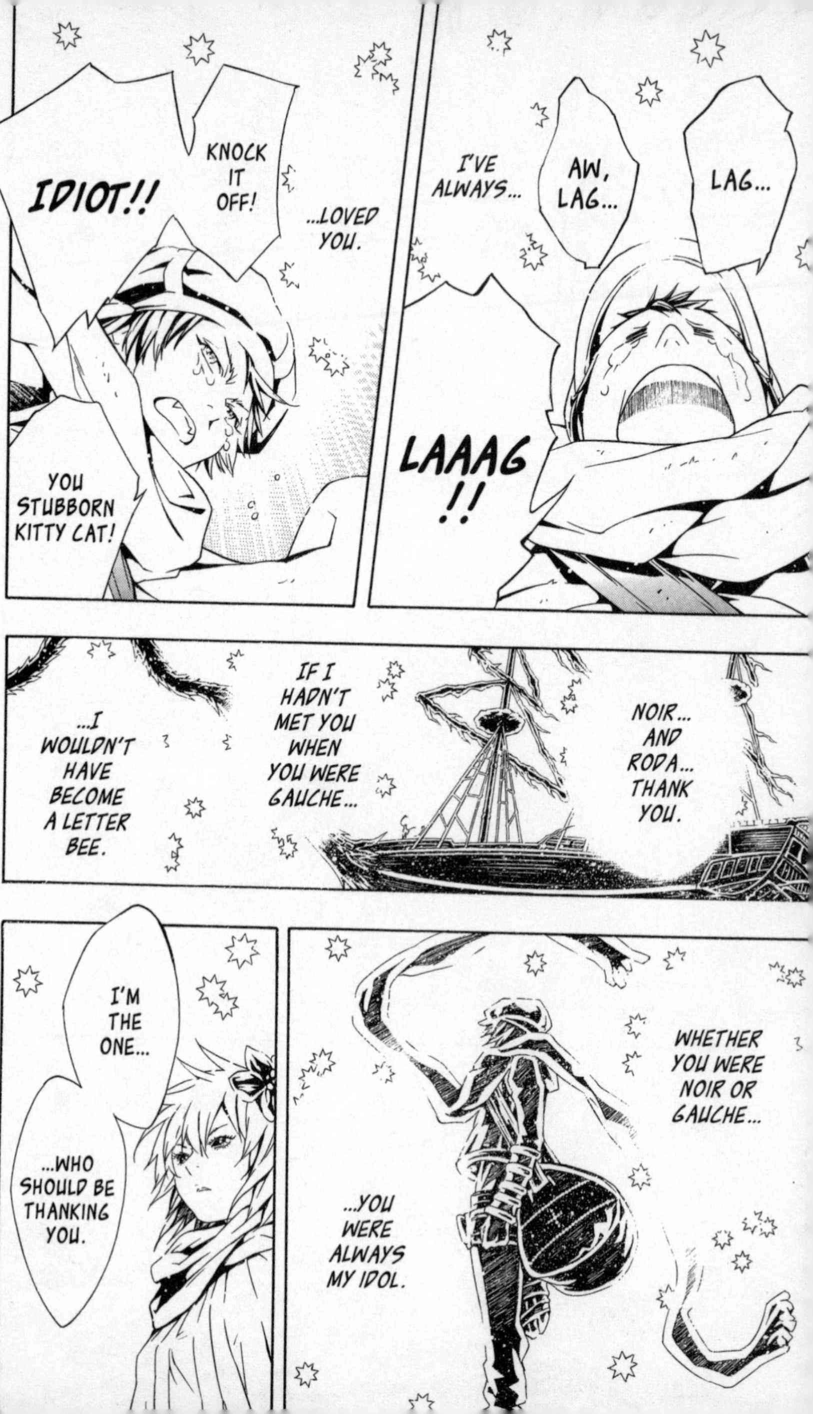

LAG...
AW, LAG...
I'VE ALWAYS...
LAAAG!!
...LOVED YOU.
KNOCK IT OFF!
IDIOT!!
YOU STUBBORN KITTY CAT!
NOIR... AND RODA... THANK YOU.
IF I HADN'T MET YOU WHEN YOU WERE GAUCHE...
...I WOULDN'T HAVE BECOME A LETTER BEE.
WHETHER YOU WERE NOIR OR GAUCHE...
...YOU WERE ALWAYS MY IDOL.
I'M THE ONE...
...WHO SHOULD BE THANKING YOU.

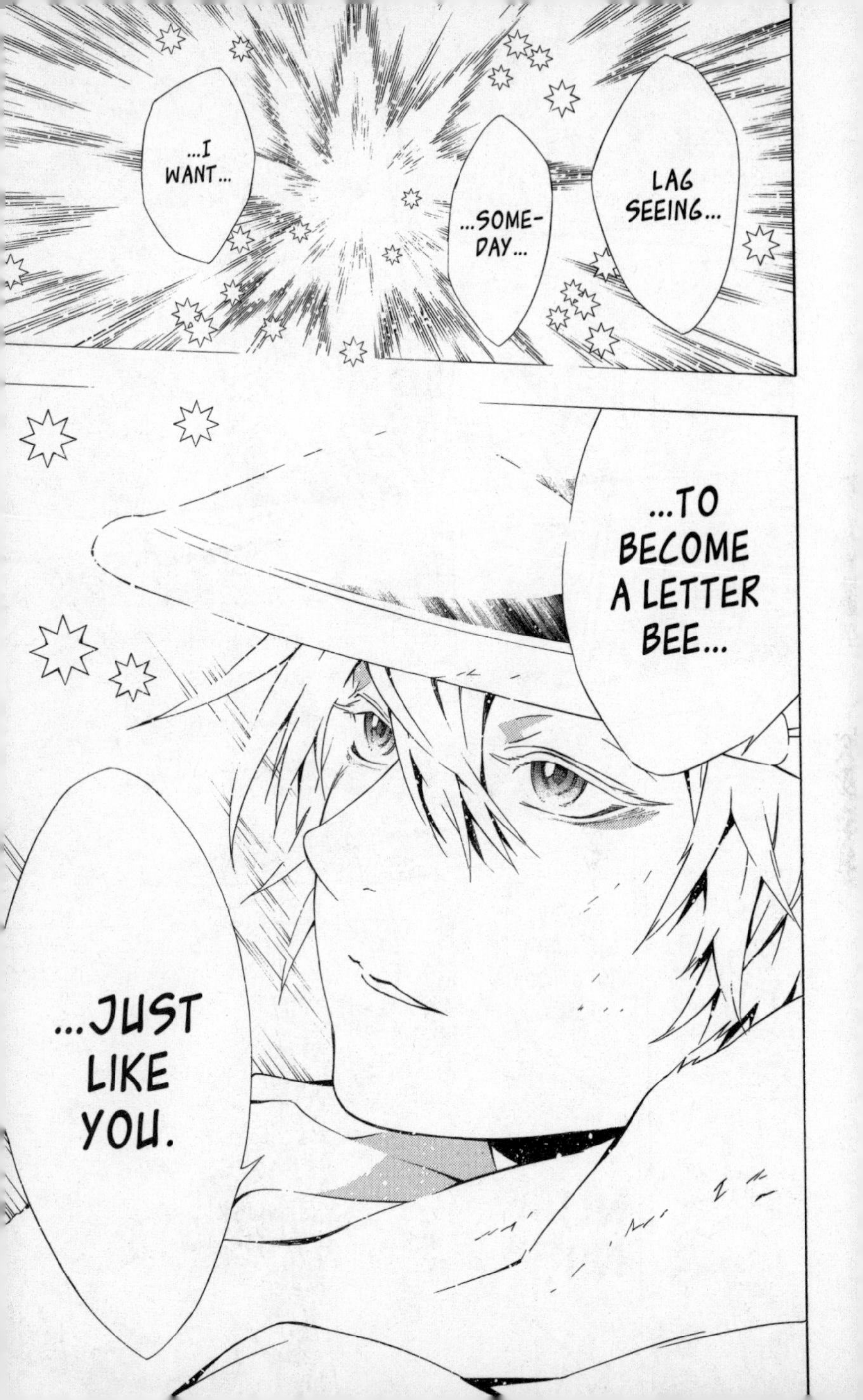
LAG SEEING...
...SOME-DAY...
...I WANT...
...TO BECOME A LETTER BEE...
...JUST LIKE YOU.

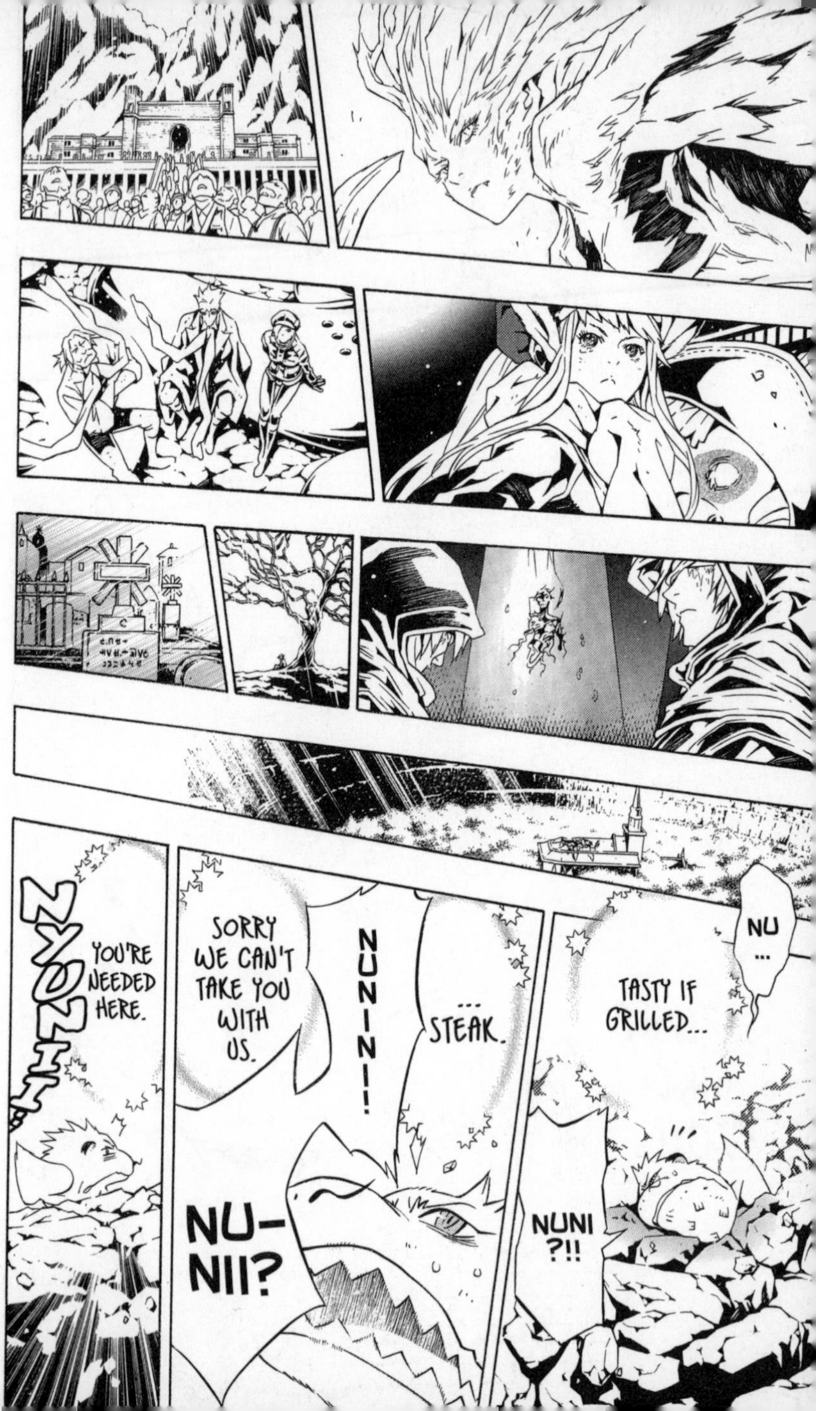
NU ...
TASTY IF GRILLED...
NUNI ?!!
... STEAK.
NUNINI!!
SORRY WE CAN'T TAKE YOU WITH US.
NU-NII?
YOU'RE NEEDED HERE.
NYONIII

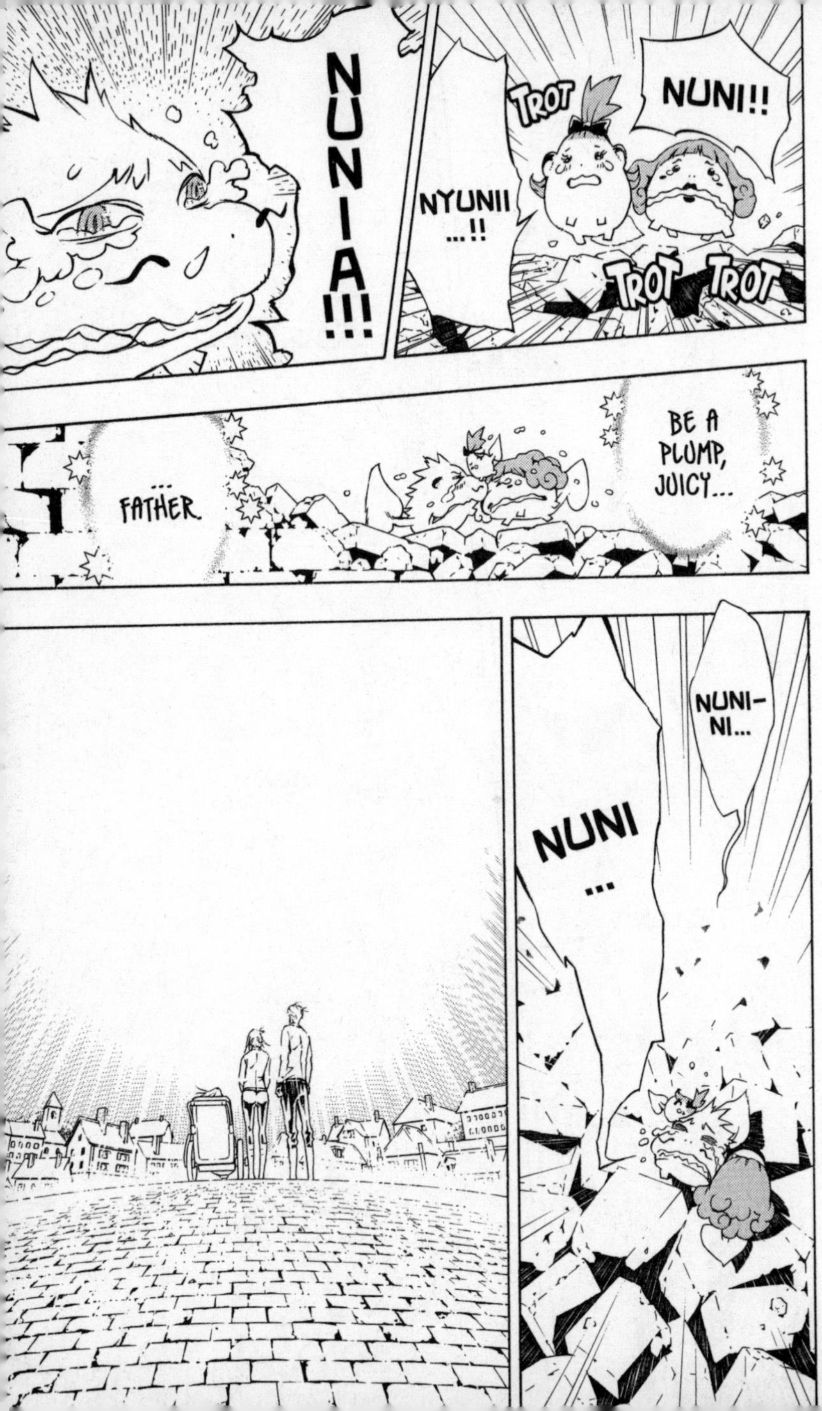
NUNI!!
TROT
NYUNII ...!!
TROT TROT
NUNIA!!!
BE A PLUMP, JUICY...
...FATHER.
NUNI-NI...
NUNI ...

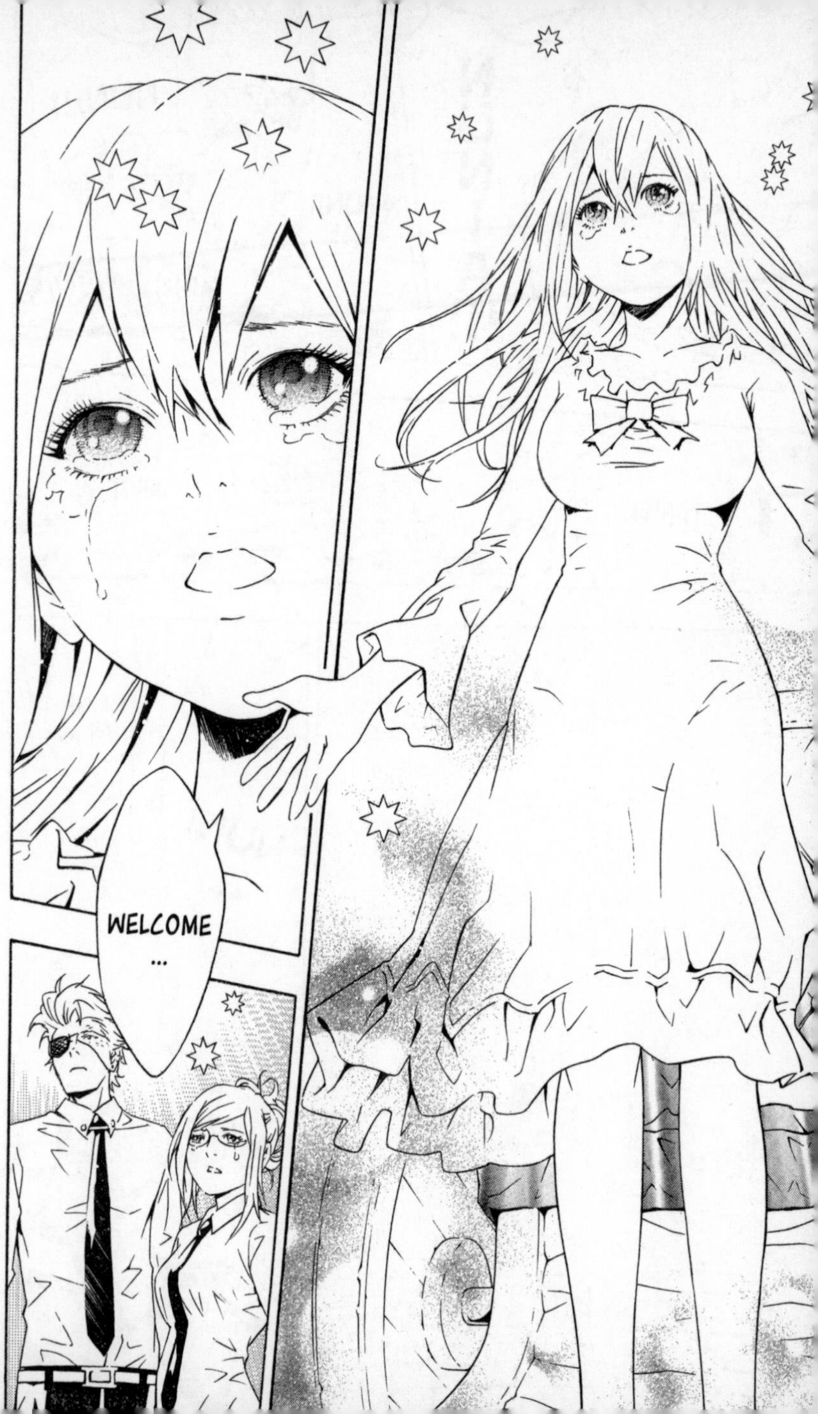
WELCOME ...

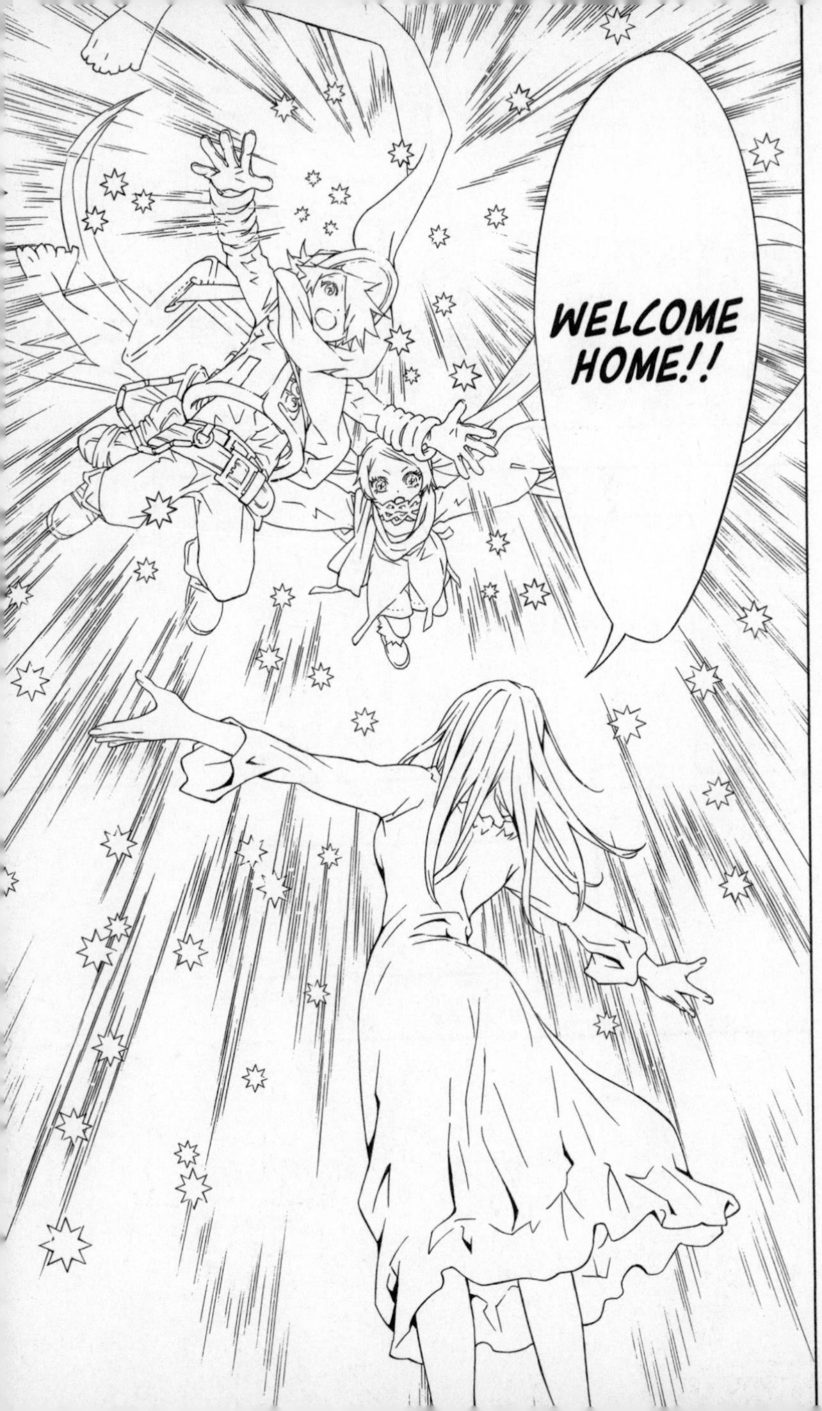
WELCOME HOME!!

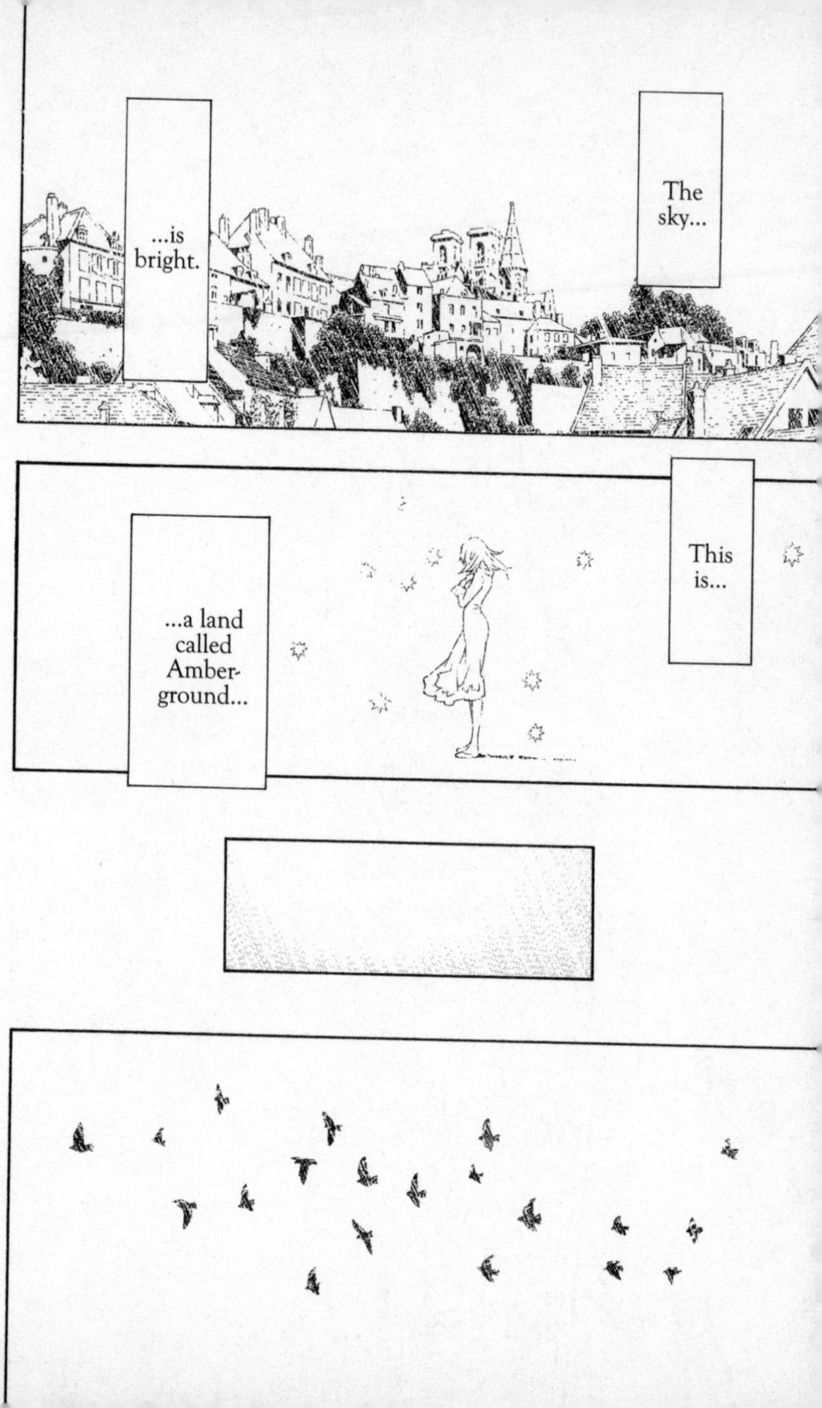
The sky...
...is bright.
This is...
...a land called Amber-ground...

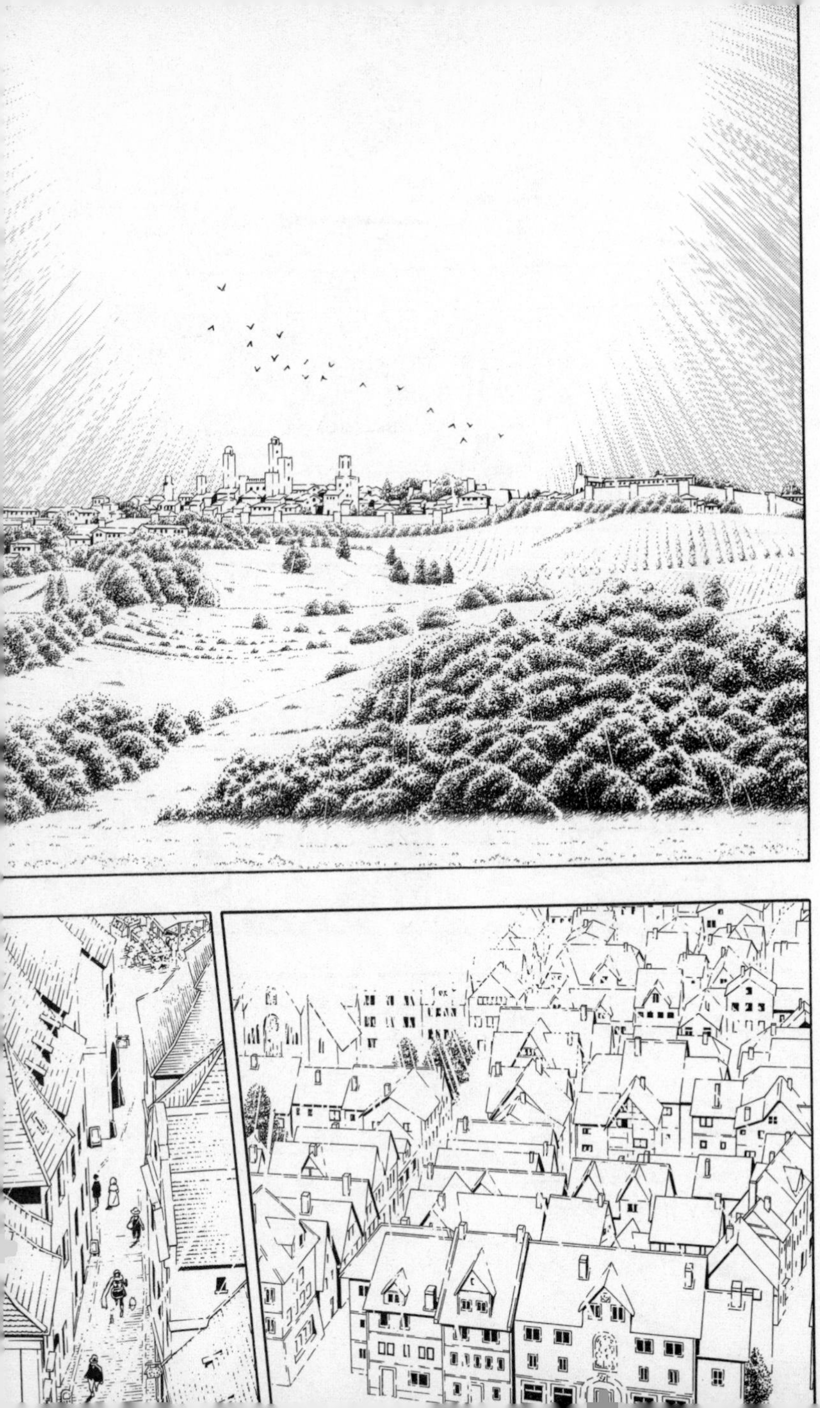

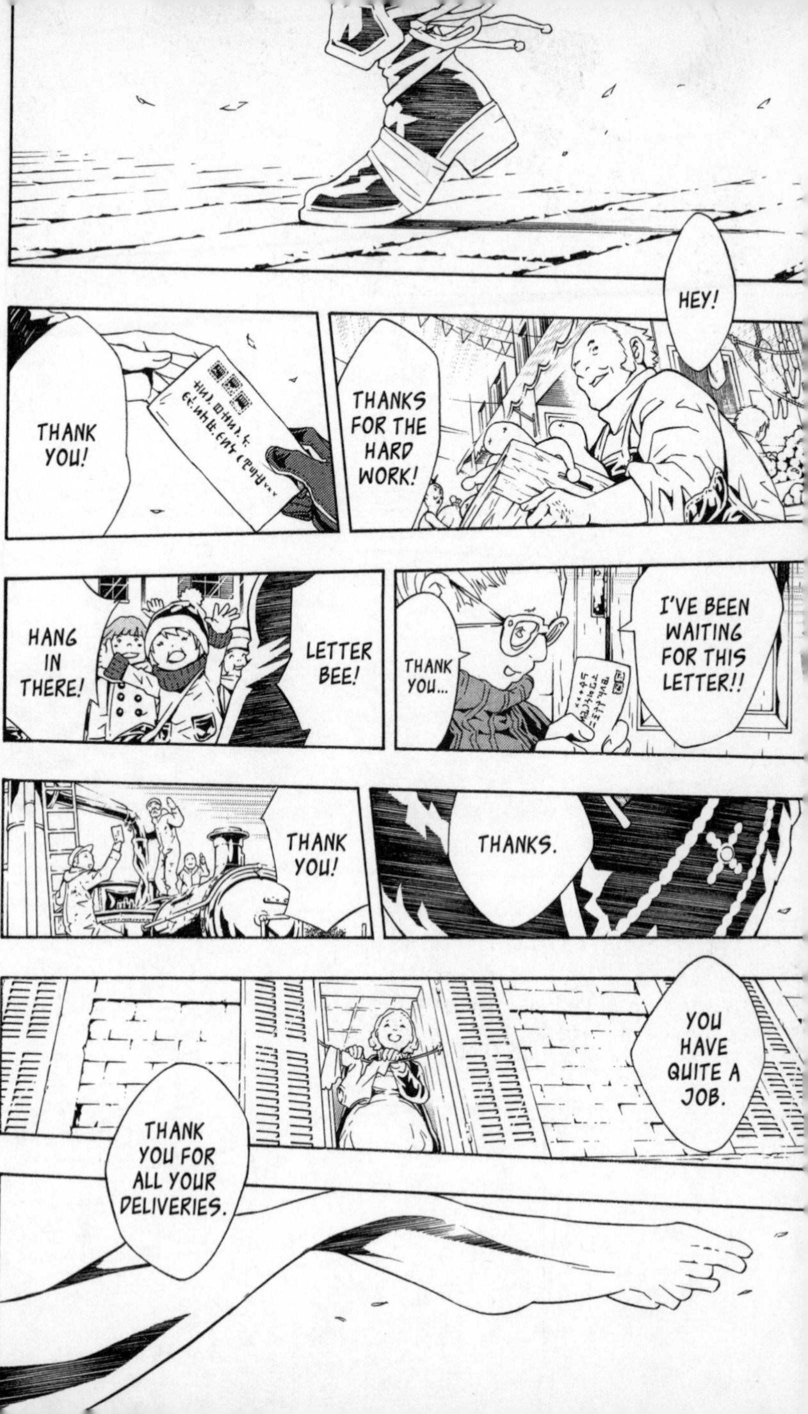
HEY!
THANKS FOR THE HARD WORK!
THANK YOU!
I'VE BEEN WAITING FOR THIS LETTER!!
THANK YOU...
LETTER BEE!
HANG IN THERE!
THANKS.
THANK YOU!
YOU HAVE QUITE A JOB.
THANK YOU FOR ALL YOUR DELIVERIES.

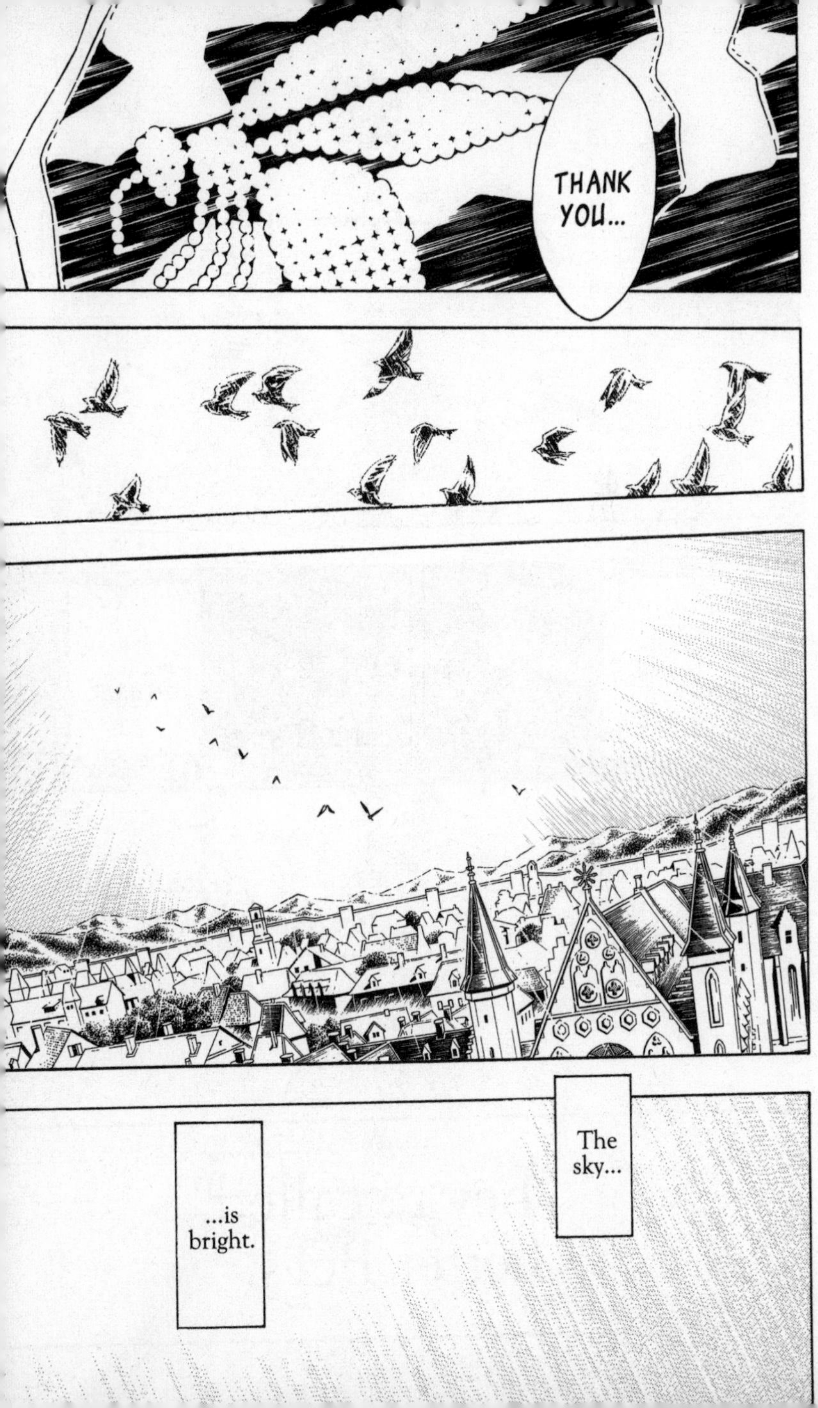
THANK YOU...
The sky...
...is bright.

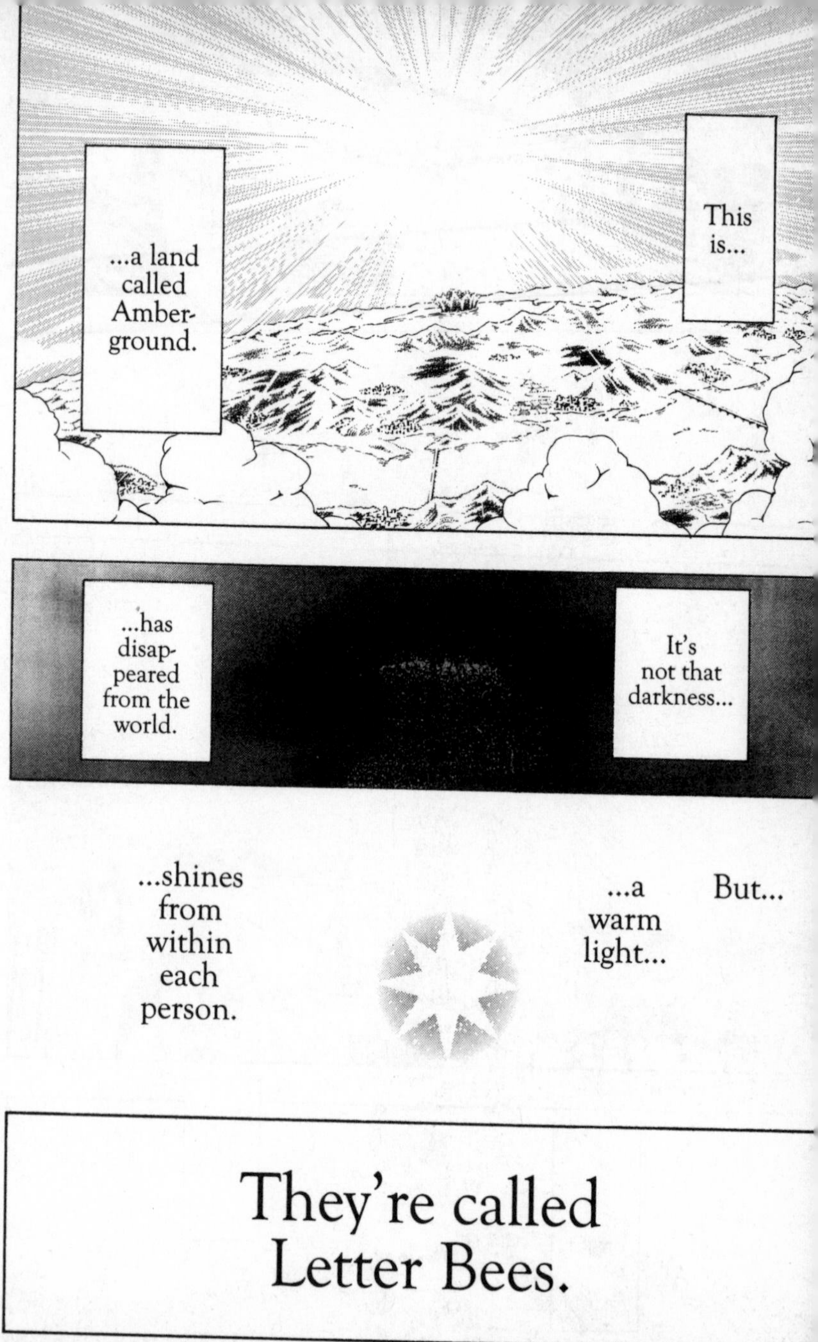
This is...
...a land called Amber-ground.
It's not that darkness...
...has disap-peared from the world.
But...
...a warm light...
...shines from within each person.
They're called Letter Bees.

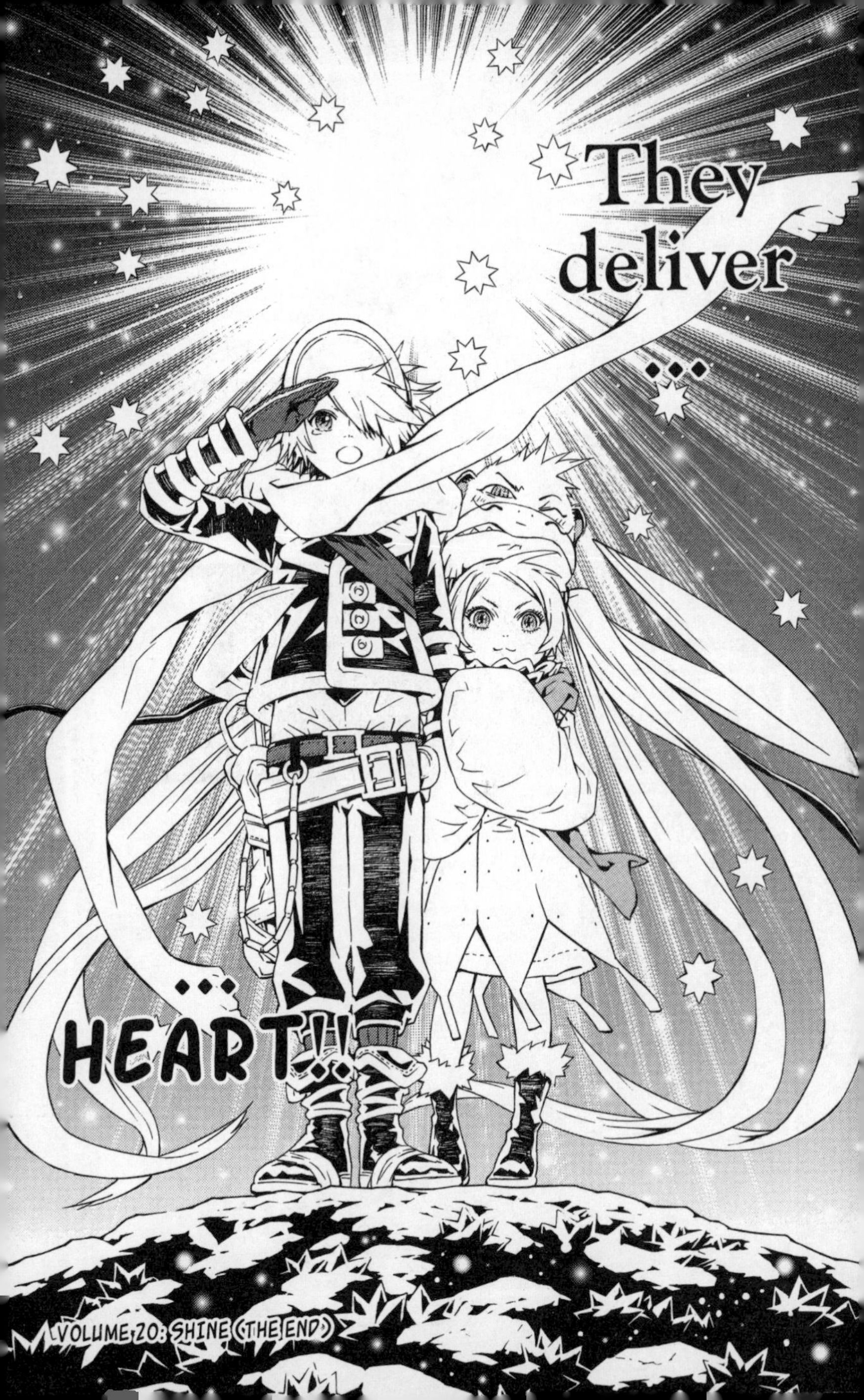
They deliver
...
...HEART!!
VOLUME 20: SHINE (THE END)

■ HEAD BEE / LOPTR SENDAK

So Kuu was the Head Bee. It seems he managed to reach the capital with his strong *heart* intact, but years of duty took a toll on his body and spirit. But because his "Kuu" personality emerged, he was ultimately able to guide Lag and the others. He gave up his life as a Letter Bee to keep the world going. I cannot but thank him. Thank you, Kuu and Loptr! *Sob!*

n.b.: Loptr / In Norse mythology, another name for the androgynous trickster god Loki.

n.b.: Maurice Sendak (1928–2012) / American illustrator and writer of children's books, including *Where the Wild Things Are.*

n.b.: Etude in C Minor, op. 10, no. 12, "Revolution" / Solo piano work by Frédéric Chopin, also known as the "Revolutionary Etude."

n.b.: Avalon / Island from the legends of King Arthur.

■ LARGO LLOYD

Lloyd had such a terrible childhood it's a wonder he managed to live so valiantly. He wanted to bring light to the world. That was probably his wish as he scrounged through ancient texts in Kagerou. However, he was not the "light." I think he had faith in Chico, but in the end every action he took guided Lag along. He laughed off his smoking when Jiggy brought it up, but I think he had a death wish. Ultimately, Lag pushed him to live and entrusted him with the future of Amberground. Lloyd always kept his true self hidden, so I wonder what he'll be like now. If only we could see into the future! *Sooob!*

n.b.: Guri and Gura / Series of children's picture books by Rieko Nakagawa, illustrated by Yuriko Yamawaki.

n.b.: Shel Silverstein (1930–1999) / American writer and illustrator of *The Giving Tree*.

n.b.: Ernest Howard Shepard (1879–1976) / British illustrator of *Winnie-the-Pooh*.

■ LAG SEEING
Lag, who gave Sylvette back her heart, saw images of ancient times when he gathered the memories of those born on the Day of the Flicker. That was when he understood his destiny. The light of ancient times was swallowed up in darkness. But Lag's *heart* was unwavering. Surely it will shine gently on the people forever and ever. After all, he has the best dingo of all, Niche, by his side... *Sooooob...*

■ AMBERGROUND
In time, scolding voices could be heard saying, "Don't do things that would make you ashamed to show your face to the sun!" A folktale spread that if you make the sun sad, you'll have a downpour. That's Lag for you. Oh, Laaag!! *SOOOOOOB!*

Flowers of gratitude are blooming all over. The world is slowly changing.

■ DR. THUNDERLAND RESTS IN PEACE HERE
Is that my grave?! Hey!! Hey, wait!!

I was dead all along! Darn it! Maybe I'll come back as a zombie next time. No, this is the final volume!!! *Sob!* But nothing's really changed. We're all still here, right next to you, waiting for you to read again. When the mood strikes you, will you come back to see us? Will you think of us?

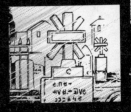

Well, thanks, everyone. Thank you from the bottom of my *heart*.

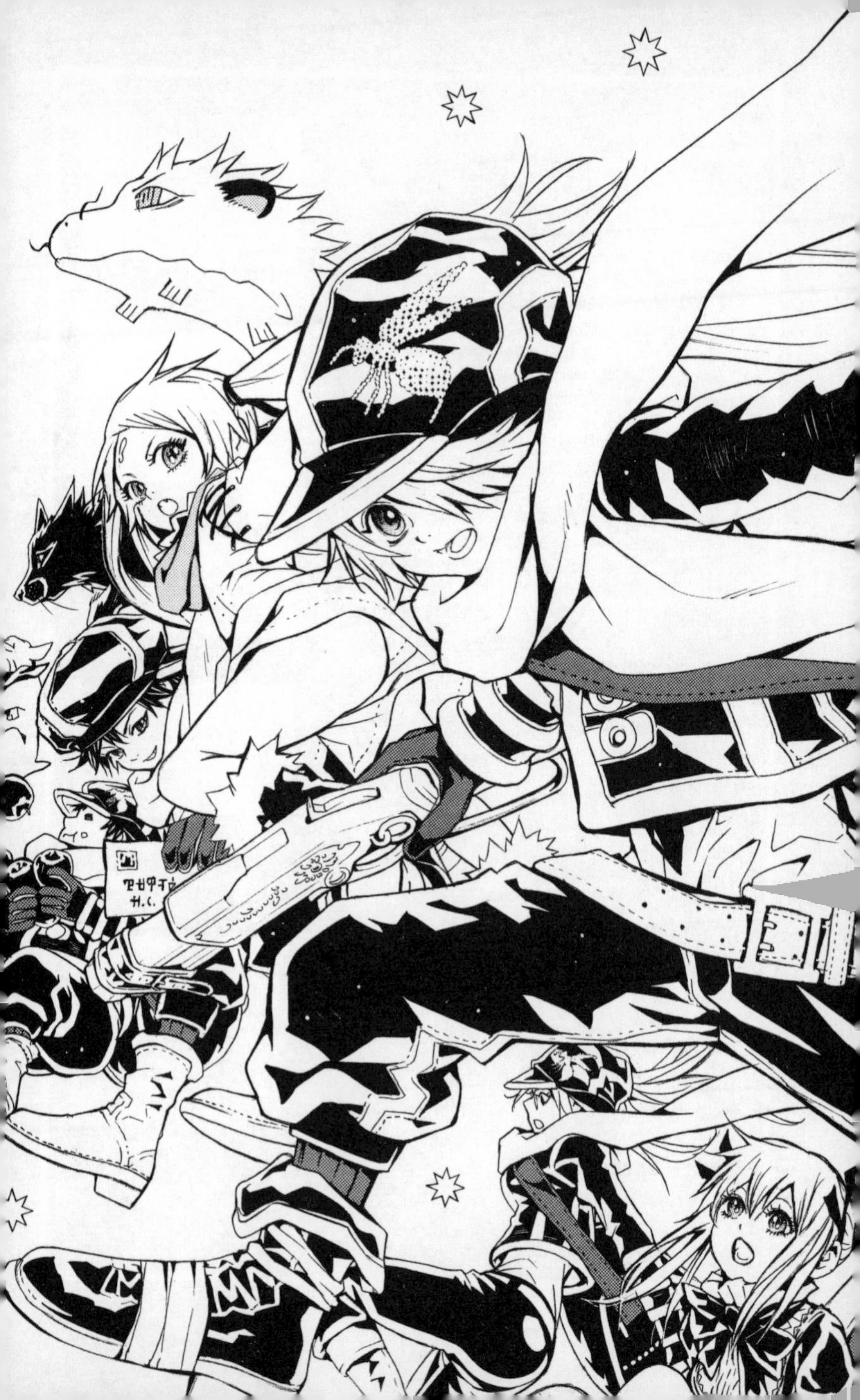

STAFF (MARIA LOTUS INC.)
JUNICHI KOSAKA
HISASHI TSUKINOKISAWA
AKIRA IWAYA
SHIGEKI NAKAMURA
DAISUKE KADOKUNI

EDITOR (SHUEISHA)
SHUHEI HOSONO
SHUNTARO KOSUGE
TAKUMA YUI
JUNICHI TAMADA

COMICS EDITOR (SHOKIKAKU)
KAZUSHIGE FUJIWARA
SHINYA TOMIYAMA

COMICS DESIGN (EARTH BREATH)
SEKI SAITOH

PRESENTED BY HIROYUKI ASADA
★

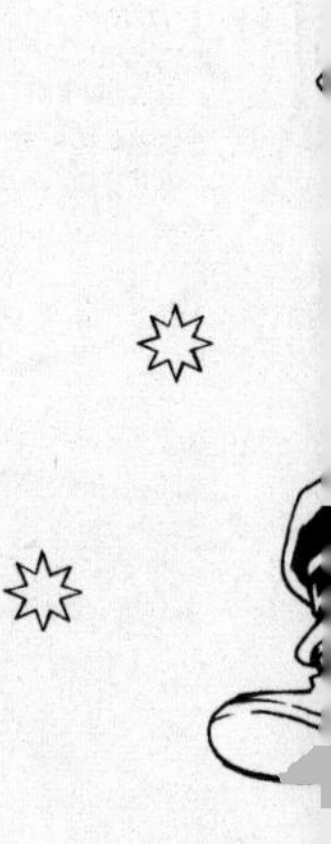

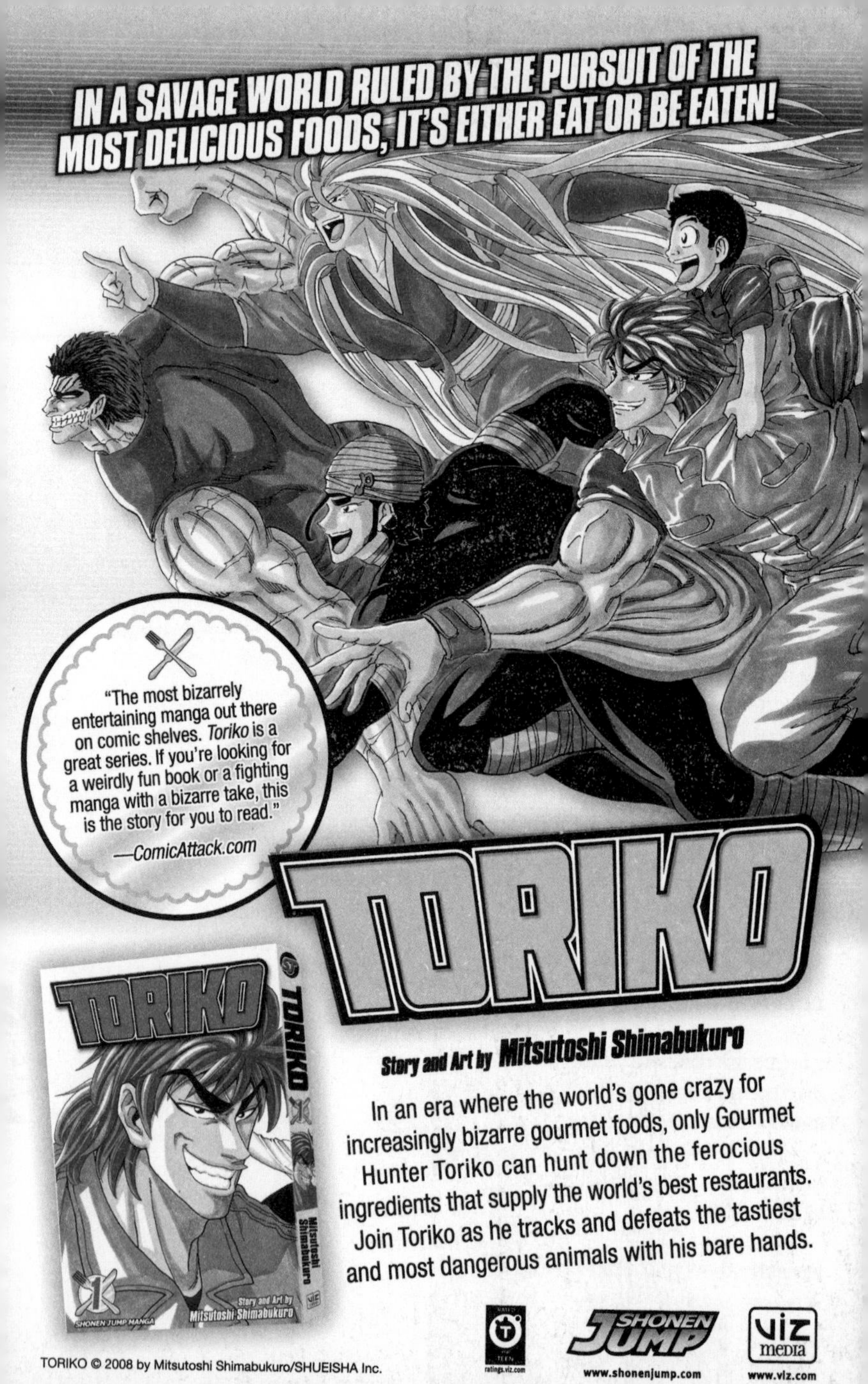

IN A SAVAGE WORLD RULED BY THE PURSUIT OF THE MOST DELICIOUS FOODS, IT'S EITHER EAT OR BE EATEN!
"The most bizarrely entertaining manga out there on comic shelves. *Toriko* is a great series. If you're looking for a weirdly fun book or a fighting manga with a bizarre take, this is the story for you to read."
—ComicAttack.com
TORIKO
TORIKO
TORIKO
Mitsutoshi Shimabukuro
1
Story and Art by
Mitsutoshi Shimabukuro
SHONEN JUMP MANGA
Story and Art by Mitsutoshi Shimabukuro
In an era where the world's gone crazy for
increasingly bizarre gourmet foods, only Gourmet
Hunter Toriko can hunt down the ferocious
ingredients that supply the world's best restaurants.
Join Toriko as he tracks and defeats the tastiest
and most dangerous animals with his bare hands.
ratings.viz.com
SHONEN JUMP
www.shonenjump.com
viz media
www.viz.com

THE ACTION-PACKED SUPERHERO COMEDY ABOUT ONE MAN'S AMBITION TO BE A HERO FOR FUN!

ONE-PUNCH MAN

STORY BY
ONE

ART BY
YUSUKE MURATA

Nothing about Saitama passes the eyeball test when it comes to superheroes, from his lifeless expression to his bald head to his unimpressive physique. However, this average-looking guy has a not-so-average problem—he just can't seem to find an opponent strong enough to take on!

Can he finally find an opponent who can go toe-to-toe with him and give his life some meaning? Or is he doomed to a life of superpowered boredom?

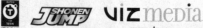

www.viz.com